GROUP PROCESSES

GROUP PROCESSES

A Developmental Perspective

Susan A. Wheelan
Temple University

Allyn and Bacon
Boston • London • Toronto • Sydney • Tokyo • Singapore

Editor-in-Chief, Social Services: Susan Badger
Series Editorial Assistant: Laura L. Ellingson
Production Administrator: Annette Joseph
Editorial-Production Service: Karen Mason
Manufacturing Buyer: Megan Cochran
Cover Administrator: Linda K. Dickinson
Cover Designer: Suzanne Harbison

Copyright © 1994 by Allyn and Bacon
A Division of Simon & Schuster, Inc.
160 Gould Street
Needham Heights, Massachusetts 02194-2310

Library of Congress Cataloging-in-Publication Data

Wheelan, Susan A.
    Group processes : a developmental perspective / Susan A. Wheelan.
        p.   cm.
    Includes bibliographical references (p.   ) and index.
    ISBN 0-205-14809-3
    1. Social groups. 2. Social psychology. 3. Intergroup relations.
  I. Title.
  HM131.W43   1993
  305--dc20   93-23768
                                         CIP

Printed in the United States of America

10 9   05 04 03 02

*To Jane, who graciously listens
again and again and again*

CONTENTS

PREFACE

Biological ecology studies the mutual influences and interdependence of living organisms and their physical environment. For centuries, humans believed that they had dominion over other species and the earth's resources. As a result of ecological research, however, we now realize the potentially fatal error of such a view. We recognize the interconnectedness of our fate and that of the earth. The quality of our individual lives is shaped by the physical environment, and our actions affect the environment in which we live. This recent awareness is changing, if slowly, the way we view our world and ourselves. The conservation movement, concern with clean air and water, and recycling efforts are but a few examples of how this shift in our thinking has influenced our actions with regard to the physical environment. How we think about things, then, can strongly affect our collective decisions and behaviors.

The social environment also profoundly shapes the quality of individual experience (Sampson, 1989). However, we have not equally accepted the reality of this concept. Instead, many of us hold tenaciously to the view that individual behavior is a matter of free will, autonomous choice, and personal psychology. If an individual has a life problem, we tend to attribute this to his or her internal mental life and to downplay the effects of the social environment in the creation and maintenance of the difficulty. We seek to alter the characteristics of the person rather than the social situation, even though research tells us that the reverse is often more effective (Pettigrew, 1988). This individualistic perspective may be as erroneous as our earlier conception of the environment.

Lewin called for an alternative view over forty years ago. He advocated the study of psychological ecology, which would help us to understand the mutual influences and interdependence of human beings and their social environment (Cartwright, 1978; Lewin, 1951). This view seeks to dispel the American myth of individualism by highlighting the profound impact of groups, institutions, and society on individual behavior. The development of an ecological perspective of the social environment requires systematic investigation of the dynamics of groups, institutions, and society and the reciprocal influence processes among social systems and their individual members. Considerable evidence for the validity of this approach can be found in the research of sociologists, social psychologists, anthropologists, educators, and the like. And yet, this body of research has failed to generate the same public interest and concern that has become associated with the work of biological ecologists.

While those who study groups and society may be passionately involved with the topic, it fails to stimulate the same passionate response in other societal groups. The individual is seen as paramount in American life, and evidence to the contrary is often met with resistance or suspicion. As a nation, we are fascinated by individual psychology. Self-help books, the war on drugs, educational reform, and social research focus, in general, on understanding and helping individuals to overcome obstacles to their growth and development. The study of group, institutional, and societal dynamics is not considered very relevant in these endeavors.

And yet, the relevance of such study could not be more timely. What could be more relevant than trying to understand the processes that produced Jonestown, Eastern Europe, Tienanmen Square, and the dissolution of the Soviet Union? What can we learn about group influences on individual choices regarding drug use? How can we learn to understand ourselves as individuals if we negate the influence of the groups to which we belong on our thinking and behavior? How can we create unity out of diversity if we do not study the role of group factors in the development and maintenance of prejudice and intergroup conflict? How can we understand society if we fail to study its basic building block—the group?

The purpose of this book, then, is threefold. First, it seeks to further the development of an ecological perspective of the social environment by integrating research and theory about group processes and development and, where appropriate, making applications to individuals and larger social systems. Second, it attempts to fire the imagination and curiosity of its readers in relation to the wonders and dangers of group and social influences on our thoughts, feelings, and behaviors. Third, it hopes to encourage people to apply the information contained in this book to support and enhance the functioning of the groups to which they belong.

The introductory chapters focus on two key issues—the reality of groups and group development. Next, the processes that result in the establishment of a relatively unified group culture are described. In the following chapters, the components of a group's culture and social structure are discussed in the context of each group's developmental stage. Next, the interdependence of the individual and the group is explored. The mutual influences flowing among groups, organizations, and society are also discussed. Research methods to further our understanding in this area are outlined and assessed. The final chapters discuss applications of this material in counseling, learning, and work groups.

Group Processes attempts to describe group processes and structures as these develop and change throughout a group's life. Previous texts on groups have tended to compartmentalize group dynamics and to discuss topics such as group goals, norms, roles, and the like without reference to each other or to group developmental phases. This provided a rather static picture of dynamic processes. Group research has also tended to ignore developmental processes and their effects on other group phenomena. And yet, groups are dynamic. Goals, for example, are understood differently by members at different stages in a group's life cycle. The leader role changes over time. The function of conflict varies as well. This book attempts to convey this dynamic process by discussing these components at different points in a group's life. While the primary focus of this work is the group, the context in which groups operate is not ignored. How groups influence and are influenced by organizations, institutions, and society is described in order to broaden our perspective on group processes.

The book intends to be both conservative and scholarly and, at the same time, controversial and unorthodox. It is conservative in that research evidence is cited continuously to support its conclusions. It is controversial in that it proposes unorthodox notions about groups and individuals that conflict with prevailing ideological views. For example, while fully aware of the anthropomorphic heresy of attributing human characteristics to nonhuman entities, this work supports the view that groups are living systems with life spans that often exceed those of human beings. Many groups, such as families, work groups, or ethnic groups, exist well beyond the life spans of individual members.

Groups have a developmental life cycle. They go through stages of development analogous to those of human beings. Thus, there is a dependent stage similar to our childhood and a rebellious stage similar to adolescence. There is a stage where trust and intimacy and preparation for work are emphasized. This stage is reminiscent of young adulthood. There is also a mature stage devoted to relational and work generativity. Like people, groups can also regress to or get stuck in a developmental stage. Thus, groups can be neurotic, psychotic, or sociopathic, even though their members, as individuals, could not be described in similar ways (e.g., Agazarian & Peters, 1981; Lewin, 1951; Luft, 1984). Some have proposed that individuals are not real. Rather, the group, not the individual, is the basic unit of our social world (e.g., Hsu, 1971; Sampson, 1989; Sullivan, 1953). While such assertions may be overstatements in an effort to compensate for our tendency to see individuals as supreme among all creation, there is evidence to support this view and a reason to explore it as well. We have learned humility as a result of biological ecology. Perhaps it is time to learn humility with regard to the social environment as well.

Hogan (1975) said that the survival of early man was not dependent on the development of superior individuals. Rather, human survival was, and is, dependent on the development of efficient groups capable of meeting new challenges. Without equal attention to the ecology of our social world, biological ecology will not be enough. The social environment is of equal importance to the quality and continuation of human life.

ACKNOWLEDGMENTS

I would like to thank the reviewers for their excellent suggestions during the preparation of the manuscript:

Rosina Chia, *East Carolina University*
George Gazda, *University of Georgia*
David Lundgren, *University of Cincinnati*
Richard Moreland, *University of Pittsburgh*
Frank Wong, *Hofstra University*

I appreciate the study leave that was granted by Temple University to complete this project. Finally, I am grateful to the hundreds of students over the years whose questions and ideas pushed me to learn more.

1

ARE GROUPS REAL?

Webster's Dictionary (1989) defines a group as "a number of individuals assembled together or having some unifying relationship" (p. 539). In contrast, Luft (1984) defines a group as:

> *a living system, self-regulating through shared perception and interaction, sensing and feedback, and through interchange with the environment. Each group has unique wholeness qualities that become patterned by way of members' thinking, feeling, and communicating, into structured subsystems. The group finds some way to maintain balance while moving through progressive changes, creating its own guidelines and rules, and seeking its own goals through recurring cycles of interdependent behavior.* (p. 2)

These two definitions could not be more different. The first suggests that the term **group** is merely a convenient way to classify individuals who have, at least at the time, some common characteristic. The second asserts that a group is a living entity that transcends and cannot be explained by individual experience. In fact, Luft's definition suggests that a group may be as real as an individual, since an individual could readily be defined in a similar way. An individual is also a living system, self-regulating through shared perception and interaction, sensing, and feedback. An individual has unique wholeness qualities, or personality, that become patterned by way of thinking, feeling, and communicating. Individuals also seek to maintain balance while moving through progressive developmental changes, creating their own guidelines and rules, and seeking their own goals through recurring cycles of interaction with others.

For nearly a century, there has been debate among social scientists about the reality of groups. In 1895, Gustav Le Bon warned that groups are very real and potentially dangerous. He proposed that a group can take over the minds of its members and, in some cases, cause individuals to behave savagely (Le Bon,

1960). In recent times, the reemergence of youthful street gangs who attack innocent strangers has renewed scientific and public interest in this phenomenon originally described by Le Bon. The term *wilding* has been applied to such incidents and discussion, concern, and public outcry have ensued.

On the other hand, F. H. Allport (1924) maintained that groups are not real. They exist only in the behavior of individuals. A group is simply the shared thoughts, feelings, and behavior patterns that exist among group members. Other theories, however, disagreed with Allport's and stressed that a group is an entity that cannot be explained by understanding the total individual psychologies of its members (Agazarian & Peters, 1981; Durkheim, 1897; Lewin, 1951; Trotter, 1916; Warriner, 1956). Still others, while not using Le Bon's term, *group mind,* used similar concepts to describe group-level phenomena. Cartwright and Zander (1968), for example, maintained that a group can be emotionally healthy or pathological. Cattell (1951) described groups as possessing different personalities.

Some social scientists have continued to describe groups from the individual perspective. Bales (1950), for example, characterized a group as:

> *any number of persons engaged in interaction with one another in a single face-to-face meeting or series of such meetings, in which each member receives some impression or perception of each other member distinct enough so that he can, either at the time or in later questioning, give some reaction to each of the others as an individual person, even though it be only to recall that the other was present.* (p. 33)

T. M. Mills (1967) defined groups as "units composed of two or more persons who come into contact for a purpose and who consider the contact meaningful" (p. 2). Bass (1960) saw a group as a "collection of individuals whose existence as a collection is rewarding to the individuals" (p. 2). These three definitions of a group focus on individual perception, individual reward, and individual purpose and meaning and are, therefore, more in line with Allport's notion that groups are real only in the minds of individuals. Finally, more in keeping with Le Bon, Lewin (1951) and Fiedler (1967) defined a group in terms of the interdependence of its members in "the sense that an event which affects one member is likely to affect all" (Fiedler, p. 6).

The debate over the reality of groups continues. Some of the reasons for this may be the result of the group processes being argued. That is, the debate itself may provide evidence to support the reality of group-level phenomena. First, if group members develop shared values, norms, and ideologies (Shaw, 1981) and if groups are influenced by their context (Lewin, Lippitt & White, 1939), then it follows that American social scientists as a group are influenced by the values, norms, and ideologies of the broader U.S. society. Many writers and researchers have described the U.S. ideological focus on individualism (Bellah, Madsen, Sullivan, Swidler & Tipton, 1985; Mills, 1959; Slater, 1966). There tends to be a bias in U.S. theories and research toward the study of the individual as opposed to the group. Zander (1979) spoke of this bias when he said that "the theories that do exist . . . seldom aid in understanding groups as such, or even the behavior of members in behalf of their groups, because the theories often are based on ideas taken from individual psychology, and these are primarily concerned with the actions of individuals for the good of those individuals" (p. 423).

Second, Americans have been described as materialistic. That is, things that can be seen are worthy of study, whereas things that cannot be seen are relegated to the realm of myth and superstition. Groups cannot be seen per se. When we look at a group, we see a collection of individuals. Individuals have a clear physical reality. The physical reality of groups is not as apparent. Therefore, we tend to study the individual members much more than the group-as-a-whole (Agazarian & Peters, 1981).

D. T. Campbell (1958) stated that differences in the reality of an object or person as compared to a group are a matter of perception. Physical objects or beings have boundaries and are solid. We can use all our senses to confirm their reality. We can touch, see, hear, and use other senses to test the reality of an object or human being. Fewer sources of data can confirm the reality of a group. However, some of the factors that organize our perceptions of physical objects can be applied to groups as well. In determining whether a number of objects or persons are an entity, we take proximity and boundaries into account. Similarity and sharing a common fate are also principles that organize our perceptions. Thus, a number of individuals, who are perceived as similar in some ways, are found in close proximity, and seem to share a common fate, can be as much an entity as physical objects meeting the same criteria. For example, we recognize an ecosystem composed of animals, plants, bacteria, and their environment as an entity. In our daily experience, we also recognize groups as entities. We speak of the team's loss, the work group's success, the government's policy, and the class's behavior. In our minds an ecosystem or a group is an entity composed of interdependent elements.

Finally, competition, private property, and boundaries are part of U.S. ideology. Consequently, little interdisciplinary theorizing or research occurs in the competitive, territorial world of science. Understanding groups, however, is essentially an interdisciplinary concern. Knowledge of group phenomena is important in many disciplines. Consequently, research on groups is found in social psychology, education, sociology, clinical psychology, business, communications, anthropology, political science, organizational psychology, and economics (Worchel, Wood & Simpson, 1992). Most textbooks on groups do not include much interdisciplinary evidence, however, due to the difficulties researchers encounter when they attempt to develop collaborative relationships, publish, or access information across disciplinary boundaries.

The U.S. tendency to focus on the individual as opposed to the group has hampered research efforts. For example, small groups have been studied without regard to the influence of other group affiliations on their members. By excluding this factor from analysis, small group research may have come to some erroneous conclusions by attributing individual differences to personality factors rather than group affiliations. For example, *personality characteristics of* group members have been associated with group behavior and roles. Dominance and assertiveness have been found to relate to leadership (Borg, 1960; Smith & Cook, 1973) and participation (Shaw, 1959a). Emotional stability has been found to relate to morale (Haythorn, 1953) and leadership (Bass, McGehee, Hawkins, Young & Gebel, 1953). Men have been found to contribute more task input (e.g., Geis, Brown, Jennings & Corrado-Taylor, 1984; Strodtbeck & Mann, 1956) and to be perceived as leaders more frequently than women (e.g., Hare, 1976; Lockheed & Hall, 1976; Wheelan, 1974). Such studies have been interpreted to mean that individual variables, such as personality and sex, influence group processes and development more than group variables. This interpretation tends to support the idea that a group is merely a collection of individuals and to suggest that ensuring group efficiency and productivity is simply a matter of finding the right mix of individual personalities to be group members.

It is possible, however, that these same data could be used to support the notion that groups shape individual behavior more than the reverse. For example, individuals are members of many groups at the same time. Merton and Kitt (1950) described two types of groups to which people belong. A **membership group** is one that an individual belongs to by virtue of birth or life circumstances. It is not voluntary. Racial, ethnic, or sexual groupings are examples of membership groups. A **reference group** is "any group to which we belong or aspire to belong and which we use as a basis for judging the adequacy of our behavior" (Jones, Hendrick & Epstein, 1979, p. 486). Political, professional, class, or relational (e.g., single, married, parent) groupings are examples of reference groups. Both membership and reference groups have profound effects on individual behavior. Gender, family, work or professional, social, ethnic or cultural, religious, regional, and national memberships have all been found to influence attitudes, values, feelings, and behavior (Caspi, 1987; Kohn & Schooler, 1969, 1978; McGoldrick, Pearce & Giordano, 1982; Wiesz, Rothbaum & Blackburn, 1984).

The study of ethnic influences on behavior, attitudes, and feelings is well documented. Ethnic differences may be more important determinants of behavior than differences of philosophy or economic system. People who would not fight over ideological or political differences will, and often do, fight over national and ethnic differences. **Ethnicity** has been defined as the characteristics of historically unique subgroups. These characteristics are transmitted in family networks and, while diminished by intermarriage, are retained for many generations (McGoldrick & Rohrbaugh, 1987; McGoldrick et al., 1982). Ethnicity has been described as a fundamental determinant of values, needs, perceptions, identity, and behavior. To assume, then, that individual differences can be attributed solely to unique personality differences without considering ethnic group differences seems in error. Personality differences observed in groups are often used to support the notion that groups are simply the sum of individual characteristics. If, however, what we call personality characteristics are, in some cases, ethnic characteristics, then substantial support is lent to the reality of the group origins of individual behavior.

As has already been stated, much research points to the presence of sex differences in the functioning of small groups. Here again, differences in the behavior of men and women support the idea that membership groups influence our behavior as much as, if not more than, personality differences. Reference groups also affect the behavior of individuals. Training for a particular profession, for example, is not just technical or theoretical. It is also social. Candidates for membership in a particular professional group are socialized to hold similar attitudes and to live their lives in ways that are consistent with the norms of that particular profession (Janoff, 1992). As a result, we can with considerable accuracy pick out the banker, the professor, and the artist in a group by noting modes of dress, expressed attitudes, mannerisms, and behavior.

Members of a particular group, then, are not reacting and relating to that group alone. Their attitudes, feelings, and behaviors are also influenced by the other groups in which they hold membership (Tajfel, 1974, 1982). Internal conflicts may arise in individuals because of the behavioral expectations of the different groups to which an individual belongs. That is, how an individual is expected to behave in one group may be different from the expectations of other groups to which he or she belongs. These conflicts tend to be resolved in favor of the more important membership role (Killian, 1952; Reilly, 1978). If being a member of one's professional group is more important than belonging to a social group, for example, the individual may opt not to go along with the expectations of the less important social group.

Individual behavior in a group may be representative of the expected behavior of a member of a particular sex, ethnic, or professional group rather than of idiosyncratic personality characteristics. In fact, many of what we call personality characteristics might be more accurately described as normative behaviors required of members of particular societal subgroups or membership or reference groups (Ryff, 1987). Dominance, passivity, participation rate, affective expression, and the like vary among membership and reference groups. Also, association with a particular reference or membership group alters the perception of others as well. Individual behavior will be perceived as typical of the individual's most salient reference group and may be elicited by the group as well as initiated by the individual. For example, if a group expects a female member to be emotional, she may respond accordingly and confirm the group's expectation (Eagly, 1983; Eagly & Wood, 1982; Skrypnek & Snyder, 1982). In summary, by ignoring the influence of multiple group memberships on individuals, researchers may conclude that individuals are the prime factors that shape group interaction. In reality, these individuals may be reflecting the influence of other groups on the functioning of the group under investigation.

After reviewing the history of social psychology, A. Pepitone (1981) concluded that that field favors the study of the individual over the group. He stated that "theories based on intraindividual processes are inadequate to explain social behavior" (p. 972). The reality of groups is ignored. Comte (1855), considered the founder of sociology, said that social processes are very real and that to ignore this fact is a grave mistake. Durkheim (1897) contributed evidence in support of

Comte's assertion by demonstrating that different cultural norms and levels of cohesion or interdependence differentially affected suicide rates in various national groups. Hogan (1975) concluded on the basis of anthropological evidence that

> *human society throughout pre-history consisted of small groups literally struggling for survival, and survival was promoted by the quality of the group rather than the accomplishments of individuals. Specifically, an adaptive advantage was conferred on those groups that developed an efficient social organization defined in terms of leadership structure, division of labor, communication systems, transmission of knowledge, etc. Reasoning of this sort leads to two conclusions: First, culture or social organization rather than brain size was the key to man's evolutionary success; and second, the individualism assumed by many psychologists is probably an inaccurate reflection of man's biological nature. Rather, man seems to have evolved as a group-living, culture-bearing, norm-respecting animal whose survival was closely tied to his social institutions. (p. 537)*

Cassirer (1957), a philosopher, believed that human behavior could only be understood by looking at the context in which it occurred and at how societal institutions mutually influence each other and the individual. Mead (1934) said that even the contents of our minds and our self-concepts are learned in interaction with others. Lewin (1951) agreed. What motivates individual behavior is the influences and tensions affecting the individual at a particular point in time and in a particular social situation. The social situation, or group, is not merely a collection of people but a set of relationships and roles. Thus, we must learn more about these social situations and the laws that govern them in order to understand individuals.

Much of the research conducted by students of Lewin and other social scientists reinforces the validity of groups. Our perception of such an obvious thing as length, for example, can be altered by social pressure (Asch, 1951). If others say that the shortest rod is the longest, we may agree. Perception is altered by the conventions and pressures of the group (Sherif, 1936). The role one holds in a group alters individual behavior as well. Thus, when assigned the role of prison guard, we become more punitive (Zimbardo, Haney, Banks & Jaffe, 1973). Even conscience has not been found to be a stable personality characteristic. Rather, our moral choices are influenced by the groups we belong to and the norms and structures of those groups (Latane & Darley, 1968; Milgram, 1974).

Other evidence for the reality of groups includes research on the consistency of group development, regardless of individual member characteristics (e.g., Bennis & Shepard, 1956; Caple, 1978; Schutz, 1966; Tuckman, 1965). Also, group goals exert considerable influence on individual behavior (Zander & Newcomb, 1967). The physical environment in which a group is operating affects group structure and productivity (Carr & Dabbs, 1974; Glass, Singer & Friedman, 1969). The amount of cohesion in a group differentially affects morale, communication, and productivity (Schutz, 1958; Shaw & Shaw, 1962). Group rules or norms also influence individual behavior and group outcomes (Farrell, 1979, 1982; Geller, Goodstein, Silver & Sternberg, 1974).

Finally, common sense tells us that we are profoundly influenced by our group memberships. How we understand facts, events, and even ourselves depends on our memberships. How we behave and how we judge the correctness of our behavior are strongly influenced by our membership and reference groups as well. The remaining chapters describe in more depth the concepts and research referred to in this first chapter. The intention of this introductory discussion is simply to raise some of the issues and controversies surrounding the study of group phenomena. Also, the focus of this chapter is not intended to force a choice between the reality of individuals and the reality of groups. Both exist and are worthy of study. Research investigations utilizing the group and the individual as the unit of analysis are necessary to more fully understand human experience.

From this author's perspective, groups are very real. Groups vary in size from two people to millions of people, and one cannot understand a small group without reference to many larger groups and systems that influence the smaller group. Further, the study of group development and dynamics is presented as potentially critical to human survival. Groups influence our thoughts and behavior even when we are alone. There are many groups that we do not choose to belong to. We are born into a number of groups, and these groups profoundly shape who we are and what we can become. Groups expand or limit our personal choices and even the contents of our minds. At the macro level, the actions of groups expand or limit our chances for physical and psychological survival (Moscovici, 1990). Forces that are so powerful cannot be ignored or denied.

2

MODELS OF
GROUP DEVELOPMENT

Individual human beings appear to go through distinct and predictable phases over the course of their lives (e.g., Erikson, 1950). The field of developmental psychology has contributed greatly to our understanding of these patterns. Early development is clearly delineated. Adult development, while remaining a new frontier, also seems to have phases within it (Erikson, 1950, 1978; Levinson, Darrow, Klein, Levinson & McKee, 1978). Do groups develop as well? Are there predictable phases in the life of a group?

Research on this question has been ongoing for forty years. In 1951, Bales and Strodtbeck investigated the decision-making process in small groups that met for one session. They determined that when faced with a decision, groups go through a period of orientation in which information relevant to the decision is shared by individual members. This is followed by an evaluation phase in which differences of opinion, values, interpretation of facts, and proposed solutions are assessed. The control phase deals with how the group regulates member behavior and the task in order to come to a decision. They studied twenty-two problem-solving groups and found that 47 percent of the interaction in the first third of these groups dealt with orientation; 36 percent in the second phase related to evaluation; and 40 percent in the third period dealt with control. Since there was evidence of phases within one session, it seemed likely that group development occurred over a number of sessions as well. In 1953, Heinicke and Bales explored this possibility and concluded that groups do experience developmental changes across time.

Bennis and Shepard (1956) developed a theory of group development through the observation of T-groups. T-groups, unlike problem-solving groups, have two goals. The primary goal is to help individuals understand group dynamics and development through participation in an ongoing group. The secondary goal is for members to learn about how they as individuals interact in groups (Shaffer & Galinsky, 1989). In order to facilitate the accomplishment of these goals, the leadership style in such groups is nondirective. The leader comments on the processes occurring in the group but does not direct events or suggest courses of action. The leader tries not to interfere with the group's progression so that members can learn about the development and dynamics of naturally occurring groups. Bennis and Shepard proposed that there were two major phases in such groups. The first phase focuses on authority issues and structure. There are three subphases: dependency/flight, counterdependency/fight, and resolution/catharsis.

- *Dependency/Flight.* In this subphase, which occurs in the beginning of a newly forming group, members look to the leader for guidance. The anxiety of being in an unstructured situation seems to precipitate needs for certainty, direction, and safety. Members tend to think of the leader as omnipotent and benevolent. They try all kinds of strategies to gain his or her approval and direction. Simultaneously, while the group knows its task, the members avoid working on it. Interactions are not task oriented. Rather, members are more concerned with issues of psychological safety, leadership, and inclusion.
- *Counterdependency/Fight.* Because of the required role of a T-group leader or facilitator, he or she does not succumb to the group's wish for a traditional directive leader. Instead, the facilitator limits his or her comments to observations about how the group is functioning. This is frustrating to group members, and during this phase the group tends to split into two warring subgroups over this issue. One subgroup is angry at and rejecting of the facilitator's perceived lack of responsible leadership behavior. This group tends to disregard the facilitator's observations and to denigrate his or her competence. The other subgroup remains loyal to the facilitator and continues to seek his or her approval and direction. These two groups tend to argue with each other. Member attempts at leadership are thwarted by others. When members attempt to organize, develop norms, or set directions and goals, other members block these efforts at this stage.
- *Resolution/Catharsis.* Finally, the group begins to realize that the fight between the dependent, loyal subgroup and the counterdependent, antileader subgroup is inhibiting goal achievement. This realization is aided by the emergence of another subgroup that Bennis and Shepard call the independents. These individuals take on the role of mediating the fight between the counterdependents and dependents. The independents tend to view the facilitator's comments as useful but not directive or devious. Discussion of goals, structure, and norms occurs at this stage. The facilitator's role becomes less controversial and members begin to take responsibility for organizing and directing their own processes.

The second major phase proposed by Bennis and Shepard (1956) focuses on issues of intimacy and interdependence in member relationships. The subphases are enchantment/flight, disenchantment/fight, and resolution/catharsis.

- *Enchantment/Flight.* The fourth subphase appears very harmonious on the surface. Cohesion and a sense of euphoria are evident. Perhaps because of the tension experienced during the first phase of the group and its subsequent resolution, members wish to remain cooperative and pleasant with each other. Differences among members due to race, gender, ethnicity, religion, occupation, or other external roles tend to be denied or ignored. Sameness, cooperation, and agreement are strongly encouraged, and deviation from this group-imposed uniformity is strongly, if covertly, censored. Pressure to conform is very high. However, underlying tensions continue to build, since this uniformity is mythical and the group cannot communicate effectively by denying the reality of differences among members.

  Individuals, when they enter a group, bring with them the roles, values, attitudes, and behaviors required by the ongoing group memberships in their lives. Thus, the norms and behaviors of their ethnic, gender, religious, regional, and occupational groups (to name but a few) tend to define their sense of self. Inhibiting these behaviors and attitudes in order to gain membership in a new group generates tension and role conflict. Individuals begin to at least subconsciously feel disloyal to their other groups and inauthentic in their interactions in the new group. When a member says, "I can't be myself in this group," what is often meant is that he or she cannot express behaviors and attitudes that demonstrate the roles he or she plays in other groups that make up his or her sense of self. Thus, we have the feeling that we are not being real. We are not being true to ourselves and, as a result, true and loyal to the other groups of which we are a part.

- *Disenchantment/Fight.* Bennis and Shepard proposed that two subgroups emerge again: the overpersonals and the underpersonals. Overpersonal members want relationships to be intimate, while underpersonals express discomfort with that level of intimacy. The fight seems to be around how to relate to each other and how intimate and open members will be allowed to be. Questions about how much expression of feeling will be acceptable, how close members will become, and what behaviors will be allowed are the content of the feud. Again, a subgroup of independents often emerges to reconcile the two main subgroups.

- *Resolution/Catharsis.* The efforts of the independents lead to the establishment of group norms that allow for the expression of differences, feelings, and attitudes. Members begin to communicate in more valid ways. Work on the task of understanding group development and member roles proceeds in an atmosphere more conducive to learning and self-expression.

Bennis and Shepard presented this view of experiential groups but cautioned that not all groups go through all subphases. Groups can get stuck in early conflict stages and not develop further. Other groups regress for a period of time and move on with considerable difficulty. Factors that produce regression or total stalemate, while not completely understood, may include forces external to the group such as institutional racism, sexism, or political strife.

Thus, if a group contains members whose membership groups are in conflict, it may be very difficult, if not impossible, for the members to resolve role conflicts within the small group (Back, Bunker, & Dunnagan, 1972; Cohen, 1984). Other factors related to structure, norms, and the like may interfere as well.

Bion (1959) proposed that any group is really two groups—a work group and a basic-assumption group. That is, at any given moment, a group is either working on its task or acting as if it cannot work on the task due to the emotional tone of the group. Group emotionality or basic assumptions are expressed as dependency, fight/flight, or pairing. Dependency and fight/flight are defined in ways similar to the Bennis and Shepard approach. **Pairing** refers to subgroup formation and dissolution in the group. It occurs when two or more members develop allegiances to each other for periods of time. **Work** means that group interaction is related directly to goal achievement. Bion did not suggest an order or sequence of stages in which these dynamics occur. He believed that they could occur in any order or at any time.

Parsons (1961) proposed a model of small-group development based on the observation of task groups and therapy groups. He stated that four phases occur in every group. There is a period of **latent pattern maintenance** (L), the phase in which stable patterns of behavior are developed and maintained in the group. Norms for appropriate and inappropriate group behavior are developed and agreed to by the members. **Adaptation** (A) is the period in which group structures and roles are determined. **Goal attainment** (G) is the time in which the group works on and ultimately achieves its goal. **Integration** (I) refers to the period in which group structures and subsystems are adjusted in order to achieve effective functioning of the group-as-a-whole. Parsons, Bales, and Shils (1953) found that task groups tend to follow the AGIL sequence of phases. Learning and therapy groups utilize the LIGA sequence. Much later, Hare (1976) noted that most groups follow the LAIG sequence, although the A and I phases may be reversed.

In 1965, Tuckman reviewed the available developmental theories and research and came up with an integrative model of his own. Groups, he maintained, go through identifiable periods of forming, storming, norming, and performing. In 1977, Tuckman and Jensen added a fifth phase that they referred to as adjourning. Phase one, or **forming,** is a period devoted to issues of membership, inclusion, and dependency. **Storming** is similar to the conflict or fight stage described by Bennis and Shepard (1956) and Bion (1959). **Norming** is the period in which a group determines its rules, structure, and roles. **Performing** is similar to Parsons's goal attainment phase, in which the group actively works on its task. **Adjourning** refers to termination, in which a group deals with the fact that it has finished its task and is, as a result, disbanding.

Schutz (1966) presented a theory of group development based on the needs of members at certain periods in the group's development. According to Schutz, the first need to emerge in a group is the need for inclusion. **Inclusion** refers to the need to belong to the group and to be included in group interaction. This is followed by a **control** phase in which issues of power and authority among members are sorted out. Finally, the **affection** phase is characterized by work on the interpersonal relationships of members in order to meet needs for positive interpersonal interaction.

Zurcher (1969) observed 174 meetings of different neighborhood committees during a nineteen-month period. He determined that the stages these groups went through were orientation, catharsis, focus, action, limbo, testing, and purposiveness. Fisher (1970a) studied decision-making groups. He found the sequence to be orientation, conflict, emergence, and reinforcement.

Spitz and Sadock (1973) studied groups of student nurses and determined that these groups went through three stages: guardedness and anxiety, interaction and trust, and finally disengagement. LaCoursiere (1974) also observed student nurses during a weekly ninety-minute meeting. The group met for ten weeks. He found the stages to be orientation, dissatisfaction, production, and termination.

Dunphy (1974) observed two classes that were studying social relations. He analyzed student reports to obtain his results. His findings confirmed the following sequence: External norms and behaviors are maintained by group members; individual rivalries develop; conflict emerges and negativity among members is evident; concern with feelings is the focus of the next phase; and positive feelings and affection develop in the last stage.

Like Tuckman before him, Braaten (1974/1975) reviewed fourteen previous studies and determined that collectively they suggest that groups go through several phases: lack of structure, conflict, a focus on norm development and work, and lastly, termination.

Yalom (1975) based his findings on therapy groups. He found that these groups go through an orientation phase, a conflict phase, a period characterized as interpersonally close, and a termination phase. Mann, also in 1975, used an observation procedure to reach his conclusions. He described a sequence of phases: leader dependency, anxiety, and resistance; frustration and hostility; intimacy, integration, and work; and separation.

Near (1978) studied therapy groups in an attempt to test Schutz's model. She found that leader abdication and response to that was phase one. This was followed by a period of emotionality and norming. Issues of control and another period of emotional expression related to member leadership came next. The final phase dealt with inclusion and role differentiation. Caple (1978) offered the following sequence meant to be applicable to all types of groups: an orientation phase; a period of conflict; and integration, achievement, and order. Babad and Amir (1978) systematically investigated Bennis and Shepard's (1956) model, and their results were consistent with this early theoretical formulation.

Research that does not confirm the existence of group developmental patterns is minimal. Yalom (1975) suggested that research that does not support group development has been inconclusive. Cissna (1984) reviewed several studies that did not confirm a developmental sequence in groups. He also concluded that conceptual and methodological problems accounted for the negative findings.

AN INTEGRATIVE MODEL OF GROUP DEVELOPMENT

A number of theories and research studies related to group development have been outlined in the preceding section. While there are differences in terminology, there is considerable overlap among them. Where differences occur, they seem to be due to the nature of the group's task. Thus, research on experiential learning and therapy groups, taken together, suggests that such groups go through a period of orientation and dependency, followed by conflict. The third phase is characterized by the development of trust and interpersonal relationships. Termination issues dominate the fourth stage. Task groups also experience periods of orientation and conflict. The third stage is devoted to the development of structure and norms. Work and goal attainment dominate phase four, and if the group is temporary a termination phase occurs near its end.

Conspicuously absent from many investigations of experiential learning and therapy groups is a work phase. Likewise, a stage dealing with trust and the development of interpersonal relationships is absent from many studies of task groups. With regard to experiential learning and therapy groups, it may be difficult for researchers to define the work of the group since it frequently deals with relational issues. Thus, the work phase may be subsumed under phase three, which deals with the development of trust and interpersonal relationships. Work occurs but is rarely identified in most studies of therapy or learning groups. In task-oriented groups, stage three, which focuses on the development of norms, structure, and roles, undoubtedly includes attention to issues of trust and the development of interpersonal relationships. The way in which this is expressed, however, may make it difficult to identify using conventional observation systems, since the language and tone tend to be different in work settings than in learning and therapy settings. Group and societal norms are different in these contexts. Trust issues are generally dealt with in more covert ways (such as joking, teasing, or testing) in task groups and in more overt ways in learning and therapy groups.

In all types of groups, regardless of their task or the length of time they were studied, there are many more similarities reported in the literature than differences. The following is an attempt to describe in some detail what appears to be the process of group development across all types of groups (Wheelan, 1990).

Stage One: Dependency and Inclusion

A major characteristic of this first stage of group development is the significant amount of member dependency on the designated leader. When individuals enter a group situation, tension and anxiety frequently occur because the situation is new and, consequently, not clearly defined. Will the group be safe? Will the individual be accepted as a member? What will the rules of conduct and procedures be? Is the leader competent and capable of protecting individual members from attack and harm? Such questions are consciously or unconsciously on the minds of most members.

Since members have not yet interacted sufficiently with each other to establish relationships, they cannot rely on each other for support or structure. Consequently, the members are very leader focused. The implicit assumption is that the leader is capable and benevolent. He or she will provide protection and structure, which will relieve member tensions. The leader is deified in a sense, since his or her actual competence is not known but is taken on faith by members. Thus, groups during this early stage are solicitous of the leader and are eager to please this authority figure.

At the same time, members are testing the waters with regard to initial attempts to get to know each other and to determine what the rules, roles, and structures of this group will be. This initial exploration is very tentative and polite, since there is much fear of being perceived as deviant by other members. Fears of being excluded or attacked are high at this point. Few if any challenges of either the authority figure or each other occur. Reliance on the leader for direction and support is very much in evidence.

Independent action at this stage of group life occurs rarely, if at all. Human fears of abandonment or punishment run deep. No one voluntarily chooses to alienate others during this stage, since most of us have had experiences that lead us to assume that the price for deviance will be exorbitant. Members have not yet developed the relational connections that give rise to civilized, accepting behavior. It is much easier to attack or challenge an unknown person than it is to behave in such a manner with persons with whom we are involved. Even if members have known each other in different contexts, this situation is different and not yet defined. Also, since members tend to be anxious and fearful, they assume, with some justification, that some members may attempt to secure their own safety at the expense of others. Thus, politeness, tentativeness, and defensiveness are prevalent in this initial stage with regard to other members. Since work might precipitate conflict, members tend to avoid work by engaging in flight or discussions unrelated to the group's task. Work occurs, of course, but at minimal levels. With regard to the authority figure, members tend to be solicitous and to perceive this individual as all knowing and all loving. This hope, while clearly not realistic, tends to reduce member anxiety and concern to some extent.

Stage Two: Counterdependency and Fight

This stage is characterized by conflict between a member and a leader, among members, or among members and leaders. It also includes flight from task and continued attempts at tension avoidance. Conflict has been described as essential to the development of cohesion (Coser, 1956; Deutsch, 1971; Northen, 1969). It has also been described as a way to delineate areas of common values (Theodorson, 1962). Lewin (1936) wrote that the tension produced by conflict provides the opportunity to clarify psychological boundaries. This has the potential to create additional stability for the group through the establishment of shared values and norms. Rendle (1983) stated that group conflict is a means of balancing the differences found between extreme positions or views held by members. "It is in the balancing of polar extremes that conflict may be understood and described as an 'energy source,' which is available to drive the system of the small group"(p. 3).

Essentially, the group's task at this stage is to begin to struggle with how it will operate and what roles members will play. The anxiety and fear of the previous stage have produced an undifferentiated mass of participants dependent on authority for direction. As with individual human development, however, this rather merged and regressed stage becomes frustrating and confining. Consequently, individual members seek to define their roles more clearly, and the group seeks to liberate itself from the perceived control of the authority figure.

In order to achieve more independence, individual members begin to articulate their goals and ideas about group structure. Coalitions begin to form among members with similar ideas and values. Splits occur as a result, and conflict inevitably ensues. Simultaneously, the leader is alternately attacked by some coalitions and defended by others for perceived transgressions or positive actions.

All this struggling is, in large measure, an attempt on the part of the group to define itself and to begin to tentatively outline the structure of the group and the roles that various members will play. The motivation behind this is to reduce anxiety by clarifying the goals and structure of the group. Conflict is a necessary part of this process, since from divergent points of view one relatively unified direction must be achieved if group members are to be able to work together in a productive way.

On a more psychological level, conflict is necessary for the establishment of a safe environment. While this may seem paradoxical at first glance, conflict is helpful to the development of trust. We know from our own experience that it is easier to develop trust in another person or in a group if we believe that we can disagree, and we will not be abandoned or hurt for our differences. It is difficult to trust those who deny us the right to be ourselves. Thus, marriages become more solid and real after the first fight. The same could be said of all human relationships. To engage in conflict with others and to work it out is an exhilarating experience. It provides energy, a commonly shared experience, and a sense of safety and authenticity, and it allows for deeper intimacy and collaboration.

We also know from experience that conflict can lead to the destruction of relationships. Many groups get stuck in this stage and cannot progress. Longstanding wars, feuds, divorces, and the breakup of business partnerships are examples of the potential negative outcomes of conflict. Thus, while this stage cannot be avoided, since it is the only route to mature collaboration, most of us would rather bypass the conflict stage of group development. As with individual development, however, groups that avoid this stage remain dependent, insecure, and incapable of true collaboration, unitary action, or productive work.

Stage Three: Trust and Structure

Assuming that the conflict stage is successfully navigated, members of the group will feel more secure with and trusting of each other and the leader. Now the group can begin a more mature negotiation process about group goals, organizational structure, procedures, roles, and division of labor. Norms or rules of conduct can be decided upon. Communication, at this point, is more open and task oriented. Power struggles, while always still occurring, lessen in intensity. Feedback is possible and tends to be more related to the task at hand than to hidden agendas or emotionality. Information is shared rather than used as a way to gain status or power.

In a sense, the group at this stage is designing itself. It is laying the groundwork and planning the way in which it will function to accomplish its task. In so doing, the group is preparing for work. Work occurs at every stage of group development. However, the attention to structures and roles that occurs during this stage significantly increases the group's capacity to work effectively and productively. Of course, at the same time, relationships are becoming more defined, and role assignments can be made on the basis of competence and talent rather than fantasy or wishes for safety or power.

Stage Four: Work

Once goals, structure, and norms are established, the group can work more effectively. Work begins as an idea and ends with a product that has real effects on some part of the environment. Thus, committees that meet again and again but never produce a report or a product are not working. Such groups are most likely stuck in one of the earlier stages of development.

In order to work, people must be able to communicate freely about ideas and information. If individual group members fear reprisals for offering suggestions or feedback, necessary information will be withheld from the group, and its product, should there be one, will be inferior as a result. Another factor required for work to occur is an awareness of time. Work occurs within a time frame. Thus, groups who are always working probably are not working effectively, and those who start late are definitely not working effectively. This does not mean that groups will spend the majority of their time working. Human beings and human groups need time to deal with emotional and relational issues throughout their lives. Efficiently functioning groups spend about 60 percent of the time allotted actually working (Bales, 1970). The remainder is used for group maintenance, dealing with interpersonal issues that arise, and the like. Workaholic groups, like workaholic individuals, are unlikely to produce their best possible results.

For work to occur, groups must also be able to use available resources. Resources include such things as information, individual expertise, and materials, if these are necessary to accomplish the task. Most of us have been members of groups who refuse to listen to certain information because the individual who offers it is somehow devalued by the group. Such groups have not adequately resolved the issues of previous stages, such as trust and roles, and as a result are unable to utilize input necessary to their work.

Stage Five: Termination

Most temporary groups have an ending point. Of course, some groups continue beyond the tenure or, in some cases, the life span of individual members. Family groups and institutional groups are examples of continuous groups. Even in continuous groups, however, there are various endings: Tasks are completed, children leave home, and members retire or leave. At each ending point, functional groups tend to evaluate their work together, to give feedback, and to express feelings about each other and the group (Lundgren & Knight, 1978). Of course, many groups do not do these things. This is unfortunate, since this type of processing is invaluable to individual members and can significantly enhance their ability to work effectively in future groups.

Impending termination alters the structure of a group, and regression to earlier stages is very likely. As a result, termination points can cause a reoccurrence of conflict and negativity (Farrell, 1976; Mills, 1964). During this period, members also discuss their reactions to being separated from each other and the group (Dunphy, 1968; Gibbard & Hartman, 1973; Miles, 1971; Slater, 1966).

The preceding formulation of group development assumes that these stages occur in all groups. There has been considerable argument about whether sequenced stages are the best way to describe group processes. Bion (1959), for example, does not assume an order to his basic assumptions. Thus, dependency could follow work or precede it, and any basic assumption could occur at any time. Schutz (1966), Bennis and Shepard (1956), Tuckman (1965), and many others do pose an invariate order. This author agrees in part with both views. Experience, logic, and research suggest that some processes or stages occur before others in group development. Dependency is less likely to occur after trust and structure are established, for example. Also, our knowledge of individual development supports the notion that certain psychological phenomena must, of necessity, occur prior to others. As an example, it is difficult to envision a rebellious antiadult newborn.

On the other hand, regression occurs in individuals with great regularity. Under conditions of severe stress, the most mature adult may become helpless and dependent for a period of time. Changes in the environment, disturbing new information, structural changes, new sets of demands, and the like affect an individual's ability to operate in a mature manner. So, too, groups may fluctuate widely based on the circumstances and forces affecting the group at a given moment.

Changes in the membership, external demands, changes in the psychological state of a member, and changes in leadership can all affect the structure and the work of a group. In work groups, turnover rates, reassignments, and new managers or group leaders often produce regression and require a rebuilding of the group. Unfortunately, this fact is frequently ignored or unknown by members or leaders, wreaking havoc with productivity.

Groups, like people, can get stuck in a particular stage, often with serious consequences. Frequently, groups remain in the counterdependency and fight stage for extended periods. Such groups spend an inordinate amount of time fighting with the leadership or with each other, to the detriment of the task. Other groups may get stuck in the trust segment of stage three. Such groups expend considerable energy dealing with the emotional aspects of group life, but fail to establish structural agreements that would allow them to work on the task. These groups are reminiscent of love-ins in that they are concerned with developing relationships and good feelings. Usually, basic fears regarding performance and differentiation underlie the group's refusal to focus on work.

Finally, some groups remain dependent for extended periods of time. Thus, if the leader is not present, the group cannot work. These groups are, in general, avoiding the conflict that accompanies further development. One serious consequence of this is that such groups are incapable of collaborative, thoughtful work. They do what they are told and not much more. Questioning, challenging, or constructive feedback cannot occur. Such groups are ripe for being led into negative actions. Some cults, work groups, classes, and families arrested at this stage have done quite destructive things.

VALIDATION STUDIES OF THE INTEGRATED MODEL

The integrated model of group development was derived from previous work. An analysis of theoretical models and research was conducted to determine their common threads, and these commonalities formed the basis for the model. To date, validation studies with six groups have been completed (Verdi & Wheelan, 1992; Wheelan & McKeage, 1993). Six groups who met from a minimum of four-and-a-half hours to a maximum of seven-and-a-half hours were investigated using a systematic observation system. The Group Development Observation System (Wheelan, Verdi & McKeage, in process) classifies each verbal unit expressed in a group into one of seven categories. The categories include dependency, counterdependency, flight, fight, pairing, counterpairing, and work. A unit was defined as a complete thought or simple sentence. "I like you" would be classified as pairing. "I'm not interested in friendship" is an example of counterpairing. "I don't know what to do" is a dependent statement. "The leader is incompetent" is a counterdependent statement. "Did you watch the ball game last night?" is a flight statement. "I don't want to be in the same group with you" is a fight statement. "Let's focus on the task at hand" is an example of a work statement (Verdi & Wheelan, 1992).

The integrated theory would predict that the number of dependency statements would be highest during the first two stages of a group. Fight and counterpairing should peak during the second and last stages. Work statements should be most frequent during the fourth stage and decrease during the termination stage. In general, these predictions were confirmed in five of the six groups. In one group, flight increased and pairing decreased from beginning to end. This group was considerably larger than the other five, which suggests that size may influence group development to some extent. However, the results of these studies support the validity of the proposed theory.

A content analysis method was employed to study twelve groups. Content analysis is a method used to determine conversational themes in groups (Glaser & Strauss, 1967; Holsti, 1969; Spradley, 1979, 1980). The results of these analyses also lent support to the integrated model. Discussion themes tended to occur as predicted. For example, conflict and competition themes were most frequent during the second stage, and intimate personal discussions did not occur until the third stage of these groups (Wheelan & Krasick, 1993). More studies are needed to fully investigate the utility of the integrated model. However, results to date seem promising.

GROUP PSYCHOLOGICAL ADJUSTMENT

Given the fact that groups develop, like people, a question arises: Do groups suffer from developmental and psychological problems the same as people do? As has already been stated, it does appear that groups can regress or suffer arrested development, as is the case with individuals. Family groups, for example, may be unable to adapt to the demands of the next stage of family development and, as a result, may develop significant problems. Work groups may also fail to progress to later stages of group development and productivity and member morale may be negatively affected as a result. Also, mature, well-functioning groups, like mature individuals, can regress because of stress or perceived negative input. New company rules, a labor dispute, and many other factors may profoundly affect the development of a work group. For example, an effective work team may regress when its manager is replaced or promoted.

On the broader macro level, famine, war, economic depressions, significant changes in government policy, and the like can wreak havoc with the work effectiveness of innumerable groups within a society all at once (Staub, 1990). Extended civil war, for example, could be compared to a group stuck at the conflict stage of development. In such cases, and there are many throughout the globe at any moment, the conflict becomes the primary focus of group energy. Economic development, education, ecological concerns, and even food distribution may be neglected as a result.

At the micro level, many consultants, including this author, have seen organizations and work groups stuck at the conflict stage to the detriment of the work task. In some cases, companies literally go bankrupt rather than work to resolve the conflict. While individuals within the organization may be painfully aware of the consequences of such a protracted fight, they seem unable to mediate the necessary settlement.

Some organizations do not go out of business. Government agencies, schools, or hospitals may continue to function but at considerable cost to personnel and to the public they serve. Many schools in the United States right now, for example, are mired in conflict. Standards are perceived to be lessening.

Educators, parents, students, and the community at large are very distressed by this. Conflict among the various constituent groups is significant. In one particular case, the teachers blamed the principal. In their view, student performance was suffering due to the repressive, dictatorial leadership style of the principal. Simultaneously, they blamed each other for not working hard enough. They blamed students for their lack of motivation and parents for their lack of involvement. The principal, on the other hand, was convinced that the teachers were at fault. If they would only use better teaching techniques and work harder, students would learn. Even with considerable outside intervention, however, no change occurred. It proved too difficult for the various sides in the controversy to give up blaming and attempt to mediate differences in order to work on the task of educating children. This case is not unique. Nor are there any villains in the piece. These are people of good will stuck in a mire of dissension and unable to extricate themselves. So, conflict and task avoidance prevail over cooperation and productive work (Wheelan & Conway, 1992).

Groups can also elevate the functioning level of the individuals within them. Mature, effective groups can facilitate the individual development of members. Individual desires for membership and inclusion lead people to conform to group standards and norms. Thus, in a highly motivated, work-oriented group, individual performance often improves (Johnson, 1980; Rosenthal & Rubin, 1978).

Finally, because of our societal lack of awareness of group development and processes, individuals are often blamed for things over which they have little control. For example, periodically there is a violent incident and passersby do not help. Public outrage is expressed, and editorials are written about the immorality of the individual bystanders. However, the bystanders may be caught in a group dynamic process. Had there been only one bystander, the individual most likely would have responded in some way. Or if an organized group, such as a team or a group of coworkers, had observed the incident, they most likely would have responded. In the case of an individual, there is no diffusion of responsibility. That is, the person cannot assume that someone else will respond to the situation. He or she alone is present. In the case of an organized group, development has occurred, and there are roles and norms already established. The group can act in concert.

However, when strangers just happen onto a scene at the same time, there is no structure. No interaction rules, no trust, and no roles have been established. By virtue of simultaneously viewing the event, they have a common focus and share a common problem. Thus, they are the beginning of a group. But they are at stage one, dependency and inclusion. Group action is highly unlikely, and individual action, at that stage, is equally unlikely. If a societally acknowledged authority figure, such as a police or military officer, were present, he or she could possibly lead the group to act. Otherwise, the probability of group or individual action in that situation is very remote. Such situations are very difficult to research, because they are spontaneous occurrences. But our understanding of group development makes this a compelling argument.

RECENT GROUP DEVELOPMENT RESEARCH

A great deal of group research was conducted between 1940 and 1970. Since then, however, research investigations have decreased in number. Group research conducted after 1970 was often done to look at the therapeutic or educational effects on individuals of particular models of group leadership or structure. Less basic research was conducted to enhance our understanding of group development.

In the past few years, there has been a resurgence of interest in group dynamics and development. Renewed interest has been fueled by the increasing need to utilize teams in the workplace. Efforts to understand the nature of productive work teams have stimulated a revival of interest in basic research in this area. This is a very positive development, since much of the previous research on groups was conducted on training or laboratory groups (Heinen & Jacobson, 1976; Moreland & Levine, 1988). Studying more groups with different types of tasks will add to our understanding of these phenomena. In addition, it will provide the opportunity to determine whether workplace groups have similar or different patterns of development than groups operating in other contexts.

Recent research noted that a set of work teams did not follow the general sequence of development outlined in this chapter. The punctuated equilibrium model, developed by Gersick (1988), suggested that work teams go through periods of stability that are punctuated by brief periods of considerable change. These are followed by periods of stability. The change periods occurred at approximately the midpoint of the group's life. Gersick studied teams that had project deadlines and found that these midpoint transitions occurred in the groups whether they met for seven days or six months. Glickman and his associates (1987) studied thirteen navy gunnery teams during their training. In these teams, the initial focus was on teamwork or coordination. The next phase focused on taskwork or goal achievement. These studies suggest that the developmental sequence of organizational groups may differ from that of training or laboratory groups.

The idea that the type of group and the environmental conditions in which groups operate influence the sequencing of group development is not new. Bell (1982) noted that the sequence of phases or stages does vary in different research investigations. As Brower (1986) stated, there is more than sufficient evidence to conclude that all groups face a basic set of issues or developmental tasks. This conclusion is supported by other researchers as well (Bales, Cohen & Williamson, 1980; Bell, 1982; Hartman, 1979). However, even modest environmental differences may influence the sequencing of development and the emphasis placed on specific developmental tasks. For example, the sex of the leader (Reed, 1979), the historical time period in which groups are studied (Gustafson & Cooper, 1979), the type of group, and its context (Gersick, 1988) have all been found to influence developmental processes.

Another recent model of group development (Worchel, Coutant-Sassic & Grossman, 1992) may serve to elucidate environmental effects on groups. The authors of this model were interested in understanding how groups form as well as how they function once established. The researchers analyzed books describing the development of groups. Literature detailing the development of the civil rights and women's movements, community political action groups, divisions of professional societies, labor unions, environmental groups, and work groups operating during periods of crisis was examined. A political group in Poland and two small political parties in Israel were also investigated.

By analyzing the common developmental processes in these groups, the researchers constructed a six-stage model of group development. The first stage is a period of discontent in which individuals are members of a group that is not meeting their needs. Individuals feel alienated and frustrated. They become passive and withdrawn and often drop out of the group. Sometimes members resort to violence or vandalism to express their frustration. If the group members or leaders attempt to change things by meeting member needs, the group may survive intact. However, this does not usually occur. Instead, conditions proceed to the next stage, identified by the occurrence of a precipitating event.

Worchel, Coutant-Sassic, and Grossman use the killing of students at Kent State University as an example of a precipitating event that led to the emergence of the anti–Vietnam War movement. Precipitating events are not always so dramatic, but they are distinct and always symbolically represent the issues surrounding the discontent and alienation of members of the current group. The event causes a split in the original group, between those who remain loyal to and those who are alienated from the original group.

During the third stage, the alienated splinter group works to develop a sense of identity as a separate group. Ideology, norms, leadership, and structures of the new group are established, and contact with the original group is severed. Member conformity with the new ideas and procedures is adamantly enforced. This stage is followed by a productive period in which goals and tasks are identified and worked on. New members are recruited, and conformity demands lessen to some extent.

Individuation characterizes the fifth stage. Individuals attempt to negotiate with the new group in order to get personal needs met. Leadership becomes less centralized, and members seek personal freedom. Individuals may even use the threat of leaving the group in order to influence the group to make changes. During the sixth stage, described as a period of decay, members begin to feel alienated from this group as well. Leaders are challenged and distrust increases. This phase sets the stage for another phase of discontent and begins the cycle once again.

The model proposed by Worchel, Coutant-Sassic, and Grossman fits well with many other theories discussed earlier in the chapter and adds another dimension. It is similar to other approaches in that the stages of discontent and the precipitating event resemble the conflict stage described in many previous formulations (e.g., Tuckman, 1965; Wheelan, 1990). The stage of group identification is very similar to the dependency and inclusion stage described in earlier work. The characteristics of the group productivity and individuation stages fit well with descriptions of the conflict stage and the trust and structure stage, although in reverse order. The decay of stage six seems to suggest an inability to resolve key conflicts and a return to conflict.

Worchel, Coutant-Sassic, and Grossman's model adds a new dimension to our understanding of what happens in groups who become mired in conflict and unable to meet member needs. Ultimately, such groups splinter, and new groups emerge who attempt to operate more effectively. In this model, however, the inability to meet member needs or to resolve conflicts seems inevitable and cyclic. More research is needed on this point, since many groups do seem to be able to resolve problems and function effectively over long periods of time. Whether this model can be applied to all groups is questionable. However, it does add to our understanding of what occurs when dissension becomes intractable.

In summary, groups do develop. They can also regress or arrest in their development. Groups are confronted with apparently universal developmental tasks. The order in which they approach these tasks can vary depending on the circumstances in which groups are operating. Groups do appear to behave in ways that can be described as healthy and mature or pathological and destructive. Their influence on the behavior of individual members is profound. Certainly, phenomena as powerful as these are worthy of study, since they impact individual, institutional, societal, and international life so greatly. And yet, while much research has been done, a tremendous amount remains to be done. A new group of interested scientists is needed to expand our efforts to understand these powerful phenomena.

To that end, the next chapter discusses the elements that comprise group culture and social structure. With these basic elements in mind, the subsequent chapters consider these elements in the context of group development. Research methods that are used to study group development and dynamics are detailed and applications to a variety of groups are discussed. Hopefully, new recruits to the study of group phenomena will be found among the readership of this book.

3

ELEMENTS OF GROUP CULTURE AND STRUCTURE

Slater (1966) described the small group as a microcosm of the society at large. That is, the culture and structures of an individual group are influenced by and reflective of the larger society. The way in which the group's processes and structures are developed, maintained, and changed will also reflect societal methods for the development and alteration of similar elements. This is not surprising, since society and culture are products of small group interaction. Early humans lived in small face-to-face groups (Mayr, 1963; Washburn, 1962). As was stated previously, the ability of these ancestral groups to survive depended on their skill at organizing to meet their basic needs and adapting their organizational structures to deal with the new challenges that emerged. "An adaptive advantage was conferred on those groups that developed an efficient social organization defined in terms of leadership structure, division of labor, communication systems, transmission of knowledge, etc." (Hogan, 1975, p. 537).

The processes that create a small group's cultural system and organizational structures are precursors of the processes occurring at the macro level of culture and society today. Historically, the small group predates current mass societies. The origins of the organizational processes of mass society are found in the small group. They are not the same, of course. With increasing size, technological advances, and the like, mass society has evolved more complex dynamics than those found in the small group. However, many similarities remain. The study of smaller groups, then, does much to aid our understanding of larger social systems, and vice versa.

Small groups have also become more complex over the millennia. An isolated tribe with little or no interaction with other groups would logically require less complex systems of organization than the small group of today. The modern small group exists within the context of mass society. Norms, values, and conventional ways of organizing at the societal level influence small groups in profound ways. Also, members of a modern group are rarely members of that group alone. They come to the group holding multiple memberships. Consequently, members may represent considerable diversity in background, status, roles, attitudes, and behavior. Group integration and the development of consensual views and plans are, as a result, more complicated and difficult (Back et al., 1972). Mobility, another fact of life in modern times, makes group cohesion, loyalty, and stability more difficult than they would be in sedentary, isolated groups. As a result, even the study of small groups has become more difficult, since the number of factors influencing them has increased. There are many thorough compilations of research on group dynamics (e.g., Forsyth, 1990; Hare, 1976; Shaw, 1981). In general, however, these works do not deal with the complexities of group life. The contexts in which groups operate are not examined to any great extent. The influences of internal, external, and historical factors on the development of culture and social organization in groups are typically not addressed. This chapter attempts to describe the development, maintenance, and adaptation of small group culture and social structure. It does so with reference to the larger contexts that influence intragroup processes. It outlines the basic elements of group culture and structure. It also emphasizes the interconnectedness of these internal elements and similar elements occurring in the larger contexts in which a particular group operates. Later chapters describe how these elements change as a result of group developmental processes.

GROUP CULTURE

Culture, from the sociological perspective, is the collective script that dictates how a society is to be organized and built. Culture, in this view, is to society what DNA is to the biological human. As DNA dictates the characteristics and physical organization of a unique human being, so culture defines the characteristics and social organization of a unique human society. Societies are not the only social systems that develop cultures. All social systems do, and small groups are no exception. When a new group forms, the primary task is to create an organized system capable of achieving goals. In order to do that, the group's members need to develop shared perceptions of how the system is to be organized. That is, the members need to create a group culture that will dictate its social structure. Logically, group culture would develop first and social organization second. However, the demands of survival, the influence of past group experience, and the interconnectedness between group culture and structure necessitate simultaneous development.

In no case does a modern-day group begin from scratch to develop its culture. Through the process of socialization, individuals internalize the culture of the society in which they live. Socialization enables people to take on social roles and to learn cultural values, norms, and ideologies. As a result of interactions in many social situations and groups, individuals learn how to think and act like other members of their culture. Individuals learn the customs, roles, beliefs, accepted behaviors, and attitudes of members of their particular society. Socialization serves to reconstitute society across generations. It ensures that traditions, modes of behavior, beliefs, and roles will be carried on in the future. It reproduces culture across time. Each generation inherits the cultural blueprint of its ancestors. No generation invents its culture from scratch.

When individuals come together to form a new group, they bring with them the internalized cultural blueprint of their society. In addition, they bring with them the internalized blueprints of the gender, ethnic, occupational, and other subgroups to which they belong. To the extent that member backgrounds and cultural subgroups are similar, developing shared perceptions about how they will interact and organize this particular group is a relatively simple matter. The greater the diversity of cultural subgroups represented in the new group, however, the greater the difficulty of developing shared perceptions regarding the culture of this particular group. In U.S. society, given the amount of cultural diversity it contains, the melding of individuals into an interdependent unit can be quite a task.

Schein (1990) defines **culture** as:

a) a pattern of basic assumptions, b) invented, discovered, or developed by a given group, c) as it learns to cope with its problems of external adaptation and internal integration, d) that has worked well enough to be considered valid and, therefore, e) is to be taught to new members as the f) correct way to perceive, think, and feel in relation to those problems. (p. 111)

Culture is a response to challenges that all groups or organizations must deal with (Ancona, 1987; Schein, 1985, 1988). Agreement about values, norms, and ideologies reduces member anxiety and increases the ability to predict and understand the events that occur. Consensus on these issues helps individuals to know how to respond in various situations. The building blocks of a society's culture include values, norms, and ideologies. They are the same in groups as well. These elements combine to build a coherent group culture. Their role in the development of group culture is discussed in the following sections. Of course, for group members to come to agreements about what they value, how they will behave, and how they will interpret their experiences, they must communicate, or exchange information, thoughts, and feelings with each other. Therefore, group communication is described first. This is followed by discussions of the basic elements of group culture—values, norms, and ideologies.

COMMUNICATION IN GROUPS

Communication is the most basic necessity in groups. "People can only form groups when they communicate or interact regularly with each other" (Nixon,

1979, p. 65). Communication is essential, since the group needs to build a relatively uniform culture and social structure. To do this, members must share and compare their beliefs, values, and attitudes with each other in order to establish balance and develop consistency in these areas (Festinger, 1954). Communication, then, is an essential process in the development of group culture.

The ways in which members communicate with each other are not haphazard. Communication patterns or networks that determine, among other things, who may talk to whom, are established very quickly. Once established, these patterns are quite resistant to change (Mills, 1967). On the one hand, the rapidity with which communication patterns are developed helps the group get on with its work. It is the first part of the group's social structure to emerge and is useful in facilitating organized discussion of group culture and additional structural needs. On the other hand, the type of communication structure that develops at this early stage greatly influences future organizational structures and social processes. The type of communication structure that is adopted has been found to affect leadership, group morale, problem-solving efficiency, cohesion, and group integration (Kano, 1971; Lawson, 1965; Leavitt, 1951; Schein, 1958).

For example, before a group's communication structure is firmly established, members tend to communicate more frequently with others whom they perceive to be of lower status than themselves. The initial status of an individual is largely determined by his or her most salient membership and reference groups. Other factors that determine initial status include titles, previously known information about an individual, observed behavior, credentials, and information provided by the individual him- or herself. This initial communication pattern is interpreted as an attempt on the part of individuals to establish high positions in the emerging pecking order of the group by communicating in a downward direction. Once the communication structure stabilizes, however, members begin to communicate more frequently with members of higher status than with those of lower status. This is thought to be an attempt on the part of lower-status members to move up in the hierarchy by identifying with and currying the favor of higher-status members. This shift from downward communication to upward communication is a consistent research finding (Crosbie, 1975; Larsen & Hill, 1958).

In larger, formal organizations we find the same tendency to communicate upward within status levels once communication stabilizes, but not outside that particular group. That is, within a unit or department, members communicate more frequently with higher-status individuals but not with higher-status individuals outside the group. Thus, a middle-level manager in a production unit will communicate more frequently with upper-level managers within that unit but is unlikely to attempt frequent communication with an upper-level manager in sales. This is thought to be due to the sanctions imposed on this type of behavior and the increased risks involved (Blau & Scott, 1962; Collins & Guetzkow, 1964; Simpson, 1959).

From the very beginning, the act of communicating serves to aid discussion of group concerns but, at the same time, begins to establish the structure of the status-leadership hierarchy. While the group is still tentatively attempting to define its needs and wishes concerning its goals, culture, and organizational structure, it is, albeit unwittingly in most cases, establishing a status hierarchy. The hierarchy that is established may or may not meet the group's needs in the future but, nevertheless, it becomes quite stable at this early period.

In work groups, for example, leadership is frequently designated before the group meets. These designations are often made on the basis of rank within the organization rather than competence with regard to the task of the group or leadership skills. Such a designated leader may not be the best choice for the role and can inhibit discussion and communication. This may keep the group from developing beyond stage one (dependency) and, as a result, inhibit the group's ability to work effectively on the task.

When leadership is not designated beforehand, problems can also emerge due to initial group perceptions of status. For example, a member who might be suited to the leadership role is overlooked by the group due to his or her membership or reference group status. A competent woman, for example, may not be perceived as capable of assuming a leadership role. Reference group status may also interfere with perceived leadership. Type of profession or professional status may preclude a capable individual from being perceived as leadership material. Initial communication patterns, then, can produce a status-leadership hierarchy in the group that ultimately may doom the group to failure.

We know from experience that the way people communicate in groups is not random. Some people talk more than others and some are talked to more than others. This might be attributed solely to personality characteristics. However, it also has to do with one's physical placement in the communication network of a particular group. A series of experiments has been conducted over the years to investigate this question. Different kinds of communication networks have been studied. Based on the early work of Bavelas (1950) and Leavitt (1951), researchers have experimented with different kinds of three-, four-, and five-person communication networks. Four of the more typically used networks are pictured in Figure 3–1.

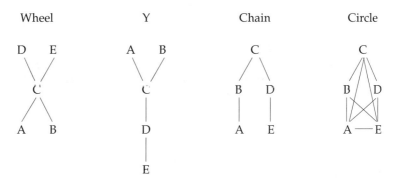

FIGURE 3–1   Types of Communication Networks

Only individuals connected by lines can talk to each other in these experiments. The wheel and Y networks are called *centralized,* since they tend to funnel communication through a central person (C). The circle is called *decentralized,* since there is no central person or persons. Many studies were conducted on these and other network arrangements. One important result is that the person in the most central position in a network is most likely to be perceived as the leader (Leavitt, 1951; Shaw, 1954a). This has been found to be true of cross-cultural subjects as well (Hirota, 1953). This result, confirmed in a number of studies, is thought to be due to the fact that the central person has access to more information and can coordinate the activities of other members.

The type of network used affects not only leadership but also the way a group organizes to do its work. Centralized networks lead to the development of centralized organizational patterns. That is, all information goes to one person, who solves the group problem and checks with another member to confirm the solution. In decentralized networks, a decentralized organizational pattern develops in which all information goes to all members, who solve the group problem independently, and then results are checked with everyone. The wheel, Y, and chain communication networks generate centralized organizational patterns. The circle produces a decentralized organizational pattern (Cohen, 1962; Guetzkow & Dill, 1957; Leavitt, 1951; Schein, 1958; Shaw, 1954b; Shaw & Rothschild, 1956). When the type of communication network is unrestricted, a decentralized pattern emerges.

While these experiments may seem unrealistic and manipulated to the reader, many work groups are organized in these different ways. In some work groups, individuals confer with the leader or manager only. In other cases, upper-level managers confer with a middle manager who relays the information downward in the chain of command. Other groups meet together frequently to discuss and come to shared agreements about work goals and plans. These choices about how communication can occur may be conscious or unconscious, or based on traditional values and structures. They are usually not decided on the basis of efficiency or productivity. So a question arises: Which type of communication network is most efficient and produces the best results?

Initial research investigations found the centralized wheel and Y communication networks to be most efficient and to produce the best results. The circle was found to be least efficient in terms of time and results (Guetzkow & Simon, 1955; Hirota, 1953; Kano, 1971; Lawson, 1964a; Leavitt, 1951). However, in these early investigations, the problems groups were asked to solve were relatively simple. When more complex problems were used, the circle was found to be most efficient (Kano, 1971; Lawson, 1964a; Mulder, 1960; Shaw, 1954b). This lends support to the current effort to decentralize work groups. As the problems faced by institutions have become more complicated and interconnected, traditional hierarchical communication networks tend to inhibit the generation of solutions. A movement toward decentralization is occurring in some work organizations as a result (Sundstrom, DeMeuse & Futrell, 1990). There is considerable resistance to this change since, as was previously noted, groups resist changes in their communication structures (Mills, 1967). However, awareness of the need for decentralization is growing (Hollander & Offermann, 1990).

Another question of interest to researchers was: Which type of communication structure is most satisfying to members? Member satisfaction is one of the factors that aids group cohesion. Group cohesion is "the resultant of all forces acting on the members to remain in the group" (Festinger, 1950, p. 274). Efficiency, then, may not be the only criterion for choosing a communication network (if the type of network is consciously chosen). Member satisfaction and group cohesion are important to the stability of the group and, ultimately, to efficiency and productivity. In investigations of this question, group member satisfaction has been consistently found to be higher in decentralized communication networks such as the circle (Cohen, 1961, 1962; Lawson, 1965; Leavitt, 1951; Shaw, 1954a; Shaw & Rothschild, 1956).

In summary, then, centralized communication networks facilitate the emergence of leadership and speed organizational development in groups, but inhibit solving complex problems and decrease member satisfaction (Shaw, 1981, p. 161). Decentralized communication networks are less time efficient and slow organizational development and the emergence of leadership. However, they aid in solving complex problems, increase member satisfaction, and increase group cohesion.

Another way to interpret these results is to view them in relation to group development theory. Centralized communication structures are very likely to inhibit group development. In effect, the group is forced by such structures to remain in the dependency or counterdependency stage of group development described in Chapter 2. Remaining in these early stages of group development impedes problem solving and increases member dissatisfaction with the group. The findings of research on the effects of communication structures are similar to the findings on the processes involved in group development. Thus, one of the ways to impede group development may be to establish a centralized communication network.

Decentralized communication networks, on the other hand, may help groups to develop to the work stage. The process takes longer but facilitates complex problem solving. Most modern-day work group goals require complex problem solving and, therefore, a decentralized communication network. The fact that many groups do not initiate decentralization may be due to traditional notions about hierarchy and control rather than to considerations of outcomes. It may also be due to a lack of awareness about the importance of communication processes in group and organizational effectiveness.

Different types of communication structures might be needed for different tasks and to meet the emotional needs of group members. However, as has already been stated, groups resist changes in their communication structures (Cohen & Bennis, 1962; Mills, 1967). The often unconscious choice of a communication structure, which occurs very early in the life of a group, may not work to its advantage. However, a group tenaciously resists altering the structure once it has stabilized. Group and organizational consultants are often painfully aware of this fact when organizations and groups refuse, or prove unable, to alter a communication structure that is obviously impeding the group's morale, integration, and goal achievement.

Communication structures, as we have seen, clearly affect morale and group integration. Hare (1976) stated that integration was related to the manner in which members get along or the sense of group harmony or solidarity. It also refers to how the various parts of the emergent group social structure work together. The various aspects of integration are referred to as *cohesiveness* or *cohesion*. Groups that develop high levels of cohesion interact more (Back, 1951; Lott & Lott, 1961). They are more satisfied and cooperative (Shaw & Shaw, 1962). They also exert more control over members' actions and attitudes, thus developing a more unified group culture (Back, 1951; Deutsch, 1959; McGrath, 1984; Seashore, 1954; Wyer, 1966). Cohesion is often, but not always, found to be associated with greater productivity (Stogdill, 1972). High cohesion and shared rules or norms in support of quality work, however, do result in higher productivity (Hackman, 1987).

The content of group communication also affects group cohesion, efficiency, and outcomes. Bales (1950, 1970) undertook extensive analyses of the content of verbal communication in small groups. He outlined two broad types of communication in groups—task statements and maintenance statements. **Task statements** are those that directly relate to goal accomplishment. They give information, ask for information, make suggestions, and the like. **Maintenance statements** are those that directly relate to the socio-emotional life of the group. They offer support, encourage, compliment, and reduce tension. There are also negative maintenance statements that are critical, discouraging, and nonsupportive. The number of task and maintenance statements in groups has been found to affect cohesion and task performance. Too many task and not enough positive maintenance statements, for example, decrease morale and productivity. Too many maintenance and too few task statements can have the same effects. Bales (1970) suggested that efficient and cohesive groups have a 60:40 task:maintenance ratio.

If, as Hogan (1975) suggested, an adaptive advantage is conferred on groups that develop efficient organizational structures, then the importance of the communication structure, content, and process in a group cannot be overestimated. The structure of communication, as we have seen, does much to determine the other structures to follow. It influences the status hierarchy, leadership, and roles. It influences morale and cohesion. It limits or enhances productivity. The content of communications also affects productivity and cohesion.

In naturally occurring groups with members who are unaware of the significant impact of early emergent communication patterns, these initial unconscious choices may seal a group's fate. All other group issues will be discussed within the confines of the adopted communication system. Attempts to reach agreement on values, norms, and ideology occur within the emergent communication structure. All work will occur within this framework. And as we have seen, once stabilized, communication structures are resistant to change. If the emergent structure restricts communication or is too centralized to allow for adequate resolution of complex problems, the likelihood of creating a unified culture and social structure becomes remote. If the type of communication structure inhibits group development, task success is equally remote. Thus, from the very beginning, a group is in the grip of powerful initial structures that will impact all future developments.

Most group and organizational members are unaware of the effects of initial communication structures or the content of communication on future efficiency and goal achievement. Most management training does not include these research findings. Universities do not, as a rule, include this content in schools of business, education, or psychology. Politicians are, in the main, unaware of these dynamics. And yet, the effectiveness and efficiency of all groups hinge, in part, on these processes.

It would be interesting to study the effect of awareness of these issues on newly forming groups. Would knowledge of the effects of these initial choices on group culture, structure, and development aid members in the creation of a communication structure more likely to support group success? How much difference would preknowledge make? Are the ways we develop these structures so embedded in our cultural inheritance that knowledge alone would not make a significant difference? Also, since most new groups form within the context of a larger institution or social system, is the nature of the emergent structure in essence predetermined by the culture of the larger system? How can resistance to change in a stabilized group communication structure be reduced? More research is needed in this area.

From a practical perspective, it would be useful to make recommendations to individuals and groups with regard to the findings of communication research. Reasonable recommendations might include the following:

1. Group goal achievement might be enhanced if members were familiar with the findings of communication research.
2. The choice of a communication network might be more effective if the choice were more conscious.
3. It takes more time to develop a decentralized communication network. If that type of network is desired, time must be allotted for development to occur, and urges to stabilize the structure too early must be resisted.
4. Employing the services of a consultant whose task is to observe the group's process and make comments to the group regarding its process may facilitate the development of a more effective communication structure.

Based on what we know about the emergence of communication patterns and structures to date, these recommendations seem helpful. More research is needed, however, to verify their utility. Certainly, a more general awareness of the effects of communication processes would be beneficial.

There are a number of other variables that affect the communication process as well. This discussion is not meant to be inclusive, since there are many other excellent sources of information on this topic. Instead, an attempt has been made to describe how communication affects, from the outset, the development of a group's culture and social structure. All other processes and structures emerge within the context of the established communication patterns. The next section looks at how values, norms, and ideologies emerge to form a coherent culture in a group.

VALUES

In order to develop a consistent view or culture, a group must work to create shared beliefs and values. A **belief** is defined as a conviction or opinion. **Values** are beliefs that we determine to be important. They are ideals that arouse an emotional response, for or against them, in individuals. Thus, an individual may believe that all persons are equal. If this belief is considered very important by the individual, he or she will be emotionally upset when this belief is not shared by others with whom the individual interacts.

Our beliefs and values are the products of interaction with significant others, initially in primary groups such as the family. They are reinforced, or in some circumstances altered, in other group situations such as schools, friendship groups, or significant membership or reference groups such as race, sex, or profession. Thus, people come to new group situations with already established sets of beliefs and values. These beliefs and values will be similar among group members to the extent that they have similar backgrounds. If they were raised in the same society and share a number of similar reference or membership groups, they are likely to find considerable agreement in their beliefs and values. The greater the diversity in background, however, the less agreement in beliefs and values will be found. Increased diversity in member backgrounds, therefore, increases the difficulty that a group will encounter in creating the stable set of beliefs and values necessary to coordinated group activity.

Holding similar beliefs on important issues is a determinant of interpersonal attraction (e.g., Byrne, 1961; Byrne & Griffitt, 1966; Heider, 1958; Newcomb, 1956). This has been found to be true in both laboratory and field studies (Griffitt & Veitch, 1974; Newcomb, 1961). Other similarities that are important determinants of attraction include personality (e.g., Griffitt, 1966; Izard, 1960a, 1960b), attitudes (Good & Good, 1974), economic status (Byrne, Clore & Worchel, 1966), and race and sex (Smith, Williams & Willis, 1967; Sykes, Larntz & Fox, 1976). In high school students, for example, the best predictors of attraction are sex, ethnicity, and age (Kandel, 1978).

It is important to notice that most of these variables found to be predictive of attraction and group cohesion are directly related to distinctions in background or may be the result of these distinctions. Race, ethnicity, sex, and economic status are clearly background variables. They represent unique societal subgroups.

Such groups produce similarities in beliefs, attitudes, and behaviors among their members. Through the same and similar processes described throughout this book, these unique subgroups build their own cultures and social structures. Individual members of these groups are socialized to believe and act in ways similar to other subgroup members. For example, evidence of sex and ethnic differences in attitudes, values, and behavior abounds. Age, too, constitutes a unique subgroup. This is so in two ways. First, as a result of the process of human development, individuals of a particular age are likely to be dealing with similar psychological and social concerns. Second, they represent a cohort group, which Neugarten (1979) describes as a group that is experiencing the same social conditions at a particular historical time. Thus, the beliefs and values of individuals raised during the Depression will typically be different from those raised during the post–World War II economic boom.

Consequently, much of the research findings on interpersonal attraction may be related to the attraction or antipathy of societal subgroups to each other as represented by their emissaries—individuals. When we as individuals enter a new group, we display our group memberships to others in many ways. Some we wear on our sleeves, such as race, sex, or age. Some we demonstrate through our actions, such as behavioral characteristics that distinguish ethnic groups or socioeconomic groups. What others see is how different or similar we are to them as a result of our revealed memberships and resultant attitudes and behaviors. Similarity is seen as comforting and familiar. Difference is often perceived as threatening and problematic, in part because it makes the coordination of group culture and organizational structure more stressful and difficult (Back et al., 1972). More research is needed in this neglected area. Research on differences among U.S. ethnic groups, for example, has far outstripped its application or replication in research on group behavior. Gender research has done so as well. It is necessary to incorporate and attempt to replicate these findings if we are to more adequately explain research results in this and other areas of group research.

For the group in which similarities outweigh differences in terms of beliefs and values, the development of a shared view or culture is relatively easy. Members will rely on previously internalized values and will smoothly move to the establishment of rules of conduct or norms for group membership. For those in which differences abound, however, the struggle will be greater. It intensifies the conflict stage described in Chapter 2. The attempt to clarify values described by Lewin (1936) will be much more difficult. While conflict during this stage is inevitable in order to establish commonly held views, highly diverse groups have an even more difficult time. This is especially true if the reference or membership groups of different members are actively engaged in conflict at the macro levels of society. Thus, issues of race, sex, age, and socioeconomic status, for American groups, are issues that will intensify this struggle, since these continue to be issues of conflict at the macro level. Some groups will fail as a result. Some will succeed. The variables that enhance the likelihood that a group with highly diverse members will succeed in developing a cohesive, unified group culture have been investigated in research on the types of contact or interaction that facilitate interpersonal attraction between members of conflicted membership groups.

Cook (1978) proposed that

attitude change favorable to a disliked group will result from equal status contact with stereotype-disconfirming persons from that group, provided that the contact is cooperative and of such a nature as to reveal the individual characteristics of the person contacted and that it takes place in a situation characterized by social norms favoring quality and egalitarian association of the participating groups. (pp. 97–98)

Research in support of Cook's contact hypothesis has found the following factors to be necessary for attitude change to take place:

1. Cooperation positively affects subgroup relations (Aronson et al., 1978; Blanchard & Cook, 1976; Cooper et al., 1980; Slavin, 1985; Weigel et al., 1975).
2. Relations improve when the contact leads to successful outcomes (Cook, 1969, 1978, 1984).
3. Participants of equal status increase the probability of a positive outcome (Cohen, 1984).
4. Support of authority figures increases the probability of improved relationships (Cohen, 1984).
5. The contact should be intimate and personal in nature to maximize the effect (Slavin, 1985).

While these variables have been found to be very important and have facilitated attraction and integration of members from diverse primary membership groups, they do not always guarantee success. Other variables have been found, however, that in concert with those previously mentioned significantly add to the probability of success. Research has demonstrated that the following variables are also critical:

6. Relations are enhanced if the situation allows for the expression of behavior that disconfirms our stereotypic expectations of members of a disliked group (Rothbart & John, 1985).
7. Significant and frequent disconfirming contact with many members of the other group is necessary for attitude change (Rothbart & John, 1985).
8. Members of the other group should be seen as typical of that group as opposed to special or unique (Royle, 1983).
9. The goals and activities of the group should make it necessary to utilize more refined and specific categories (other than sex, race, religion or ethnicity) to evaluate the individual or the subgroup (Brewer & Miller, 1983).

We see, then, that for groups containing members from dissimilar reference or membership groups, the task of group formation or the development of a cohesive culture and social structure is fraught with pitfalls. For this endeavor to be successful, many factors in addition to the normal group processes need to exist. While many of these research findings were derived in laboratory settings with the hope of discovering factors that would reduce racism or sexism at macro levels of society, they are relevant to a growing number of naturally occurring groups in the United States. The demographic characteristics of the U.S. workplace are changing at a rapid rate. White males, once the dominant group in the U.S. workforce, now represent less than 50 percent of all workers. Even this number is expected to decline rapidly (Copeland, 1988). Women and Blacks and other minorities will constitute 75 percent of all people hired to work in the United States in the 1990s. By the year 2010, Whites as a group will represent less than 50 percent of the total U.S. population. These demographic shifts may make it more difficult to develop cohesive, integrated, and productive work or educational groups.

Attention to variables known to enhance interpersonal relations, such as those just described, has become a matter of critical importance from both an ethical and an economic perspective. Cohesion, as we have seen, has been associated with group productivity (Goodacre, 1951; Shaw & Shaw, 1962; Strupp & Hausman, 1953). Its lack increases the probability of lowered morale, decreased goal achievement, and lowered productivity.

As a result, research on group processes has become more critical to U.S. society. For example, from what is known so far, it is logical to predict decreases in group cohesion, efficiency, and productivity in U.S. work and school groups. In fact, many say this is already occurring. This prediction is based on the extensive research documenting the relationship between similarity and attraction, cohesion and group integration already described in this chapter. It is also based on the research and theory presented in Chapter 2 regarding group development.

For example, many of the factors found to increase cohesion and successful group integration occur at later stages of group development. Cooperation, personal interaction, frequent interaction, and successful outcomes are characteristic of stages three and four of the integrative model of group development described in Chapter 2. These stage are preceded by the dependency/inclusion and conflict/fight stages of development. These early stages are also influenced by the type of communication structure adopted by the group, its resultant leadership, and the content and process of communications. Stages one and two are also where the bulk of the work is done to create a group's culture. Stage three tends to focus on trust, the development of group structure, and refinement of member roles. It is likely that groups with members from more diverse reference and membership groups will develop communication structures, status hierarchies, and input distinctions among members that will make the resolution of the inevitable conflict of stage two more difficult.

Some researchers have concluded that even when cooperative goals are established, members of societal subgroups will still seek advantages for their subgroups even when doing so interferes with goal achievement for the group-as-a-whole (Komorita & Lapworth, 1982; Kramer & Brewer, 1984). Tajfel (1974, 1982) attributes this to the tendency of individuals who are members of different societal subgroups to compete for status. Individuals actually seek distinctions between their groups and those of others in order to ensure or increase the status of their groups. As a result, even the most favorable group conditions may not be enough to overcome this tendency of group members to champion their respective groups.

The United States is undergoing great demographic shifts in its population. These shifts may have regressed the U.S. group-as-a-whole to the conflict stage of group development. This seemed to happen during the civil rights movement of the sixties and may be happening again. As minorities become majorities, a period of conflict and unrest seems inevitable. When major demographic shifts occur, some redefinition of culture will be necessary. The previous consensus about U.S. cultural elements is being challenged. This tends to produce conflict and tension among societal subgroups. Increased tension among U.S. subgroups has been noted. Acts of racially motivated violence have increased significantly. Religiously motivated violence and vandalism are also on the rise (Coates, 1987; Schwartz, 1988; Tye, 1990). Awareness of these processes and attempts to create the conditions necessary to navigate these difficult waters can help. More research is needed to find ways to help our increasingly diverse work, school, and social groups.

Every group attempts to develop shared beliefs and values. Without agreement in these areas, it is difficult for group members to work together. If beliefs and values were not shared, it would be difficult for members to organize to accomplish goals and tasks, since the meaning of the goals might be understood differently by different members. Also, members would be less inclined to continue their membership in the group, since the lack of shared values decreases the group's attractiveness to its members. If shared beliefs and values are arrived at, the group can begin developing other aspects of its culture.

NORMS

Once a set of shared beliefs and values has been established, the next task is to create norms or rules of acceptable group behavior. The amount of agreement among members about emerging norms will depend on all that has preceded this stage. Norms represent collective value judgments about how members should behave and what should be done in the group. Norms are necessary if the group is to coordinate its efforts and accomplish its goals. Without behavioral predictability, chaos reigns. For example, it would be dangerous to drive a car if we were uncertain whether others would obey traffic signals. Since we can predict that most citizens will obey them, we feel safe when driving. In like manner, a group has a task. That task requires members to behave in certain ways in order to succeed. If member behaviors were unpredictable or chaotic, there would be little hope of task accomplishment. Thus, norms are established.

Depending on the degree of member similarity, some rules of behavior are assumed by the group. For example, when an individual enters a group, he or she assumes that the group will not be physically violent and will conform to other important rules of humanity in general and his or her society in particular. These rules, if accepted by the group, are sometimes referred to as *unconscious norms,* since they require no discussion. Also, depending on the institutional context in which a group is forming, adherence to the rules of the broader institution is assumed. For example, when a teacher moves to another school district, he or she assumes that the new faculty group will have many normative similarities to the old one. There will be differences, of course, but important norms will be the same. Such rules, if accepted by the group, are called *formal* or *institutional norms.* In the main, the teacher is likely to be right in assuming adherence to formal norms. However, on some occasions, a particular group may not adhere to formal or institutional standards.

It becomes apparent from this discussion that while a standard of behavior can be imposed upon a group by society or a larger unit of society, it is not a norm until the particular group accepts it. In a company, for example, the rule is that work begins at 8:30 A.M. The norm of a particular work group within the company may be different, however. Work might begin earlier or later. Also, while it is much rarer, unconscious or societal rules of behavior are not normative among certain groups or individuals. Gangs, for example, may in fact injure or kill a member under certain circumstances. Incest, rape, murder, and the like, unfortunately, increasingly violate societal norms.

Groups do not establish rules to govern all member behavior. Norms are established with regard to behaviors considered important by the group. Norms may also "apply to all members of the group or only to the occupants of certain positions in the group. Role specifications are norms that apply to positions, but not all norms are role specifications" (Shaw, 1981, p. 265). Some norms may apply to leaders or high-status members only and others may apply to all members. For example, low-status members (students, for instance) must be on time for class but high-status members (professors) are typically allowed to be fifteen minutes late.

Once a norm is accepted by the group, member violation of that group rule is usually met with some form of punishment or sanction (Schacter, 1951). The severity of sanctions imposed on norm violators varies depending on the consequences of violation and the circumstances under which a norm is violated (Shaw & Reitan, 1969). Violations of norms that cause severe negative effects on the group or a member are generally dealt with harshly unless there are mitigating circumstances. If the effects are less negative, norm violation may be tolerated. Toleration levels are different depending on the status the norm violator holds in the group. For example, leader deviation from norms is tolerated better by a group than deviation by lower-status members.

When deviation occurs, other members tend to increase their interaction with the deviant in order to induce conformity. If this is unsuccessful, however, communication with the deviant will decrease dramatically (Schacter, 1951). The deviant is essentially shunned by others. The timing of the deviation has been found to affect the severity of group sanctions. Deviation early in the group's history is more severely sanctioned than deviation that occurs later in the group's life (Wahrman & Pugh, 1974).

CONFORMITY

Why do members conform to group norms? What factors increase conformity to or deviation from group norms? As has already been stated, we conform with norms in order to create order, stability, and predictability in our dealings with other group members. These conditions are necessary for unified work to occur. Even norms that seem irrelevant to task accomplishment may indirectly be useful to group success by creating a sense of safety or simply positive feeling. Forms of greeting may be prescribed to reduce tension or anxiety. Seating arrangements are quickly determined to reduce competitiveness among members. Such norms can also reflect the status hierarchy and may work to reinforce the group's authority structure. They can inhibit or enhance group functioning depending on the degree of agreement with and the utility of the established norms.

Factors that increase conformity have been the subject of a number of research investigations. Conformity increases as the unanimity of the majority increases (Asch, 1951; Morris & Miller, 1975). The degree of attraction among members increases conformity as does a decentralized communication network (Goldberg, 1955; Shaw, Rothschild, & Strickland, 1957). As the size of a unanimous majority increases, so does conformity (Asch, 1951; Mann, 1977). The more ambiguous the group situation is, the more conformity there will be (Sherif & Sherif, 1956). This is thought to be due to the anxiety evoked by ambiguity, which tends to cause quicker acceptance of direction. Membership and reference group identity also affect the degree of conformity. For example, there is less conformity in all-male or all-female groups than in groups containing both women and men (Reitan & Shaw, 1964). High-status members and leaders conform both more and less than members of lower status, depending on the task (Gergen & Taylor, 1969).

A few individual characteristics have been found to influence the degree of conformity. More intelligent members have been found to conform less than other members (Crutchfield, 1955; Nakamura, 1958). Self-critical persons and those who tend to defer to authority conform more (Costanzo, 1970). In general, however, group cultural, structural, and task variables and reference group memberships have been found to have the most influence on member normative conformity. The more of these factors existing in the group, the higher the degree of conformity.

Conformity with established group norms is essential to the creation and maintenance of a stable group culture and organizational structure. It has also been found to increase altruistic and socially responsible behavior (Berkowitz & Daniels, 1963). However, since conformity appears to be a quite natural response of individuals to the requirements of group membership, the goals and norms of the group become critical issues. For example, conscience has not been found to be a stable personality trait but rather has been described as situational and, thus, changeable. It is subject to group pressures for conformity (Latane & Darley, 1968; Milgram, 1963). The role one is playing within a group can change one's behavior, since the norms associated with different roles are variable. Thus, when we are assigned the role of prison guard, we become less kind and more punitive (Zimbardo et al., 1973). When assigned the role of subject in an experiment, we do as we are told even if we believe that this means injuring another person (Milgram, 1963). Pressures to conform can even change our perception of things as basic as length (Asch, 1951). Loss of individuality and creativity and increased mediocrity can also result from conformity (Asch, 1951; Milgram, 1964; Whyte, 1957).

On the plus side, these same pressures to conform can lead us to collectively defy directives from an authority figure whom we perceive to be wrong (Milgram, 1963). Conformity to group pressures for tolerance can reduce discriminatory behavior. It can also increase socially responsible actions and create positive change. For some, these effects emerge as a result of individual needs to belong and thus conform to these more positive norms. For those who initiate these changes, however, the results are due to their willingness to deviate from group or societal norms. The relationship between conformity and deviation, then, is an important one. Conformity allows for the establishment of order, coordination, and predictability. This is critical to group and societal survival. However, when the norms or goals of a group are destructive or restrictive, deviation from and destabilization of the norms and structures are necessary in order to create a more positive group or social order. Gandhi and Martin Luther King would be examples of deviants who produced positive change. Hitler, on the other hand, is the quintessential example of a deviant who produced horrific outcomes.

IDEOLOGIES

At the societal level, as shared beliefs, values, and norms multiply, ideologies emerge that organize and simplify our overall understanding of what is important, what should be done, and how people should behave. Ideologies are belief systems that tell people how to live, why life should be lived that way, and why certain values and norms are important. They tell us not only what to value and why but also what to believe. Ideologies justify our norms and values and make it extraordinarily difficult to see things in any other way. In general, ideologies are taken for granted. They tend to be such givens that we are unaware of them

(Berger & Hansfried, 1981). Ideologies also inhibit the development of values and norms inconsistent with their world view. Thus, in novel situations, groups and individuals do not usually flounder in their attempts to determine how to respond. They are guided by their society's ideological views and will usually develop values and norms consistent with these views. In effect, as the philosopher Cassirer (1957) stated, reality recedes as ideology emerges. We understand not only what to do but also what to believe, based on our internalized ideological views.

For example, some of the ideological components that undergird the U.S. world view include individualism, materialism, competition, and continuing progress (Bellah et al., 1985; Slater, 1970). These ideological elements are translated into norms and structures that can be identified in groups and organizations throughout the country. Common sayings such as "Up by your own bootstraps," "I am the captain of my own ship," and "Do your own thing" attest to our favoring the individual over the group or society. While there are many positive outcomes from such a world view, including the protection of individual rights, this emphasis also makes it difficult for us to see our interconnectedness. When things go well or poorly, we tend to look for the individual who produced the result rather than to look at the influence of the group in determining the result. Our belief in individualism also leads some researchers to study the effects of individual personality on group functioning rather than the effects of group culture or social structure on individuals and groups. We become, in a sense, ideologically blinded to the tremendous influence of group processes on individual behavior.

Our allegiance to materialism is manifested in sayings such as "What is he worth?" or "The business of America is business." It is further demonstrated in consumerism, our adherence to empirical scientific evidence over other approaches, and our faith in economics as a way to improve the human condition. Again, the positive side of this view has led to a high standard of living for individuals and many useful scientific discoveries. However, it also leads us to devalue endeavors that do not directly lead to profit. Thus, educators and social service and community workers have lowered status in U.S. society. Product and profit become more important than people or the environment in many cases.

"May the best man win," "Climbing the corporate ladder," and "Watch out for the other guy" are all sayings that relate to the value we place on competition. Again, this has led us to work hard and achieve many positive results. It has also made it difficult to cooperate or collaborate. "Progress is our most important product" attests to the U.S. emphasis on continuing personal, professional, and societal growth and development. Things will—in fact must—get better. This hopeful ideological view supports our work ethic and faith in scientific advancement. However, we may overemphasize progress and underemphasize our past and present as well.

When a group composed of Americans is forming, it does not do so in a vacuum. Prevailing U.S. ideologies will guide its formation and functioning. Many things will be assumed rather than debated. Most U.S. groups will develop similar norms and structures. Views about authority, roles, sex roles, intimacy, conflict, task accomplishment, status, reference and membership groups, and other issues will, in the main, be consistent with prevailing U.S. ideological views. When this is not the case, it is usually due to the presence of a number of members whose primary membership or reference groups are ideologically at odds with mainstream views. The more diversity is represented in the membership, the less unity will be evidenced in ideologies.

GROUP SOCIAL STRUCTURE: CULTURE ENACTED

Culture dictates how the group is to be organized. It outlines shared assumptions about the structures that will be necessary for the group to accomplish its work. Society as a whole also establishes an organized social structure to meet basic human needs. Shared societal assumptions or culture dictate what these needs are, how division of labor is to occur to meet these needs, what roles individuals and groups will play in order to accomplish necessary tasks, how decisions will be made, how communication will occur, and how transmission of knowledge and socialization will be accomplished. Culture provides the blueprint from which social structures are built.

Institutions are systems established in society to address important human needs. The institutions of the family, education, economy and work, religion, government, recreation and leisure, and the media form the basic institutions in most modern societies. Each institution has the responsibility to accomplish specific societal tasks and goals. The family is charged with the physical and psychological nurturance of the young. It also has the task of socializing children. That is, families teach children the values, norms, and ideologies of their particular culture. The educational institution continues the task of socialization and transmits the knowledge and skills necessary for productive adult membership in the society. The task of the economy and work is to produce the goods and services necessary for physical survival. The production of food, shelter, clothing, health care, and the like are some tasks of the institution of economy and work. Existential meaning is also perceived as an essential need. This task is given to religious institutions and, increasingly, the arts. Members of society also need play and relaxation. This is the task of the newly emerging institution of recreation and leisure. Mass communication is the task of the media. Finally, all these activities must be coordinated and organized. The government or state is the institution charged with this necessary function.

Institutional division of labor outlines the basic structure of society. Within each institution, however, more structure is needed to accomplish specific goals. Each societal institution requires mechanisms to articulate its goals and tasks. A communication structure is necessary. Roles and status must be clarified in order to accomplish further division of labor. Leadership and power need to be defined. Processes must be developed to promote conformity and reduce deviance among institutional members. Ways to promote cohesion and reduce conflict are also necessary. The relationship between the individual and his or her institution requires clarification. How the institution will relate to other institutions and the institution's relationship to the total society must also be clarified. One outcome of all this is that each institution, through the establishment of its own culture and social structure, develops a unique character. Thus, the behavior of teachers or clergy is expected to be different from the behavior of journalists or government officials. Within each primary institution, language, values, norms, structures, and the like will vary to some degree.

While a description of this process seems quite logical and rational, it is necessary to keep in mind that cultural and organizational processes operating in society are subject to both the same and additional inhibiting, emotional, traditional, and nonfunctional factors as smaller groups. A glimpse at the newspaper on almost any day makes this obvious. Governmental policies often inhibit the effectiveness of other institutions, for example. Institutional rivalries can cause difficulties. Goals may be unclear or overlapping. Intrainstitutional and interinstitutional communication is often obstructed. Division of labor still occurs, and work is done. However, these processes are subject to the same blocks as smaller groups. In fact, the degree of difficulty in establishing effective social structures at the societal level is greater.

Institutions are large social systems made up of smaller groups. Each group, then, is part of an institution and shares its goals and tasks. Each group's goals and tasks are related to the larger institution and to the society as a whole. Within each group, the culture and social structure that emerge will mirror the larger institution of which it is a part (Deutsch, 1990a; Markova, 1990; Slater, 1966). As a result, each group's social structure contains some of the structural and cultural elements of its parent institution.

Cartwright and Zander (1953) described group structure as the relationships among the different aspects and parts of the group. These aspects and parts include ways to organize and manage goals and tasks, communication, status and roles, leadership and power, conformity and deviation, cohesion and conflict. The parts of a group's structure are interdependent. That is, each part affects each other part. The communication network that is established, for example, will influence individual role assignments and vice versa. It will also affect other structural elements as well. As a result, it is difficult to talk about or research structural elements in isolation.

In 1968, Cartwright and Zander suggested a number of factors that help to determine group structure. Group performance requirements affect the structure that the group will adopt, for example. Task difficulty, deadlines, need for high performance, or need for cohesion are examples of performance requirements that can influence structure. Member abilities, personality variables, and motivations also influence group structure. For example, if a group contains members with high needs for safety, it is likely to develop a hierarchical structure. Groups with members with high esteem needs, on the other hand, will be more likely to develop a more egalitarian structure (Messe, Aronoff & Wilson, 1972). These same researchers found that a man was more often chosen as leader in groups containing members with high safety needs than in groups with high esteem needs. Intellectual abilities of members have also been noted to influence group structure. Groups with members who are intellectually capable of abstraction and conceptualization tend to adopt a more flexible group structure than those with members who are less conceptual (Turney, 1970). The physical and social environment of the group affects the structure as well. Physical position in the group may influence one's role and status assignment.

Finally, the broader social context in which the group is operating influences the group's structure (Gaskell, 1990; Staub, 1990; Tajfel, 1982). While there will be similarities, certain structural differences will exist in groups functioning in different nations by virtue of macro-level cultural factors and customs regarding structure. Also, as has been noted, each group functions as a subset of a particular institution (Cummings, 1981; Gladstein, 1984). Institutions have different values and norms with regard to structural factors. Thus, a senate subcommittee's structure will be more formal than a family's or a recreational group's structure. Within the educational institution, one can see the influence of other institutional structures on classrooms in various disciplines. For example, the law classroom tends to be more traditional and hierarchical than the social work classroom. It seems that the education of students preparing to assume roles in different institutions includes not just technical aspects of that role. The classroom structure tends to reflect the structures of the institutional groups that students will join. Thus, resistance to alternative teaching methodologies may be due not only to individual teacher preferences but also to the threat that alternative classroom structures might pose to the continuation of institutional structures.

Unfortunately, much of the research on group structure is done with groups that exist temporarily and are not seen by members as institutionally based. College students participating in a temporary experiment, for example, have only their experience in similar experiments and their experience in the educational institution to guide their structure choices. They are, most likely, less influenced by institutional structural variations than a work group consisting of members from a single profession. This may be why some researchers report that personality differences tend to be significant initial determinants of group structure.

Differences in individual rates of talking, assertion, and the like are thought to initiate the process of role and status assignment. The group parts, or structures, are said to reside in individuals at first. Later, however, when the structure is more established, it becomes fairly independent of individuals. Thus, a particular role will have a certain status and requirements regardless of who is in that role. Norms become independent of individuals as well. Jacobs and Campbell (1961), for example, demonstrated that a well-established norm continues to exist even after the original members are no longer in the group. Norms were found to persist for five generations after the last original member was removed. While it is true that arbitrary or inconsequential norms disappear faster, even these are still quite persistent (MacNeil & Sherif, 1976).

It is only logical to assume that ideas about how a particular group should be structured initially reside in the minds of individuals. However, it is not logical to assume that individual personality traits determine group structure. Structure is in the minds of members as a result of their experience in other groups. Members may have different ideas about how things should be organized based on past or concurrent membership in other groups. Groups do not arbitrarily determine how to organize themselves. Past institutional and group experience strongly affect their choices.

Research on noninstitution-based, temporary groups may tell us as much about the historical evolution of society as it does about contemporary group structural development. Contemporary groups develop within the context of institutions with customs and methods of organization that have been in operation, in some cases, for hundreds of years. Consequently, when naturally occurring groups form, they do so already constrained to a large extent by structures of the larger institutions of which they are a part. Their structural choices will be limited by the institution in which they reside. Some structural options are not available, since they are not customary within that institution. For example, a military group would be unlikely to establish an egalitarian structure regardless of the personalities, motivations, or desires of its members.

Of course, exceptions do exist, and institutional changes do occur. Business is beginning to undergo structural changes at this time. Customary hierarchical structures have been found unsuitable and ineffective as we have moved from a production-oriented economy to a service economy (Hollander & Offermann, 1990). Ever so slowly, the institution of the economy and work is shifting from an autocratic, hierarchical structure to a more democratic, participative structure (Weisbord, 1987). Social scientists observing this slow shift note the awkwardness and uncertainty of individual members as they try to adapt. Confusion and conflicting norms and structures exist. Simultaneously, some would say that the educational institution is becoming more autocratic and centralized due to national concerns about decreases in the quality of education (Schmuck & Schmuck, 1990). The effects on institutional members are similar, however. Confusion, conflict, and resistance abound.

We see from this discussion that the development of group culture and structure is a very complex process. This chapter is intended to introduce the reader to the basic elements that comprise group culture and structure. The following chapters describe the emergence and maintenance of these elements. This is done in the context of group development. That is, each of these cultural and structural elements exists throughout the life of a group but manifests itself in different ways depending on the developmental stage of the group at the time. For example, norms, goals, and tasks will be less clearly defined at stage one than at stage four. Leadership will be different at various stages of development. Consequently, these mechanisms are discussed with attention to how they function at different stages in the group's life.

4

STAGE ONE: DEPENDENCY AND INCLUSION

In Chapter 2, the first stage of group development was described as one in which individuals are concerned primarily with being accepted as members. The newness of the group situation creates anxiety due to the relative lack of structure and relational bonds. The new group has not had time to develop its own culture and social structure. Things are not predictable. If the group has, as many groups do, a designated leader, he or she tends to be perceived as benevolent and competent. At this early stage, individuals place their trust in the leader more readily than in other members. If the group does not have a designated leader, anxiety will be high, since stability and safety are perceived as less certain.

The following sections will look at the elements of the group's social structure and processes, as these are manifested during this first stage of group development.

GROUP STRUCTURES

The Communication Structure

In the initial stage of group development, the communication structure is being determined. During stage one, the establishment of this structure is as important as the content of communication, since the adoption of a communication structure signals the beginning of order and provides the medium in which all future processes will occur. As we have seen, the type of communication structure that is adopted does much to determine the status and leadership hierarchy, group morale, problem-solving efficiency, cohesion, and group integration (e.g., Kano, 1971; Lawson, 1965; Leavitt, 1951; Schein, 1958).

The fact that this structure stabilizes during the earliest stage of group development poses some potential hazards for the group. For example, at this stage of group development, members have not interacted long enough to develop rational views, based on experience, about each others' leadership potential, competence with regard to the group task, or social skills. Preliminary determinations are frequently based on status and credentials external to the group. Early member self-revelations, obvious membership and reference group identities such as race, sex, and class, and initial behaviors form the basis for assigning members status and roles in the new group. If the group judges incorrectly, difficulties will ensue later on. Also, the type of communication structure chosen limits or enhances the group's future problem-solving ability, and at this stage the group does not have enough goal clarity to determine the complexity of the problems it will face in accomplishing its goal. As a result, it may establish a communication network that proves inadequate to the facilitation of goal achievement or group integration.

The establishment of a group's communication network occurs in a climate of tension, anxiety, ambiguity, and dependency. Members tend to be overly polite and conventional in an attempt to ward off potential group rejection. These conditions are not the best for thoughtful consideration of future needs, since current concerns are so paramount. Thus, groups often choose conventional, societally established communication structures rather than assessing their particular group's structural needs. As a result, groups tend toward the establishment of centralized communication networks where information is filtered through one or two persons, since this is a typical communication structure in U.S. society (McGregor, 1960). The choice of a centralized communication network, however, may limit a group's ability to solve complex problems and accomplish complex goals, since it limits input. Consequently, classrooms that could benefit from more student input may not be structured to allow for it. The same may be true of work groups, community groups, and the like. The communication network is critical, since it provides the avenue for the development of group culture and social structure. Discussion of values, norms, goals, tasks, roles, leadership, and the like are only possible through communication. Who can talk, and to whom, will limit or expand the group's ability to clarify goals, organize rules and roles, and develop a coherent culture.

Realistically, communication networks are usually flawed in some ways. Societal customs and traditions often impede the free flow of communication. For example, members with higher external status due to their membership or reference groups are likely to get more air time in the group. This will limit, from the outset, the input of lower-status members. Some members may be ignored by the group even if their input might be valuable. This is especially true during the dependency stage of group development, when anxiety is high and needs for inclusion are paramount. Members do not wish to offend or appear to deviate from societal conventions. Lower-status members will not usually push to be heard. Most members will wish to go along with prevailing group views and emerging rules. Our need to belong is extremely strong.

As a consequence of customs that we inherit and our overriding need for inclusion, we tend not to challenge our place in the communication network for fear of being rejected by the group. Valuable input may be lost to the group as a result. Also, since most people are unaware of how groups function, there is not likely to be any discussion of the importance of early group decisions regarding the communication network or any other group issues, for that matter. Many group decisions are not discussed at all. In fact, group decisions at this stage are frequently made without the awareness of any members of the group. They just seem to occur.

How these covert or unconscious decisions are made is the subject of much discussion in the literature, but not much research. We know the results, but little about the process. It is assumed, for example, that verbal communication has overt meaning and covert meaning (Watzlawick, Beavin & Jackson, 1967; Watzlawick, Weakland & Fisch, 1974). A discussion of goals, for example, has at least two purposes. Its overt purpose is to clarify and gain consensus about the group's goals. Its covert purpose is to establish the type of communication network the group will employ. This will help to determine member status and influence in that emerging network. Individuals are usually aware of the overt purpose of the discussion. They are typically not conscious of the discussion's covert purpose. Even though individuals are not aware of the covert purpose of a discussion, they generally respond to its demands by communicating in accordance with their place in the emerging communication network.

So far, this discussion has focused on verbal communication. Nonverbal communication is also influential in determining the communication network and group decisions regarding culture and structure. Volumes have been written about nonverbal communication (e.g., Lott & Sommer, 1967; Shaffer & Sadowski, 1975; Sommer, 1969). It is a powerful medium for interpreting meaning. Suffice it to say that many cultural and structural choices are decided without words. Gestures, eye contact, physical position in the group, and the like convey significant amounts of information to group members. This fact intensifies the unconscious nature of much of what occurs in groups. We respond to nonverbal communication and act in accordance with its messages, and we are likely to be unaware of these nonverbal messages or of our responses to them.

The communication structure is the vehicle for the discussion of goals, values, norms, beliefs, and other group issues. We also know that the type of communication structure determines who contributes to discussions and decisions. What is less clear is how unified beliefs and values emerge in the group. How do themes, ideas, and values gain acceptance in the group and become the basis for a unified culture and social structure?

Whitaker and Lieberman (1964) concluded that group themes and beliefs develop as a result of conflicts among group members. Certain conflicts become focal conflicts in the group. That is, the members communicate wishes and fears about group culture or social structure that must be resolved. Discussion continues until an enabling or restrictive solution emerges. **Enabling solutions** or norms are those that facilitate group goal achievement. **Restrictive solutions** or norms are those that inhibit group goal achievement in the long run.

Bennis and Shepard's (1956) formulation differs from that of Whitaker and Lieberman concerning how beliefs and other group content and process decisions are made. They maintain that the group leader is responsible for presenting themes to the group. Farrell (1982) argues that not just the leader but any vocal member may initiate discussion of a content or process theme. Argyris (1957) contends that themes do not emerge from one individual. Rather they are the product of ongoing group discussions. Thus, themes are the result of interaction. Sherif and Sherif (1956) side with Argyris. Their research leads them to conclude that theme transmission and acceptance is a long process of presentation, discussion, modification, and acceptance by the group. Neimeyer and Merluzzi (1982) support Sherif and Sherif's conclusion that lengthy dialogue is necessary for the emergence of unified themes. All would agree, however, that the themes or beliefs that result are determinants of a group's culture and social structure (Hill & Gruner, 1973).

The different views regarding how unified themes, beliefs, and values develop in a group might be clarified if group development were taken into account. For example, a recent study of a number of groups interacting within the same social system found that the content of discussion was related to the current stage of group development. That is, when a group was determined to be at stage one, its conversational themes focused primarily on issues of belonging and acceptance. At other stages, conversational themes also related directly to group development issues. In that same study, leaders initiated only nine out of 336 themes that were discussed (Wheelan & Krasick, 1993). It appears that the emergence of unified themes may be related to group and organizational development rather than the needs or wishes of individuals. Studies that investigate how groups develop unified themes, beliefs, and values is minimal at this point. Additional research of this type is sorely needed. While such research is difficult and time consuming, it is essential to further our understanding of this complex and important process.

The fact that the communication structure powerfully affects group culture and structure is well established. It is also known that this structure solidifies and stabilizes early in a group's life. It begins to stabilize at a time when communication is inhibited by anxiety and when dependency needs and fear of rejection are at their peak. The consequences of this for group development and productivity are very significant.

Some groups may develop communication structures that will severely restrict their ability to mature and work effectively. Others will develop communication patterns that, while flawed, will allow for development. Communication, both verbal and nonverbal, is the medium in which all group activity occurs. If communication is blocked, activities and development will also be blocked. An analogy with the arteries in the human body can be made. There is usually some blockage in all human veins and arteries. Human beings can live and function in that condition. However, if blockage builds up, it can seriously impair human functioning. Human groups are similar. Communication networks are never perfect; they can never allow for maximum communication. Groups can live with that. However, if communication is seriously blocked, it will impair all aspects of group functioning.

Goals and Tasks

All groups form to accomplish some goal or end. "A group forms and continues its existence for some purpose; when this purpose no longer exists, the group disintegrates unless a new purpose can be established" (Shaw, 1976, p. 293). Groups may have one or many goals. For example, a committee may be formed to establish company policy with regard to worker absenteeism. Once this is accomplished, the committee disbands. However, if that committee's charge is to determine personnel policy in a broader sense, it may have many goals concerning areas such as benefits, promotion policies, dress codes, worker safety, and many other issues. Such a group may continue permanently, since these issues and goals are ongoing.

The goals of a group may be predetermined by groups or individuals who are not members of that group. They may also emerge as a result of member interactions. A work group, for example, may be brought together to accomplish specific goals outlined by company executives. This is the group's initial goal. The group may adhere to that goal or it may change it due to group members' needs, their interpretation of the goal, internal group problems, or changes in the environment in which the group is operating. For example, a work group may be formed to meet a specific production quota established by company higher-ups. If the group accepts this goal as reasonable and in their best interest, members will work to accomplish the goal. If, on the other hand, the group determines that the quota is too high and the incentives (such as wages) for goal achievement are too low, the group may establish a new goal. That goal might be to organize effective ways to reduce the quota or to keep workers from meeting it (Roethlisberger & Dickson, 1939).

Goals are also subject to interpretation. Recently, a human resources department was asked to establish a program to help newly hired minority and female employees. The goal was to increase the number of these employees eventually promoted to management positions in the company. The human resources group, however, interpreted upper management's actual goal to be window dressing. That is, they believed that management was not committed to the progress of minorities and women, but wanted to appear to be. Therefore, they were slow to begin working on this goal, since they assumed that it was not a real goal. When work on the program was undertaken, it was minimal. The program that was planned was too brief and cursory to have any real effect on the progress of women and minorities in the organization.

Goals can also be in conflict. For example, when hospital employees are asked what the primary goal of the hospital is, some say quality patient care and some say profit. If it is a teaching hospital, some will see teaching as the primary goal. Still others will choose research as primary. All four of these goals are true goals, and they are inherently conflictual. Research and teaching, for example, may interfere with quality patient care by requiring patients to undergo extra examinations for teaching or research purposes. Profit may interfere with the other goals by reducing the length of patient stay, which may reduce treatment effectiveness and limit research and teaching possibilities.

There may also be a difference between what the group says is its goal and what the group is actually working to accomplish. Thus, a group such as a sensitivity training group may set as a goal the development of intimacy among members. However, the behavior of all members throughout the group's life may act to inhibit intimacy. The actual goal, then, may be to avoid rejection rather than to establish intimacy. There may be a difference between a group's overt goal (in this case, intimacy) and its covert goal (safety). The potential existence of covert goals seems to suggest that the only way to determine a group's actual goal would be to see what purpose the group accomplishes at its conclusion. But this may not be accurate either, since groups may fail to accomplish their goals. The end point that they reach may not be what they intended. Goals may be achieved, partially achieved, or not achieved at all.

The problem of defining a group's goal, then, is a difficult one. Further, the problem of determining the process whereby groups establish goals is equally difficult. Most researchers state that a group's goal is a composite of individual members' goals for the group (Shaw, 1981). Evidence for this position includes the fact that individuals react to group goals the way they react to their own individual goals (Cartwright & Zander, 1953).

Research on individuals has demonstrated that when an individual is successful in accomplishing a personal goal, the individual will raise his future level of aspiration by setting more difficult goals. If he or she fails to accomplish the goal, he or she will not raise his or her level of aspiration (Lewin, Dembo, Festinger & Sears, 1944). Shelley (1954) found that the same holds true for groups. Zander and Medow (1963) also found this pattern and stated that group level of aspiration is more often raised after success than lowered after failure, which is also true of individuals (Lewin et al., 1944). This pattern is found in natural groups as well. Zander and Newcomb (1967) studied United Way groups in 149 cities. If the United Way group met its goal for the year, it increased the goal in the following year. If it did not meet its goal, it rarely reduced the goal the next year.

What this research suggests is that the motivational processes that apply to individuals with regard to goals can also be applied to groups. This has been interpreted to mean that individual member goals, achievement motivation, and level of aspiration are determining factors in the establishment of group goals. Thus, a group goal is the end state desired by the majority of members. One can determine the goal, then, by asking members and observing group actions (Shaw, 1981).

While there is much to be said for this line of reasoning, there are some problems as well. First, the research on group goals has not taken into consideration the stages of group development. Questions such as whether group goals are changed or clarified by the processes of group development have not been sufficiently studied. How goals relate to developmental processes has also not been adequately addressed. Second, the process whereby a group establishes a goal and individual members commit to and adopt these goals as their own has not been clearly articulated. The research has been relatively rarefied. That is, the study of goals has been undertaken in relative isolation from the other variables that may influence their formation and achievement.

For example, new groups have an overriding concern for safety, tension reduction, inclusion, and dependable leadership. Members are reacting to the lack of structure and direction associated with the beginning stage of a group. This is the context in which initial discussion of group goals takes place. Besides clarifying its goal or goals, then, the new group is doing many other things. Members are sizing each other up. They are trying not to say or do anything that would result in rejection by others. Members are tentative, polite, and unlikely to challenge the leader or each other. Discussion of goals in this context may serve more as a medium to work on more pressing issues, such as tension reduction and inclusion, than as a way to clearly establish group goals.

Discussion of goals provides a forum for initial exploration of many other issues. Member values, status, reference and membership groups, competence, and trustworthiness can be explored using the discussion of goals as the vehicle to do so. Leader dependability and competence can be tested as well. There will be member pressure on the designated leader, should there be one, to tell the group what its goals are. If the goals of the group have been predetermined, as in the case of a work group, few members will be willing to risk rejection by disagreeing or asking for clarification. Most people who have led a first meeting of a group know that when the leader asks if there are any questions about the goals, there rarely are. So, it often appears during this stage as if group members understand and agree with the goals being discussed. Usually, however, this is not the case. Only later on will confusion or disagreement surface.

Commitment to goals at this point is tentative at best. Individuals may have varying ideas about group goals and tasks or methods to accomplish the goals. However, these will not be stated clearly during this stage. Instead, individuals are pursuing more primary goals concerning personal safety, position or status in the group, relationship to the designated or emerging leader, and the like. Since all members share their humanity in common, they are likely to be more concerned with these personal issues at this stage than with the more rational task of goal clarification.

Tasks and goals are often confused. However, they are not the same. Tasks represent the work that must be done in order to achieve a goal. Hackman (1969) stated that the task "consists of a stimulus complex and a set of instructions which specify what is to be done vis-a-vis the stimuli. The instructions indicate what operations are to be performed by the subjects with respect to the stimuli and/or what goal is to be achieved" (p. 113). Group members choose tasks because, in their collective wisdom, they believe that the chosen set of tasks will help the group to accomplish its goal.

It would be, at best, very difficult for a new group to choose tasks that would lead to goal accomplishment. As we have seen, goal clarity and commitment are usually not achieved at this stage of group development. Also, members do not yet know how to assess their new group's capabilities. There is no history of successful or unsuccessful task completion at this early stage. Zander (1971) found that when the quality of a group's past performance is unknown, the group cannot adequately assess the tasks necessary to accomplish a goal. Therefore, the group will choose tasks based on their incentive value without regard to the probability of group success or failure in task accomplishment. Beginning groups, then, are likely to bite off more than they can chew. That is, they may choose tasks that are too difficult to accomplish. Also, they often choose tasks based on, at best, an ambiguous understanding of the group's goals.

The group at this stage is still engaged in accomplishing more universal and primary goals related to the group itself. Members are attempting to establish a coherent group culture and a rudimentary organizational structure. They are far from being ready to work on goal accomplishment and its requisite tasks. Frequently, due to external or internalized pressures to achieve, groups assume goal clarity and begin task sequencing too early. Not only does this waste time, since much of this work will need to be redone, but also it may frustrate and demoralize a group, since failure is much more likely.

Some groups and organizations are beginning to understand the hazards of not allowing sufficient time for goal clarification, task analysis, and planning. Group and organizational consultants have played a major role in educating group members to the fact that you cannot push group development without consequences. Unfortunately, experience alone does not always produce this understanding. Many individuals and groups continue to set unrealistic timetables for establishing and clarifying goals as well as determining tasks and their sequencing. Often, if enough time is allotted to these processes, the results are much better, and time can be saved in the long run.

Status and Roles

Logically, in order to accomplish goals, a group must organize its members to work on different aspects of the task. It must also maintain itself as a group while it works on the task. Therefore, some members will perform task roles at various times in the group and others will perform maintenance roles such as the promotion of unity and cohesion. A role consists of a set of expectations shared by members about the behavior of an individual who occupies a given position in the group (Babad, Birnbaum & Benne, 1983; Gross, McEachern & Mason, 1958; Hare, 1962). Position in the group refers to the prestige and importance to the group of the role and the role occupant. It is the "total characterization of the differentiated parts associated with an individual group member" (Shaw, 1981, p. 263). Position, then, relates to the preexisting personality and status of an individual, the role he or she occupies, and other performance variables, such as rate of inter-action, perceived contribution to the group, and the like. Role is just one aspect of position.

Personality and role are not the same. "Role is imposed by the context, by the person, and by others; personality expresses itself from within. These two patterns may match perfectly, partially, or not at all" (Luft, 1984, p. 21). In order to function, the group assigns roles to individual members. This is referred to as the **expected role** or what others expect the individual role occupant to do. What the individual thinks he or she should do in the role is called the **perceived role.** The **enacted role** is what the individual actually does. If the enacted role devi-ates too much from the expected role, other members exert pressure on the indi-vidual to conform to expectations. Usually, the individual will conform. If not, he or she may ultimately be rejected by the group.

Functional member roles are related to task accomplishment. Some exam-ples of task-oriented roles include opinion or information giving or receiving and initiating. Group maintenance roles relate to behaviors that increase or decrease group cohesion and organization, such as agreeing or disagreeing and supportive or nonsupportive behavior (Bales, 1970). Other roles relate to organi-zational needs. The roles of leader and recorder are examples of these.

How are roles assigned? If the group makes the assignments, what are the criteria for its decisions? If roles have not been assigned before the group meets, the degree of anxiety associated with stage one is significantly greater. Typically, in everyday life, at least some roles are defined from the outset. For example, it is hard to imagine a class of students waiting for a teacher to emerge from among them. The teacher is provided beforehand. So are bosses, government officials, and the like. The role of designated leader, then, is usually predeter-mined.

Most roles, however, are not predetermined. It is up to the group to decide which member will take on what role. In most cases, during stage one members are sizing each other up. Sources of data that the group uses to make role assign-ments include outside roles that individuals occupy. Thus, someone who occu-pies a leadership role outside the group might be selected as a jury foreman. Individuals help the group along by supplying information about themselves and their outside roles. Professional roles, relationship status, and place of resi-dence offer a great deal of information about an individual. Our membership groups are easily discerned. Sex, race, and ethnicity are usually obvious. Clothing, regional or national accents, nonverbal behavior, and initial self-pre-sentation offer a host of information about our qualifications for certain roles.

Of course, during stage one, the information that the group gains about its members is much more limited than it will be later on in the group. Also, at this stage individuals are behaving in cautious, careful, and ingratiating ways in order to secure their membership in the group. Nevertheless, role assign-ments are made during this early stage. Assignments may turn out to be good or bad matches later on. However, they are made quite early. If mismatches occur, roles can be shifted, but with great difficulty. Especially in stage one, the group is unlikely to overtly discuss role assignments. Assignments are made covertly, not overtly. It would be difficult to talk about something that the group is usually unaware that it is doing. Individuals may simply find themselves in a role.

Position in the group, which includes role, carries with it varying amounts of status. Some roles, such as leader, are highly valued and carry great amounts of status. Other roles, such as recorder, will provide less status to the role occupant. High status is not just ceremonial or something that confers certain privileges or respect from others. High-status members can more directly influence group direction and processes. Low-status members have less influence and their attempts to influence are weaker and more indirect (Kipnis, 1984; Kipnis, Schmidt, Swaffin-Smith & Wilkinson, 1984).

The power of social roles to influence the behavior and attitudes of both the role occupant and others viewing the role should not be underestimated. Roles shape attitudes and behavior. Once a person assumes a role, the role creates a new mental perspective in the individual. If assigned the role of manager, for example, an individual often begins to perceive workers differently than he or she did previously. The role we occupy changes our attitudes and behaviors. This process is helped along by the fact that the expectations of others regarding an individual's role influence that person's performance and behavior as well (Rosenthal, 1971, 1976; Rosenthal & Rubin, 1978). This is especially true if these others have power over the role occupants.

Once in a role, we are perceived differently by others. Our behavior is viewed through the role and compared with expectations for that role. Sometimes those expectations cloud perceivers' judgments. For example, Rosenhan (1973) and some associates assumed the role of inpatients in a psychiatric facility. They did not change their behavior to match other patients. Rather, they behaved as they normally would. However, they were not perceived as normal by staff. No staff ever questioned whether they were in need of inpatient psychiatric care.

Milgram (1963, 1974) and Zimbardo and associates (1973) dramatically demonstrated that the role we play can even cause us to behave in ways that normally would be unconscionable. Milgram found that when they were in the role of subject in a scientific experiment, individuals who believed they were inflicting pain on others would often continue to do so if told to by the scientist experimenter. Zimbardo noted that individuals in the role of prison guard became more punitive and aggressive. Roles powerfully influence our perceptions, attitudes, and behaviors. The roles others have in relation to us strongly influence us as well. It would be comforting to imagine that we have complete control over the roles we assume in the groups to which we belong. However, this does not appear to be the case. While we have some control, the group has input as well.

We can influence our role assignment by what we wear, what we reveal to the group, and how we behave during early meetings (Goffman, 1967; Stone, 1962; Strauss, 1977). However, we cannot hide such things as sex, age, or race.

We also cannot control how the group perceives what we reveal. Also, we cannot always determine what the group needs are at the time. The group may need an individual to assume a certain role necessary to its functioning. If we are available, the job may be ours.

We have all found ourselves from time to time in unfamiliar roles. We may not know how we ended up in the role, but here we are. While it is possible to extricate oneself from a role, it is very difficult. It entails changing the perceptions of quite a number of people, and this is no easy task. The more one knows about roles and group processes, the more likely one is to be able to influence the group's role choices. Even with knowledge and skill, though, this is perhaps most difficult to do during stage one. One has been assigned a role by other group members. The role assignment is based on limited information and first impressions. However, to challenge one's role assignment during this stage may threaten one's membership. Most individuals will not challenge during this early stage of group development.

Given what has been said about the formation of goals and roles during the initial stage of group development, one can conclude a number of things. First, goals established at this stage will not necessarily be clear or consensual. Task assignments emanating from these goals will most likely be unclear as well. However, attempts to clarify this confusion are unlikely to occur, since such conversations pose risks to one's group membership. The group is not safe enough to question or challenge prevailing views.

Role assignment, as we have seen, is not entirely the product of rational assessment of each member's skills and talents. Rather, it is based on first impressions, external status, and initial self-presentation as well as the group's needs at the moment. Members may or may not secure a role that will facilitate group goal achievement. On an individual level, a member may find him- or herself in a role that is comfortable and allows for positive contribution to the group effort. On the other hand, the member may find his or her assigned role inhibiting and unfamiliar.

Leadership: A Special Role

Leadership has been defined as the process of influencing group goal setting and goal achievement (Stogdill, 1950). Fiedler (1967) described leadership as behavior that directs and coordinates the work of group members. While essentially correct, these definitions do not adequately convey our collective fascination, admiration, hatred, avoidance, love, or envy of those in leadership roles. Even in modern times, leaders are sometimes thought to be gods or devils. They are worshiped, placed on pedestals, and made into heroes. They are also hated, villainized, banished, or killed. Objectively good and objectively bad leaders often share similar fates. They are alternately loved and hated, made into heroes, and banished by the groups, organizations, or nations that they lead. In this author's lifetime, for example, Gandhi, two Kennedys, and Martin Luther King have been assassinated. Ceausescu, the hated dictator of Romania, was executed. The Shah of Iran, Duvalier, and Marcos were banished. Noriega is in prison, and the fate of Saddam Hussein is, to date, undecided.

People who have been in leadership roles have experienced overestimates and underestimates of their power or skills by others. They know the respect and disdain accorded them. They may have, at times, overestimated their role or questioned their own competence. Some survive both physically and psychologically. Others do not. Many receive praise and rewards for performing this role. Others end up bankrupt and broken human beings. Scientific descriptions of this role seem tame in light of the tremendous emotional reactions that human beings have to individuals in leadership roles.

Volumes have been written about leadership and its importance in groups, organizations, and nations. Our fascination with leadership has led to tremendous research efforts to understand this special role. Interest in the leadership role is understandable, given the power we attribute to leaders. Hitler's Germany, the Reagan years, and the McCarthy era, for example, are terms used to describe complex historical and societal processes and events. It is important to note that we use the name of the period's leader to denote these historical periods. It is as if the leader is thought to be solely responsible for the events that occurred at a particular time. If that is so, and leaders are primarily responsible for events that occur in the group, organization, or society that they lead, then our research focus should be on the identification of the characteristics of good leaders. If we could simply outline the personality characteristics of good leaders, then we might be able to identify leaders who would act for the common good.

This line of reasoning led to research efforts to identify the individual characteristics of persons who emerged as leaders in groups. The results of these investigations were very disappointing. The trait approach to leadership did not result in many consistent findings (Stogdill, 1948, 1974). Three clusters of traits were identified. Effective leaders tend to have more task-related abilities. They are also more social and more motivated to be leaders than others (Stogdill, 1948, 1974). Carter (1954) identified three similar clusters that he called group goal facilitation, sociability, and individual prominence.

While these findings indicate that personal characteristics do influence leadership to some extent, it is also clear that task-related abilities will vary in different situations. The same is true of the kinds of social skills required of leaders in different social situations. Thus, the same individual will not necessarily be leader in different situations. As a result, researchers turned their attention to identifying the requirements of different social situations and their effect on leader emergence. The notion here was that an individual may be leader in one situation but not in another, due to differences in the required leadership skills necessary in a given situation. This line of research led to some interesting findings. Many situational variables affect who will lead, how the leader will behave, and how successful he or she will be (Shaw, 1981). Again, however, the situation alone does not fully explain leader role expectations or who will occupy that role in a given situation. Consequently, researchers looked for more complex models to explain leadership. These models sought to identify the interactions among individual, situational, and group variables in leader emergence and behavior.

Hollander (1978) saw leadership as related to the situation, leader characteristics, and follower characteristics and expectations. Fiedler (1964, 1967) discussed the interaction between leadership style and situational variables. These approaches, and many others like them, seem to be most promising in exploring leadership behavior. However, there is much more to be learned about this important social role.

Stogdill (1974) stated that research on leadership does identify six leadership functions. These are: (1) defining objectives and maintaining goal direction, (2) providing the means for goal achievement, (3) providing and maintaining group structure, (4) facilitating group action and interaction, (5) maintaining group cohesion and satisfaction, and (6) facilitating group task performance.

The problem with this description of the leadership role is that it could equally well describe the functions of the group itself. All group members participate in these activities to some extent. While leaders perform these functions, others do so as well. The interconnectedness of leader and group becomes obvious in our efforts to define one without the other. Leadership has been defined in many ways. However, it is generally accepted that leadership is the process of influencing a group's goal setting and achievement. Leaders direct and coordinate the work of the group. At the same time, leaders are influenced by the group and behave in accordance with group expectations just like other members in other roles (Hollander, 1978, 1985). We discuss this important role in subsequent chapters as well. Now, however, we focus on looking at the leadership role in the initial stage of group development.

In the first stage of group development, dependency and anxiety and needs for inclusion and safety are at their height. The leader, whether appointed or emergent, is likely to be seen as benevolent, competent, and the provider of safety for anxious group members. The leader's main job during this time may be to reduce the anxiety of the group. His or her expected role, at least, is to provide direction and safety for the members.

The leader has a symbolic function during this stage of group development. This is so because he or she usually occupies the most clearly delineated role in the group. Frequently, the role of leader is defined prior to group formation. If not, this role is usually the first to emerge. As a result, the leader becomes the focal point for role differentiation among members and for initial development of group culture and social structure. The leader may symbolize a parental figure (Freud, 1950). At this stage, due to the lack of a coherent culture and social structure, the group is incapable of choosing a collective course of action, ensuring psychological safety, or organizing effectively. Therefore, it may expect the leader to act as the parent of a young child might and perform these functions for the group.

While leadership and power are not synonymous, power is an aspect of the leadership role (Maccoby & Jacklin, 1974; Maccoby, 1980; McClelland, 1975). Lewin (1951) described power as the ability to influence others even if they attempt to resist that influence. French and Raven (1959) added that power is the capacity to get others to behave in a certain way despite resistance. Leaders are not the only group members with power. Other high-status group roles and subgroups that may emerge assume, and are accorded, certain amounts of power as well. This led Hollander (1985) to define power as the capacity to control people and events and the capacity to defend against others' attempts to exert power.

During the first stage of group development, leaders tend to use power tactics more readily than other group members. Other roles are not clearly established yet, and members seem to want the leader to be forceful and directive. Given the pressure exerted by the group on the leader to act as benevolent dictator, most individuals in leadership roles respond accordingly. The group, in turn, rewards the leader by conferring higher status, privileges, and respect for the role. Of course, the way a leader uses power may have repercussions later on. For example, Schaible and Jacobs (1975) suggest that in the beginning of a group, positive feedback from the leader increases cohesion. Using power to reward rather than punish members, then, may facilitate group development. Initially, however, groups tolerate a wide range of power tactics from leaders.

At this early stage, the role of leader is a fairly safe one. The leader is usually treated with deference and respect. Many new leaders are lulled into complacency by this phenomenon. They begin to expect member compliance throughout the life of the group. However, as parents of young children soon find out, when children begin to mature, compliance with parental authority decreases. In fact, it must decrease if the child is to develop into a competent and independent adult. This is equally true of groups. If groups are to develop, the expected role of leader will have to change. The enacted leader role must change as well. This change is frequently conflictual. The ensuing power struggles are described in the next chapter.

GROUP PROCESSES

The previous section described how communication structures, goals, tasks, and roles begin to emerge during the first stage of group development. Usually, when we think about the functioning of groups, these structural elements are what come to mind. However, these factors alone are not enough for the group to function. It requires methods to encourage member conformity with norms, roles, and procedures. Also, in order to ensure the group's continuity, processes to deal with conflict must be developed and cohesion maintained.

A group's structural elements are the building blocks of the group. Goals, tasks, and roles allow members to coordinate their individual activities in order to accomplish the group's work. These structures tell individual people what they should do in the group. The processes described in this section are akin to the cement necessary to hold these elements or building blocks together. They act to keep members attracted to the group and interested in continuing as members. Group processes also operate to promote behavioral and attitudinal conformity with the group's emerging culture. This section describes the emergence and operation of these processes during the first stage of group development.

Conformity and Deviation

Research confirms that conformity and dependency are higher in ambiguous situations (Sherif, 1936; Asch, 1952; Sherif & Sherif, 1956). As a result, conformity will be high during the first stage of group development. This stage is characterized by a lack of structure, a lack of a unified group culture, anxiety, and fear of rejection. Very little is clearly defined. In such an ambiguous situation, members tend to conform in order to reduce anxiety and to secure their inclusion in the group. Member dependence on the leader is high at this stage as well. The group focus tends to be on pleasing the leader. Much discussion of what is proper group behavior occurs at this stage. Agazarian and Peters (1981) describe the stage-one group as dependent, conforming, and compliant. They add that the most conforming and controlling member or subgroup often dominates group discussion.

Pressures on individual members to conform with prevailing beliefs and behaviors will be high at this time. Conformity will also be easy to achieve, since members are unlikely to risk group rejection by deviating in any way. Those who do deviate are likely to do so unwittingly. That is, members may be seen by others as deviant because they display attitudes or behaviors that are unacceptable in that group. However, the member labeled as deviant may be merely displaying attitudes or behaviors that have gained him or her acceptance in other groups. All of us have had this experience at one time or another. We enter a new group and say or do something that would be acceptable in other groups to which we belong. However, in this new group we are met with disapproval. The emerging beliefs, values, or processes of the new group are different from those of other groups of which we have been a part. The culture and social structure of our other groups may be different in ways that elicit negative reactions in the new group. Most of us quickly learn to alter our behavior to match the expectations of the new group, since not to do so means to risk rejection.

The leader's beliefs and behaviors carry significant weight with group members at this point. This is so whether the leader wants to be influential or not. Members at this stage look to the leader for protection, safety, and stability. They are eager to please the leader and tend to watch for cues about what to say and how to behave. Members are anxious to determine what is acceptable to say or do in this new group. Since other member roles are not clarified yet, members tend to focus on the leader for direction (Bennis & Shepard, 1956; Bion, 1959; Rioch, 1975).

The degree of conformity expected during the dependency stage seems excessive. However, it may serve a very useful purpose. Conformity quickly creates a more predictable environment, which allows for discussion of goals, roles, and processes to begin. Of course, the discussion is inhibited, since opposing views tend to be censored. A kind of false harmony develops, which reduces anxiety and creates a sense of order. Differences of opinion are stifled in the interest of group conformity. As a result, tentative, polite exploration of the leader and other members ensues. Eventually, this enforced conformity of belief and behavior will reduce in intensity and the group will allow some dissension. If this reduction in conformity does not occur, the group may become stuck at this stage and remain dependent and compliant for a long period of time. Such a state of affairs will certainly inhibit the group's ability to meet goals or be productive.

At this stage, however, conformity and dependence may be necessary conditions for the establishment of order and some degree of safety. It may not be a condition to fix or cure. Many would argue that the degree of conformity and dependence at this stage is unnecessary and correctable. However, research and theory on group development speak to the universality of conformity and dependence during stage one. Efforts to push the river (that is, speed the process) may result in group disintegration rather than group development. Initial conformity may be a kind of member initiation rite. Perhaps we have to join before we have the right to challenge.

Cohesion and Conflict

Festinger (1950) defined group cohesion as "the resultant of all the forces acting on the members to remain in the group" (p. 274). Cohesion is the result of member attraction to the group, interpersonal attraction, group morale, group effectiveness, methods of conflict resolution, and the timing of leader feedback. During the first stage of group development, cohesion is primarily associated with member attraction to the group, the timing of leader feedback, and interpersonal attraction. This is so because group morale, effectiveness, and methods for conflict resolution are not yet fully operational, since they take longer to emerge.

Member attraction to the group refers to the reasons why people join a particular group in the first place. One primary reason why people join groups is because human beings seem to have a primary need to affiliate with others. While this may seem obvious, there has been significant research in the area, and it supports this conclusion (Gewirtz & Baer, 1958a, 1958b; McClelland, Atkinson, Clark, & Lowell, 1953; Pepitone & Kleiner, 1957; Schacter 1959; Singer & Shockley, 1965; Stevenson & Odom, 1962).

Another reason why people join groups is because they agree with and value the goals of the group (Latane, Eckman & Joy, 1966; Reckman & Goethals, 1973; Sherif & Sherif, 1953). People join groups whose goals are consistent with their values and beliefs. They also join groups whose activities are likely to be rewarding and attractive (Sherif & Sherif, 1953; Thibault, 1950). Finally, member attraction is enhanced if the group is perceived as being able to satisfy needs outside the group. If outside needs for status, economic security, and the like can be met through membership, individuals are more likely to join (Rose, 1952; Ross & Zander, 1957; Willerman & Swanson, 1953).

The leader also plays a role in increasing group cohesion. Schaible and Jacobs (1975) found that it is important that initial feedback from the leader to the group be positive rather than negative. If this occurs, cohesion is increased. This seems to relate directly to the importance members place on the leader at this stage. If the group is attempting to please the leader, then members will be encouraged by positive feedback from him or her. This may have the effect of reducing anxiety and increasing feelings of safety.

Interpersonal attractiveness is another factor associated with the development of group cohesion. Once an individual joins a group, he or she is usually confronted with many new people. If the individual finds other group members compatible and attractive, and vice versa, cohesion is increased. Physical attractiveness has been associated with cohesion (Kleck & Rubinstein, 1975; Krebs & Adinolfi, 1975; Walster, Aronson, Abrahams & Rottman, 1966). Attitude similarity among members increases interpersonal attraction (Byrne, 1961; Byrne & Nelson, 1964, 1965a, 1965b; Newcomb, 1961). Personality similarity has also been demonstrated to increase interpersonal attraction and cohesion (Byrne et al., 1967; Griffitt, 1966; Izard, 1960b). Economic similarity (Byrne et al., 1966) and racial similarity are associated with attraction and cohesion (Kandel, 1978; Smith et al., 1967). Need similarity is associated with attraction as well (Rychlak, 1965).

Taken together, this body of research suggests that the more alike group members are, the more cohesive the group will be. Also, the more members value group goals and activities, the more cohesive the group will be. Finally, leaders in this initial stage who give members positive feedback will effect an increase in group cohesion.

High levels of cohesion increase conformity in the group (Bovard, 1951; Lott & Lott, 1961; Wyer, 1966). High cohesion also increases the influence the group has over its members (Berkowitz, 1954; Schacter, Ellertson, McBride, & Gregory, 1951). Thus, with reference to the earlier discussion of conformity as a characteristic of groups at this stage, it seems reasonable to assume that one function of conformity is to increase group cohesion. Conversely, a function of cohesion might be to increase conformity.

Perhaps the essential goal of increasing cohesion and conformity during this early stage is group survival. In order to develop and mature, an organism must first survive intact. Maslow (1962) described this as the most basic individual need. The same appears to be true of groups. To survive, the group must stay together. Thus, cohesion and conformity and the avoidance of conflict become paramount at this early stage. Processes and procedures necessary for constructive conflict and disagreement are not yet in place. It is too risky for the group to allow conflict or disagreement. Group integration and the establishment of a coherent social structure that would allow for conflict and disagreement have not yet occurred. Thus, in order to survive, the major portion of the group's time and energy goes into increasing cohesion and conformity. Early deviation or conflict might be likely to cause the the group to dissolve.

Groups at this stage are not yet in a position to solve complex problems, come to consensual and informed decisions, or work to their full capacity.

However, such groups are often expected to do all these things. For example, it is common practice in industrial settings to put a team together to respond to an environmental demand. Such groups may be charged with developing a proposal, creating a new product, or generating new processes or procedures. Usually the teams are composed of individuals who are thought to be experts in the various tasks necessary to accomplish the goal. They are often from different departments and may not have worked together before. A project manager is selected to lead the team. Almost invariably, the team is given a deadline for completing its work. Given the pressures of the business world, the time allotted for project completion tends to be short.

In this situation, the group is forced into premature decision making, role and task assignment, and the like. Outcomes in such circumstances tend to be inferior, since there is no time for the development of a group culture and social structure that will facilitate the free flow of ideas. Unfortunately, there are many examples of this in work situations, community groups, and other kinds of groups. Understanding the process of group development and the time necessary for it to occur might help organizations to improve the effectiveness and productivity of project teams.

The reviewed research is summarized below in the form of a list of factors that are generally associated with stage-one groups. This is provided to assist the reader in making the leap from understanding to identification of these factors in the real groups of which he or she is a part. The intention is to aid the transfer of learning. Readers are encouraged to use the lists as the basis for observing and attempting to determine the developmental level of ongoing groups with which they have contact.

Identifying a Stage-One Group

1. Members are concerned with personal safety in the group.
2. Members are concerned with acceptance and inclusion.
3. Members fear group rejection.
4. Members communicate in a tentative and very polite manner.
5. The members behave in ways that suggest a need for dependable and directive leadership.
6. The leader is seen as benevolent and competent.
7. The leader is expected and encouraged to provide members with direction and personal safety.
8. The leader is very rarely challenged.
9. Goals are not clear to members, but clarity is not sought.
10. Members rarely express disagreement with initial group goals.
11. The group assumes that consensus about goals exists.
12. Role assignments tend to be based on external status, first impressions, and initial self-presentation of members, rather than on matching member competencies with goal and task requirements.
13. Member compliance is high.

14. Communication tends to be centralized.
15. Participation is generally limited to a few vocal individuals.
16. Overt conflict is minimal.
17. Conformity is high.
18. A lack of group structure and organization is evident.
19. Member deviation from emerging norms is rare.
20. Cohesion and commitment to the group are based on identification with the leader rather than other factors.
21. Subgroups and coalitions are rare at this stage.

5

STAGE TWO:
COUNTERDEPENDENCY
AND FIGHT

The second stage of group development has been described as stormy (Tuckman & Jensen, 1977), hostile and conflictual (Braaten, 1974/1975), a time for testing boundaries (Mills, 1964), antiauthority (Bennis & Shepard, 1956), and a phase characterized by premature enactment in which groups attempt to work before they are mature enough to do so (Mann, Gibbard, & Hartman, 1967). Essentially, the group's tasks at this stage include clarifying goals, values, and boundaries (Lewin, 1936; Rendle, 1983), establishing norms (Stanford, 1977), and trying out and clarifying role assignments (Mills, 1967). While all these tasks seem reasonable and rational, the processes that groups go through to accomplish these tasks can be fraught with conflict and hostility. In fact, some have argued that another important task of this stage is to engage in conflict. The conflict generated provides the medium for the accomplishment of all the other tasks. Successful resolution of conflicts is seen as necessary for further group development (Lewin, 1936; Rendle, 1983).

In Chapter 2, conflict was described as a way to develop shared values (Theodorson, 1962). It has also been seen as necessary to the development of cohesion (Coser, 1956; Deutsch, 1971; Northen, 1969). What these writers and researchers suggest is that conflict and tension provide the energy needed by the group to continue to develop and clarify its culture and social structure. The reader will recall that the first stage of group development is characterized by conformity, dependency, fear of rejection, anxiety, and overly polite agreement with emerging goals, roles, and processes. While this first stage clearly inhibits valid communication, it does serve to decrease member anxiety and increase feelings of belonging and safety. The members join the group at stage one, but at the cost of suppressing certain aspects of the self for fear of group rejection. The safety engendered at stage one, however, does make it possible for group members to begin to disagree and present more aspects of themselves at stage two.

The tension of this stage comes mainly from two sources. Individuals who have hidden certain views from the group often experience increasing divergence between their self-perception and their inhibited self-presentation to the group. The tension that this discrepancy engenders may provide individual members with the energy or incentive to speak up or object to issues, roles, or processes being decided by the group.

Another source of tension for group members is a shift in their perceptions regarding the leader. Some members will continue to see the leader as benevolent and competent. However, in most cases a subgroup begins to form who opposes the leader. This subgroup tends to perceive the leader as autocratic, incompetent, or emotionally distant from the group. These two subgroups argue over their opposing views during this stage (Bennis & Shepard, 1956). The actual competence of the leader does not seem to affect these dynamics to any great extent. Both objectively competent and objectively incompetent leaders may become the target of a rebellious subgroup. What the group-as-a-whole may be doing by arguing about the leader seems to be related to the group's need for increased interdependence as opposed to dependence on any one leader. The group is working to establish a coherent culture and social structure that allow for communication and participation from many members. The group may or may not succeed in establishing a participatory social structure. However, during this stage of group development all groups seem to try.

GROUP STRUCTURES

The Communication Structure

It is during the conflict stage of group development that a group attempts to clarify and agree on its goals, norms, roles, power distribution, and the like. All of this is accomplished through communication. If the structure established during stage one does not allow sufficient participation in these discussions, agreement is unlikely. For example, in some groups only certain influential members speak. Decisions that are made do not necessarily represent a convergence of the views of all members. Consequently, commitment to these decisions may not be shared. This can seriously affect group morale and productivity. Crucial to the successful resolution of the inevitable conflict of stage two is a communication structure that allows for participation and discussion of different member values, goals, and strategies for goal accomplishment. The communication structure must allow members the freedom to express their views and to disagree with each other. If it does not, member alienation, resentment, decreased attraction to the group, and decreased drive for goal accomplishment will be the results.

Unfortunately, examples abound of communication structures that inhibit the free flow of ideas and emotional reactions. At the macro level, representative governments that do not faithfully represent the views of the citizens breed apathy and feelings of powerlessness among the electorate. Hierarchical communication structures in organizations often reduce and inhibit the upward flow of information. Decisions are made with less input from members, resulting in poor or uncreative decisions and apathy or hostility among organization members.

At the level of the small group, committee members may feel too unsafe or inhibited to express their views. After such a meeting, it is common to hear participants asking each other why no one spoke up at the meeting. "Why didn't you say something?" is frequently heard. Such behavior outside the meeting suggests that the communication structure of that committee acts to instill fear of reprisals or rejection in lower-status members. Such a state of affairs will inhibit the committee's ability to deal successfully with the naturally occurring conflict of stage two. The communication structure continues to enforce dependency and conformity. It also acts to maintain an excessive amount of anxiety about group membership and fears of rejection or reprisals. The group will be severely limited in its ability to develop a social structure that will meet the emotional needs or achievement requirements of the group.

Such a state of affairs is often attributed to the the malevolent intentions of the leader or the more powerful high-status members of the group. Members often feel that the power elite of the group is consciously trying to inhibit lower-status members' participation. While this is undoubtedly true in some cases, it is often due to the unconscious choices made by the group during stage one. The communication structure is established very quickly and without much conscious thought. Thus, the type of structure established by the group may not meet the group's future requirements. Often the type of structure chosen is based on the past experiences of members or on the social conventions of the day. As has been stated previously, no modern group begins from scratch to develop its culture and social structure. Therefore, a new group forming within an institution or culture that tends to be autocratic and hierarchical will, most likely, establish a hierarchical communication structure. All members, not just the leadership, will expect this to occur, and so it will. Even if the leader and higher-status members want increased member participation, it may not occur. Members, based on their past experience in that institution, may not trust the motives of the leadership and will not participate in a more egalitarian structure.

For example, leaders of economic institutions have come to realize that increased worker participation in management decisions is an important factor in increasing U.S. economic productivity. They have reached this conclusion based on the perceived effectiveness of participatory management practiced in Japan and that country's resultant productivity. Interestingly, much of the research supporting this conclusion was conducted by U.S. social scientists in the 1960s and 1970s. At that time, however, U.S. business rejected the idea. Only after Japan began to significantly improve its economic standing as a result, in part, of adopting participatory practices did U.S. business leaders begin to entertain the idea of change.

However, regardless of managements' reasons for wishing to increase worker participation, there is a significant movement underway to accomplish this goal. Organizational consultants are working to assist industry in this change. The process is a slow one, however, since workers are often suspicious of the reasons for the change. Employees, operating on historical assumptions and their own previous experience, often resist efforts to involve them more in the management of their companies. The change will be very time consuming and difficult since it requires ideological change in group and organizational culture.

While some progress is being made in the effort to increase worker participation in the private sector, the public sector is having even more difficulty moving to a more participatory communication structure. For example, teacher empowerment is being encouraged across the nation. **Teacher empowerment** is a term used to describe attempts to increase teacher input into educational decisions. Resistance to the change, however, remains high. Once they are established, structures and patterns of communication are very difficult to alter, even if change is in group members' best interests. Such a change will take a considerable period of time, if it occurs at all. We see, then, that there are not always villains to be blamed for the existence of communication structures that inhibit group development and productivity. Group processes and dynamics are interactive. All participate in their establishment and maintenance and all must participate in changing them.

The effectiveness or ineffectiveness of a communication structure becomes most apparent during the conflict stage of group development. It is during this stage that the utility of the communication structure receives its most important test. The resolution of conflict and the development of a shared group culture is the primary task of this stage. This cannot occur unless the communication structure allows for adequate discussion, disagreement, and conflict resolution strategies.

The content and process of communication are also critical at this stage. If conflict must occur, then the content of the conflict and how it is expressed will either facilitate or inhibit its resolution. On the level of content, if the opposing views being expressed in a group are too divergent, the probability of developing unified views is decreased. A current national example of this is the debate over abortion. Some citizens see abortion as always wrong in all cases. Others see it as acceptable under certain conditions. The fight goes on and on. There has been, to date, no evidence of a move toward reconciling these very disparate views. The nation is locked in an ideological conflict with, as yet, no hope of resolution. The intensity of this fight, and our national focus on it, divert our attention from other pressing issues such as the environment, poverty, and drugs. This type of protracted fight can occur in small groups as well, with the same debilitating results. Unless the conflict is resolved, the group will be severely restricted in its ability to organize or to accomplish its work. The fight will be the focus of attention, to the detriment of other aspects of group life.

The content of the conflict, or what is said, is very important at this stage. However, how things are said is also significant. It is important to the successful resolution of this stage that members feel that they can disagree and not be punished by the group. If a member voices disagreement and is disparaged, shunned, or ridiculed for his or her views, the likelihood of developing enough trust in the group to enter stage three is minimal.

Goals and Tasks

The agreement concerning group goals that appears to exist at stage one generally disappears during the second stage of group development. This early agreement may be superficial, since disagreement is not considered safe at this stage. The discussion of group goals at stage one provides a context for tentative exploration by individual group members. It allows for the establishment of a communication structure and preliminary role assignments. These structural tasks take precedence over actual goal clarification. The establishment of certain elements of the social structure helps to create a less anxiety-ridden and more predictable group environment. Members begin to feel a bit safer and more certain of their group membership. At the same time, members begin to feel constrained by the strong pressures to conform imposed by the group in order to facilitate the establishment of an initial social structure. These two elements, a feeling of increased safety coupled with a growing feeling of discomfort regarding the degree of conformity, provide members with the motivation to disagree and to challenge initial group decisions. Conflict is the inevitable result.

Wheaton (1974) stated that there are two types of conflict. **Principled conflict** focuses on disagreements about basic values. **Communal conflict** occurs when there is agreement about basic values but not on specifics. Wheaton noted that principled conflict negatively affects group cohesion. Communal conflict, however, positively affects cohesion. Essentially, once agreement on basic principles and values takes place, conflict over how to enact those principles and reach goals serves to remind members of their consensual values. This aids cohesion, cooperation, and group integration.

The conflict that erupts at the second stage of group development tends to be principled conflict as opposed to communal. Basic values, ideals, and goals are being explored. The group is seeking to establish the degree to which members agree or disagree about these basic issues. Group members hope to establish a consensus regarding basic values and group goals. The more divisive and severe the conflict is at this stage, the less likely it is that the group will become cohesive and integrated. Consequently, the way in which differences of opinion or values are discussed may be as important to the process as the objective diversity of views. The type of communication structure that has been established will also influence the search for consensus. If, for example, only certain members can or do speak, agreement is jeopardized.

The search for agreement about basic values, goals, and commitment to these goals is a critical one. Agreement about goals and, ultimately, the paths to those goals affect many other aspects of the group. Cohen (1959) found that when goal-path clarity is poor, members report less motivation and security. Members also evaluate themselves more poorly and work less efficiently. Raven and Rietsema (1957) noted that high goal clarity is associated with increased attraction to the group tasks and increased member conformity. Anderson (1975) reported that when goal-path clarity is high, so are cohesion and liking.

Deutsch (1949a) defined a competitive group as one in which the goal achievement of one member hinders to some degree the goal achievement of other members. In contrast, a cooperative group is one in which the goal achievement of one member facilitates the goal achievement of others. In essence, then, Deutsch equates cooperation with homogeneous or consensual goals. Cooperative groups have consensual or homogeneous goals. He reported that productivity is higher in groups with homogeneous goals than in other groups (Deutsch, 1949b). It appears that the time and effort expended in seeking consensus and clarity about goals are well spent. If the group achieves consensus and clarity, productivity and many other aspects of group culture and social structure will be positively affected.

Status and Roles

Role assignments are made early in the group. As a result, individual role assignments may or may not be useful to the individual or to the group. Also, it is important to remember that individuals are unlikely to disagree initially with their assigned roles. This is so, in part, because individuals tend to be unaware of the process of role assignment in groups. It is also due to the fact that even if a role feels particularly inappropriate and the individual is aware of his or her role assignment, the climate of stage one makes it very risky to challenge the group. Individual members fear rejection or punishment if they do not conform and go along with the group.

At stage two, however, conflict and disagreement become more permissible. During this stage members try out their roles. A member may object to his or her role assignment and argue for another. Other members may be dissatisfied with an individual's enacted role and may press the individual to conform to the expected role. These discussions and disagreements usually are more indirect than direct discussions of roles. Since most people are unaware of the role they are occupying in a particular group, discomfort with a role is often expressed as anger with the expectations of others regarding one's behavior.

Many of us have found ourselves in rather uncomfortable situations in which others seem to expect something of us that we either cannot or do not wish to enact: other members may be looking to us for advice and direction, and this makes us uncomfortable; they may expect us to know things that we do not know; or they may expect us to be silent and subservient when we do not wish to behave that way. These are examples of group role assignments and expectations for behavior. When the fit between the role occupant and the role is not a good one, the occupant will feel discomfort, and some occupants will begin to express this discomfort during the second phase of group development.

The individual is unlikely to say, "I am uncomfortable with my role assignment. Can I have another?" More likely, an individual will say, "You seem to think I know things that I don't." Another might say, "I keep feeling pressured to be quiet and agreeable." These are examples of individual role occupants' attempts to alter their role assignments by expressing discomfort.

On the other hand, a role occupant may be comfortable with his or her role assignment. However, the group may not be happy with his or her performance. When this occurs, the group tends to communicate a great deal with the role occupant in an effort to gain conformity with expectations. Ultimately, if the role occupant does not conform, he or she will be shunned or ignored by the group.

At stage two, then, members try out their role assignments. The fit between the individual and the role may be a good one or a source of tension and conflict within the individual. He or she may try to influence the group for a role change. Also, if the individual's enacted role does not fit the group's expectations, the group may try to influence the role occupant to change his or her behavior to conform with group expectations. Conflict and disagreement about role assignment or performance are likely at this stage. It affords the group the opportunity to correct blatant errors in role assignments. It also allows individuals the opportunity to fine tune their roles to fit them better. Keep in mind, however, that role shifts and changes do not occur very frequently. Once a group member is in a role, it is very difficult to get out of it. However, some shifts and changes do occur.

Leadership

In the first stage of group development, leaders have considerable influence. Members tend to be dependent on the leader for direction and safety. Leaders have a good deal of influence with regard to initial definition of goals and preliminary decisions about the types of group structures being established. The leader is expected by group members to provide direction, safety, order, group goals, and structures. During stage two, however, member expectations and reactions to the leader change markedly. Members will begin to resent what is now perceived as undue influence on the part of the leader. The leader's competence may be challenged. Some members may feel manipulated by the leader. Members question the leader's competence and ability to provide safety. Suspicion and challenges to the leader's authority begin to take place.

Not all members become disenchanted with the leader. Some remain loyal. Bennis and Shepard (1956) reported that the group splits into two factions over this issue. One faction is supportive of the leader, and the other is not. These two factions often fight about their expectations of the leader and his or her performance with regard to these expectations. Some of this conflict may be due to actual leader behavior in the group. Much of the conflict, however, is about things that go beyond the role of the leader. In essence, the conflict with and about the leader is a way for the group to discuss who can have input into decisions. Roles, decision making, power, status, and communication structures are being clarified in this process. Efforts to redistribute power begin to occur.

During the first stage of group development, the role of leader is the most differentiated and important role. Other roles are just being assigned. The role of leader, however, is either predetermined or assigned very quickly. The leader role is necessary to the establishment of some sense of safety and order. In effect, the role of leader and members' reactions to that role are the impetus for the emergence of other roles and structures in the group. The prominence of the leader at stage one and member dependence on the leader, then, allow for initial structures to form. Once these are in place, the group can begin to define its structure even further. A major way that the group does this is by redefining the leader's role and reducing, to some extent, the power associated with the role. This redistribution of power clears the way for other structures and roles to emerge.

So far, this seems like a reasonable and natural transition. However, leaders have used their power during stage one. People with power generally use it (Deutsch, 1973). We also know from research that when individuals use power successfully they experience considerable self-satisfaction. They also tend to overestimate their power and to view themselves unrealistically (Erez, Rim, & Keider, 1986; Kipnis, 1974). The acquisition of power tends to make individuals want more power, not less (Cartwright & Zander, 1968; McClelland, 1975, 1985). Thus, the redistribution of power necessary for further group development is not an easy process. When leaders are met with resistance, their efforts to exert power and influence tend to increase.

French and Raven (1959) outlined five bases for power. The ability to deliver positive or negative reinforcers to others is **reward power. Coercive power** is the capacity to punish individuals or the group for noncompliance. **Legitimate power** exists when others believe that one has the right to expect compliance. That is, the powerholder is authorized by the group or organization to have power over others. This type of power base stems from group structure and member agreement with group norms and values. When members identify with, feel attracted to, and respect the leader, he or she is said to have **referent power.** This type of power is sometimes referred to as charisma. Finally, if members feel that a person has superior abilities or skills, the individual is said to have **expert power.**

The basis for a particular individual or leader's power does affect member reactions to the individual's efforts to influence them. For example, reward and coercive power may gain compliance. However, these power bases can be problematic. If the group is successful in meeting its objectives (Michener & Lawler, 1975) and the leader is trusted (Friedland, 1976), the group will tolerate these power bases and their resultant power tactics. These tactics will also be tolerated if group norms support rewards and coercion as power bases (Michener & Burt, 1975a). However, if the group is not successful, these power bases and tactics will increase group hostility and resistance (Johnson & Ewens, 1971; Schlenker, Nacci, Helm & Tedeschi, 1976). Coercion may work for a while, but resistance builds with the passage of time (Youngs, 1986).

Members tend to respond to legitimate power quite differently, since the powerholder is seen as having the right to expect compliance. Also, compliance is consistent with group norms. Members comply because they accept these norms. Thus, legitimate power, while it will also be challenged, produces less resistance and is more effective than reward or coercive power (Wrong, 1979).

The tactics that leaders or powerholders use to influence others are numerous. Direct tactics include threats, demands, and faits accomplis such as presenting the group with a decision. Indirect tactics include manipulation and covert attempts to influence. Tactics can be rational, such as persuasion and bargaining, or nonrational, such as evasion and ingratiation. Finally, some tactics, such as demands, faits acomplis, and evasion are unilateral in that the influence goes only one way. Bilateral tactics such as discussion and negotiation allow influence to flow in both directions (Falbo, 1977; Kipnis, 1984).

High-status individuals tend to use direct power tactics while low-status people use indirect tactics (Kipnis, 1984). Also, the more individuals resist attempts to influence them, the more likely a leader or other powerholder is to use direct tactics (Kipnis, 1984; Michener & Burt, 1975a). Unfortunately, people do not respond well to some direct tactics. We tend to like people who use discussion, persuasion, and expertise as opposed to other power tactics (Falbo, 1977; Shaw & Condelli, 1986).

Hollander and Offermann (1990) describe three types of power. There is **power over,** which they associate with dominance. **Power from** is the ability to resist unwanted influence and demands. **Power to,** or **empowerment,** is the ability to act more freely through power sharing. Power-over strategies tend have negative affects on group relationships and goal achievement (Kipnis, Castell, Gergen & Mauch, 1976). Such tactics often lead others to attempt to take power from the leader. Power-to or empowering strategies facilitate group development, since no leader can perform all the functions of leadership alone. Redistribution of power is essential to facilitate group structural development and productivity (Hollander & Offermann, 1990).

Given the previous discussion, a group is not always successful in altering its perceptions, or the leader's perceptions, of the leadership role. Also, even if the group's perceptions change, the leader may force or coerce the group into continuing to respond as they did in stage one. Should the group fail to alter its perceptions, it will regress to the dependency stage of group development. Should the leader and group disagree about the leader role and be unable to resolve this controversy, a prolonged fight for power and control is likely to occur. The group remains in stage two for an extended period of time. Should this happen, the group's cohesion, social structure, and productivity will be very adversely affected. Power struggles, fights, and the like will take precedence over goal achievement, efficiency, and productivity.

Examples abound of groups that do not succeed in altering their perceptions of the leader role. These groups tend to remain dependent on the leader. Such leader prominence severely limits the group's structural development. Other roles do not develop. Consequently, individual members may work only in the presence of the leader. This is because the group's social structure is very deficient. The other roles, structures, and processes needed for the group to continue its work in the absence of the leader have not developed. As a result, the group cannot work on its own.

Elementary school classrooms are often examples of this type of prolonged dependency on the leader/teacher. Of course, given the age of the class members and the nature of many educational tasks, this may not inhibit individual learning. However, if cooperative learning tasks or tasks requiring student initiative are attempted, the classroom group will be unsuccessful unless the teacher–student relationship is changed, and group development is not only allowed but encouraged.

Adult work groups sometimes fit the description of a group stuck at stage one. Such groups work well in the presence of the leader/manager. However, when the manager is absent, productivity is significantly reduced. These groups are capable of following orders. But group decisions are not possible, since the structures necessary for decision making are not in place. Extreme examples of this phenomenon on a larger level include Nazi Germany and Jonestown. Small-scale examples of this protracted dependency and limited development are, of course, quite common in the workplace, families, and many other group settings.

Examples of groups who are unable to resolve the conflict over the role of the leader are also common. These groups tend to be in conflict for extended periods of time. The inability to resolve the conflict inherent in the second stage of group development is a major block to cooperation, integration, efficiency, and productivity in all types of groups and organizations. The group's energy is directed toward the resolution of power struggles rather than toward goal achievement and productivity. Group and organizational consultants see the consequences of this prolonged fight all too frequently in their work. Such groups, organizations, or nations are intent on winning power or overthrowing the leader. Work, rationality, and the like seem forgotten.

One of the reasons why groups fail to resolve the tension and conflict inherent in this stage of group development is that members tend to personalize the experience. That is, when an individual member's views are challenged by others, the individual has a natural tendency to feel hurt and attacked personally. Leaders who are attacked and discounted a great deal at this stage also perceive these as personal affronts. As a result, individuals may become quite defensive and combative themselves. This escalation of tension to unmanageable levels may significantly reduce the group's chances to resolve the conflict and create a unified group culture and social structure.

Adopting a group perspective can be very helpful to members and leaders, especially at this stage. If the events of stage two are viewed from this perspective, they are understood very differently. Rather than feel personally attacked, a leader with a group perspective could view the attack as a sign that the group was ready to further define its social structure. The leader would view his or her role at this stage as a focus or catalyst for continued development. He or she would not feel as threatened by the loss of some power or influence. Rather, he or she might come to view this redistribution of power roles and tasks as essential to group productivity and goal achievement (Banas, 1988).

In like fashion, a member whose views are challenged by others could see the challenges as necessary to the establishment of homogeneous goals and an integrated group culture and social structure. Instead of reacting defensively, he or she might focus on clarifying his or her views and the views of others in an attempt to gain consensus. A group perspective makes it possible for individuals to view conflict as normal and necessary at this stage of group development.

In real situations, the author has seen the effects of adopting a group perspective on numerous occasions. If a group or organization that is stuck in the conflict stage of group development can adopt a group perspective, it may be able to free itself and move to higher functional stages. The first step, then, is learning about group development and dynamics. Simply knowing about these phenomena, however, is not enough. The group and its members must be able to give up blaming each other in order to begin to resolve the conflicts. This is not easy. Even though we know intellectually that conflict, attacks, and disagreements are normal and necessary parts of group development, on an emotional level we feel hurt or angry. Our emotions may overwhelm us and lead us to seek revenge or vindication rather than reconciliation and consensus. In many cases, groups would rather get even than succeed.

While this tendency for groups and human beings to choose emotionality over rationality is very frustrating, it is also very normal and natural. People are not purely rational. We are emotional *and* thinking persons. Our rationality is easily overwhelmed by the intensity of our feelings. This is especially true in groups, since the prevailing emotional tone of the group is infectious. For example, groups can easily become hostile or aggressive even if their members would not if they were alone. Rational decisions and actions are very difficult for individuals and even more difficult for groups. These are facts. We cannot change our nature—at least not within a generation. However, awareness of these dynamics and the powerful hold emotions have over individuals and groups can help us to make decisions that are in our best interests.

Coalitions and Subgroups

A sign of increasing organization and maturation at this stage is the appearance of coalitions and subgroups. During the first stage of group development, few if any coalitions or subgroups form. Individual members tend to focus their attention on the leader as the source of safety and reward. Members do not know or trust each other enough to align themselves with some members over others. However, this changes during the second stage of group development. The necessary but confining conformity of stage one allows members to begin to explore each others' views and behavior. Anxiety over inclusion lessens to some extent, and individuals begin to reveal themselves and their opinions more readily. These events herald the beginning of stage two and the advent of the subgroups and coalitions that members will form for a variety of reasons.

Bennis and Shepard (1956) state that subgroup formation occurs first in relation to the leader. The group tends to split into two subgroups based on their view of the leader. The dependent subgroup maintains its loyalty to the leader, while the counterdependent subgroup begins to challenge the authority of the leader. These two subgroups debate their positions until some resolution is reached regarding how the group-as-a-whole will view the leader.

Subgrouping occurs when "two or more members develop ties with each other on the basis of some common understanding, feeling, or mutual need" (Luft, 1984, p. 35). For example, a particular subgroup may contain the members of the group who are most similar with regard to their membership or reference groups. Mutual attraction may serve as the basis for a subgroup. Similarity of assigned group roles or the need to work together to accomplish part of the group's task may also serve as the basis for a subgroup. Emotional or communication style might be the criterion for membership in a subgroup. Similarity of goals or values is another possible reason for subgroup formation.

Whatever the reason for subgroup formation, it undoubtedly threatens the existing order of conformity and unity established at stage one. Thus, subgroup members are often challenged by the other members and accused of exclusivity or disloyalty to the group. Regardless of how benign a subgroup may be, it upsets the group's infant structure and disturbs the new-found safety achieved during stage one. Issues of inclusion and exclusion resurface as the group-as-a-whole tries to cope with this new phenomenon.

In fact, the emergence of subgroups does signal a change in the group, but not necessarily a negative one. If the group is to develop a social structure capable of accomplishing its goals, it will be necessary for the group to allow subgroups to form. Mills (1967) stated that one of the criteria for group growth and development is the capacity to differentiate into subgroups while maintaining a feeling of group-as-a-whole unity. Luft (1984) stated that subgroups grow out of the need to organize to do work. Groups are systems made up of subsystems that are governed by relational ties and the requirements of the groups' goals and tasks (p. 16).

While the emergence of subgroups is perceived as threatening to total group unity, it is essential to group development. The group's social structure will remain primitive unless members are allowed to organize in ways that will facilitate goal achievement and morale. People must be allowed to be different and to establish different relationships with other members. Otherwise, work and emotional requirements will not be met.

Subgroups and membership in subgroups are subject to change over the course of the group. The basis for their formation will vary depending on the prevailing conditions and phase of group development. The interaction among different subgroups is thought by many to be an indicator of group development. Thus, when friendly relations exist among subgroups, the group is thought to be at a higher level of development than when relations are strained or hostile.

During stage two, relations among emergent subgroups are likely to be tense and strained. This is due to the fact that the existence of any subgroup threatens the tentative unity so recently established. Th emergence of subgroups also signals the beginning of a period of conflict, which group members would rather avoid. However, there is no avoiding the conflict and anxiety engendered by the overt expression of individual differences and allegiances.

A coalition is seen by some as identical to a subgroup. Borgatta (1961), for example, defined a coalition as joint activity. Mills (1953) described a coalition as providing mutual emotional support. These definitions are not unlike the description of a subgroup provided above. However, most researchers define a coalition as a joint use of resources to affect the outcome of group decisions (Gamson, 1964). According to this definition, then, a coalition is a special type of subgroup formed to influence group-as-a-whole decisions. Other types of subgroups exist for a variety of reasons but not primarily to gain advantage in influencing group decisions.

Coalitions involve two or more people who join forces against at least one other person. The assumption is that this joint action will produce a better result than would individuals acting alone (Bond & Vinacke, 1961; Caplow, 1959; Gamson, 1961a, 1961b, 1964; Komorita & Brinsberg, 1977; Lawler & Youngs, 1975; Pearce, Stevenson & Porter, 1986; Vinacke & Arkoff, 1957). Like other types of subgroups, coalitions are usually not permanent and shift with internal and external group conditions. They are influenced by group norms and structures and the attitudes of group members.

While any subgroup causes anxiety and potential conflict, coalitions are always associated with conflict. Those excluded from the coalition respond with hostility toward coalition members. Frequently, the excluded members attempt to forge their own coalition to counteract the influence of the original coalition. Another reason for the hostility of excluded members is that coalitions tend to form and work outside the boundaries of the formal group structure (Cyert & March, 1963; Pearce et al., 1986; Stevenson, Pearce & Porter, 1985). For example, coalition discussions may take place outside of the group or on breaks rather than within the hearing of other group members.

Coalitions may contain members who disagree about many other things but join forces to influence the direction of the group on some issue that they agree is important (Murnighan, 1978). In some cases, considerable bargaining and negotiation occur within the coalition in order to maintain the alliance (Murnighan, 1986).

Given the tasks of groups during the second stage of group development, coalitions are inevitable. The task of the group-as-a-whole is to develop a unified group culture and social structure. Inevitably, individuals will differ in their views on the group's mission and goals and how the group should organize to meet these goals. It would be difficult for an individual member acting alone to have much influence on this process. However, by forming temporary coalitions, group members increase the probability of influencing decision making. Coalitions form to influence group goals, norms, structures, power distribution, roles, and many other issues. Coalitions for and against a particular position work to impose their views on the group. Ultimately, compromise on a particular issue may be reached. Current coalitions may then be dissolved and new ones formed based on differing views of another decision facing the group.

Coalitions form to gain power from or the power to resist unwanted influence being exerted by the leader or other high-status members. Sometimes coercive tactics used by a leader contribute to the formation of rebellious or revolutionary coalitions and subgroups (Lawler, 1975; Lawler & Thompson, 1978, 1979). As was stated earlier, if the content of the divergent views is extremely divisive, coalitions will battle for extended periods of time, often with no resolution. This will seriously impede group development. Group morale, cohesion, and productivity will be negatively affected as a result. Subgroups and coalitions present a special challenge to groups. They are necessary to group growth and development in that they allow for differentiation and organization essential to goal achievement. On the other hand, if coalitions cannot reach agreements and subgroups cannot be tolerated by the group-as-a-whole, group effectiveness and development will be seriously compromised.

GROUP PROCESSES

Conformity and Deviation

One of the hallmarks of the conflict stage of group development is a reduction in the amount of conformity required of group members. Decreased conformity is necessary to allow freer communication and discussion of differences. It is also necessary to the establishment of a more democratic form of leadership. Finally, a reduction in conformity is essential to the formation of a social structure that can tolerate the subgroups and role differentiation necessary to do work.

Even though a reduction in conformity is necessary for further group development, individual deviators are met with considerable pressure to continue to conform. Thus, one reason for the emergence of subgroups and coalitions is to provide strength in numbers and protection for individuals with views different from others'. It is more difficult to reject or shun a subgroup or coalition than it is an individual. The task of the group at stage two is quite delicate. The group must allow deviation in order to promote group development and achievement. On the other hand, if deviation does not lead to coordination and unity, the group may disband or become dysfunctional.

Cohesion and Conflict

At this point, the reader may have come to the conclusion that cohesion is seriously impaired by the conflict that occurs at stage two. While this can be the result, cohesion can also be positively affected by conflict. Although this sounds paradoxical, it is important to note that in any relationship, the freedom to be oneself and to disagree without fear of rejection or retribution increases rather than decreases cohesion and trust. Also, as was stated earlier, conflict provides energy to the group and allows for clarification of group values, goals, and structures. All of these have been found to be associated with increased cohesion and trust. Cohesion and conflict are inextricably linked. You can't have one without the other, so to speak.

Of course, how conflict is dealt with is the crucial factor in determining its effect on cohesion. Inevitably, conflict is resolved. How it is resolved will determine whether group cohesion is positively or negatively affected. Six methods of conflict resolution have been described by a number of researchers (Blake & Mouton, 1964; Burke, 1970; Pruitt, 1983; Pruitt & Rubin, 1986; Sternberg & Soriano, 1984). These include:

1. Imposition, in which the position of an individual or subgroup is forced on other members.
2. Withdrawal of an individual or subgroup from the group.
3. Inaction, in which one or both sides of a conflict do nothing to resolve the conflict.
4. Yielding, in which one side gives up its position.
5. Compromise, in which the parties find a solution somewhere between their respective positions.
6. Problem solving, in which the source of the conflict is located and a mutually agreeable solution is found.

The first four solutions have many negative repercussions. Imposition can result in hostility and passive-agressive behavior on the part of group members. Withdrawal threatens the life of the group and reduces its resources through member loss. Inaction can result in simmering discontent, apathy, or alienation. Yielding may also elicit alienation and covert hostility. Compromise can be viable if the resolution of the conflict seems reasonable and acceptable to all concerned. However, problem solving has the best results, since it requires an actual resolution of differences and a new group conceptualization of the issues involved in the conflict.

Some groups navigate their conflicts well, and others disband or become dysfunctional by dealing with their differences through ineffective means. What do successful groups do to promote positive conflict resolution? One answer can be seen from the previous discussion of communication structures, content, and process. Successful groups, or individuals for that matter, communicate their views clearly and explicitly. They avoid generalizations and are specific in their communication. They talk about trust and cooperation during the discussion (Lindskold, 1986; Lindskold, Han & Betz, 1986; Swingle & Santi, 1972). Members also initially respond cooperatively to others who are behaving competitively (Brickman, Becker & Castel, 1979). If others continue to respond competitively, successful group members demonstrate their willingness to compete by arguing their position. While this sounds like an inappropriate strategy, research suggests that this may result in cooperation from others since not to cooperate would result in continued stress or personal losses (Axelrod & Hamilton, 1981; Orkin, 1987). Sometimes demonstrating a willingness to compete will bring about cooperation from others (Sermat, 1964; Solomon, 1960). Demonstrating a willingness to compete may also result in being viewed as a more formidable opponent (McGillicuddy, Pruitt & Syna, 1984).

All of these strategies help to maintain a reasonable trust level to allow negotiations to proceed. Negotiation is an important conflict-resolution strategy (Druckman, 1977, 1987; Pruitt, 1981, 1987; Rubin & Brown, 1985). Seeking a mutually agreeable solution is sometimes referred to as **principled negotiation** and has been found to increase communication (Deutsch, 1973) and cooperation (Worchel, Axsom, Ferris, Samaha & Schwietzer, 1978). It also tends to reduce the conflict by breaking it down into specific issues that can be dealt with one at a time (Fisher, 1964).

Sometimes the intensity and depth of the conflict are too great to be solved by the group members themselves. In such cases, seeking the aid of a third party can help to resolve the conflict. Group and organizational consultants are often asked to assist groups stuck in stage two as a result of seemingly insurmountable conflicts. This can be a useful strategy for conflict resolution (Carnevale, 1986; Folberg & Taylor, 1984; Raven & Rubin, 1976). However, third-party intervention should be sought only if all parties desire the intervention and if the intensity of the conflict is high (Hiltrop & Rubin, 1982). In some cases, however, the techniques used by the intervener may serve only to exacerbate the conflict (Rubin, 1980). This last-resort strategy requires a willingness on the part of the group and considerable skill on the part of the third party.

Much remains to be learned about conflict resolution. However, we do have considerable information about it. And yet groups, organizations, institutions, and nations often get trapped in the conflict stage of development, with serious consequences. The task of this stage is to forge unity out of diversity. It is a difficult task, fraught with dangers and pitfalls. For some groups, the conflict will be conducted in such a way that resolution, trust, and cohesion are strengthened. These groups move relatively smoothly to higher stages of development. For others, the wounds, resentments, and angers generated by the conflict overwhelm reason and mire the group in insoluble struggle. Such groups disband or become seriously dysfunctional.

It is important to remember that successfully navigating the conflict stage does not mean that groups cannot and do not experience conflicts at other times. Development is ongoing and cyclical. Thus, other issues or outside factors may cause a group to engage in conflict again. Successful past conflict resolution, however, should help a group to manage recurrent conflict in more constructive ways in the future. Successful conflict resolution strengthens cohesion and morale. It signals the group's movement from stage two to the next stage, which is characterized by trust and the establishment of an effective social structure to facilitate group goal achievement.

Identifying a Stage-Two Group

1. Conflicts about values surface.
2. Disagreements about goals and tasks emerge.
3. Increased feelings of safety allow dissent to occur.
4. Dissatisfaction with roles may surface.
5. Clarification of goals begins.
6. Role clarification also begins.
7. Members challenge the leader.
8. Subgroups and coalitions form.
9. Group intolerance of subgroups and coalitions is manifest.
10. Increased member participation is evident.
11. Decreased conformity begins.
12. Deviation from emerging group norms occurs.
13. Attempts at conflict management are evident.
14. If efforts to resolve conflicts are successful, increased consensus about group goals and culture become evident near the end of this stage.
15. Conflict resolution, if successful, increases trust and cohesion.

6

STAGE THREE:
TRUST AND STRUCTURE

The third stage of group development has been described as a time when norms are refined (Braaten, 1974/1975; Tuckman, 1965). Hare (1976) saw this phase as a period of integration, in which group structure is adjusted in order to increase the likelihood of goal achievement and productivity. It is also a period in which trust and cohesion are emphasized (Schutz, 1966). Essentially, this stage of group development is characterized by more mature negotiations about goals, roles, organizational structure, and procedures. These negotiations are made possible by an increase in the trust level in the group.

The events of stage two were stormy and conflictual. However, conflict about values, goals, and other elements of the group's cultural system are essential to group maturation. If the conflict is resolved and the group develops a coherent culture, then it can begin to design or, more accurately, redesign its social structure to increase the probability of group success.

Stage two also provided a success experience for the group, in that it engaged in significant internal conflict and survived intact. Some basic conflicts have been successfully resolved. There will, of course, be other conflicts in the group. Not all conflicts have been resolved. However, basic differences have been addressed and the group has forged a more unified group culture. The anxiety and tension of the stage have been faced and, while members may have experienced considerable distress, the group remained together. Increased trust in each other is the logical result of these events. Having arrived safely at stage three, the group's next tasks are to consolidate the gains in trust and cohesion and to forge a more efficient social structure that will support group goal achievement and productivity.

GROUP STRUCTURES

The Communication Structure

Tuckman (1965) stated that during the third stage of group development communication becomes more open and task oriented. Feedback tends to be more straightforward, readily given and received. The communication structure, which allowed for successful resolution of conflict at stage two, is altered further by the events of stages two and three. That is, if conflicts over goals, roles, values, and leadership are reasonably resolved, then group structures, including communication, are adjusted to increase the probability of goal achievement and group productivity (Hare, 1976). The struggles encountered at stage two cannot be resolved unless the communication structure allows expression of different opinions and points of view. Thus, communication at stage three will be more open and freer of hidden agendas. The increased clarity about group goals attained at stage two also helps to facilitate the communication process (Shaw, 1976).

As was stated previously, a centralized communication structure enhances early group development and the establishment of stable leadership. However, this type of communication structure also impedes problem solving of complex tasks and reduces member satisfaction (Shaw, 1981). Ideally, then, groups need to shift communication structures to manage different group tasks and goals. The reader will recall, however, that groups tend to resist changes in the established communication structure (Cohen & Bennis, 1962; Mills, 1967).

What this suggests is that groups that arrive at stage three either had a more flexible communication structure from the start or managed to alter the existing communication structure enough to allow for a freer flow of information and a more decentralized communication network. While alteration of communication structures is difficult, it is not impossible.

The content of communication is also altered during this stage. Member communication becomes more task oriented. Many of the socio-emotional needs of members have been addressed by this time. Needs for inclusion, safety, affection, status, and the like have been dealt with to some extent. Therefore, members can focus on group tasks more directly without being overly concerned about their emotional needs. Of course, emotional needs are ever present. Human beings always require reassurance, praise, support, and the like. Maintenance statements continue to be essential to successful individual and group functioning. Such statements do not necessarily decrease in frequency. In fact, they may increase in this more open climate. The number of task statements, however, significantly increases at this stage.

This increased focus on group tasks is a hallmark of stage three. The group is preparing to work on goal and task accomplishment. Stage-three groups have two primary tasks to accomplish in order to prepare for work. They must continue to build trust and cohesion among group members. They also must decide how to accomplish their recently clarified goals. That is, such groups must determine the best methods to reach their goals. Division of labor, steps to goal achievement, problem solving, idea generation, decision-making strategies, and other organizational structures must be decided upon. The newly renovated communication structure facilitates this organizational process.

Goals and Tasks

As a result of the group's struggles at stage two, goal clarity has increased. Raven and Rietsema (1957) found that goal clarity increases member attraction to group tasks. Member conformity also increases as a result. When goal-path clarity is high, liking among members is also high (Anderson, 1975). These studies lend support to the necessity of stage two, where time is spent and effort is expended to clarify goals. The studies also suggest a relationship among goal clarity, trust, and cohesion. The group enters stage three with a shared vision of its mission and, as a result, is more trusting and ready to work cooperatively. Deutsch (1949a) described a cooperative group as one in which the goal achievement of an individual member is perceived as furthering the goal achievement of the group-as-a-whole. Homogeneous group goals, then, facilitate effective group functioning (Blau, 1954; Deutsch, 1949a; Shaw, 1958). This is due, in part, to the positive effect of a shared vision on cohesion. It becomes easier to establish a workable group social structure with which members are more likely to conform willingly.

A group's level of aspiration is raised following a success (Shelley, 1954; Zander & Medow, 1963). Resolving conflicts and developing a shared sense of mission and goals constitutes a major success experience. This provides the group with actual evidence of their ability to perform as a group. Zander (1971) stated that when group performance is unknown, a group is likely to choose tasks that are too difficult for the group to achieve. Stage-one groups tend to make this mistake, since they do not have any way to gauge the group's performance level. However, as a result of a group's performance at stage two, it can be more realistic in determining the degree of task difficulty that it can manage.

The greater members' desires for group success, the more likely the group is to choose tasks of intermediate difficulty (Zander, 1971). High levels of group cohesion also lead to the choice of tasks of intermediate difficulty (Zander, 1971). If the group must choose difficult tasks, performance is improved if members can openly communicate their feelings about the group's progress (Maier, 1950; Shaw & Blum, 1965). Events at stage two tend to expand channels of communication, allowing for increased member input. As a result, group decisions about tasks and organizational structures made at stage three are more likely to be based on input from more people. This makes the establishment of a more realistic and efficient organizational structure possible.

Members of groups that reach the third stage of development, then, tend to be enthusiastic about participating and hopeful about the likelihood of group success. Member commitment to and interest in group tasks is high as a result of an emerging sense of shared goals. A sense of 'we-ness' has replaced individualism as a common value.

Status and Roles

It sounds as if there is smooth sailing ahead for a stage-three group. Much work remains to be done, however. It must be remembered that the group's social structure begins to form and solidify from the very beginning. Thus, a stage-three group may have developed, albeit unwittingly, a social structure that could inhibit its further development. Some alterations of that structure undoubtedly occurred at stage two. In the process of clarifying values and goals, the group inevitably alters various elements of group structure. The communication structure, for example, is altered to allow for the expression of differing views. Role conflicts and ambiguities are identified and discussed. At stage three, the group has the important and difficult task of redefining or reassigning roles that have been identified as dysfunctional.

Role conflict and ambiguity have been found to increase tension, decrease job satisfaction, and increase turnover among employees (Kemery, Bedeian, Mossholder & Touliatos, 1985). Fisher and Gitelson (1983) reviewed forty-two studies of role conflict and ambiguity and found that increases in either factor resulted in member tendencies to leave the group. Lowered commitment, involvement, and job satisfaction were also noted. Participation in decision making also decreased as a result of role conflict or ambiguity.

Having identified role conflicts and ambiguities during stage two, a group must resolve these conflicts and clarify role ambiguities at stage three. As has already been stated, however, role redefinition or reassignment is an arduous task. It is sometimes difficult to change the perceptions of the role occupant, and it can be equally difficult to change the expectations of other members regarding an individual role assignment. Position in the group, you will recall, results from one's role and status in the group. Role reassignment, then, may result in decreased status and position. Individuals may resist reassignment as a result. Other members may resist the reassignment of an individual if this is perceived as threatening their own positions.

Since trust and cohesion are higher at stage three than previously, role redefinition and reassignment are more likely. However, the process remains difficult. Unfortunately, little research has been done on how this occurs when it occurs. Clues to this process, however, can be found in research on factors that produce changes in the group status of women and minorities. Women and minorities tend to be assigned lower status in groups. As a result, they are assigned less influential group roles. They report dissatisfaction with their lower status and other group members report uncertainty about the status of minority and female group members (Crosbie, 1979; Hembroff, 1982; McCranie & Kimberly, 1973).

With all members, group performance suffers when member role and status assignments are inappropriate. Potentially valuable contributions are overlooked and goal achievement and productivity suffer as a result (Kirchler & Davis, 1986). Researchers have identified individual strategies and group conditions, however, that increase the status of women and minorities in groups. These results may also apply to any individuals whose group role or status is not commensurate with their abilities.

Cohen (1982), Katz (1970), and Riordan and Ruggiero (1980) all reported that individuals who do not accept the lower status assigned to them increase the likelihood of improving their position in the group. Also, women and minorities who demonstrate their competence and abilities to the group tend to increase their status. Simply claiming the right to higher status has not been found to be an effective strategy (Freeze & Cohen, 1973; Martin & Sell, 1985; Pugh & Wahrman, 1983). Women and minorities who act in group-oriented as opposed to individual-oriented ways tend to improve their group status (Ridgeway, 1982).

Time is an additional factor in increasing the status of minorities and women in groups. Bias and lower status can be overcome if minorities demonstrate their competence (Cohen & Roper, 1972). Eventually, other group members see these demonstrated abilities, and there is no longer a need for the minority member to prove his or her worth to the group (Hembroff & Myers, 1984; Markovsky, Smith & Berger, 1984).

On the individual level, then, resisting an inappropriate role assignment or status, demonstrating one's competence and abilities, and acting in a cooperative, group-oriented way increase the likelihood of positively altering one's role and status in a group. On the group level, time aids the process of redefinition or reassignment of roles and status.

While the research is limited in this area, the available evidence does suggest some ways in which roles, status, and position are altered. That some groups are successful in redefining or reassigning roles and status is obvious, since certain groups develop more effective social structures than others. The importance of this midcourse correction is also clear in that if efficient, productive group structures are to be established, role conflict or ambiguity must be reduced (Kirchler & Davis, 1986).

Leadership

It may be apparent to the reader that member perceptions of the role of the leader change at different stages of group development. In stage one, the leader is perceived by the group as benevolent and powerful. He or she is perceived as the source of member safety and reward. At stage two, members begin to challenge the leader's authority and control. In order for the group to mature, such challenges are necessary. The role of the leader must be redefined if the group is to move into stage three. Power is redistributed and all leaders of groups at stage three experience some loss of influence and prominence in the group.

Groups that successfully move into stage three do so, in part, by changing the relationship between members and the leader. The leader, once benevolent and then authoritarian in the eyes of members, emerges in stage three in a more realistic way, as a group facilitator and coordinator. Earlier mythic qualities ascribed to the leader by members are stripped away, and a human being with a job to do emerges. Leader prominence is less necessary at later stages of development, since goals and roles have become more clear. Member roles have emerged that take over aspects of the leader's role. The elaborated group social structure makes leader prominence unnecessary and potentially disruptive. The leader moves into a more consultative role with the group. Leadership is still necessary for coordination. However, the role no longer carries the symbolic qualities it had at earlier stages.

These changes in status and perceptions take their toll on the bravest of leaders. Since most people who assume a leadership role are not aware of these naturally occurring group processes, they may feel defeated as a result of stage two. However, in order for the group to develop further, the leader's perceived, expected, and enacted roles must be significantly altered.

To this point we have focused on the group's perceptions of and reactions to the leader and how changes in these reactions facilitate group development. How should the leader behave during these stages? Logically, the enacted leader role can facilitate or impede group development. The leader and the members form an interacting system. Each part of the system affects the other parts. It is reasonable to assume, then, that some leadership styles will be better than others. The question is, which style is best?

Stogdill (1974) says that research results concerning the best leadership style are not clear. In fact, results tend to be contradictory. Leadership styles have been identified, but debate continues about which style is best. One reason for the confusion is that most investigators have not taken the stages of group development into account in researching this question. If they did, the research question would change from "What leadership style is best?" to "What leadership style is best at what stage of group development?" Fortunately, there is some research that addresses this second question.

On the basis of their research, Vroom and Yetton (1973) describe five different leadership styles. These are:

1. *Autocratic I:* In this leadership style, the leader solves group problems based on the information he or she has at the time. The leader does not seek input from group members.
2. *Autocratic II:* In this leadership style, the leader gets information from group members and then solves the problem alone. Members provide information only.
3. *Consultative I:* In this leadership style, the leader shares the problem with relevant individuals and gets input and ideas from these individuals. Then the leader makes the decision alone.
4. *Consultative II:* Here the leader discusses the problem with the group and solicits members' ideas and suggestions. Then he or she makes the final decision.

5. *Group II:* In this leadership style, the leader and the group discuss the problem together and jointly decide what to do.

Vroom and Jago (1978) noted other styles in their research (e.g., Group I or delegation). However, they focused on the five styles outlined above. They concluded that no one style was best in all situations. Rather, different styles work better in different situations. They were unable to ascertain a single style that leaders should employ in specific situations. However, they were able to determine what styles leaders should not use in certain circumstances. Seven rules for choosing a style were put forward. These are summarized below:

1. *The Leader Information Rule:* Leaders should not use the Autocratic I style if the quality of a decision is an important consideration and the leader does not have enough expertise or information to solve the problem alone.
2. *The Goal Congruence Rule:* Do not use the Group II style of leadership if the quality of the decision is important and members are not likely to keep the group goal in mind in solving the problem.
3. *The Unstructured Problem Rule:* Leaders should not use the Autocratic I, Autocratic II, or Consultative I styles if the quality of the decision is important, the leader lacks information, and the problem is unstructured.
4. *The Acceptance Rule:* When member acceptance of a decision is important to implementation, don't use Autocratic style I or II if it is unclear whether an autocratic decision will be accepted by the group.
5. *The Conflict Rule:* When acceptance is important and disagreement is likely, do not use the Autocratic I, Autocratic II, or Consultative I styles.
6. *The Fairness Rule:* Do not use autocratic or consultative styles if decision quality is unimportant and acceptance is critical.
7. *The Acceptance-Priority Rule:* Do not use autocratic or consultative methods if acceptance is critical but unlikely if these methods are used, and members will adhere to group goals (Vroom & Jago, 1978, pp. 151–162).

Initial research seems to suggest that the rules proposed by Vroom and Jago are useful (Hill & Schmitt, 1977; Jago, 1978; Vroom & Yetton, 1973). More important for the purposes of the current discussion is the relationship between these results and group development.

The model proposed by Vroom and Jago for choosing a leadership style in different group situations fits well with research on the stages of group development. For example, when the quality of a decision is important and the leader has sufficient information to make a decision, the model suggests that he or she can use the Autocratic I style of leadership if the group will accept the decision. The group is likely to accept such a decision at stage one, but not at other stages of group development. At stage two, the leader would be wiser to choose a consultative style, since autocratic styles would not be accepted by the group and the group has not yet developed shared goals. The group style of leadership would be risky in such a situation, since the group is not yet capable of goal-directed action.

If the quality of a decision is important and the leader does not have enough information, the Autocratic I style is unwise at any stage of group development. In stage one, however, the Autocratic II style might work. At stage two, avoidance of both autocratic styles is advised. At later stages of development, the picture is less clear. However, since the group has developed shared goals by then, consultative and group styles seem best. When the quality of a decision is less important, the model suggests avoidance of autocratic styles at any stage of development.

In light of Vroom and Jago's findings, a key shift in leadership style seems to occur during the second stage of group development. In stage one, leaders may use the two autocratic styles in certain circumstances. At stage two, however, autocratic styles are not recommended under any circumstances. While more research is clearly needed, some support for this conclusion is found in the results of Vecchio's (1987) study of new versus seasoned employees. New employees, Vecchio concluded, both need and appreciate greater task structuring by leaders than seasoned employees do. In effect, leaders are expected to be more decisive and autocratic in the beginning.

Further support for the necessity of different leadership styles at different stages of group development is found in the work of Hershey and Blanchard (1976, 1977, 1982). They maintain that leadership style should mesh with the needs of the group. Group needs, they add, are determined by the group's maturity level (Hershey & Blanchard, 1976). According to these authors, leadership styles are composed of different amounts of two essential dimensions—the task dimension and the relationship dimension. The task dimension includes an emphasis on results and productivity. The relationship dimension emphasizes concern for people and interdependence. Many other social scientists have investigated these dimensions and their impact on leadership effectiveness (e.g., Blake & Mouton, 1964, 1978, 1980; Bowers & Seashore, 1966). In general, researchers have concluded that effective leadership is the result of creating a balance between these two dimensions (e.g., House, 1971; Kerr, Schriesheim, Murphy & Stogdill, 1974; Likert, 1967; Misumi, 1985; Reddin, 1970; Yukl, 1981). What that balance is and whether the balance should shift at varying stages of group development remains a debated question.

Some investigators argue that the most effective leaders pay equal attention to both task and relationship dimensions of the leadership role throughout the life of the group (e.g., Blake & Mouton, 1982; Nicholls, 1985). Hershey and Blanchard (1977) disagree. They argue that the ratio of task to relationship behaviors must shift at different stages of group development to ensure overall leadership effectiveness. New groups require a leader high on the task dimension and low on the relationship dimension. At the next stage, the most effective leader is high in both task and relationship. During the third stage, low task and high relationship produces good results. In a mature group, a laissez-faire or low task–low relationship style is advised. These four leadership styles are characterized by

Hershey and Blanchard as telling, selling, participating, and delegating (Hershey & Blanchard, 1977).

While more research in this area is needed, studies utilizing the situational approach to leadership have yielded good results (Blanchard & Johnson, 1981; Vecchio, 1987). Taken in conjunction with Vroom and Jago's (1978) results, research on role theory, and group development, it suggests that leadership style is affected by and affects group development. A rigid leadership style can adversely influence both group development and productivity.

Coalitions and Subgroups

Coalitions are always associated with group conflict. They emerge when three or more members join forces to affect the outcome of a group discussion or decision (e.g., Bond & Vinacke, 1961; Caplow, 1959; Komorita & Brinsberg, 1977; Pearce et al., 1986). Coalitions are minimal to nonexistent during stage one. At stage two, coalitions are very prevalent. Given that the second stage focuses on the identification and resolution of conflict, one can expect a significant number of coalitions, with varying membership, to form in order to influence the group's direction and decisions. Coalitions continue to emerge, function, and dissolve at the third stage of group development as well. The prevalence of coalitions, however, tends to be less than at the previous stage.

Since coalitions form to influence the resolution of conflict, their presence during stage three reminds us that not all group conflicts were resolved during the previous stage. Because a primary task of groups at this stage is deciding on methods for goal accomplishment and group procedures, conflicts are inevitable. Coalition formation is, therefore, equally inevitable.

Subgroups in which two or more members form a bond based on some shared understanding, need, or feeling also continue to emerge during stage three. What changes at this stage is the group's response to coalitions and subgroups. In previous stages of development, coalitions and subgroups were met with considerable hostility from other group members. Their existence seemed threatening to the tentative unity that the group was attempting to forge. Coalitions or subgroups were seen as a threat to the group's survival. They were perceived as potentially capable of splitting the group apart. At stage three, however, coalitions and subgroups are met with less negativity and more tolerance.

Mills (1967) stated that the capacity to form subgroups while maintaining group-as-a-whole cohesion and unity is essential for group development. Luft (1984) concurred and added that the group system is made up of subunits, of which subgroups are one, which are connected to the system as a whole by relationships and task requirements. Without subgroups, the group-as-a-whole could not organize to get its work done. Imagine a society in which there was no division of labor. How would its needs be met? Who would do what? Subgrouping is needed in order to organize and subdivide the work necessary for goal achievement. Coalitions, while less long lasting, are also necessary to group functioning in that they provide members with a way to influence the group-as-a-whole.

The more tolerant response of other group members to subgroups and coalitions during the third stage of group development seems to be due to the fact that they are perceived as less threatening than they were at earlier stages. The group at this stage is more solid and cohesive. Members have dealt with conflict successfully in the past without breaking apart. In fact, members have learned that coalitions may influence the group in positive ways.

Subgroups are also trusted more. Other group members assume that the subgroup will conform to the group's norms and will work for the good of the whole. Of course, as with all group processes and dynamics, there is always the potential for a coalition or subgroup to negatively affect the group. They may not act in the best interests of the group or may gain enough power to return the total group to the dependency stage of development. Thus, while essential to group development, coalitions and subgroups continue to be a potential threat, albeit to a lesser extent. Given the pressures to conform, however, the risks are worth it, since the benefits usually outweigh the risks.

For example, coalitions and subgroups are inherent in the U.S. system of government. Competing interest groups (coalitions and subgroups) are expected to form in order to influence the leadership structure to respond to their needs or demands. In general, this system works. As these subgroups gain strength and support, they can influence the government. Occasionally, however, a particular coalition or subgroup gains too much influence and may threaten the solidarity or rights of other members of society. Of course, which coalitions or subgroups qualify as threatening to the cohesion or fabric of the society-as-a-whole depends, to some extent, on your political perspective. The pro-life or pro-choice groups, the National Rifle Association, animal rights activists, the National Organization for Women, the Moral Majority, the emerging coalition to ban flag burning, and the small but vocal group that wishes to restrict the kinds of art funded by the National Endowment for the Arts are all thought of by some people as threatening to the society-as-a-whole.

In general, society brings into line those subgroups deemed threatening by the majority or by our system of law. However, the fact that most threats to the society are neutralized depends on the emergence of other coalitions and subgroups that form to counter their effects. Citizens cannot assume that their rights, norms, or customs will be protected automatically. Participation in political coalitions and subgroups is essential to the maintenance of the society. So it is in small groups as well. While coalitions and subgroups are necessary to group functioning, they are also a potential hazard. Tolerance of subgroups and coalitions is a sign of group maturity. Vigilance is as well.

GROUP PROCESSES

Conformity and Deviation

As Tuckman (1965) and others have demonstrated, norms are reworked during this third stage of group development. Norms that inhibit group development are altered to increase the likelihood of goal achievement. The reader will recall that pressures to conform were very high during the first stage of group development. During stage two, pressures to conform are reduced, which allows for the expression of differences of opinion and disagreements. This reduction in conformity at stage two is essential. It allows conflicts hidden at stage one to surface and be addressed. As conflicts are resolved, a more consensual, unified group culture emerges. Members forge agreements about goals, roles, and group processes during stages two and three. These agreements result in a shared sense of direction and increased commitment to the group.

During the third stage of group development, pressures to conform increase again. While this may seem regressive, there is evidence to support the reemergence of conformity and a rational explanation for the increase. We know from research that conformity increases with increasing member unanimity (Asch, 1951; Morris & Miller, 1975). Stage-three groups have struggled to gain agreement on goals, roles, procedures, and the like. Thus, it is logical that pressures to conform with these revised norms and agreements would increase.

In addition, decentralized communication networks produce more conformity (Goldberg, 1955; Shaw et al., 1957). Stage-three groups tend to establish more decentralized communication networks in order to prepare for work on group goals and tasks. Decentralized communication networks increase member satisfaction with the group and a sense of unity. They also make the solution of complex problems more likely. Thus, members are more willing to conform.

Conformity increases as member attraction increases (Goldberg, 1955; Shaw et al., 1957). Conformity also increases as cohesion builds (Bovard, 1951; Lott & Lott, 1961; Wyer, 1966). Increases in trust, member attraction, and cohesion are all typical of stage-three groups. Increases in pressures to conform are a logical outgrowth of these dynamic changes.

Finally, conformity increases with group success (Hollander, 1960; Kidd & Campbell, 1955). The resolution of conflicts that emerged at stage two is a major group success. It is logical, then, that pressures to conform with the norms of this more unified group would increase in strength.

The reader may have determined already that the conformity being described here is different from the conformity described as typical of stage one. Conformity at stage one is based on fear of exclusion, needs for safety, and concern with the ambiguity inherent in a beginning group. Stage-three conformity is based on shared agreements and a sense of belonging. In short, members more willingly conform and encourage others to conform with the requirements of the culture they have built together. It is qualitatively different to conform to a norm because you want to and agree with the norm's requirements than to conform out of fear of rejection.

Deviation during stage one is dealt with quite harshly. However, deviation that occurs later in a group's development is subject to less severe sanctions (Wahrman & Pugh, 1974). Thus, while conformity increases at this third stage of group development, punishment for deviation does not. In fact, it lessens. This, too, is different from the processes surrounding conformity and deviation during stage one. Perhaps some additional research findings will shed some light on why this is so.

In general, member deviation or nonconformity with group norms eventually leads to exclusion or rejection by the rest of the group (Schacter, 1951). The group will attempt to get the deviant to conform, but if he or she does not comply, severe consequences will accrue to the deviant. However, if the task is facilitated by a member's deviance, group sanctions are lessened (Kelley & Shapiro, 1954). Since stage-three groups have experienced the positive effects of deviation during stage two, such groups are more likely to allow deviation that proves to be helpful in moving the group toward its goal.

Prior conformity also reduces the severity of sanctions a deviant receives (Hollander, 1960; Katz, 1982). Individuals who have been together for a period of time and have not been previously rejected or shunned for deviance have a record of prior conformity. Members of a stage-three group are less likely to receive severe sanctions for deviance, since they have conformed to group norms in the past. Finally, if group norms encourage innovation, then deviance will be more tolerated (Moscovici, 1976). Again, stage-three groups are more likely to have norms that encourage innovation than groups at earlier stages.

We see, then, that while conformity increases during the third stage of group development, its effects are not debilitating. Rather, conformity at this stage is based on trust and agreements reached by the group-as-a-whole. While conformity in its extreme can result in coercion or even unconscionable group actions, the conformity described here supports coordination of group activities, order, and altruism when individuals place the good of the group above their own. Members can be more socially responsible due to the positive pressure to conform (Berkowitz & Daniels, 1963).

Cohesion and Conflict

An increase in group cohesion is a main feature of the third stage of group development. There are a number of reasons for this increase. First, research tells us that when goal-path clarity is high, cohesion will be high (Anderson, 1975). As a result of the efforts expended at stage two to clarify and agree on the group's goal and of efforts being expended at stage three to determine the path to goal achievement, cohesion logically increases.

Second, successful resolution of conflicts at stage two reduces individual fears of rejection and increases intermember trust. A feeling of "we-ness" or cohesiveness results. Third, while it is rarely clear what causes what in an interacting system, increased communication is associated with increased cohesion and vice versa (Back, 1951; French, 1941; Lott & Lott, 1961). Given the increases in the types and amount of communication allowed at stage two, increases in cohesion are a likely outcome.

What effects does increased cohesion have on the group? Increased conformity has already been cited as one noticeable effect (Bovard, 1951; Lott & Lott, 1961; Wyer, 1966). The group has more influence over its members when cohesion is high (Berkowitz, 1954; Schacter et al., 1951). Member satisfaction with the group increases as cohesion increases (Exline, 1957; Gross, 1954; Marquis, Guetzkow & Heyns, 1951; Van Zelst, 1952). Finally, high levels of cohesion produce increased cooperation and facilitate group integration (Back, 1951; Shaw & Shaw, 1962).

The significance of cooperation in groups cannot be overestimated. Cooperation, which is facilitated by cohesion and homogeneous goals, has many positive effects on group functioning (Deutsch, 1949a). Deutsch, who has spent his career researching the effects of cooperation (and competition) on group functioning, has identified a number of characteristics of cooperative groups. These include: (1) more effective communication, (2) a friendlier group atmosphere, (3) stronger individual desire to work on the group task, (4) stronger feelings of commitment to the group, (5) greater division of labor, (6) greater coordination of effort, (7) greater group productivity, (8) increased trust and the development of stable agreements, and (9) increased ability to resolve conflicts (Deutsch, 1949a, 1949b, 1973, 1990a).

The stage-three group, with its increased levels of cohesion and cooperation, is ready and able to organize in effective ways to work on its task and to accomplish its goals. Cohesion is a significant catalyst in this process.

A word of caution with regard to cohesion is appropriate at this point. High levels of cohesion, in conjunction with specific additional factors, can have deleterious effects on groups. Groupthink, or "a deterioration of mental efficiency, reality testing, and moral judgment that results from in-group pressures" can occur under certain conditions (Janis, 1972, p. 9). That is, a group can make poor or, in some cases, dangerous decisions due to an overriding wish to maintain unity and cohesion. This leads the group to overlook other choices or courses of action (Janis, 1982).

Janis (1972) outlined four causes of groupthink. Of these he identified high levels of cohesion as the most important. He stated that "a high degree of group cohesiveness is conducive to a high frequency of symptoms of groupthink, which, in turn, are conducive to a high frequency of defects in decision making" (p. 199). Janis's observations seem to contradict the positive effects of cohesion outlined earlier in this section. However, he does not maintain that cohesion alone produces this negative group condition. Other factors must be present as well. These are isolation, a particular type of leadership style, and significant stress on the group to make the proper decision (Janis, 1972, 1989; Janis & Mann, 1977).

When groups deliberate in relative isolation and do not report or check their conclusions with others outside the group, the possibility of groupthink increases. Also, if the group's leader controls the discussion and makes his or her positions clear from the outset, groupthink is more likely. Finally, if the group is faced with a major and stressful decision, the tendency to decide quickly in order to reduce the stress is enhanced. This, too, increases the probability of groupthink (Callaway, Marriott & Esser, 1985).

Janis stated that two or more of these conditions must be present for groupthink to occur. Thus, cohesion alone does not pose a threat. In fact, as we have seen, cohesion has many positive effects on groups. However, if one or more of the other outlined factors are also present, a group may fall victim to group-think.

A number of case studies support Janis's contentions. Herek, Janis, and Huth (1987), for example, analyzed nineteen international crises that were dealt with by high-level U.S. officials. They examined the contents of these delibera-tions for symptoms of groupthink. The findings indicated that the more symp-toms of groupthink that were present, the more negative the outcome of a group's decisions. Other case studies and experiments have lent support to Janis's conclusions as well (Flowers, 1977; Hensley & Griffin, 1986; Janis, 1985; Moorhead, 1982; Moorhead & Montanari, 1986). Some researchers, however, while supporting Janis's general conception, suggest that cohesion may not be the primary factor in all cases. The leader's style may be more significant in inducing groupthink (Flowers, 1977; Leana, 1985).

From a group development perspective, groupthink appears to be a phe-nomenon more closely associated with the first stage of group development than the third. Three of the factors outlined by Janis could occur at stage three (cohe-siveness, isolation, and decision stress). However, the leadership style described by Janis is inconsistent with descriptions of leadership at stage three. A group that becomes embroiled in groupthink apparently has been unable to change its perception of the leader and still holds illusions about this powerful role. Communication during groupthink is not open and honest, and pressures to conform are reminiscent of stage-one conformity rather than stage three.

While more research is needed to clarify this phenomenon, it is clear that groups need to monitor their functioning in order to avoid reaching unfavorable decisions. Research is also needed to clarify the connection between groupthink and the stages of group development. Given our current knowledge of group development, it seems safe to conclude that a more mature group would be less vulnerable to groupthink.

This discussion also reminds us of the interactive nature of group processes and structures. Cohesion alone does not predict positive group functioning or the existence of the third stage of group development. A number of interactive factors must be present to identify the presence of a particular stage of group development or the presence of groupthink, for that matter. High levels of cohe-sion, in the presence of a number of other distinct group factors, such as open communication and a collaborative leadership style, produce many positive group effects. The presence of cohesion and the absence of these other support-ive variables can produce groupthink, cults, and other potentially harmful out-comes.

Despite the resolution of significant conflicts during the second stage of group development, conflicts continue to occur throughout the group's life. In fact, group conflict is as common as group cooperation (Bales et al., 1980; Fisher, 1980; Tuckman, 1965). The types of conflict and the way conflict is dealt with, however, change during this trust and structure stage of group development. Types of conflict include **false conflicts,** in which one member misinterprets another's position or actions (Deutsch, 1973). This type of conflict is also referred to as *autistic conflict* (Holmes & Miller, 1976; Kriesberg, 1973). **Contingent conflicts** are those that can be solved in a relatively simple way by requesting that a member or the group change a particular behavior or position. **Escalating conflict** may begin over a minor issue, but quickly extends to more basic issues. This type is more difficult to resolve since it tends to encompass value differences (Deutsch, 1973). Wheaton (1974) described two other types of conflict. **Principled conflict** is the type that relates to basic values. **Communal conflict** occurs when there is agreement on basic values but disagreement on how to operationalize these values to accomplish group goals and tasks. Wheaton stated that principled conflict can adversely affect cohesion while communal conflict increases cohesion.

At stage two, principled and escalating conflicts are frequent. Given that the group is engaged in defining its culture, which rests on beliefs and values, conflicts over principles and values are plentiful. Also, conflicts can escalate more readily at this stage due to the instability of the group's social structure. The social structure does not stabilize until principled conflicts are dealt with to some extent (Bennis & Shepard, 1956; Deutsch, 1969).

At stage three, communal conflict is more prevalent. If stage-two conflicts have been successfully resolved, there is agreement on principles and group goals. The group's task now is to determine the methods it will use to enact its principles and accomplish its goals. Conflicts about how to do these things inevitably occur. False and contingent conflicts occur as well but are less likely to result in escalating conflicts at this stage. This is due to the fact that other group structures and processes are now in place that facilitate the resolution of conflict. Communication is more open at this stage, and this enhances the likelihood of conflict resolution (Deutsch, 1973). Cooperation in seeking solutions also facilitates conflict resolution (Worchel & Yohai, 1979). As we have seen, cooperation and cohesion increase at this stage as well.

The threshold theory of group tension posits that each group has an optimal level of conflict (Bormann, 1975). If the amount of tension in a group remains above its optimal level for prolonged periods, productivity decreases and hostility increases. If the group is below that level for an extended period of time, members may become bored or apathetic. According to Bormann, effective groups experience frequent tension and conflict, but not prolonged amounts either above or below their optimal level. This would reduce the probability of escalating conflict, which threatens group functioning and integration.

Stage-three groups are better equipped to manage conflict as a result of successful resolution of principled conflicts occurring at earlier stages. Again, members must be ever vigilant, since conflicts at this stage can escalate and return the group to previous developmental levels. As in any relationship, trust, open communication, negotiation, and compromise facilitate conflict resolution whenever it occurs. The old adage "familiarity breeds contempt" is perhaps not accurate. Rather, as we learn to know and trust each other, we may forget that the maintenance of relationships requires attention and work. So it is with groups.

Attaining a more mature level of development does not guarantee that that level will be sustained or enhanced. It requires work and commitment to maintain the levels of trust, communication, cohesion, and other factors that facilitate group development and conflict resolution.

If the group successfully fine tunes its culture and social structure during the third stage of group development, it is ready to vigorously engage in working on its tasks and goals. As a result of the developments at this stage, the group has determined how it will work toward its goals. Its members are more trusting, more committed to the group, and more motivated to accomplish the group's goals. The group's norms have been refined to support task accomplishment and cohesion. Roles and division of labor have been established, and individuals and subgroups are clear about the parts they will play in goal achievement. Communication is more open, and methods for decision making and conflict resolution are in place. The group is ready to work.

Identifying a Stage-Three Group

1. Increased goal clarity and consensus are evident.
2. Roles and tasks are adjusted to increase the likelihood of goal achievement.
3. The leader's role becomes less directive and more consultative.
4. The communication structure appears to be more flexible.
5. The content of communication becomes more task oriented.
6. Pressures to conform increase again.
7. Helpful deviation is tolerated.
8. Coalitions and subgroups continue to form.
9. Increased tolerance of subgroups and coalitions is evident.
10. Cohesion and trust increase.
11. Member satisfaction also increases.
12. Cooperation is more in evidence.
13. Individual commitment to group goals and tasks is high.
14. Greater division of labor occurs.
15. Conflict continues to occur.
16. Conflict management strategies are more effective.
17. The group works to clarify and build a group structure that will facilitate goal achievement and productivity.

7

STAGE FOUR AND FIVE: WORK AND TERMINATION

STAGE FOUR

The fourth stage of group development focuses on group performance and productivity (Tuckman, 1965; Tuckman & Jensen, 1977). Of course, some work occurs at every phase of group life. At this stage, however, the group is preoccupied with goal achievement. Having established a unified culture and structure at earlier stages, the group can now turn its full attention to working on its goals and tasks. Performance and productivity, problem solving and decision making are characteristic of this period of group life.

Research confirms that task performance and work activity occur at higher levels later in a group's development. Hare (1967, 1982) found this to be the case in a variety of groups, including an anthropological expedition, factory work groups, and experiential groups. Other researchers have also found the same pattern (Bales & Strodtbeck, 1951; Borgatta & Bales, 1953). Therapy and growth groups follow suit as well (Hill, 1977; Hill & Gruner, 1973; Stiles, Tupler & Carpenter, 1982). Even the productive outcomes of the Camp David Summit on the Middle East were accomplished near its end (Hare & Naveh, 1984).

Research also reminds us that not all groups reach the work stage of group development. Time together is not enough to ensure productivity (Gabarro, 1987). For example, Goodacre (1953) studied sixty-three combat units and determined that only thirteen became productive. In a study of community action groups, one in twelve reached this phase (Zurcher, 1969). A study of eighteen personal growth groups determined that five reached the work stage of group development (Kuypers, Davies & Hazewinkel, 1986). The road to group productivity is fraught with difficulties.

This section discusses what is known about the impact of group structures and processes on productivity. Before turning to that, however, we must address a prior question. Are groups more productive and capable than individuals working alone? Conventional wisdom offers little help in answering this question. Some would answer that groups are more productive since two heads are better than one. Others would cite the adage "a camel is an animal put together by a committee" as evidence of the ineffectiveness of groups. Clearly, there is disagreement surrounding this question. Perhaps examining the findings of social scientists will shed some light on the matter.

Group and Individual Performance

Very early in this century, two processes were discovered, each of which lent weight to a different side of this argument. **Social facilitation,** or the effect of the presence of others on performance, was proposed by some social scientists (Allport, 1920; Dashiell, 1930; Travis, 1925; Triplett, 1898). Triplett (1898) was the first to study this question, and he found that the presence of others had a positive effect on individual performance. Therefore, he termed the influence of others *social facilitation*. Later research found that the presence of others could also have negative effects on performance, but the term social facilitation continued to be used to describe this area of research.

The **Ringelmann effect** was also discovered (Ringelmann, 1913; Ingham, Levinger, Graves & Peckman, 1974). The Ringelmann effect is sometimes referred to as **social loafing** (Latane, Williams & Harkins, 1979; Williams, Harkins & Latane, 1981). Research on social loafing suggests that while a group may outperform an individual in many cases, there is a tendency for groups to work below their maximum capacity. Social facilitation suggests that individual performance can be positively or negatively affected by the presence of others. Social loafing suggests that individuals in the presence of others sometimes do not work as hard as when they are alone.

Later research did little to resolve this controversy. Sometimes working in the presence of others seemed to enhance performance (Carment, 1970; Dashiell, 1930). However, others found that working in the presence of others decreased performance (Burwitz & Newell, 1972; Martens & Landers, 1972; Travis, 1928).

In an extensive review of 241 studies of social facilitation, Bond and Titus (1983) concluded that the presence of others does not improve the quality of performance for simple or complex tasks. It does, however, increase the quantity, or rate of performance, for simple tasks. Zajonc (1965) concluded that performance of simple tasks that are easy to learn is enhanced by the presence of others, while performance of complex tasks that are difficult to learn is reduced in the presence of others. As a result, Zajonc (1965) would advise a student to study for a difficult exam alone and to take that exam in the presence of many other students. This should result in improved performance, since learning the complex material is best achieved alone and demonstration of that learning (now a simple task) is enhanced by the presence of others.

However, other research contradicts Zajonc's conclusion and, in fact, asserts that working in cooperative, interdependent groups enhances student learning and member performance in other work settings (Blau, 1954; Johnson, 1980; Johnson, Maruyama, Johnson, Nelson & Skon, 1981; Schmitt, 1981). This has led a number of researchers to conclude that learning in cooperative groups should be strongly encouraged (Johnson, 1980; Johnson, Johnson & Smith, 1986; Slavin, 1986).

These seemingly contradictory research results and conclusions can perhaps be reconciled by a more careful look at what kinds of groups the researchers investigated and at group development factors embedded in the results. The research on social facilitation was conducted with individuals who performed in the presence of a passive audience or in situations of coaction. **Coaction** refers to a situation in which individuals work on the same task, but not together. The situations being described are at best nominal group situations. Interdependence and interaction are nonexistent or quite minimal. Also, in most of these studies, groups were assembled for the purpose of the experiment. The groups were new and, consequently, subject to the dynamics of a stage-one group. In contrast, the studies that suggest that performance or learning is enhanced in cooperative groups more often study naturally occurring classroom and work groups that are together for extended periods of time. In addition, research suggests that cooperative as opposed to competitive groups facilitate performance (Deutsch, 1990a). Since cooperation is associated with later stages of group development, one can reasonably conclude that more mature groups, with interdependent goals, can enhance individual and group performance.

Evidence to support this conclusion can be found in research on methods to reduce social loafing. For example, social loafing is reduced when group tasks are involving and interesting (Brickner, Harkins & Ostrom, 1986; Harkins & Petty, 1982; Zacarro, 1984). Social loafing is also reduced if members see each other as competent and willing to work (Jackson & Harkins, 1985; Kerr, 1983). If member input is identifiable and members believe that their input will affect group decisions and products, social loafing is reduced (Hardy & Latane, 1986; Kerr, 1983; Kerr & Bruun, 1981, 1983). For these conditions to exist in natural groups, time and group maturation are required. What can be concluded, at this point, is that groups have the potential to surpass individual performance under certain circumstances. However, whether groups maximize this potential depends on their ability to create a culture and social structure that facilitate performance and goal achievement.

GROUP STRUCTURES

Communication

If a group's task is relatively simple, a centralized communication network tends to increase effectiveness. If the task is complex, a decentralized communication network enhances group productivity (Kano, 1971; Lawson, 1964a; Mulder, 1960; Shaw, 1954b). Member satisfaction, however, is lower in centralized networks regardless of the requirements of the task. Given the demands of the goals of modern groups, most tasks are relatively complicated. Technological advances and the complexities of modern life suggest that most groups will require a decentralized communication network in order to facilitate goal achievement.

Unfortunately, most organizational groups adopt a centralized, hierarchical communication network (Goetsch & McFarland, 1980). This may be a remnant of our past production-oriented work culture. However, in a service-oriented economy, and in increasingly complex production areas, a centralized communication structure may negatively affect productivity. For example, upward and downward communication tend to be very different in centralized, hierarchical networks (Browning, 1978; Katz & Kahn, 1978). Communication downward is initiated by higher-status members and focuses on suggestions and directives about what lower-status persons should do or how they should behave. Explanations for these suggestions and directives and feedback about performance of lower-status persons are also transmitted downward.

Upward communication is initiated by subordinates and directed at higher-status members. In general, the content of these upward communications does not contain suggestions, directives, or feedback about the performance of superiors. Instead, upward communication focuses on facts, information about the performance of lower-status individuals, complaints about peers, grievances, and expressions of distrust. Also, upward communication occurs less frequently than downward. It is more guarded and brief than downward communication (Bradley, 1978; Browning, 1978; Manis, Cornell & Moore, 1974).

It is immediately apparent that a centralized, hierarchical communication network has the potential to inhibit group productivity in most organizations, given these descriptions of the types of communication that occur within it. Interaction is limited and constrained. Important feedback that might affect group productivity may not occur, since more good news than bad is communicated upward. It also inhibits the rate of communication and what can be said.

If a group has a complex task, a decentralized communication network will increase member satisfaction and group productivity. U.S. business organizations are becoming increasingly aware of this fact, and some are taking steps to change from centralized to decentralized communication structures. Employee involvement groups, often called **quality control groups** or **quality circles,** are an example of one attempt to change communication patterns. It has been estimated that several hundred thousand U.S. workers participate in quality circles (Ledford, Lawler & Mohrman, 1988). Such groups usually meet for a few hours a month (Thompson, 1982). The intent of quality circles is to increase upward communication by providing a regular forum for employee input. The groups are set up to reduce fears about expressing negative feedback or innovative ideas. This strategy can be successful but, as you will recall, groups resist changes in their traditional communication patterns. Some quality circles have not had the desired effect as a result. Also, some organizations have failed to decentralize other aspects of communication beyond the initiation of quality circles. The organizational group remains centralized and hierarchical except for a few hours a month. This will reduce the likelihood of positive results from the initiation of quality circles.

The content of communication is also associated with group productivity. Stage-four groups tend to increase their rate of task-oriented communications. While socio-emotional communications remain necessary to support group integration and cohesion and to reduce tensions, a high rate of socio-emotional communications at this stage will decrease productivity (Schacter et al., 1951). Also, feedback increases at this stage. Effective groups get, give, and utilize feedback about their performance (Ketchum, 1984; Kolodny & Kiggundu, 1980).

Problem Solving and Decision Making

One of the distinguishing features of stage-four groups is their emphasis on task-related decision making and problem solving. Utilizing the plans, strategies, and methods for problem solving and task accomplishment established during stage three, the stage-four group's primary task is to implement these strategies to resolve problems, make decisions, and accomplish tasks.

Effective methods for decision making and problem solving have been studied by a number of researchers. Their results are, in general, overlapping. For example, Shaw (1981) stated that effective group problem solving and decision making consists of four steps: recognizing the problem, diagnosing the problem, decision making, and accepting and carrying out the solution. Maier and Solem (1952) suggested that productive group problem solving begins with a brief discussion of each member's views on the issue. Next, important factors related to the problem are listed. Finally, the list is used as a guide in determining the final solution.

Others have outlined a process similar to Shaw's description, including an orientation phase, a discussion phase, a decision phase, and an implementation phase (Fisher, 1980; Hoffman, 1982; Simon, 1976; Zander, 1982). Each of these phases has significant impact on the quality of a group's solution and/or its overall productivity and effectiveness. For example, during the orientation phase the problem is defined, and strategies are outlined for solving the problem. Strategies include such things as ways to gain needed information about the problem, how to analyze the information, and how to make the final decision. Research tells us that groups that outline these strategies in advance are more successful than those that do not (Hackman, Brousseau & Weiss, 1976; Hirokawa, 1980; Vinokur, Burnstein, Sechrest & Wortman, 1985). Unfortunately, many groups spend little or no time planning strategies for problem solving and decision making. Some groups consider it a waste of time, even if members have been made aware of the fact that planning improves solution quality and group performance (Hackman & Morris, 1975).

The amount of time spent in the discussion phase of the decision-making process improves the quality of the outcome (Harper & Askling, 1980; Katz & Tushman, 1979; Laughlin, 1988). Harper and Askling (1980) found that the rate of participation relates to the quality of the group's solution and overall effectiveness. Again, many groups do not spend adequate time discussing an issue. In some cases, a group will only discuss a few alternative solutions (Janis & Mann, 1977; Stasser & Titus, 1985).

Groups can make the actual decision in a number of ways. The group may delegate the responsibility for the final decision to an individual, subgroup, or expert. Member inputs could be averaged to form the basis for the decision. Group members can vote on alternative proposals or may choose consensus as their decision-making method (Davis, 1982; Kerr, 1982). **Consensus** refers to reaching a decision that is agreeable to all members. Efforts to determine which of these methods is best have been unsuccessful (Hirokawa, 1984; Rawlins, 1984). Individuals like the consensus method, but it does not necessarily produce better decisions. In general, people tend to like any method as long as they agree with the final decision (Miller, Jackson, Mueller & Schersching, 1987).

It is certain, however, that participation in the decision-making process does increase member satisfaction. It may also improve performance to some extent (Miller & Wong, 1986). Sashkin (1984) stated that nonparticipation may have negative physical and psychological effects on individuals. He concluded that since participation increases member satisfaction and may improve, or at least not degrade, performance, it would be unethical not to advocate participatory decision making.

Implementing and evaluating group decisions are key elements in the process. Ideally, evaluation is built into the process, and the results of the evaluation form the basis for the group's next problem-solving process (Lewin, 1943, 1951). Many of us have sat on committees and made recommendations that were never implemented. This is often the case when the group making the decision does not have the authority to implement its solution. Nothing is as demoralizing to a group. It is incumbent on the group, then, to interact with other groups that will be involved in implementation throughout its deliberations. This increases the likelihood of successful implementation of group outcomes.

The findings outlined in this section suggest that problem solving and decision making are enhanced when groups outline, in advance, the strategies that they will use to solve problems and make decisions. Lengthy discussion of alternative solutions, ensuring implementation and evaluation, and involving all members in these processes are also associated with quality problem solving and decision making. These steps, supported by research, seem reasonable and are likely to help groups make better choices, but other factors must be considered as well.

Group Decisions and Members' Views

When a group makes a decision, we tend to assume that the decision reflects the views of the individual members of that group (Turner & Killian, 1957). Allison and Messick (1985a) referred to this as the **group attribution error,** since in some cases, group decisions or actions do not reflect member preferences. They stated that "groups can and do produce decisions that fail to correspond to members' preferences. More than that, . . . group decisions may have properties that do not characterize any of the individuals" (Allison & Messick, 1987, p.138).

This conclusion sounds illogical to most people, especially those who base their faith in democratic principles on the belief that those principles ensure that the will of the majority prevails. And yet, in some cases, group decisions do not reflect majority rule, or even minority rule, despite our tenacious belief that they do. People tend to perceive a group as a single entity similar to an individual (Allison & Messick, 1987). Therefore, individual group members are assumed to hold the same views as the group. We believe, for example, that the views and actions of nations reflect those of their citizens (Allison & Messick, 1987; Morgenthau, 1970; Wolfers, 1959). Logically, not all citizens agree with every government policy, and in some cases, no citizens might agree. However, this does not stop us from believing that group decisions do reflect the attitudes of group members. Of course, sometimes there is a correspondence between group decisions and member preferences, but not in every case. Therefore, it seems important to discover what factors may account for group decisions that do not reflect the preferences of members.

Allison and Messick (1987) identified two general categories—social influences and group structures—that can create divergence between group decisions and member views. The social influence category includes the phenomenon of social loafing described earlier in this chapter (Ringelmann, 1913; Harkins, Latane & Williams, 1980). This process can reduce the motivation of individual members to participate up to their capacity in group decision making, thus reducing the chances that decisions will reflect their views.

Discussion can also produce a phenomenon referred to as **group polarization,** in which member positions become more extreme than they were prior to the discussion (Stoner, 1961; Lamm & Meyers, 1978). This tendency to adopt a more extreme position may be the result of individual desires to be accepted by other group members. During discussion, members attempt to determine the prevailing group view and then espouse a more extreme position of that view in order to gain the favor of others (Goethals & Zanna, 1979). It may also be that the discussion causes individuals to think about more factors, which leads them to alter their position (Vinokur & Burnstein, 1974). Pressures to conform may be operative as well.

Groupthink (Janis, 1972) is another social process that can result in decisions that do not reflect individual preferences. Also, members may erroneously believe that others hold a certain position and, as a result, individual members adopt and vocalize this position. This phenomenon, referred to as the **Abilene paradox,** may result in a decision that does not reflect the views of any group member (Harvey, 1974).

Allison and Messick (1987) also noted that certain structural elements of groups may contribute to decisions that do not reflect the wishes of members. For example, at the macro level, individuals may make choices that are good for them but that collectively result in a decision that no one actually desired. Hardin (1968) referred to this phenomenon as a **social dilemma.** Pollution and deforestation are examples of individual decisions that generate collective results that no one actually desired. Individuals may make such decisions because they have difficulty delaying gratification (Cross & Guyer, 1980) or because they wish to keep up with their peers (Messick & Thorngate, 1967). Lack of knowledge may also be a factor (Allison & Messick, 1985b).

How do these factors relate to group structures? Cultural elements dictate group or societal structures to a large extent. Therefore, ideological perspectives such as the supremacy of the individual and the value of competition create beliefs that lead people to organize their social groups in particular ways. Most Western societies, for example, believe that individual self-interest will create positive effects for the society as a whole. Laws tend to favor individual rights over the rights of the collective. These structures, then, make it more likely that individuals will make choices alone and that their right to do so will be supported by governing bodies. Discussion of collective consequences is less likely when rules are organized around individual freedom.

How a decision is made can also increase the probability that group choices and individual preferences are divergent. For example, if the decision process of a committee requires that all members agree on the finalists in a competition, it may be that the finalists will include none of the people favored by individual committee members. Typically, committee members review all the candidates and make their individual choices prior to meeting as a committee. If their individual choices do not correspond with others', then alternatives acceptable to but not preferred by anyone may be chosen as finalists. Researchers have failed to discover which decision-making procedures are best at producing quality decisions that reflect member views. It may be that all decision procedures are flawed and, in conjunction with other group processes, can produce nonrepresentative decisions. Allison and Messick's (1987) work suggests that research in this area would be more fruitful if group structures and dynamics were taken into consideration.

The factors outlined by Allison and Messick (1987) also suggest that groups should monitor member motivation during decision making. Symptoms of groupthink and polarization should be monitored as well. Finally, group structures and decision-making procedures should be assessed to determine how they influence decisions.

Goals and Tasks

While it is not quite accurate to identify one factor in an interactive and interdependent system as more important than others, it is fair to say that a high level of goal consensus is crucial in determining the ultimate level of group productivity. Homogeneity of goals is not enough to ensure productivity, of course. Many other factors and processes can interfere with group achievement. For example, a number of researchers remind us that high goal consensus must be accompanied by high levels of agreement about member and leader status in order to ensure group productivity (Heinicke & Bales, 1953; Klein & Christiansen, 1969; Melnick & Chemer, 1974). However, homogeneous goals significantly increase the likelihood of effective group functioning and productivity (Blau, 1954; Deutsch, 1949b; Shaw, 1958).

Group tasks also influence group productivity. The reader will recall that tasks represent the kinds of work that must be done in order to accomplish the group's goal. With increasing task difficulty, group performance tends to decrease (Lanzetta & Roby, 1956, 1957; Shaw & Blum, 1965). However, this is not inevitable. If the group has a communication structure that allows for discussion about the difficulty of the task and the group's progress, group performance and productivity are enhanced (Maier, 1950; Shaw & Blum, 1965).

Group performance will be better than individual performance on some tasks and not on others. Our common sense tells us that this is so. For example, certain tasks only require one person to accomplish them. Only one person is needed to paint a picture. More than one person would, most likely, reduce overall performance. To paint a house, however, more than one capable house painter would be helpful. Thus, factors to be considered in predicting group performance and productivity include the inherent demands of the group's task. Task demands include whether a task is divisible or unitary, the type of output required, and the methods used to combine member contributions to the task (Steiner, 1972).

Divisible tasks, as their name implies, can be broken down into subtasks to be accomplished by an individual or subgroup. **Unitary tasks,** such as portrait painting, cannot be divided. If the output desired is quantity, Steiner (1972) refers to the task as **maximizing.** If quality output or performing up to a given standard is required, the task is **optimizing.** Finally, the methods for combining member inputs vary with different tasks. **Additive tasks** require adding member inputs to determine the group's productivity. **Compensatory tasks** require the averaging of all member inputs to determine the group's solution or product. **Disjunctive tasks** require a yes-or-no solution. **Conjunctive tasks** require each member to complete certain behaviors or actions before the task is finished. Finally, in some cases, the group is free to choose its own method of combining member inputs. Steiner refers to these tasks as **discretionary.**

Any group task can be described in these terms. For example, building a house is divisible, optimizing, and conjunctive. Playing a team sport is usually divisible, maximizing, and conjunctive. The tasks of a project team at work are divisible, optimizing, and discretionary. A committee task would generally be divisible, maximizing, and discretionary. The task of a work group formed to decide whether or not the company should move to a new location would be divisible, optimizing, and disjunctive. The task of a school committee deciding how many new teachers to hire based on anticipated enrollments could be divisible, optimizing, and compensatory. It could also be discretionary, depending on the methods that the committee members chose to employ.

Under what task conditions, then, do groups do as well as or better than individuals? Groups outperform all or most of their members on additive and compensatory tasks (Latane et al., 1979; Shaw, 1981). On disjunctive tasks, groups outperform individuals in most cases (Davis, 1973; Marquart, 1955; Smoke & Zajonc, 1962). Sometimes, groups working on disjunctive tasks do not accept the proposed solution. In such cases, groups will not perform as well as individuals on disjunctive tasks (Bray, Kerr & Atkin, 1978; Maier & Solem, 1952).

When faced with a unitary conjunctive task, the group will perform only as well as its worst individual performer. This is due to the nature of unitary conjunctive tasks, which require all members to complete some action in order to assess group performance. For example, the performance of a violin section in an orchestra is not judged by the average number of players who complete the passage skillfully. Rather, it is judged by its worst performer (Frank & Anderson, 1971; Steiner, 1972). On divisible conjunctive tasks, such as building a house, groups do better than individuals as long as member subtasks match individual ability levels (Steiner, 1972). Group performance on discretionary tasks varies, of course, with the method or methods that the group chooses to complete its task.

Group performance and productivity, then, surpass or compare favorably with individual performance on additive compensatory and divisible conjunctive tasks. They also compare well with individual performance on disjunctive tasks, if the group is capable of accepting the proposed solution. Only on unitary conjunctive tasks do individuals always perform better than groups. In the case of divisible conjunctive tasks and some disjunctive tasks, groups have the potential to outperform individuals. If other group structures, such as role assignment and communication networks, are supportive, group performance on these types of tasks will be quite effective.

Groups can perform better than or as well as individuals on most kinds of tasks. Of course, attention must be paid to other variables in order to facilitate task accomplishment and goal achievement. In 1972, Steiner proposed a law of group productivity that suggests that a group's actual productivity is equal to its potential productivity minus group process losses. **Group process losses** are decreases in productivity due to the ineffectiveness of relevant group structures or dynamic processes. Thus, a group with a disjunctive task that has not made appropriate role assignments or has an inefficient communication structure will suffer losses in productivity. If, on the other hand, the group had made effective role assignments and created an efficient communication structure, group process gains would occur, enhancing productivity. If the group is operating in a context that supports goal achievement, and has created a culture and social structure that facilitate task accomplishment, group productivity will be enhanced (Hackman, 1983; Hackman & Morris, 1975; Hackman & Oldham, 1980).

Roles and Status

As has already been stated, high consensus about group goals and tasks, in and of itself, is not sufficient to ensure group productivity. Member agreement about their roles is another important factor. In Chapter 4, the early process of role assignment was described. The reader will recall that role assignments are not necessarily made on the basis of individual competencies. As a result, individuals may find themselves in unaccustomed or unacceptable roles. Role conflict is usually the result. Also, role ambiguity or a lack of clarity about what is expected of a person in a particular role is possible. Another potential hazard for the group is that role assignments may have resulted in the wrong man or woman occupying a particular role. That is, the role occupant may not have the abilities necessary to perform his or her assigned role.

Role conflict or ambiguity can result in tension and lower satisfaction (Kemery et al., 1985). It can also result in high turnover in work groups. Lower commitment, involvement, and participation are other potential effects of role conflict or ambiguity (Fisher & Gitelson, 1983). All of these outcomes will negatively affect a group's ability to be productive in, or even to reach, the work stage of group development.

Groups must be careful to match member abilities and skills with their roles. Group effectiveness is enhanced when member role assignments relate to the group's tasks (Steiner, 1972). Then, when tasks are subdivided, member task assignments can be made on the basis of ability to complete the task. If, however, a member's role does not allow for effective task assignments, group productivity will be compromised. A recent example of inappropriate task assignments due to role occurred at a large university. Racial tension had erupted at the school. In an attempt to work to resolve the tension, a task force consisting of students and administrators was formed. However, faculty members with expertise in intergroup conflict were not asked to work on this task. Perceptions of faculty roles was a clear factor in their exclusion. That is, the resolution of this conflict was seen as the role of administration rather than faculty. The task force, as a result, reduced the likelihood of successful task completion by excluding important resource persons. Unfortunately, this is a far too frequent occurrence in all types of groups.

Status, a consequence of role and position in the group, must also be acceptable to group members if productivity is to be high (Klein & Christiansen, 1969). If the role and position of a member do not confer status that is acceptable to him or her or to other group members, group effectiveness may be compromised.

Leadership

There has been considerable argument over the years about what style of leadership increases group productivity. For example, a number of studies have found that a democratic leadership style facilitates group productivity (e.g., Argyle, Gardner & Ciofi, 1958; Lyle, 1961). Other studies, however, conclude that an autocratic leadership style increases group effectiveness (e.g., Lyle, 1961; Mahoney, 1967; Shaw, 1955). Still other studies found that democratic leadership had no effect on productivity (e.g., Adams, 1952; Anderson, 1959; Mahoney, 1967; Snadowsky, 1969). To confuse things even further, another set of studies determined that an autocratic leadership style had no effect on group productivity. A democratic style, however, has been consistently associated with increased member satisfaction and group cohesion (e.g., Foa, 1957; Mullen, 1965; Shaw, 1955; White & Lippitt, 1960).

Stogdill (1974) conducted an extensive review of the relationship between leadership style and group productivity. He concluded that productivity was associated with a leadership style high on consideration for members and high on initiation of structure. His conclusion continues to be supported by more recent research findings (e.g., Blake & Mouton, 1982; Nicholls, 1985).

Vroom and Jago (1978) concluded that the most effective leadership style varies with the current situation in the group. The situations they describe generally correspond with the stages of group development. For example, an autocratic leadership style can be effective during the first stage of group development but not at later stages. A consultative style would be more appropriate at stage two. Depending on the circumstances, either a consultative or a group-oriented leadership style seems best at stages three and four. (See Chapter 6 for a more detailed discussion.)

Hershey and Blanchard (1976, 1977, 1982) directly link leadership styles to the stages of group development. Their findings lead them to conclude that leadership style should be determined by the group's maturity level. Thus, the leadership style most likely to increase group effectiveness and ultimate productivity will be different at each stage of group development. According to Hershey and Blanchard, the most effective leadership style at stage one is high on task and low on relationship. At stage two, a leadership style high on both task and relationship dimensions is advised. A low task and high relationship style seems most effective at stage three. Finally, they suggest a style low on both task and relationship during the fourth stage of group development. Hershey and Blanchard describe these stages as telling, selling, participating, and delegating.

The work of Hershey and Blanchard meshes well with the descriptions of the stages of group development outlined in this book. Their model fits with the needs of the group at each stage and with the research evidence presented. An analogy with individual development may be illuminating. A child is in no position to make his or her own decisions. Parents tell little ones what to do much more than at other stages of individual development. In a child's adolescence, faced with a more rebellious teenager, some parents abdicate responsibility. Developmental findings, however, conclude that this is a mistake (e.g., Silberman & Wheelan, 1980). Adolescents require task-oriented parents who also work at building and maintaining lines of communication and affection with their teenagers. Young adults, however, need parents who are supportive and encouraging but not controlling or directive. Finally, parents delegate all responsibility to their adult children. They also, in general, are less interactive on a daily basis.

This description of changes in parental leadership style parallels the description suggested by Hershey and Blanchard (1976) for group leadership.

Beginning groups are not yet capable of functioning independently. Stage-two groups need a task-oriented and relational leader. Stage-three groups are testing their ability to organize and prepare for successful work. A leader who is supportive and participatory but not directive seems to facilitate the group's growth. When a group reaches the work stage, leadership is not as critical as at earlier stages. If the group has developed an effective cultural and social structure, it is capable of working with little input from the leader. In fact, more directive leadership would likely interfere with productivity.

While more research on leadership style and productivity is clearly needed, a rudimentary picture has emerged. Effective leaders do vary their styles to meet the current needs of their groups. The connection between leadership style and group development is an important step in our understanding of group productivity.

Coalitions and Subgroups

Coalition and subgroup formation continues to occur during the work stage of group development. Coalitions emerge to influence group decisions or direction. Subgroups are formed on the basis of organizational requirements or member affiliative needs. Members who are attracted to each other for any number of socio-emotional reasons may become an identifiable subgroup. These friendship, interest, or subtask groups were perceived as threatening during the early stages of group development. However, at stages three and four, the group's capacity to form subgroups while maintaining group-as-a-whole cohesion is greatly increased (Mills, 1967).

What helps organizational subgroups or work teams to be effective and productive? A number of researchers have studied this question, and their findings provide a picture of the factors that facilitate work team effectiveness. A primary factor influencing subgroup success is the subgroup's relationship to the organizational group (Kolodny & Dresner, 1986; Luft, 1984). Successful subgroups are integrated into the group-as-a-whole by task requirements and relationships. Ongoing interaction and feedback between the subgroup and the total organization are important to subgroup productivity. Work team tasks that are perceived by the members as significant and important facilitate productivity. Tasks that provide variety and challenge to members also increase subgroup productivity (Hackman & Oldham, 1980). Work teams that produce a total product or work on a complete project are more productive than those that work on only a portion of the product or project (Cummings, 1981). Subgroups are more effective if they contain the smallest number of members necessary to accomplish the task (Hackman, 1987). Groups that contain additional members have lowered productivity.

Other factors that the subgroup cannot provide on its own affect productivity as well. That is, the organization must provide certain supports to the subgroup to ensure effectiveness. For example, subgroup effectiveness is dependent on access to resources necessary to accomplish its task (Goodman, Devadas &

Hughson, 1988). The subgroup may require the technical or interpersonal expertise of individuals outside the group to complete its task. Teams that have access to training in necessary technical or interpersonal skills may be more effective than those that do not. Subgroups that have a defined work territory also tend to be more productive (Miller, 1959; Sundstrom & Altman, 1989). If team members work in close proximity to each other, effectiveness is enhanced (Sundstrom, 1986). Team members also need sufficient time together to establish a mature working unit (Heinen & Jacobson, 1976). Finally, if the subgroup is rewarded and recognized by the larger group for its efforts and accomplishments, productivity is increased (Pritchard, Jones, Roth, Stuebing & Ekeberg, 1988).

The factors described in the preceding paragraph are achieved only with the cooperation and support of other groups within the organization. This fact acts as a reminder that the effectiveness of any group is dependent, to a large extent, on the context in which it is operating. If a team is functioning well within itself but is operating in a competitive, conflictual environment, the likelihood of success is diminished. Small-group effectiveness depends on factors internal and external to the group. Functioning well within the group can, to some degree, facilitate the development of cooperation with essential individuals and units external to the group. Such subgroups may be able to plan strategies to elicit cooperation and support from external sources. However, mature internal functioning may not be enough to overcome external resistance or interference. In predicting team effectiveness, then, the role of external individuals, groups, and other contextual factors cannot be underestimated. Being a working group in a dysfunctional, nonsupportive environment is akin to being in an airtight compartment in a sinking submarine. Viability and success, in both cases, are quite limited.

GROUP PROCESSES

Conformity and Deviation

Conformity remains high during the work stage of group development. The increased consensus about group culture and structure gained at stage three results in increased conformity, which persists at stage four. This type of conformity, which is based on member agreements, supports the work of the group. Deviation is also more tolerable to a mature group if it is task related. Innovation is important if a group is to be successful, and innovation usually requires stretching or breaking norms initially. Deviance from accepted norms may result in changes for the better. Mature groups are more tolerant of task-related deviant behavior as a result. Other forms of deviance are also tolerated at this stage due, in part, to familiarity among members, group cohesion, and past conformity on the part of the current deviator (Hollander, 1960; Katz, 1982).

The question arises at this point: What are members of a stage-four group conforming to? That is, what norms encourage productivity? Norms that encourage high performance standards and effectiveness increase group productivity (Bassin, 1988; Hackman, 1987). Shared expectations of success also support productivity (Shea & Guzzo, 1987a). A group culture that encourages innovation increases the likelihood of higher productivity as well (Cummings, 1981; Moscovici, 1976). Peters and Waterman (1982) concluded that norms and values that support superior quality, service, innovation, and attention to detail significantly increase group effectiveness and productivity.

Cohesion and Conflict

Cohesion has been found to increase group productivity (Evans & Dion, 1991; Greene, 1989; Littlepage, Cowart & Kerr, 1989). However, most researchers agree that cohesion in conjunction with high performance norms is more predictive of group success than cohesion alone (Hare, 1976; Stogdill, 1972). Interpersonal attraction has also been shown to increase group effectiveness (Goodacre, 1951; Hare, 1976; Husband, 1940). Cohesion aids the development of cooperation, and cooperation increases group productivity (Deutsch, 1949a, 1949b, 1973, 1990a).

Group size affects this process. For example, the addition of unnecessary members to a group reduces the level of cohesion and, as a result, may negatively affect productivity (Gladstein, 1984; McGrath, 1984). The presence of extra members results in increased difficulties in coordination that may affect cohesion (Steiner, 1972). Social loafing occurs more frequently in groups that are larger than necessary (Latane et al., 1979). This, too, may negatively affect cohesion.

Sundstrom, DeMeuse, and Futrell (1990) conclude that cohesion does facilitate group performance if it is accompanied by high performance norms and effective decision-making methods designed to avoid groupthink. Groups at the work stage of group development tend to have relatively high levels of cohesion. However, high performance norms are not guaranteed outcomes of group development. Skill in decision making is also not automatic. Stage-four groups need to pay attention to these areas in order to maximize their chances of success. Training in decision-making strategies may help some groups to avoid groupthink and increase their productivity (Sundstrom et al., 1990).

Conflict continues to occur throughout the life of a group. Mature groups experience frequent periods of conflict. This conflict or tension occurs during periods of significant disagreement. Bormann (1975) noted that well-functioning groups have frequent brief periods of tension or conflict. Such groups have developed conflict-management strategies, however, that help to resolve these episodic conflicts before they escalate or continue beyond the group's established toleration level. Periodic conflicts have positive results, such as clarification of issues, increased member interest, and increased understanding among members.

Conflict can escalate and threaten group effectiveness or survival at any stage of development. It can also have many positive outcomes if managed well. A group at any stage of development must learn to handle naturally occurring conflict in ways that will support group cohesion and performance. Conflicts are natural, but human beings do not have innate skills in conflict management. Thus, a successful group is one that learns and practices good conflict-management skills throughout its developmental life.

As a result of the research reviewed in this chapter, a number of factors have been identified that enhance group effectiveness and productivity. These factors also serve to identify a stage-four group. Clearly, all the factors that facilitate productivity have not yet been discovered. Also, the relative importance of each factor is unclear. However, groups interested in increasing the likelihood of goal achievement and productivity would be wise to monitor the occurrence of the outlined processes. To that end, a list of the factors associated with group effectiveness and productivity is provided next.

Identifying a Stage-Four Group

1. Members are clear about group goals.
2. Members agree with the group's goals.
3. Tasks are appropriate to group versus individual solution.
4. Members are clear about their roles.
5. Members accept their roles and status.
6. Role assignments match member abilities.
7. The leadership style matches the group's developmental level.
8. During the work stage, delegation, or unleadership, is the prevailing leadership style.
9. The group's communication structure matches the demands of the task.
10. The group has an open communication structure in which all members participate and are heard.
11. The group has an appropriate ratio of task and socio-emotional statements.
12. The group gets, gives, and utilizes feedback about its effectiveness and productivity.
13. The group spends time defining problems it must solve or decisions it must make.
14. The group spends time planning how it will solve problems and make decisions.
15. The group spends enough time discussing the problems and decisions it faces.
16. The group chooses participatory decision-making methods.
17. The group implements and evaluates its solutions and decisions.
18. Voluntary conformity is high.
19. Task-related deviance is tolerated.
20. The group norms encourage high performance and quality.
21. The group expects to be successful.

22. The group encourages innovation.
23. The group pays attention to the details of its work.
24. The group accepts coalition and subgroup formation.
25. Subgroups are integrated into the group-as-a-whole.
26. Subgroups work on important tasks.
27. Tasks contain variety and challenge.
28. Subgroups work on a total product or project.
29. The group contains the smallest number of members necessary to accomplish its goal or goals.
30. The group has access to the technical and people resources necessary to accomplish its task.
31. The group has access to technical or interpersonal consultation as needed.
32. The group has access to technical or human relations training as needed.
33. The group has a defined work territory.
34. The group is allotted sufficient time to develop a mature working unit and to accomplish its goals.
35. Subgroups are recognized and rewarded by the group.
36. The group is highly cohesive.
37. Interpersonal attraction among members is high.
38. Members are cooperative.
39. Periods of conflict are frequent but brief.
40. The group has effective conflict-management strategies.

STAGE FIVE

Many natural groups are continuous. That is, they continue to exist beyond the tenure, and in some cases the life span, of their members. The U.S. Senate, for example, has been in continuous operation for two hundred years. Members have been replaced over time. However, the senate group continues to function. Faculty groups are usually continuous, as are work units in other institutions or organizations. Such groups do not experience a termination phase as such. Individuals leave, and this may cause disruption and a shift in dynamics and developmental processes. Rapid turnover among group members can cause serious problems for a group, regression to earlier developmental levels, and significant decreases in productivity. However, the group continues to exist.

Other groups do experience a definite end. Some groups are time limited from the outset. A classroom group begins in September and ends in June. A therapy group is designed to run for fifteen weeks. Other groups end when their goals are accomplished or their resources are depleted. Thus, the project team ends when the project is finished and the laboratory team disbands when the grant money runs out. In all these examples, the group's eventual end is known to members from the beginning. In essence, termination is planned into the process from the outset.

Sometimes, however, groups end when unexpected problems occur that make continued interaction impossible. A plant closing, for example, means the termination of individuals' employment but also of the work groups to which those individuals belonged. An individual loses not only a job but also a work group that may have been a source of support and pride for the individual. Sometimes, member dissatisfaction and internal conflict precipitate a group's end. When members are dissatisfied with a group and can join another group or believe that continuing membership is too costly, they may precipitate termination (Rusbult, 1983; Rusbult, Zembrodt & Gunn, 1982).

Whether planned or unplanned, impending termination causes disruption in a group and may generate internal conflict, attempts to reintegrate and expand the group's life, or increased work activity (Farrell, 1976; Mann et al., 1967; Mills, 1964). Sometimes, termination stimulates increased solidarity and expressions of positive feelings among members. Problematic issues may be avoided, which can result in a decline in the group's task-oriented activity (Lundgren, 1971).

While not all theories of group development view termination as a separate stage, a number of theorists do include a termination stage (e.g., Braaten, 1974/1975; Dunphy, 1964; Gibbard & Hartman, 1973; Mann et al., 1967; Miles, 1971; Mills, 1964; Slater, 1966). The termination phase has also been identified and described in therapy and counseling groups (e.g., Gazda, 1989; Kramer, 1990; Yalom, 1975).

Less is known about this final period of group life. It has received more attention from psychologists who view the termination phase as an important part of treatment (e.g., Corey & Corey, 1992). However, it has received only minimal attention from group researchers in general. This is unfortunate, since what is known suggests that this period of group life is stressful for members (Johnson, 1974; Mayadas & Glasser, 1985). This is especially true when a group's end was unexpected. In such cases individual apathy, conflict among members, and the tendency to blame others for the group's failure may increase (Kushnir, 1984).

During the termination phase, members may strive to establish the fact that they have produced something of enduring value. The group's difficulty with termination is often quite evident. Some researchers have even characterized discussions during this period as regressive (Mills, 1964; Schutz, 1958; Slater, 1966).

Flapan and Fenchel (1987) suggested that debriefing sessions can reduce the stress of termination. During such sessions, members are encouraged to share their concerns over the group's ending and discuss the group's accomplishments and their individual plans for the future. Mayadas and Glasser (1985) recommended that leaders attempt to reduce group cohesion by focusing on the independence and individuality of each member. Corey and Corey (1992) outline a set of tasks for leaders and members of counseling groups that are ending. They suggest that feelings of separation be explored, feedback exchanged, and unfinished business dealt with. A review of the group experience should occur, and strategies for continuing personal development outside the group should be explored. While their suggestions focus on counseling and therapy groups, much of what they propose would be useful in other group contexts as well.

We live in a society that does not deal well with endings. Death and loss are generally not discussed very openly. Separation from family and friends is often not marked in any special way. Little attention is paid to departures. We are a mobile people. Work demands often include frequent moves. Our reluctance to discuss endings may be a way to defend ourselves from the pain of separation and loss. However, this reticence may also rob us of the opportunity to learn from our experiences and to resolve things with the people whom we are leaving.

Our national reticence regarding endings may account, in part, for the lack of research on the termination phase of group development. More research is clearly needed to clarify the dynamics of this phase and to determine the effects of different kinds of endings on individual members.

Since less research has been done on this stage, the following list of characteristics associated with the termination phase is less definitive than those describing the other stages of group development.

Identifying a Stage-Five Group

1. Group members know that the group will be ending soon.
2. The group's ability to manage conflict may begin to degenerate.
3. Members may discuss ways to continue the group beyond its designated ending point.
4. Work activity may increase or decrease abruptly.
5. Feelings of solidarity among members may increase.
6. Increased expressions of positive feelings among members may occur.
7. Problematic issues may be avoided.
8. Stress and anxiety among members is evident.
9. Some members may become apathetic with regard to the group.
10. Members discuss group achievements.

8

THE INDIVIDUAL
AND THE GROUP

This chapter addresses two primary questions. First, how does knowledge of group dynamics and development increase our understanding of individual personality development? That is, do membership and reference groups influence the enduring psychological characteristics of the person? Are personality characteristics such as values, needs, attitudes, and behavior unique to the person or the product of group influences experienced by an individual throughout his or her life? Second, if group membership does influence individual personality development, how can personal knowledge of group functioning be helpful to individuals? Can awareness of group processes assist individuals in the development and maintenance of a positive self-concept? Can such knowledge aid individual problem solving, increase quality of life, or reduce psychological distress?

The first seven chapters of this book outline much of what we know about group development and dynamics. This chapter focuses on the effect these group dynamics have on individuals and whether awareness of group processes can help people understand and manage themselves in the various social contexts they encounter throughout their lives.

TWO VIEWS OF THE PERSON

In the modern era, increasing emphasis has been placed on the individual as the basic unit of society (Nisbet, 1969; Spence, 1985). Individuals are thought to freely shape their own identities, choose their own goals, and stand accountable for their own actions. The person is seen as separate from his or her context. Personal identity, in our time, is thought to precede and be distinct from group memberships (MacIntyre, 1988). Individuals freely choose the roles they will play in the groups they opt to join. The real self, however, is distinct from and only minimally influenced by these group memberships (Sampson, 1989).

The supremacy of the individual is a relatively new concept in human history. In the premodern era, the family was the basic unit of society. Individuals were defined by their social contexts and were the subjects and products of the social environments in which they lived (Sampson, 1989). Roles and persons were the same. A real self, separate and distinct from group memberships or roles, was inconceivable.

Thus, we have inherited two views of the person. One describes the individual as the product of his or her group, institutional, and cultural memberships. The other views the individual as separate from and antecedent to these memberships. While the latter view clearly has the upper hand in current Western thought, both views still influence the thinking of social scientists and cause great debate and consternation (Kihlstrom, 1987).

While at first glance this intellectual debate may seem interesting but irrelevant to everyday life, the view that we hold has real effects for society and the individual. For example, if individuals are products of their groups, then individuals have no influence in shaping the groups, institutions, and cultures of which they are a part. In fact, when this view was prevalent, democracy was not. Individuals had little or no influence in society. Progress was not the motivator that it is today. Since individuals were born into many of their roles and enacted these roles in socially prescribed ways, stability, not progress, was the goal. Also, if individuals are created by their groups, then individually initiated change would be impossible, since individuals do not influence. They are influenced. Thus, the quality of one's life is totally out of personal control. Quality of life depends on the circumstances of one's birth and group memberships.

If, on the other hand, individuals freely create their own lives, relatively unencumbered by their membership or reference groups, a different picture emerges. Society is shaped by the goals and desires of the individuals who live within it. The role of government is to ensure that individuals are free to pursue these goals and do not interfere with each other's pursuits. Governments would feel little responsibility for individuals, since the quality of life is in the hands of each person. If a person is in economic difficulty, the fault is his or hers. Individual psychological problems are also the responsibility of the person rather than other social institutions. Problems are overcome individually through will power, as opposed to changes in educational, health, or other governmental policies.

While both of these views are presented in slightly exaggerated form, the reader will recognize the description of the individualistic view as representative in the modern-day United States. The view of the individual as the product of society is reminiscent of feudal and monarchial societies. Thus, the perspective that a society takes with regard to the individual has real implications for the structure of that society and the lives of persons. Whether we see issues as personal or social problems will be determined by our view of the individual. How we solve these problems will be determined this way as well. For example, if drug abuse is a personal problem, little institutional intervention can be expected. However, if we view the addicted individual as a product of his or her environment, institutional intervention would be the only alternative.

From another perspective, human desire to understand the world in which we live drives us to attempt to resolve the question elegantly posed by Allport in 1968. He asked:

> *How can his nature depend indisputably upon the prior existence of cultural designs and upon his role in a predetermined social structure while at the same time he is clearly a unique person, both selecting and rejecting influences from his cultural surrounding, and in turn creating new cultural forms for the guidance of future generations? (p. 9)*

How can individuals be both created by and creators of the groups, institutions, and societies of which they are a part? Which view is true? Are both true? Or is neither?

To the reader of the preceding chapters, it is clear that the point of view espoused in this book does not coincide with the individualistic perspective. Throughout this work, it is argued that individuals are profoundly affected by their social environments. It is suggested that much of what we call individual personality characteristics could be more accurately described as normative behaviors of particular societal subgroups. Clearly, the author rejects extremely individualistic theories of personality. This rejection is based on the evidence presented in earlier chapters regarding the impact of group membership on individual thoughts, feelings, and actions. One cannot conclude, in the face of such evidence, that individual personality or identity is unaffected by social contexts. However, it would be equally unreasonable to assume that individuals have no input whatsoever into their thoughts, feelings, or actions. Individuals are both the products and the producers of their social world. The individual and his or her groups are inextricably locked in a system of mutual influence.

Of course, the amount of influence exerted by individuals and groups is not necessarily equivalent. For example, an individual who aspires to be an artist in a culture that does not support the arts economically or socially will be hard pressed to achieve his or her goal. On the other hand, the expression of unique personality characteristics can be supported by the social environment. For example, the courage, values, and attitudes of Nelson Mandela are admired by many throughout the world. This international support and the enduring encouragement of the African National Congress and other groups have enabled a unique personality to influence the values and norms of groups, institutions, and nations. One's aspirations and self-expression can be limited or expanded by the concrete realities of the culture and social structure of which one is a part (Kleiner and Okeke, 1990).

A SOCIAL PSYCHOLOGICAL VIEW OF PERSONALITY

Volumes have been written about individual personality development. It is well beyond the scope of this work to describe this area of inquiry in any detail. Suffice it to say that research in this area reflects the two views of the individual described in this chapter. The first view, represented by many personality psychologists, assumes that individual personality characteristics are relatively stable across time and minimally affected by the groups and social situations one encounters. One's personality is seen as predictable and stable. The focus of this research, then, is to demonstrate this stability and to determine the origins of individual personality.

The second view, represented by social psychologists and some personality psychologists, is that individual personality changes in different social contexts. That is, the groups and social situations that persons encounter influence their thoughts, attitudes, and behaviors. Research in this area, then, attempts to demonstrate the changeability of individual personality and to describe the effects of different social situations on individuals.

Both views have significant research support for their conclusions. Individual characteristics have been found to be stable across time (Buss, 1985; McCrae & Costa, 1982; Mischel & Peake, 1982). The influence of groups and social situations on individuals is equally well documented (Asch, 1955; Latane, 1981; Lewin, 1943; Milgram, 1965; Zimbardo, 1975). The weight of the evidence does not solidly fall on either side. This has led many social scientists to conclude that both views have validity and should be integrated into a more systemic or relational perspective. That is, there is both stability and change in individual characteristics. People are not just conformers to social norms, nor are they just reasoning beings unaffected by their families, groups, or cultures (Wrong, 1961). They are both. Discovering the processes that allow individuals to be both consistent and malleable, then, is the task of current social research.

This view, that individuals and their social environments operate in a system of mutual influence, is not new. Lewin (1951), Mills (1959), and others articulated this perspective decades ago. However, in an era that held up the individual as the center of the social world, their views went unheeded. In essence, this perspective went counter to the prevailing views of modernism, in which the individual is supreme. It is beginning to be heard now, however, which may indicate a loosening of the grip of modernism on Western thought. The call for this more integrated view is evident in the writings of many contemporary social scientists (e.g., Buss, 1987; Magnusson, 1981; Magnusson & Endler, 1977; Pepitone, 1981, 1990; Ryff, 1987; Wheelan & Abt, 1990).

Lewin's (1951) formula, $B = f (P, E)$, still stands as a reasonable way of describing this integrated view of the person. Behavior is a function of the person and the person's psychological environment. What a person does in a situation depends on his or her characteristics, drives, and needs operative at the moment, and the norms and social structure of the situation he or she is in. Lewin believed that the individual's perception of these norms and values was key to understanding how he or she would behave. Thus, the environment influences the person to the extent that the individual perceives and responds to that influence. Since Lewin's time, others have argued that the environment has real effects, in many cases, whether the individual perceives these effects or not (Gold, 1990). Sampson (1989) stated that people are affected not just by those with whom they have face-to-face contact, but also by the actions of individuals, groups, and governments at great distances. Ecological or economic policies of distant nations, for example, may limit or support individual expression or aspirations. Such remote events may promote stability or change in the personality characteristics (beliefs, values, needs, and so on) of an individual.

Understanding the individual alone, then, is not adequate. The individual cannot be the basic unit of society, since he or she is part of a system of mutual influence that includes the groups he or she interacts with, the groups he or she is born into, and the physical and social factors operating in the world around him or her. This influence system, then, may be the basic unit of society. $B = f (P, E, PE)$: Behavior is a function of the person, the real environment, and the individual's perception of that real environment.

What does this mean in concrete terms? We know, for example, that many personality characteristics are relatively enduring over time. How can this be, since it is also true that groups and social contexts influence these characteristics? One process that helps to account for this is selective interaction (Swann, 1987). Swann proposed that people seek out groups and social contexts that confirm their perceptions of self and allow expression of their unique personality characteristics. Swann also said that the individual's search for compatible groups is aided by displaying identity cues. We wear clothes and use titles and self-descriptions that attract people to us who will confirm our self-concepts. If we meet others who perceive us in ways that are inconsistent with our sense of identity, we try to convince them to adopt our view of ourselves. Failing that, we may dismiss those who see us differently as incompetent observers, or we may distort what they say in order to maintain our sense of self.

One way that we maintain a consistent sense of self, then, is by selecting, as much as we can, the social situations we will participate in. We also attempt to change situations that do not support our self-identity (Baron & Boudreau, 1987). As a result, individuals, by choosing to interact in social contexts that support their sense of identity, do have some control over the factors that influence personality and identity. This is so whether people have positive or negative self-concepts. Individuals who view themselves as inadequate will seek out social situations that confirm their inadequacy (Swann, 1987). The need for a stable self-identity seems very strong.

It also seems likely that people seek to maintain a stable self-concept out of loyalty to the groups that initially helped to forge that self-concept. The earliest shapers of our personality and eventual self-concepts are the membership groups that we are born into. Our sex, racial, and ethnic memberships are predetermined and, with rare exceptions, immutable. Significant others respond to us on the basis of these memberships and teach us how to be members of these groups. All unique characteristics of the person from birth are expressed and responded to by others in the context of these and other membership and reference groups. Thus, many innate or biological characteristics will be expressed in ways that are consistent with group norms, due to the strong human need for inclusion and acceptance. Pressures to conform with group norms are great from our earliest days.

Individuals observe their own behavior and people's reactions to it. They compare their behavior with others' and slowly build a stable view of self (Mead, 1934). Once a person's self-concept is established, he or she will resist change in it in order to avoid feelings of instability and possible rejection by the primary groups in his or her life.

A person's identity, then, is the product of innate personality characteristics, singular experiences, individual choices, and group memberships. Personality emerges in the context of interaction with others who reinforce the norms and values of these groups and shape our unique qualities to assure conformity with these norms and values.

Each person is a complex profile of group identities or socio-identities as a result of this process (Babad et al., 1983). Socio-identities include race, gender, ethnicity, age, vocation, religion, and political affiliation (Babad et al., 1983). With each of these identities come prescribed ways of thinking, feeling, and behaving which individuals must integrate along with unique or innate aspects of their emergent personalities.

These most basic group memberships leave fairly permanent imprints on our personalities. They also lead others, throughout our lives, to respond to us as members of these primary social groupings. Others, then, will relate to us according to the prevailing cultural assumptions regarding our basic membership groups. For example, people will respond to assertion or extroversion differently, depending on the race, gender, or ethnic membership of the individual displaying the characteristic. Ultimately, the person may increase or decrease the expression of this characteristic as a result of positive or negative responses from others.

It is important to keep in mind that groups do not create norms for all behaviors, attitudes, or feelings. Norms are created to ensure conformity with essential and important group values and beliefs. Consequently, while the impact of groups on individuals is very significant, this influence is felt only in relation to certain core values and beliefs. In other areas, the individual has some latitude to express his or her uniqueness. As a result, individual differences will be noted even within groups composed of persons with similar socio-identity profiles.

The fact that not all attitudes, feelings, and behaviors are legislated by groups and society is key to understanding the stability and variability of individual personality. Only some of the unique characteristics of the person come under the influence of social norms. We learn to express or inhibit certain parts of ourselves in different social settings to conform with the norms and values in that setting. Other aspects of the self, however, are unaffected by this process and remain relatively stable throughout the life of an individual.

It is clear that individual personality and self-identity are profoundly affected by the membership groups into which a person is born. Reference groups and other groups impact on self-expression and identity as well. An individual typically seeks out these latter types of groups because he or she perceives them as groups that will support his or her sense of self. If the person is mistaken or is forced to interact with a group whose view of him or her is discrepant, the individual will attempt to change the group's view. Failing that, the individual may dismiss the inconsistent view as misguided or in error. Failing that, the individual may change his or her self-perceptions to accommodate the new view.

It is also clear that individuals can change aspects of the groups to which they belong. This can happen in at least two ways. First, since groups do not legislate all aspects of member self-expression, unique personal qualities can influence elements of a group's culture or social structure. Second, a group may require or need the unique characteristics of an individual in order to accomplish its goals. In this case, the group may support and encourage these qualities in the person.

Individuals, groups, and the broader social context in which they all operate mutually influence each other. The development of individuals, groups, institutions, and societies are inextricably linked. The health of each affects the others. How can knowledge of this mutual influence and knowledge of group processes and development assist the individual in the process of self-discovery and actualization?

CREATING HEALTHIER HABITATS FOR HUMAN BEINGS

Webster's Dictionary (1989) defines *habitat* as "the place where a plant or animal naturally or normally lives and grows" (p. 545). One definition of the word *environment* is "the aggregate of social and cultural conditions that influence the life of an individual or community" (p. 416). Another definition of *environment* is "the complex of physical, chemical, and living things that act upon an organism or an ecological community and ultimately determine its form and survival" (p. 416). *Ecology* is defined as "the totality or pattern of relations between organisms and their environment" (p. 395). Finally, *psychology* is defined as "the mental or behavioral characteristics of an individual or group" (p. 951).

All that has been discussed here is captured in these definitions. It can be summed up in the following way. The mental or behavioral characteristics of individuals are influenced by the physical and social conditions operating in their environment. The social habitat where individuals naturally or normally live and grow is the group. The interrelationships among individuals and their social environment as these are enacted in social groups affect the psychology of individuals and groups and can affect the condition of the broader social environment. That is, the well-being of individuals, groups, and the totality of the social environment are interdependent. A functional, mature group facilitates the effectiveness and maturity of individuals within it, and vice versa. The broader social context in which the individual and group are operating influences and can be influenced by individuals and groups. The importance of this connection between the individual and the social environment led Lewin (1951) to advocate the study of psychological ecology, which seeks to understand the mutual influences of human beings and the social environment enacted in human groups (Lewin, 1951; Cartwright, 1978).

Human beings, as members of groups in which aspects of the social environment are enacted, have a vested interest in the habitability of these groups. Since the groups one belongs to significantly affect personal attitudes, behaviors, and feelings, the well-being of these groups is crucial to the well-being of the individual. The values, beliefs, and norms of these groups can limit or enhance individual self-expression, self-determination, and self-concept. Learning to participate in ways that facilitate the development of a healthy, mature, and accepting group is not just a matter of enhancing the likelihood of group goal achievement. It is also a matter of enhancing personal well-being or, in some cases, survival.

There are many things that individual members can do to facilitate the development and well-being of groups. For example, people who express liking for, respect for, and trust in others facilitate social interaction and cohesion in groups (Haythorn, 1953; Sorrentino & Sheppard, 1978). Individuals who are assertive and prominent in groups influence others to participate and communicate. They tend to have leadership roles and creative input (Borg, 1960; Shaw & Harkey, 1976; Smith & Cook, 1973). A positive self- concept and emotional stability also facilitate group functioning (Bass, Wurster, Doll & Clair, 1953; Buck, Miller & Caul, 1974; Haythorn, 1953; Leonard, 1975). Acting in a responsible manner in relation to the group promotes effectiveness as well (Mitchell, 1975; Stogdill, 1948).

Conversely, expressing anxiety or defensiveness reduces group effectiveness (Kogan & Wallach, 1967; Ryan & Lakie, 1965; Teichman, 1974). Expressing dislike, distrust, or competitiveness also has negative effects on group functioning (Deutsch, 1990b; Haythorn, 1953; Sorrentino & Sheppard, 1978). In short, individual member behavior in groups can influence group dynamics and development.

How individuals perceive group events and the behavior of individual group members can significantly affect group functioning. In 1958, Heider proposed that individuals tend to attribute the behavior of others to the enduring personality characteristics of the individual. This seems to be the result of our need to be able to predict future events. If a person behaves in a particular way, we assume that he or she always acts in that way and respond accordingly.

Jones and Davis (1965) described a theory of inference to explain this human tendency. When we observe the behavior of another, we attempt to determine whether the actor is aware of the consequences of that behavior. If he or she is not aware, we assume that the behavior is unintentional. In the same way, we determine whether the actor has the skills to intentionally behave in a certain way. If we decide that knowledge of consequences and skill are present, we attribute the behavior to the person.

While this seems reasonable, it is not always true that individual characteristics are causal. Sometimes, behavior is influenced or restrained by the social environment in which it occurs. Ross (1977) referred to this tendency to attribute actions to personality characteristics without taking into account environmental constraints as the **fundamental attribution error.**

Our tendency to blame the boss for negative group performance without taking into consideration budgetary constraints is an example of an attributional error. This attribution has real effects on the group. If we attribute poor group performance to a person or persons, conflict is very likely to escalate. However, if we attribute poor performance to other factors, group members might be able to develop collective strategies to overcome budgetary constraints (Horai, 1977; Messe, Stollak, Larson & Michaels, 1979).

Some general patterns regarding the ways in which individual members interpret group successes or failures have been identified. For example, leaders and members in central positions tend to take responsibility for both group success and failure while followers and peers take more responsibility for success than failure (Caine & Schlenker, 1979; Zander, 1971). The tendency for individuals to feel personally responsible for group success but not for failure is called the self-serving bias and has been identified in a number of research investigations (e.g., Beckman, 1970; Forsyth & Schlenker, 1977; Medow & Zander, 1965).

Some groups attribute success to positive group characteristics and failure to environmental constraints. This is referred to as a group-serving bias (Caine & Schlenker, 1979; Forsyth & Schlenker, 1977; Leary, 1978). The self-serving bias tends to decrease group cohesion, while the group-serving bias increases cohesion (Dion, Miller & Magnan, 1971).

Individuals tend to misinterpret the behavior of others (Kelley, 1979; Orvis, Kelley & Butler, 1976). This tendency is exacerbated in conflict situations (Regan & Totten, 1975; Rosenberg & Wolfsfeld, 1977). This natural tendency to distort events and actions, however, can have very negative consequences for the group and its members. However, we can, with awareness and training, reduce the number of attributional errors that we make.

For example, teachers generally take credit for student successes, but not for student failures (Beckman, 1970; Johnson, Feigenbaum & Weiby, 1964). But when teachers are made aware of this tendency and are trained not to blame students, they correct this attributional error (Ames, 1975; Beckman, 1973). What this suggests is that individuals can reduce the number of attributional errors they make in group situations and, by doing so, can contribute to group success directly. How members think and act in group situations can be very influential.

Chapter 7 outlined factors that have been found to influence group productivity and development. These factors easily translate into prescriptions for individual actions that can promote positive group development. They are:

1. Individuals encourage the process of goal, role, and task clarification and agreement.
2. Members in leadership roles adjust their style of leadership to match the group's developmental level.

3. Individuals encourage the adoption of an open communication structure in which all member input and feedback are heard.
4. Members promote an appropriate ratio of task and socio-emotional communications.
5. Individuals are aware of and promote effective problem-solving and decision-making procedures.
6. Members encourage the establishment of norms that support productivity, innovation, and freedom of expression.
7. Members discourage any group tendency to overlegislate individual behavior through the adoption of excessive or unnecessary norms.
8. Individuals voluntarily conform with norms that promote group effectiveness.
9. Members support division of labor, such as coalitions and subgroups, necessary to accomplish group goals.
10. Members promote group cohesion and cooperation.
11. Members interact with others outside the group in ways that promote group integration and cooperation with the larger social context.
12. Members are aware of and encourage the use of effective conflict-management strategies.
13. Members are familiar with research and theory on group development and productivity and utilize this information in the group.
14. Individuals encourage the group to frequently assess and alter, if necessary, its functioning in order to facilitate individual and group well-being and productivity.
15. Individuals guard against misinterpreting group events or individual behavior and encourage others to do the same.

Individuals are encouraged by this list to promote the establishment of a group culture and social structure that facilitate group and individual goal achievement. Both are necessary, since it is unlikely that groups can be effective if members feel unnecessarily inhibited or restricted from expressing their uniqueness. Likewise, individual goals and needs cannot be met in a dysfunctional social environment. Groups and individuals need each other in order to promote their mutual well-being.

Freud (1950) saw the individual and the group or society as combatants. That is, society seeks to inhibit individual self-expression in an attempt to promote order. It was reasonable for Freud to come to this conclusion, given the overly restrictive Victorian era in which he lived. However, the individual and the group need not be in constant struggle. Their well-being is intertwined. Individual self-expression is enhanced by effective social organization, and vice versa.

Responsible individual group membership is important for the group and for individuals. Groups do shape individual personality to a great extent. Well-functioning groups promote the reduction of psychological distress and facilitate positive self-concepts in individuals (Bednar & Kaul, 1978; Yalom, 1975, 1985). Such groups aid the reduction of stress and physical or psychological problems in individuals (Barrera, 1986; Cohen & Wills, 1985; Dalgard, Anstorp, Benum, Sorensen & Moum, 1990). Finally, groups help us to learn about ourselves and our social world (Lieberman, 1980; Yalom, 1975). Larger social groupings, institutions, and organizations also impact on the physical and psychological well-being of individuals (e.g., Argyris, 1964; Cooper & Marshall, 1976; Ivancevich & Matteson, 1980).

In the same way, then, that we have become increasingly concerned about the well-being of our physical habitat, it behooves us as individuals to care about our social habitat as well. Each of us has a vested interest in fostering supportive, open, healthy, and productive groups. In so doing, we help to create habitats that encourage self-expression, protect us from stress, and work with us to meet our psychological, physical, and social needs. Individual and group well-being are one and the same.

9

GROUPS, ORGANIZATIONS, AND SOCIETY

The preceding chapters have focused primarily on describing the dynamics of small groups. Periodically, the reader has been reminded that modern groups rarely operate in isolation. Most groups function within the boundaries of organizations and institutions. Groups operate within a particular society and, in the age of mass communication, can be influenced by macro-level phenomena that transcend national boundaries. World events, international economic and social conditions, alternative ideologies, and the like are just some of the macro-level phenomena that can influence small groups.

While a full description of the organizational, societal, and international environments in which small groups operate is beyond the scope of this book, not to include some reference to these environments would be misleading. For many years, groups have been discussed as if they were isolated entities whose operations were unaffected by larger systems, but nothing could be further from the truth. Groups are almost invariably parts of larger systems. Therefore, this chapter briefly sketches the terrain of these larger environments. Key questions that the chapter attempts to answer are:

1. How does the organizational affiliation of a group influence its dynamics?
2. Are groups capable of influencing the organizational environment of which they are a part?
3. How are groups and organizations influenced by their societal contexts and by international macro-level phenomena?
4. Are groups and organizations capable of influencing the societal contexts in which they operate?

ORGANIZATIONS DEFINED

Groups help individuals accomplish goals and tasks that they could not accomplish alone. For many goals and tasks, a small group may be sufficient to ensure goal accomplishment. To plan a party, paint one house, or harvest a small crop, one group is ideal. However, to cater a dinner for 500 people, to paint twenty houses in two weeks, or to harvest crops from 5,000 acres, many groups will be needed, and their activities will require coordination. The development of an organization is necessary to accomplish these larger and more complex tasks. Organizations, then, grow out of the need to coordinate the activities of numbers of groups in order to achieve common goals and objectives.

Schein (1980) described an organization as a cluster of groups. These groups become subgroups of the total organization and are influenced by the culture that develops in the organization as a whole. In turn, the subgroups and the organization are influenced by the institution, society, and cultures of which they are a part. Caplow (1983) also defined an organization as a cluster of subgroups. Each subgroup is an organization in its own right, and its features resemble those of larger organizations, and vice versa. Caplow stated that all human organizations have similar characteristics. Each organization has a collective identity, members, goals and tasks, a schedule, a structure in which to accomplish its work, a territory, norms, division of labor, a shared history, and the like. Thus, the dynamics of small groups and larger organizational systems have much in common. Larger systems, however, are more complex. Developing shared goals, communication patterns, structures, management systems, cohesion, mechanisms for conflict resolution, and other necessary systems among multiple groups increases complexity within organizations. The coordination of multiple groups in pursuit of common goals can be a difficult task. Katz and Kahn (1966, 1978) described organizations as multidimensional systems. Organizations consist of group systems operating within the larger organizational system. The various subgroups of the organization may cooperate or compete, trust or distrust, share or not share information, and value similar or different things.

It is evident from these descriptions that an important characteristic of an organization is that most of its work is done in groups or teams. The work group or team has been described as the "basic building block" of the organization (French, Bell & Zawacki, 1989, p. 82). If organizational groups function effectively, the organization does as well. If the internal functioning of organizational groups or their ability to relate to each other is impaired, the probability of organizational effectiveness becomes remote (Ivancevich & Matteson, 1987).

We know that developing a shared small-group culture and social structure is a difficult task. It is much more difficult to create a shared culture and efficient social structure in complex organizations. The fact that organizations function at all is quite an accomplishment. And yet, many organizations do quite well. Products are made and distributed. Education is provided to the young, and trash is usually collected on time. In some cases, the activities of tens of thousands of individuals and thousands of groups are coordinated well enough to achieve organizational goals. Most organizational subgroups do take on the culture and social structure of the organization (Schein, 1990). Things work, not always well, but most organizations do function.

Two major factors influencing an organization's viability and success are the ability to influence its constituent groups to work toward organizational goals and the ability to create and maintain collaborative intergroup relations. These two factors are explored in some detail in the following sections.

HOW ORGANIZATIONS INFLUENCE THEIR MEMBER GROUPS

Group behavior is a function of the group and its psychological environment (Agazarian & Peters, 1981; Lewin, 1951). That is, how a group operates is affected by intragroup factors, such as its developmental level, cohesion, communication structure, and the like. These factors have been described in detail in previous chapters. However, these processes are also affected by the environment in which a group is operating. According to Ancona (1987), the group environment is "the organization in which the group is situated and its external task environment. The external task environment consists of entities outside the organizational boundary that either provide input or receive output from the group" (p. 209).

Examples of entities that might be part of a group's external task environment include governmental agencies, consumers, local political groups, and suppliers. These external entities may enhance or inhibit an organizational group's effectiveness through such activities as increasing or decreasing regulations concerning a group's task or product, increasing or decreasing access to resources necessary to group task accomplishment, increasing or decreasing demand for a group's product, or increasing or decreasing positive public opinion regarding the group.

There are a number of theoretical views on the question of how an organization influences the dynamics of its member groups. Open systems theory, attributed to von Bertalanffy (1968), is based on the notion that dynamic systems exist through a continuous exchange of components. Organizational groups, for example, exchange information and physical and human resources. These exchanges may explain how groups become more alike over time. Von Bertalanffy observed that eventually the same events begin to happen at the same time in different subsystems within an organization. He related an anecdote about workers within the same organization, but in distant locations, arriving at similar conceptions and conclusions at the same time. Access to similar information, people, technical resources, and other factors influence groups to structure themselves and respond in parallel ways.

Kernberg (1978) stated that the environment is a suprasystem that affects the systems operating within it. Burke (1982) added that a change in one part of a system affects all other parts and the system as a whole. According to Lewin (1951), groups should be studied in their actual settings because groups cannot be separated from their environment. To understand a group's dynamics, one must know what forces are operating on that group at that time. Groups operating within the same system or organization are interdependent. Each affects the other. The organization is part of the psychological environment of its member groups, and vice versa. That organizational groups become more alike over time, then, is not so surprising, since they are subject to similar environmental conditions.

The idea that systems work to achieve equilibrium has been proposed by a number of social scientists (e.g., Durkin, 1981; Festinger, 1957; Hirschhorn, 1987; Lewin, 1951; Schein, 1990) to explain why organizational groups become more alike over time. Subsystems within the organization will attempt to reduce dissonance and bring basic beliefs, norms, and behaviors into alignment. An organizational group bases its internal culture and social structure, in part, on members' perceptions of how other groups in the organization are operating. Achieving equilibrium facilitates the development of a shared organizational culture, which results in predictable behavior patterns among organization members and groups. These patterns ensure that individual members and groups will know how to respond within the organization and will be able to anticipate the responses of others. The result of this tendency to work toward balance and to create common assumptions and behavior patterns within a system of interacting groups is the ability to coordinate activities and to work toward common goals.

But how is a common culture created? How do groups begin to act in concert? Schein (1990) stated that "there are not many good models of how groups learn—how norms, beliefs, and assumptions are created initially" (p. 115). Once an organizational culture is in place, its contents can be observed. But how does the content of organizational culture emerge? Schein (1983, 1990) proposed that culture is the result of groups internalizing the values and beliefs of the founder or leader. As organizational groups implement these assumptions and experience their results, some alterations occur. Thus, the culture that eventually emerges is the result of a joint learning process on the part of leaders and members. Another mechanism for the creation of culture posits that culture emerges as a result of critical incidents (Bennis & Shepard, 1956; Bion, 1959; Schein, 1985). An anxiety-producing event occurs in the system. The response to that event tends to create a norm that becomes part of the culture. For example, if an organization member openly expresses anger, and no one responds to that person, the resulting norm may be that members of this organization will not express anger.

Another view of the creation of the content of culture suggests that people collectively create beliefs, values, norms, and shared behavior patterns through a series of conversations and arguments (Moscovici, 1990; Simmel, 1978). Eventually, shared assumptions emerge and become established in the perceptions, behaviors, and relationships of the members of the system. Shared assumptions create a particular structure of values, emotions, and behaviors that organizational members incorporate as their own. Over time, individuals and subsystems within the organization will begin to think, feel, and act in relative unison.

These theoretical views of how culture is created are based on the premise that groups operating within the same system will, over time, begin to mirror each other and that consistent patterns of response will be established. Support for this assumption is found in descriptions of variations in the content of organizational culture described in the literature (e.g., Louis, 1981, 1983; Pettigrew, 1979; Schein, 1985, 1990; Wilkins & Ouchi, 1983). Differences in assumptions, values, norms, and structures have been identified among organizations even within the same industry. Organizational systems do develop distinct cultures that can be observed. Organizational subgroups do, in most cases, conform to the overarching culture that is created. How this occurs, however, remains unclear. Some or all of the views presented here may account for this phenomenon. Research evidence supporting or negating any of these views, however, is scarce.

More is known about the operation of individual groups. The group development literature suggests that culture is the product of developmental processes inherent in groups and that these processes are manifest in member and leader discussions, disagreements, and conflicts regarding the beliefs, values, norms, and behaviors that should be adopted by group members. Group culture is shaped by the joint interaction of members and leaders as they address and eventually resolve predictable developmental issues. Two recent studies suggest that this may be true of organizations as well (Wheelan & Abraham, 1993; Wheelan & Krasick, 1993). In both these studies, groups operating within the same organizational system, but in different locations, were found to be discussing similar themes at the same time. The timing of discussion of particular themes was related to developmental processes in the groups and the organization as a whole. It is possible, then, that subgroup similarity in organizations is the result of the transmission of information about agreements, debates, and conflicts from group to group within the system until these are resolved and a relatively consistent organizational culture emerges. The behavior of groups would gradually become more alike over time as conscious or unconscious decisions about the content of culture were made.

In summary, we know that groups within an organization become more alike over time. Exactly how this occurs remains a bit of a mystery. There are several theoretical views on the subject. However, there is insufficient research evidence to favor one position over another. The paucity of studies in this area is understandable, given the difficulty of the task. Such studies require access to an emerging system from the beginning in order to determine how groups operating within the same system become more aligned over time. Also, systematic observational research in an organization is difficult, given the size of organizational systems and the resulting time, money, and personnel necessary to complete this type of research. However, research in this area is needed. Feasible research designs also need to be developed.

ORGANIZATIONAL FACTORS THAT
INFLUENCE GROUP EFFECTIVENESS

The ability of an organization to influence the culture and social structure of its member groups is essential to organizational goal achievement and productivity. A number of studies have investigated the impact of organizational variables on group processes and performance. Group or team effectiveness, for example, is enhanced when the organization of which it is a part has a clear sense of the group's mission and purpose within the organization (Shea & Guzzo, 1987b). If other groups in the organization are aware of the group's goals, coordination and cooperation are enhanced (Galagan, 1986). Clear objectives for good performance are helpful as well (Hackman, 1983). Groups also need sufficient autonomy to do their jobs (Glickman et al., 1987; Manz & Sims, 1987). The design of the group task is another important factor. Working on a project from beginning to end, for example, increases effectiveness (Cummings, 1981). Working on tasks that are important and require skill also improves results (Hackman & Oldham, 1980). The design and maintenance of technologies necessary to the task are additional factors related to group effectiveness (Goodman et al., 1988). Organizational responsiveness to group needs for decisions, information, and resources is crucial as well (Bushe, 1986).

Groups need ongoing feedback concerning their performance (Ketchum, 1984; Pritchard et al., 1988). Recognition of a group's contribution to the organization is equally important (Bushe, 1986). Group versus individual reward systems appear to enhance performance (Pritchard et al., 1988). Access to technical and interpersonal training may also improve performance (Hackman, 1983; Manz & Sims, 1987; Poza & Markus, 1980). An organizational culture that values innovation and quality can enhance group effectiveness (Peters & Waterman, 1982). Finally, an organization that is open to being influenced by the group and gives the group consistent messages about its work can facilitate group performance (Bushe, 1986).

These research findings tell us that the total organization has another kind of influence on its member groups, beyond the fact that organizational subsystems tend to conform with the overarching culture that is created. The organization can affect a group's functioning and productivity by providing or withholding resources, training, rewards, feedback, autonomy, goal clarity, appropriate technologies, and other types of support necessary to group goal achievement.

Since organizational groups are dependent on their environment for resources and other inputs necessary for them to function, group success is not simply the product of internal development and processes. Successful groups must deal with their external dependencies and adapt to external demands in order to survive and function effectively. Ancona (1987) stated that groups are not totally controlled by their environment, nor can they totally control that environment. Groups can have some control if they choose to operate in ways that may influence their environment. However, groups that isolate themselves from their environments will have difficulty surviving, since they are dependent on that environment for resources and other kinds of support. Katz (1982) found that groups, in general, have a tendency to become more isolated over time. Communication with others outside the group decreases. As a result, groups are cut off from new ideas and information. The result of this tendency of groups to isolate themselves is diminished performance. Successful groups, then, seem to overcome this isolationist tendency and to actively engage with others in their environment.

Ancona (1987) argued that mature internal group functioning is not enough to ensure group effectiveness. Groups must also engage in external activities as well. These external activities focus on influencing the larger environment in an attempt to acquire needed supports and to gain information regarding environmental demands and changes. Support and information are necessary if the group is to successfully adapt to these environmental conditions. Ancona proposed four key external activities: negotiation, information exchange and scanning, buffering, and profile management.

Negotiation with other groups and individuals external to the group is necessary to secure needed resources. For example, some group members might be designated to serve on interdepartmental committees or to meet with other groups or individuals in an attempt to influence policies concerning such things as organizational distribution of resources or procedural decisions. Negotiation with other groups is also necessary when conflicts arise (Brett & Rognes, 1986).

Information exchange and scanning involves gathering facts and impressions from other parts of the organization in order to determine current and future conditions and their potential impact on the group. These activities help the group to adapt to the environment and to make decisions regarding how to respond to these conditions (Ancona, 1987; Katz & Tushman, 1981; Mintzberg, 1973).

Buffering entails protecting the group from too much external information or pressure (Adams, 1980). Some members may perform the role of sentry or guard to insulate the group from excessive external demands (Gladstein & Caldwell, 1985). Buffering is sometimes necessary, since too much input can destabilize internal group processes (Lyden, 1975). If buffering is used as a strategy for too long, however, it may encourage an isolationist policy and become maladaptive (Staw, Sandelands & Dutton, 1981).

Strategic management and profile management involve communicating with external individuals and groups in order to influence their perceptions of and behaviors toward that group (Adams, 1980; Ancona, 1987). How a group is perceived by other groups in the organization affects the group by either increasing or decreasing the willingness of others to provide resources to or work with that group. Groups can consciously help to shape their image by planning what information they will share with others (Weick, 1980).

These external activities proposed by Ancona (1987) suggest that groups have, if they choose to use it, some power to influence the larger environment to respond positively to them and to support their efforts to be successful. She cautioned, however, that groups have difficulty changing to meet external conditions, due to inertia and natural resistance to change. Therefore, group success may be due to the fact that internal and external group processes and activities match those of the environment. In short, group success may be circumstantial in that the way a group has developed and functions fits with the larger organization and is, therefore, rewarded. Other groups in the same environment may evolve in ways that are not rewarded. It is possible that neither group could consciously change its ways in order to increase the likelihood of surviving in that environment.

In the final analysis, then, groups have less control over the environment than they might like. However, they do have some control. First, groups that manage their internal processes and development well, and function at higher levels of development, will be in a position to respond more appropriately to the external environment. Groups engaged in internal conflict or those that develop isolationist norms will have difficulty managing their relationships with the outside. If there is little internal trust, groups may not be able to delegate authority or responsibility to individual members to act on the group's behalf with outsiders. Groups that are capable of defining goals and roles, planning, and using relevant information regardless of its source increase the likelihood of success. Second, groups that consciously attempt to manage their external relationships will enhance the probability of goal achievement and high performance. No group can completely control its external environment. However, organizations are composed of many groups who mutually influence each other. Some groups, such as top management, have more power than others in the system. However, influence flows in all directions, and groups who maximize their influence in the system have a higher probability of success.

A word of caution is necessary at this point. If groups attempt to increase the likelihood of their own success at the expense of others, their efforts may backfire. Groups within an organization are interdependent. Excessive conflict among organizational subgroups decreases the organization's chances for success. While competition for scarce resources and conflicts among groups are inevitable, the management of such conflicts is crucial to organizational and group survival and success. The next section focuses on intergroup conflict and its management in organizations.

INTERGROUP CONFLICT IN ORGANIZATIONS

For an organization to achieve goals and operate effectively, its member groups must establish and maintain collaborative relationships (Ivancevich & Matteson, 1987). However, conflict among organizational groups is inevitable. Robbins (1974) outlined a number of reasons for the predictable occurrence of conflict among organizational groups. By definition, organizational groups are interdependent. As such, the behavior of one group affects other groups in the system. If, for example, the unit or group that is responsible for purchasing materials is behind schedule, the group responsible for assembling the product will also fall behind schedule. This in turn will affect the schedule of the shipping unit, which will delay payments received. Arguments and conflicts among these groups are the result.

Groups may have different goals, and these goals can be in conflict. A group responsible for the quality of a product, for example, has as its goal reducing the number of defective products that reach consumers. Such a group will want to carefully monitor production. This is likely to delay the schedule of the group or groups responsible for production. Since the goal of the production unit is to meet quotas, and the goal of the quality group is to enforce high standards, conflict between these groups, due to their competing goals, is very likely. In addition, the total organization may reward the production group for speed and the quality group for accuracy and error reduction. The way an organization rewards different groups can exacerbate competition and conflict among them.

No organization has unlimited resources. Typically, management groups have to decide how to allocate the organization's resources. Some groups' goals, tasks, efficiency levels, and other factors will lead the allocators of resources to increase their share of available funds, personnel, equipment, and other important resources. As a result, other groups will receive less. This reality adds to feelings and incidents of competitiveness among groups.

Differences in group members' roles often create different perceptions of tasks. For example, electrical engineers often have a different vision of a project than mechanical engineers have. In order to be successful, however, both groups must agree on the job's specifications. In similar fashion, administrators may see a task in terms of cost containment, and scientists may see a need for extensive research that will increase costs. These differences in perception based on professional identity are another source of intergroup conflict. Status differences among groups can be another potential source of conflict. For example, if the doctors' view of surgical scheduling differs from the nurses', conflict is more likely than compromise, since both groups may feel that power and status will be lost through compromise (Ivancevich & Matteson, 1987; Robbins, 1974).

Finally, developmental processes within the organization will cause conflicts among groups. As with smaller systems, organizations during their formation, and cyclically thereafter, experience conflicts as they try to articulate the content of their culture and social structure.

Schein (1980) outlined the consequences of intergroup conflict within a group engaged in conflict and between groups involved in a conflict. For a group involved in conflict with another group or groups, intragroup cohesion and loyalty tend to increase. Internal differences among members are deemphasized and conformity increases. The group's focus on task increases and attention to maintenance or socio-emotional issues decreases. The group leader tends to become more autocratic, and the group becomes more structured and organized. In a sense, intragroup relations improve during a conflict with another group or groups. Members circle the wagons in order to repel a perceived attack from another group. Intragroup issues and problems are set aside so that the group can focus all its attention on surviving the conflict and winning the dispute.

Groups engaged in conflict tend to decrease communication with each other. There is increased hostility toward and stereotyping of the other group. The groups' perceptions of each other become distorted, and the other group is increasingly seen as the enemy. Both groups tend to listen to each other less as a result. Schein (1980) stated that the consequences of intergroup conflict described here are the same for organizational groups and departments and even nations engaged in disputes.

The negative consequences of intergroup conflict do not necessarily end when the conflict is over. If there are perceived winners and losers in a dispute, the internal group functioning of both winners and losers can be adversely affected even after the dispute is settled (Schein, 1980). The group that wins tends to maintain or increase its level of cohesion, and tension among group members tends to decrease. However, the winning group may become complacent and less task oriented. Motivation to improve its functioning may also decrease. Schein (1980) stated that winning groups tend not to learn much as a result of winning.

Losing groups often act as if they did not lose. Tension among group members increases and internal support decreases. Such groups look for scapegoats to blame the loss on. An outsider will be blamed if possible. If not, internal conflicts increase. Losing groups continue to compete with other groups. For them the intergroup conflict is not over. A battle may have been lost, but there is still a war to be won. As a result, losing groups tend to become more task oriented and motivated to improve (Schein, 1980). Both winners and losers, then, suffer losses in terms of internal group functioning as a result of intergroup conflict.

There are other kinds of consequences that result from intergroup conflict. There are transaction costs (Brett, Goldberg & Ury, 1990). These costs refer to the money, time, and emotional energy expended during a conflict. If the outcome of a dispute is not perceived as fair or does not meet the needs of the groups involved, motivation and productivity may be affected. Prolonged conflict may negatively impact the groups' abilities to work together on a daily basis. Also, depending on the outcome of a dispute, it may reoccur, adding to the overall costs of the conflict.

Conflicts can also lead to innovation and progress (Kilmann & Thomas, 1978). If differences are resolved, new perceptions, positive changes in organizational structure, increased cooperation, and increased productivity may result (Brett et al., 1990). As is true of intragroup conflict, intergroup conflict, if successfully managed, can lead to positive changes in cooperation, coordination, and productivity.

Intergroup conflict is inevitable (Alderfer, 1987). Such conflicts have the potential to be destructive or constructive for both the organization and the disputing groups. Three general strategies have been proposed to increase the likelihood of constructive outcomes: (1) reducing the number of intergroup conflicts in order to better manage those that do occur (Ivancevich & Matteson, 1987; Schein, 1980); (2) developing procedures in advance to decrease the costs of conflicts that do occur (Brett et al., 1990); and (3) working to create cooperative systems that will be more capable of managing the intergroup conflicts that inevitably arise (Deutsch, 1990b).

In order to reduce the number of intergroup conflicts that occur in organizations, Schein (1980) suggested that superordinate goals should be emphasized. If disputing groups can be made aware of the fact that they share goals in common, resolution of disputes is easier. For example, if two departments in an organization are fighting over resources, and they are made aware of the fact that the ultimate goal is the achievement of organizational goals, conflict may decrease and both departments may seek cooperative rather than competitive solutions.

Other methods to reduce the incidence of intergroup conflict include attempting to increase communication and interaction between organizational groups by rotating members among groups, or restructuring the organization. Avoiding win-lose situations through such things as expanding the resources available to groups or encouraging compromise can also reduce conflict. Identifying a common enemy may help to reduce tension and focus groups on collaboration (Ivancevich & Matteson, 1987; Schein, 1980).

Given that intergroup conflicts are inevitable, Brett, Goldberg, and Ury (1990) suggest that systems for resolving disputes should be in place in organizations and those systems should be prepared to handle conflicts as they arise. If procedures are already in place to manage conflicts as they arise, the costs of conflicts can be reduced and their benefits increased.

A number of principles for dispute system design have been proposed. The first principle deals with prevention. Since conflicts are inevitable, the organization should take care to discuss proposed changes and issues of concern before implementation. If groups are consulted beforehand, the likelihood of future conflict among groups is reduced. Brett, Goldberg, and Ury (1990) also suggest that when a dispute does arise and is resolved, discussion and feedback about the dispute should take place so that the involved parties can learn from their experience. This also helps to prevent future conflicts.

Another important element of a system designed to resolve intergroup conflicts is focusing on resolving conflicts of interest rather than simply trying to resolve the dispute. A focus on interests rather than which group is right or wrong tends to resolve the underlying conflict and prevent a reemergence of the conflict at some later date. Negotiations should be undertaken from a cooperative perspective (Pruitt, 1981). The disputing groups should be encouraged to discuss their interests with each other (Pruitt & Carnevale, 1982). Those acting as negotiators should be trained in methods designed to resolve conflicts of interest as opposed to other negotiation strategies (Fisher & Ury, 1981; Lax & Sebenius, 1986). The use of a mediator has also been found to facilitate the resolution of conflicts of interest (Brett & Goldberg, 1983). Dispute resolution systems should provide for cooling-off periods if needed and should allow time to seek advice from knowledgeable people who are not involved in the current conflict.

If conflicts of interest cannot be resolved, alternative methods of reaching resolution should be built into the system. Brett, Goldberg, and Ury (1990) suggest arbitration and voting as two methods for dispute resolution that can be used if conflicts of interest cannot be reconciled. They suggest a sequence of intervention strategies. That is, prevention efforts should occur first. Negotiation and mediation to resolve conflicts of interest is the next step. If this is unsuccessful, a cooling-off period, or seeking advice from uninvolved parties, would be undertaken. Arbitration and voting are used as a last resort. The authors maintain that approaching resolution in this order decreases the costs of conflict. Earlier intervention strategies are the least costly in terms of time, energy, and emotion. Should they work, costs are contained. Strategies that are more costly and less likely to resolve underlying conflicts are used only if earlier efforts fail.

Brett, Goldberg, and Ury's (1990) work reminds us that preparing for the inevitability of intergroup conflict is wise. If organizations have established procedures that describe the steps to be taken in the event of a conflict, time, money, and emotional energy could be saved. Some organizations do have conflict-resolution procedures in place. Most, however, do not. This is interesting, since intergroup conflict is as common to organizational life as technical system failures, production delays, and other occurrences for which procedures are generally in place. Organization members typically know what to do in case of supply shortages, machine breakdowns, or personnel vacancies. The procedures to follow are outlined, and people have been identified to facilitate the resolution of these kinds of problems. When intergroup conflicts occur, however, people and groups are often at a loss. What should be done? How can the conflict be resolved? What kinds of interventions are likely to work? How should such a conflict be approached? Which group or individuals should be responsible for attempting to resolve the conflict? If such questions had been dealt with at an earlier time, the length and cost of conflict situations might be reduced. If conflict-resolution procedures were reviewed on a regular basis, their effectiveness might be increased over time. That conflict-resolution processes and procedures are not part of the structure of most organizations attests to our lack of awareness of group and social processes and their impact on organizational viability and effectiveness.

Finally, Deutsch (1990a) proposes that organizations should be designed intentionally to increase cooperation and equality among groups and individuals. Rather than advocating simply increasing discussion with organizational groups prior to enacting changes, Deutsch is suggesting that radical changes in the structure of organizations would reduce the number of intergroup conflicts and would have other beneficial consequences as well. Specifically, Deutsch's own research and that of many others suggests that while intergroup conflict is inevitable, the quantity and intensity of such struggles may be due to the competitive, hierarchical culture and design of most organizations. Cooperative organizational structures have been found to be more productive, friendlier places to work, and more conducive to good mental health and high self-esteem (Deutsch, 1985; Johnson & Johnson, 1989). Hierarchical organizations produce less motivation, trust, cooperation, and positive views of leaders (Katz, Kahn & Adams, 1980; Likert, 1961; Misumi, 1985; Rinat, 1987). Given that cooperation and equality have demonstrated positive effects on both productivity and organizational climate, it would seem sensible to attempt to fashion organizational cultures with these factors emphasized. In fact, many organizations are attempting to change from competitive/hierarchical to cooperative/egalitarian systems in an effort to reduce intergroup conflict and to increase productivity, motivation, and job satisfaction. However, organizational cultures do not change easily. Much resistance to changes of these types has been encountered. Organizational efforts to change from competitive to cooperative systems have had mixed success. However, the advantages associated with a successful shift to a more cooperative organizational culture continue to make efforts to move in that direction desirable in many organizations.

GROUPS, ORGANIZATIONS, AND SOCIETY

The previous sections dealt with how groups are influenced by and influence the organizations of which they are a part. This is not the end of the story, however. As was stated earlier, organizations and their member groups operate within a particular society and, in the current time period, can be influenced by socio-cultural phenomena that transcend national boundaries. Most group and organizational theory and research ignore this fact. As a result, ideas and concepts concerning the functioning of organizations and groups may be misleading, since many powerful forces that shape organizations and their member groups are hidden from view. In order to avoid presenting the reader with a limited perspective, the next sections briefly sketch the terrain of the cultural contexts in which organizations function.

Culture Defined

The concept of culture has been discussed throughout this book as it relates to individual group culture and organizational culture. Group culture is nested in organizational culture. Organizational culture is nested in larger cultural contexts as well. Occupational, regional, national, and international cultural elements are all examples of larger contexts that influence and are influenced by a particular organization and its member groups. In this sense, organizations are cultural phenomena, not just places for the development of unique organizational cultures. That is, organizations are themselves a manifestation or product of larger cultural contexts (Czarniawska-Joerges, 1991).

Modern societies, particularly Western ones, are organized societies. The way in which we meet basic needs is increasingly through the development of large-scale organizations. Currently, organizations are perhaps the most characteristic way of structuring time, activity, and direction. Their existence reflects a perception, shared internationally, that organizations represent a good way, perhaps the best way, to meet human needs and to structure human endeavors. As such, organizations have a special place in the larger cultural contexts of which they are a part. They are one of the main products of macro-level cultural phenomena and, as such, exert considerable influence over the content of the cultures that created them.

Before proceeding, it is important to describe how culture, at the macro level, has been defined. Historically, culture at this level has been equated with national boundaries. Thus, we speak of American culture, Chinese culture, and the like. However, in the age of mass communication, historically unique cultural groups increasingly penetrate each others' boundaries. Cultural elements travel and influence previously distinct cultural regions. Today, it is more accurate to look for individuals, groups, and organizations who share beliefs, values, and ideologies in common.

In this sense, culture has been defined as a way of life (Leach, 1982). Czarniawska-Joerges (1991) defined culture as "a bubble (of meaning) covering the world, a bubble that we both create and live within. Its film covers everything that we turn our eye to; it is . . . the medium of (social) life" (p. 287).

The description of culture as a "thought world" (Douglas, 1986) is very compelling. That is, members of a culture think alike about things. They do not think alike about everything, since there are often areas of ambiguity and different perspectives within a culture (Meyerson, 1991). Core beliefs, however, tend to be shared (Schein, 1991).

How Cultural Phenomena Influence Organizations and Groups

Organizations and their member groups are not closed systems. They are open systems, receiving inputs from the environment, transforming those inputs, and exporting these transformations back to the environment (von Bertalanffy, 1968). Organizations do not exist separately from their cultural environments. Rather, they are part of those environments. For example, one cultural environment to which organizations belong has been described as *the cultural context of organizing* (Czarniawska, 1986; Hofstede & Boddewyn, 1977). The cultural context of organizing refers to organizational and social processes, values, and beliefs regarding what organizations are and how they should be structured. These processes and beliefs have developed over a long period of time. As a result, unique organizational cultures are never totally unique. Rather, they are shaped by the views of this larger context. Other cultural entities—occupational, social, political, national, and international—also influence organizations.

As groups are dependent on the organization for resources, organizations are dependent on larger contexts. They are dependent, for example, on other organizations and institutions for the resources necessary to meet their goals (Pfeffer & Salancik, 1978). Economic, political, and social factors influence both the culture of an organization and its viability or survival. For example, the growing international perception that the world's ecosystem is in jeopardy has significantly affected industrial organizations, especially in parts of the world where this is a strongly held cultural belief. In areas where the belief is not as strong, these organizations are less affected (Graumann & Kruse, 1990). Beliefs of cultural and national groups concerning the value of work as opposed to leisure time also influence work organizations (Strumpel, 1990; Yankelovich, Zetterberg, Shanks & Strumpel, 1985).

How Organizations Influence Cultural Contexts

Some have argued that organizations have little control over the contexts in which they function. Astley and Van de Ven (1983), for example, proposed that either organizations fit a niche in the environment or they are selected out and fail. Others believe that organizations must adapt to changes in the cultural context in order to survive (Romanelli & Tushman, 1986). Still others suggest that organizations can partially control their environments through the use of certain strategies (Pennings, 1980; Van de Ven & Walker, 1984). Finally, some conclude that organizations both shape their cultural context and are shaped by it (Ancona, 1987; Czarniawska-Joerges, 1991).

As with groups that develop an isolationist stand in relation to the organization, organizations that attempt to operate as closed systems frequently do fail or become dysfunctional (Burns, 1977; Himmelweit, 1990). Organizations must adapt to changes in cultural contexts in order to function effectively. This requires scanning the environment and incorporating new cultural values, beliefs, and methods into the organization. Some say scanning is not necessary, since new ideas enter an organization as a result of diffusion (Rogers, 1962; Levitt & March, 1988). Diffusion is a term used to describe how new views spread rapidly among different organizations.

Czarniawska-Joerges (1991) sees the process of incorporating new cultural views as a more conscious one. She proposes that organization members, especially those in high-status positions, are expected to bring progressive ideas and practices to the organization. Consequently, they attempt to determine what is in fashion at the time. Fashion represents societal choices among tastes, ideas, and things. It is an attempt to determine what is typical and representative of a given time period (Blumer, 1973). Not all new ideas or practices, however, are incorporated into every organization. Organizations who have interactions with each other, share information, and have a sense that they belong to the same thought world tend to select similar new ideas and methods from the broader environment (Czarniawska-Joerges, 1991). Organizations within the same industry, for example, would be likely to adopt similar ideas or practices.

Organizations also attempt to control their environments through the use of certain practices. Mergers, acquisitions, joint ventures, and interlocking directorates are examples of strategies to control the environment. An organization that buys a supply company is attempting to control the supply and cost of needed resources. Computer companies that agree to create compatible machines and software are attempting to increase the market share of both organizations. Towns that band together to build a school or manage waste disposal are attempting to hold down costs and potentially improve the quality of education. Organizations often lobby political bodies for laws and policies that will be favorable to their particular organizations or industries.

Because of the special place that commercial organizations have in modern society, there is another way in which they influence larger cultural contexts. They can directly work to change the attitudes and values of larger systems. Sayings like "The business of America is business" and "Progress is our most important product" attest to the success of commercial organizations' efforts to influence larger socio-cultural contexts.

One cannot reasonably conclude that organizations and their member groups have no influence over the larger contexts in which they function. They have considerable influence and actually help to shape the thought worlds around them. On the other hand, they are influenced by these environments as well. Organizations, groups, individuals, cultures, and societies are inextricably linked. For practical reasons, we tend to study them as separate entities. However, in reality they are interdependent and ultimately not divisible. Their fates are inextricably linked.

10

STUDYING GROUPS: WHO, WHAT, WHERE?

By 1959, well over 1300 studies of group dynamics had been conducted (Hare, 1962). Today there are many times that number. And yet, some social scientists have stated that given their importance in the lives of individuals and organizations, groups receive only minimal and episodic attention from researchers (e.g., Back, 1979; Steiner, 1974, 1986; Simpson & Wood, 1992). While more research is called for, the quantity of research is not the only issue of concern. The kinds and quality of previous research studies have been questioned as well (Shaw, 1981; Steiner, 1986).

The purpose of this chapter is to briefly describe the history of group research. Research directions and examples of research questions are posed. Next, issues are discussed concerning what and who should be studied and where group research is conducted.

A BRIEF HISTORY OF GROUP RESEARCH

Generally, research in an area begins as a result of theoretical or philosophical writings that stimulate interest in exploring a particular phenomenon. Group research is no exception. In the nineteenth century, attention was focused on the influence of the group and society on the individual. Le Bon (1895) wrote about the effect of the crowd on individuals. Le Bon's ideas led to a line of research that continues to the present day (e.g., Gaskell, 1990; Moscovici, 1985). Triplett (1898) studied the effect of the presence of others on individual performance. This research line has also continued and is represented in the work of Zajonc (1965), Harkins and Petty (1982), and Harkins and Szymanski (1987).

Durkheim (1895) argued that studying individuals alone would not help us to understand social phenomena, since social processes are different from psychological processes. He proposed that a group, organization, or society "is not identical to a sum of its parts, it is something else with different properties than those presented by the parts of which it is composed" (p. 126). Durkheim (1897) went on to demonstrate the interdependence of individual and societal processes by studying rates of suicide in different European countries. He found that the level of societal cohesion predicted national rates of suicide, thus showing the influence of social forces on individual behavior.

Cooley (1902, 1909) also put forward his view of human nature and social organization. He proposed that the concept of the individual as a separate entity was an abstraction that does not occur in reality. The individual and society are inextricably linked. Trotter (1916) wrote of the influence and power of the group. Allport (1920) studied the influence of the group on association and thought. Studies of conformity and group pressure (e.g., Asch, 1951; Milgram, 1964) have also continued.

In the 1930s, Lewin (1936) and Mead (1934) primed the research pump by providing further theoretical concepts to explore. Murphy, Murphy, and Newcomb (1937) also contributed by emphasizing the influence of social systems on individual behavior. Lewin, Lippitt, and White (1939) followed by demonstrating that rates of aggressive behavior are influenced by different social climates (for example, laissez-faire, democratic, or autocratic). *The Psychology of Social Norms* (Sherif, 1936) was also instrumental in stimulating interest in the study of group and social processes. Group research began in earnest during this period.

World war in the 1940s slowed research efforts but stimulated scientific interest even further. Social norms, pressures to conform, the increase in aggressive behaviors in certain social environments, and the influence of leaders on followers were all being acted out on the world stage. Studying group, organizational, and societal processes began to be seen as crucial to the establishment and maintenance of a peaceful world.

During this period, Lewin (1943) demonstrated that individual attitudes are more readily changed in a group. Near the end of the decade, Deutsch (1949a, 1949b) began a lifetime of studies on the effects of cooperation and competition on group processes and productivity. By the end of the 1940s, group research was seen as a legitimate area of study. Emery (1990) stated that it is difficult to describe the drive and intensity of this period. The social sciences emerged from the war with an agenda focused on understanding social processes in the hope of intervening in human affairs to ensure that the chaos and atrocities of the war never happened again. According to Emery, the manifesto for that agenda was contained in Lewin's article "Frontiers in Group Dynamics" (1947a, 1947b, 1951). The article created a sense in social scientists that knowledge of group processes could serve human ends by improving the quality of group and social life.

The next decade was a time of intense exploration of group structures and processes. Fueled by the publication in 1951 of Lewin's *Field Theory in Social*

Science, a number of research programs and individual studies were begun. This work, edited by Cartwright, was published after Lewin's untimely death. Others were left to carry on his work. The 1950s were some of the most productive years for the study of groups. Bales (1950) was instrumental in facilitating the research process. He developed an observation system, known as Interaction Process Analysis, which made it possible to categorize member interaction in groups. This method, still much in use today, led to insights concerning communication patterns in groups and how member roles are established. Studies of group development began in this decade (Bales & Strodtbeck, 1951; Bennis & Shepard, 1956; Martin & Hill, 1957). The impact of structural communication networks on productivity and group satisfaction was initially explored by Bavelas (1948) and Leavitt (1951). This led to thirty years of research on this topic.

Almost every aspect of group structure and processes was investigated during this decade. In addition to communication structures and group development, leadership (e.g., Anderson, 1959; Argyle et al., 1958; Bass et al., 1953; Stogdill, 1950), member characteristics, status, and roles (e.g., Gross et al., 1958; Merton & Kitt, 1950), group goals and tasks (e.g., Borgatta & Bales, 1953; Raven & Rietsema, 1957), norms, conformity, and deviation (e.g., Asch, 1951, 1955; Bovard, 1953; Crutchfield, 1955; Kelley & Shapiro, 1954; Schacter, 1951), conflict and cohesion (e.g., Coser, 1956; Pepitone & Kleiner, 1957), coalitions (e.g., Caplow, 1959; Vinacke & Arkoff, 1957), group climate (e.g., Exline, 1957), and to a lesser extent decision making and problem solving (e.g., Hirota, 1953; Marquart, 1955) were explored. It was an exciting time period and stimulated further theoretical work as well (e.g., Bion, 1959; Heider, 1958; Lewin, 1951; Schacter, 1959; Schutz, 1958; Sullivan, 1953).

With all the studies generated during the fifties, one would assume that group research would have flourished in the sixties. While much research was conducted during this decade, there was (and is) a perception that interest and enthusiasm for group-level research declined at this time (Back, 1990; Simpson & Wood, 1992). One explanation for the decline was the triumph of the individual as the unit of analysis in the social sciences (Farr, 1990; Graumann, 1986). Also, the interdisciplinary nature of group research did not fit into the career-oriented specialties emerging in universities at the time (Back, 1990). The paucity of theory and solid, practical research methods and statistical procedures for studying groups are thought to have contributed to the decline as well (Emery, 1990; Jones, 1985; Steiner, 1974, 1986). Finally, research on groups, especially in naturalistic settings, was very difficult and time consuming. All of these factors contributed to a decline in group research.

But studies did continue during the 1960s in such promising areas as conformity and deviation, cooperation and competition. Hare (1962) published a book that documented previous group research. However, theoretical writings and models decreased in number and identifiable research programs diminished. Individuals in a number of different fields continued the work, but in relative isolation.

Relatively little theory building occurred during the 1970s. A number of books were published that summarized previous research findings (e.g., Hare,

1976; Shaw, 1976; Stogdill, 1974). However, they failed to stimulate renewed interest in groups per se. As in the previous decade, research was conducted. However, the focus of the work turned more to outcomes for individuals as a result of group participation rather than to understanding group processes and dynamics. That is, basic research that attempted to understand how groups function was increasingly replaced by applied research that focused on how particular aspects of group structure affected cohesion and productivity (e.g., Anderson, 1975; Frank & Anderson, 1971; Hackman & Morris, 1975; Hackman et al., 1976; Ingham et al., 1974).

Studies of group development actually increased during the seventies (e.g., Adelson, 1975; Babad & Amir, 1978; Braaten, 1974/1975; Caple, 1978; Hill, 1974; Hill & Gruner, 1973; LaCoursiere, 1974; Near, 1978). The flurry of studies during this time may have been stimulated by Tuckman's (1965) model of group development. Based on investigations of group development that had been conducted prior to publication of this article, Tuckman proposed a theoretical model of group development. Increased research efforts followed. This highlights the relationship between theory and research. Theories and concepts tend to stimulate researchers' curiosity. They also serve to guide research directions. In their absence, research investigations often decline in number.

Two other areas of research emerged in the 1970s that were conducted in groups but were only tangentially related to groups. Desegregation and race relations during this period led to a number of investigations focused on identifying factors that increased intergroup cooperation (e.g., Amir, 1976; Blanchard & Cook, 1976; Cohen & Roper, 1972; Cook, 1978). These studies used group variables such as status and cooperation. However, the aim was not to understand these variables further but to identify the effects of their presence or absence on interracial relations among group members.

The second area of research conducted in groups during the seventies investigated sex differences in communication patterns (e.g., Aries, 1976; Bartol & Butterfield, 1976; Chapman, 1975; Eskilson & Wiley, 1976; Maier, 1970). This line of inquiry, stimulated by the emergence of feminism, focused on determining the presence or absence of sex differences in the behaviors of group members. Again, the medium for research was the group, but the majority of studies did not investigate the effect of gender composition on group processes, structure, or development. In general, the group was the context for, not the focus of, the research.

The decline in group theory and research during the seventies prompted a number of discursive articles attempting to explain why the decline had occurred and what could be done to regenerate interest in this important area. An entire issue of the *Journal of Applied Behavioral Science* (1979) was devoted to answering these questions. This special issue, edited by Lakin, was entitled "What has happened to the small group?" A few years earlier, another article entitled "What ever happened to the group in social psychology?" (Steiner, 1974) had been published in the *Journal of Experimental Social Psychology*. Clearly, there was considerable concern over the state of group research and theory.

In the eighties, groups became teams. Increased international economic competition led to a reassessment of the role of work teams in attaining organizational goals. Efforts to create high-performance work teams became a central concern. Research studies proliferated as a result (e.g., Bassin, 1988; Cummings, 1981; Galagan, 1986; Gladstein & Caldwell, 1985; Goodman et al., 1988; Manz & Sims, 1987; Shea & Guzzo, 1987a, 1987b). These studies tended to focus on group factors that affect productivity rather than on basic group processes and development. As always, basic research on group structure, processes, and development continued, but at lower levels.

In 1981, Shaw published the third edition of *Group Dynamics: The Psychology of Small Group Behavior.* In this volume, he criticized previous group research. Shaw's critique of group research that had been conducted through the 1970s provided a partial explanation for the decline in basic research in this area. Shaw maintained that the field suffered from an overemphasis on laboratory research. That is, much of the research was conducted in university laboratories, where participants met as a group for the purpose of the study. These were ad hoc groups whose members did not have a history of working together as a group. Laboratory studies make it possible for researchers to control the situation by selecting certain kinds of subjects, tasks, seating arrangements, and many other factors. Studies of this type produce results that are clear and easy to interpret. However, the real world of naturally occurring groups is not a controlled environment. Consequently, results based on laboratory groups may not generalize to natural group settings. Steiner (1986) also criticized reliance on laboratory and experimental studies, since they limit the kinds of questions that can be asked.

Shaw also criticized the fact that groups were studied in isolation. Intragroup processes were the focus of study. Again, however, in the real world, natural groups are affected by other groups in their environment and by the organizations and institutions in which they are operating. He also argued that theories were lacking. By the end of the 1970s, thousands of studies of group processes had been conducted. However, theories that attempted to interpret and integrate these findings had not been forthcoming. As a result, we knew more than we understood. Finally, Shaw criticized the field for not applying results to the real world of social problems. To that point in time, little effort had been made to apply what we had learned to the resolution of intragroup or intergroup problems in natural groups.

In some senses, the direction of current research might be pleasing to Shaw in that more studies are being conducted on natural groups, especially in the workplace. More attention is being paid to natural groups and to the context that surrounds them. However, the research focus is primarily on what makes groups productive rather than how groups function in the more general sense. It is as if we believe that we know how groups operate and consequently have set about attempting to improve their effectiveness and productivity. This seems to be quite a leap of faith. There is considerably more to learn about basic group dynamics and development. This point was underscored by Sundstrom, DeMeuse, and Futrell (1990). They concluded that developmental processes in natural groups remain poorly understood. Until basic research on naturally occurring work groups is done, for example, it will be difficult to understand work-team effectiveness or to assist teams in becoming more effective. The influence of other groups and the organizational or institutional context on a group's dynamics and development also remain to be explored. In short, before we jump to fix something, we have to know what is broken. This requires more basic research on natural groups, with attention paid to the environments in which they are operating.

This brief history of group research seems to suggest a rather dark future for the area, and some would agree that the future is not very bright (e.g., Steiner, 1986). However, there are signs and developments that lead to a much more optimistic conclusion. First, the stranglehold that individualistic viewpoints have had on the social sciences is weakening. Significant challenges to this position are being mounted in all the social sciences (e.g., Cahoone, 1988; Gergen & Gergen, 1988; Harre, 1984; Himmelweit & Gaskell, 1990; Moscovici, 1990; Tajfel, 1984). Also, organizational psychology has become increasingly aware of the role of culture in organizations (e.g., Frost et al., 1992; Schein, 1990). Given that the group has been described as the basic organizational building block (Caplow, 1983; Schein, 1980), it will be difficult to understand organizations without a fuller understanding of group and intergroup processes.

Another sign that a resurgence of interest in group research is occurring is that the relevance of group research to the amelioration of pressing social problems is becoming clear. The interest in work groups as a way to increase economic viability is evident. The relevance of effective classroom groups to learning outcomes is being rediscovered. A number of researchers are working in this area (e.g., Johnson, 1980; Johnson & Johnson, 1989). The efficacy of group treatment for addictions and mental health issues is also clear (e.g., Altman & Plunkett, 1984; Fuhrmann & Washington, 1984a, 1984b; Yalom, 1983). Ongoing research on groups is being conducted in social psychology, education, business, political science, clinical and counseling psychology, economics, and sociology. This growing awareness of the power of groups, for good or for ill, on individuals, organizations, and societies suggests that the future of group research is assured.

An additional positive development for group research is much more practical. Many social scientists may have avoided studying groups because of the tremendous difficulties involved. In 1974, Steiner said that "no graduate student in his right mind would have elected to undertake a thesis that might have kept him busy until his own children were graduate students, especially when there were lots of easier projects that could be completed in a few months and be sanctioned by a journal editor" (p. 102). Before general access to good audiovisual equipment, group observation was extremely problematic. Trained observers could capture some interactions. However, once the group was over, findings could not be checked for accuracy. Also, the presence of visible observers may have altered group activity to some extent. Videotape equipment and tape recorders have been available for many years. However, their quality and cost were problematic until recently. The availability of personal computers has also made group research easier. Transcribing taped sessions for further analysis was cost prohibitive in the past. Now research teams can transcribe tapes themselves. This work is still very tedious, but the technology already exists to transcribe audiotapes directly from machine to machine.

Finally, while theories and models are still lacking, some have been forthcoming. Theoretical perspectives on intergroup relations have been proposed (Brewer & Kramer, 1985; Tajfel, 1981). Ancona (1987) offered a way to understand how groups are influenced by and influence the organizations in which they are operating. New models of group development are available to be tested (e.g., Worchel, Coutant-Sassic & Grossman, 1992). This book attempts to integrate previous research in ways that could provide guidance for future study. In short, optimism and interest are on the rise. This important, often neglected social phenomenon is becoming once more a legitimate and valued area of study.

CHOOSING WHAT TO STUDY

Research begins with a question or set of questions. Of course, human beings do not always approach things in such a logical way. For example, it is not unusual for graduate students to respond to a query concerning the topic of their proposed research project by stating what method they want to use, or do not want to use, rather than to state the question they hope to answer. But since form should follow function, the design of a research project should be selected based on its perceived usefulness in answering a specific question or set of questions. Questions also have a logic to them. That is, it would be difficult to answer a question concerning the impact of classroom learning groups on individual academic achievement without asking some prior questions. For example, one would want to know whether all learning groups operate in the same way. What developmental processes occur in learning groups? Does the membership composition of learning groups affect outcomes?

If a researcher were to sidestep these questions and attempt to determine whether the use of learning groups affects achievement, the results would be difficult to understand. In a particular study, for example, the use of learning groups might be found to positively affect individual academic achievement. But questions would remain. Would another set of learning groups produce the same result? What happened in these particular groups? What dynamics and developmental processes occurred? What role did the teacher play in the outcome? In our results-oriented society, we rush to apply our findings to the real world. Sometimes, however, we jump too quickly and end up finding out things that we do not understand. Research is a slow process of discovery.

In order to talk about different ways to conduct group research, then, we need to outline the questions to be answered. Identifying all the possible questions in the field of group research would be a book in itself. For the purposes of this chapter, then, discussion is limited to a specific set of questions concerning group development. Other areas of inquiry into group processes could have been chosen as well. Any number of topic areas could serve to illustrate the processes, methods, and issues involved in conducting group research. Given the focus of this book, however, questions concerning group development seem the logical choice.

FORMULATING QUESTIONS

In 1981, Shaw, on the basis of his review of previous research, stated what he concluded was a plausible hypothesis concerning group development. The hypothesis was as follows: "Group development follows a reasonably consistent pattern that involves a period of orientation, resolution of conflicts about authority and personal relations, and a productive period" (p. 116).

It is important to note that Shaw did not state a conclusion, since to do so would imply that the statement was fact. Rather, he posed an **hypothesis,** which in the sciences is an assumption based on a careful reading of previous theory and research. An hypothesis is actually a question phrased in the form of a statement. If there had been no previous research in this area, the question would have been: "Do groups go through consistent phases of development?" Shaw's hypothesis indicates that there is sufficient evidence to assume that groups do go through consistent developmental patterns, but not yet enough evidence to conclude that all groups do. The question in this case is: "Do all groups go through consistent patterns of development?"

An hypothesis indicates that more research is needed before conclusions are drawn. Shaw's hypothesis also indicates that this would be a good direction for future research. That is, future research based on this hypothesis will not lead the researcher down a blind alley. In all probability, the findings will support the hypothesis and help us to clarify the statement even further. For example, the next researcher might find that the pattern posed by Shaw is true in certain types of groups but is slightly different in other types of groups. This finding would require a reformulation of the original hypothesis, which would lead to further studies.

Shaw based his hypothesis on a **review of the literature** related to this question. Specifically, he cited studies by Bales and Strodtbeck (1951), Bennis and Shepard (1956), Near (1978), Schutz (1966), Tuckman (1965), and Winter (1976) to support this hypothesis. Other social scientists also have reviewed and evaluated the quality of previous research on group development and would agree with Shaw's hypothesis (e.g., Cissna, 1984; Kuypers, Davies & Glaser, 1986; Yalom, 1975).

If there is so much evidence of the existence of developmental patterns in groups, why is the statement still an hypothesis and not a conclusion? This brings up the nature of scientific proof. Absolute proof would require us to study all groups operating all over the world in order to conclude that all groups develop in the same way. Since this is impossible, proof, in any science, requires instead an accumulation of evidence until no one, or very few people, would disagree with the conclusion. While many people have already concluded that groups do experience consistent patterns of development, not everyone is thoroughly convinced. For example, some argue that there have been more investigations of training and therapy groups than of other types of groups (Heinen & Jacobson, 1976; Moreland & Levine, 1988). Until more studies are conducted with other types of groups, then, it would not be safe to conclude that group developmental patterns are universal. Cissna (1984) recommended that before conclusions are drawn, more studies need to be conducted of developmental processes in groups operating in different contexts, with different tasks, and different member compositions. Another concern among researchers is that studies have utilized many different methods to investigate group development. This has both positive and negative consequences. The fact that different methods of analysis have produced similar results can be viewed as positive and as further evidence of the strength of the findings. However, the lack of methodological consistency makes careful comparisons among studies more difficult.

More questions need to be answered before we can make final judgments in this area. It is fairly safe to conclude that consistent group developmental patterns exist in groups. However, we need to know more before we conclude that these patterns are consistent in all groups. Specifically, previous work suggests that the following questions need to be addressed:

1. Do groups operating within the same context, with different tasks, have consistent patterns of development?
2. Do groups operating in different contexts, with the same task, have consistent patterns of development?
3. Do groups operating within the same context, with the same task, but with different member compositions have consistent patterns of development?
4. Do groups operating in different contexts, with the same task, but with different member compositions have consistent patterns of development?

In these research questions, the term *task* is used. The **task** of a group may influence group developmental processes. In comparing groups, then, it is necessary to determine whether the groups are working on the same or different tasks. Generally, what researchers mean by task is really a combination of the group's goal and the characteristics of the activities necessary for goal achievement. A major criticism of research on group development has been that much of the research was conducted with training or therapy groups. The goal of therapy groups, for example, is to effect change in the attitudes, behaviors, or emotions of individuals. The goal of a work team might be to build a house. The issue for research is whether the dynamics and developmental processes of groups with such different goals are the same or different. Goal achievement would be measured differently in these two types of groups. In studies that attempt to determine the effectiveness of different group therapy models, effectiveness is generally measured by the percentage of group members whose psychological and interpersonal functioning is improved as a result of participating in a particular type of therapy group. If the therapy group contains members with addiction problems, an effective group is one with a high percentage of members who remain drug free as a result of group participation. Goal achievement for the team building the house would be measured by quite different criteria. The quality of the finished product, the time it took to build it, and the cost of building it would be evaluated to determine the effectiveness of the work team.

Not only are the goals of therapy and work groups different, but the tasks necessary to accomplish the goals are also different. In Chapter 7, the characteristics of tasks were discussed (e.g., Steiner, 1972). **Group tasks** are the work that a group must do to accomplish its goal. The tasks of a work group building a house are divisible. That is, the tasks can be broken down into subtasks that can be accomplished by an individual or a subgroup. From the perspective of a psychologist who is leading a therapy group, tasks are also divisible in that members may be working on different personal issues in the group, and members will perform different roles and tasks that may contribute to group effectiveness. But from the perspective of an individual member, therapy group tasks are unitary in that the individual is focused on personal goals and the tasks that he or she must accomplish in order to accomplish those goals. Theoretically, the individual could complete his or her tasks and accomplish his or her personal goals whether other members did so or not. The degree of task coordination among members that is necessary for goal achievement is also different in these two contexts. The level of group structure and organization necessary to build a house is higher than in the therapy group. The product is external and requires planning and coordinated actions on the part of members. In the therapy group, the product is internal to the individual member, and goal achievement does not typically occur on a schedule.

Many theories and models of group development include a work phase. This phase has been described as a period in which the group is actively engaged in task and goal accomplishment (e.g., Tuckman, 1965; Tuckman and Jensen, 1977). In order to study groups, then, it is critical to know what a group's goals and tasks are. Without a clear understanding of the goals and tasks of a group, it would be impossible to identify the work phase. Studies have identified a work phase in both therapy and workplace groups (e.g., Hare, 1967, 1982; Stiles et al., 1982). The definition of work in these studies is not the same, however. In a therapy group, for instance, a member is working when he or she discusses a personal problem he or she is having with his or her mother if that problem is related to his or her therapy goals. If a member of a workplace team were to discuss a similar personal problem, that would not be work since, in all probability, such a discussion would not relate to the work group's goal.

The issue of concern for research, then, is to be able to define group goals and tasks clearly. Without a clear definition of a group's goals and tasks, it would be impossible to know when a group is working and when it is not. This is also an important issue if the study is comparing the developmental processes of a number of groups. For example, if the developmental processes of four groups were observed and differences among them were found, it would be difficult to know the reasons for the differences if the goals and tasks of the groups were not clearly defined. Development may vary even among groups operating within the same context, with similar members but different tasks. As a result, all studies of group development and other dynamics need to pay careful attention to the goals and tasks of the investigated groups. In field research, it is usually difficult to gain access to natural groups who are working on the same goals and tasks. This makes it even more imperative to sufficiently describe the goals and tasks of all investigated groups.

DETERMINING WHERE TO CONDUCT THE STUDY

Another thing to consider in thinking about how to answer the questions outlined above is the **context** in which the groups are operating. Defining what is meant by context will have implications for the proposed research. For example, the context in which the group is operating could mean the institutional affiliation of the group members. If all members of the investigated groups were teachers or all members were police officers, the institutional context of the groups would be the same. This might be an interesting study. However, context may be defined too broadly, since group members could be drawn from a number of schools or police districts that might have distinct organizational cultures. This might jeopardize the study by making results difficult to interpret. In addition, groups formed in this way would be naïve groups in that they had never worked together before. If participants were randomly selected from personnel lists of a number of schools that were asked to participate in the study, another problem emerges. Groups assembled in this way may not function in the same way as groups operating within schools. A number of researchers have suggested that member anticipation of future interaction influences group processes (Katz, 1978; Shapiro, 1975; Worchel, Lind & Kaufman, 1975). The way group development occurs in a laboratory may not generalize to real settings.

Already, a few things have become clear. The definition of the word *context* must be narrowed, and participants should be members of the same organization. Also, it will probably be best to use actual groups that meet as part of the regular work responsibilities of their members. If the goal is to avoid the mistakes of **laboratory studies,** such as assembling groups only for the purpose of research and not worrying about the institutional and organizational affiliations of study participants, these decisions seem best. However, laboratory research on human groups has advantages. The researcher has more control over who is in the group and what occurs during the investigation, but results may not be typical of natural groups. Choosing to do **field research,** that is, to study groups in their natural settings, avoids this problem, but has other disadvantages. For example, it is more difficult to study initial phases of group development due to the problems involved in locating and gaining access to such groups from their first meeting. Also, even within the same organization, there may be subcultural differences among various departments. It would be best, then, to define context even more narrowly and investigate groups within a particular department, or at least within the same building in the case of a large organization. Timing becomes a factor as well. Organizational theory suggests that groups operating within the same context will be similar at the same point in time because the groups will be subject to the same forces operating in the larger system. This suggests that developmental processes could vary among groups from the same department when observation occurs at different periods of time. Therefore, ideally, it would be best to study a number of groups operating within a particular department during the same period of time.

DETERMINING WHO TO STUDY

In a laboratory setting, a researcher could select participants on the basis of certain criteria, such as sex, age, intelligence, and the like. This would be done to ensure that the personal characteristics, or **member composition,** of a group does not account for the results of the study. The researcher could also select participants at random from a large pool of possible participants. The assumption underlying random assignment is that if members are assigned to groups in this way, their personal characteristics are less likely to influence the study results. While this makes results easier to interpret, it is not the way our social world operates. People are not randomly selected to be police officers or teachers, for example. They are selected because of their personal characteristics and similarity of experience. As a result, the design of a field study will have to take into account member composition in some way. At minimum, participants' ages, sex, occupations, and other characteristics that might influence study results should be obtained.

What all this means is that the potential researcher will need to find a location for the investigation that meets the following requirements: (1) an organizational unit housed in one building or one department within an organization, (2) that has several work groups meeting during the same period of time, (3) that contains members who are willing to participate in the study (preferably from the group's beginning), (4) who are willing to fill out questionnaires about themselves and about the group or their reactions to the group, and (5) who are willing to allow themselves to be observed by outsiders while they attempt to do their jobs.

It is easy to see why more laboratory research has been done with college classroom groups and training and therapy groups than with work groups. College students are a captive audience. Training and therapy groups are studied frequently, since participants tend to be more amenable to participation. This may also explain why military groups have been studied quite a bit. Military groups are also a captive audience. It is much more difficult to gain the participation of civilian work groups who would be required to spend time in the service of science rather than in the completion of work responsibilities. With the growing awareness of the importance of groups or teams in increasing productivity, morale, creativity, and the like, organizations are becoming more willing to collaborate with social science researchers, since findings in this area may be helpful to these organizations. However, it is incumbent on researchers to develop research designs that are as unobtrusive as possible and to share study results with participating groups and organizations. If group research is to answer the questions outlined previously, collaborative relationships with natural groups are essential.

Locating groups that are amenable to participation in a research project can be daunting. Suggestions for finding willing participants include the following:

1. *Look for groups that will benefit from participation in the study.* Organizational consultants and trainers work with groups regularly. Members of the organizations that they work for are often willing to participate in research projects because the findings may help them improve the effectiveness of their member groups. Organizational consultants and trainers may be researchers themselves. If not, researchers may be able to negotiate collaborative relationships with consultants and trainers. Consultants and trainers work in a wide variety of organizations. Not only business and social agencies but also community groups such as neighborhood associations, churches and synagogues, political groups, and the like use consultant services. Developing stronger ties between researchers and practitioners would dramatically increase the kinds of groups included in research studies.

2. *Plan research designs in advance and be ready to take advantage of opportunities to do research when they arise.* Recently, a researcher was at a meeting whose purpose was unrelated to research. However, a person at that meeting stated that a task force was being formed to work on developing health-care policies, and the members might be amenable to participating in a research project. The first meeting of the task force was to be held in two weeks. This is a rare and wonderful opportunity. If the researcher has a prepared research design or strategy for conducting group research, he or she can take advantage of such an opportunity to study a natural group from its inception.

3. *Develop collaborative relationships with other researchers and share the data or information that has been obtained.* One of the impediments to group research has been that an individual researcher may not be able to gain access to enough groups to answer a particular research question. Also, even with technological advances, group research is still quite time consuming. Developing collaborative relationships with others engaged in studying groups can solve both of these problems. If each of four researchers, for example, has audiotapes of three groups that met for a minimum of five sessions, collectively they have twelve groups. By sharing the work involved in preparing the data for analysis, each researcher substantially increases the number of groups available to him or her and reduces the amount of time involved. The data can be analyzed in various ways in order to answer several questions, or the same question can be analyzed in different ways. Collaborative relationships are sorely needed in the study of group processes and development. The development of cooperating research teams would significantly speed up our acquisition of knowledge in this area. The advantages and pitfalls of sharing data and ways to do so effectively are currently being discussed more in the social sciences as we attempt to tackle questions that exceed the abilities of isolated individual researchers or research teams (Sieber, 1991).

4. *Consider conducting research on temporary groups and organizations.* Some questions are difficult to answer in longstanding groups, and it is difficult to gain access to groups from their inception. These difficulties limit the kinds of questions that can be asked. Early stages of group development cannot be studied in groups that have been meeting for some time. In order to ask questions about the early phases of group development, then, researchers often resort to laboratory studies. However, there are temporary organizations that form naturally that could be used to collect information regarding early group development or other aspects of group dynamics. One example of a temporary organization that contains groups that meet for specified times is the think tank, which brings together a number of people to discuss specific issues. For another example, working conferences are held by many professional organizations to set policies, review procedures, or deal with any number of other issues. In such settings, groups may meet for a week or two. While it cannot be assumed that these groups are identical to naturally occurring work groups, since they are time limited, they can serve as models. Results from studies in these settings may help us to refine research designs that could be implemented in other kinds of settings as well.

In determining the member composition of study groups, the following guidelines are offered:

1. *In general, natural groups contain members who have been selected on the basis of some external or internal criteria. In field research, it is incumbent on the researcher to determine what those criteria are.*

An employee who is assigned to work on a particular project team was chosen on the basis of some criteria. The individual may have been selected because of special skill or knowledge related to the team's goal. The group may contain members with similar or different areas of expertise. Decisions about who should become a member of the group can be made by people outside the group or by the group itself. Other criteria may be used as well. For example, a research team was engaged in study that required diligent attention to detail and considerable drive on the part of members, since the work was sometimes tedious. In discussing possible new members, the group tried to select people who were like themselves. Members jokingly described themselves as obsessive-compulsive. Differences in how individuals are selected for membership may have no influence on group development. On the other hand, they may. Therefore, it is helpful to determine what selection criteria were employed.

2. *If members of a group chose to belong to that particular group, selection criteria were also employed. Again, the researcher should determine why members chose to belong to that group.*

The reasons why people join groups may or may not influence group development or other group processes under investigation. However, it is best to determine members' reasons for joining the group, since these reasons may help to explain the research findings.

3. *Determine the membership and reference groups of participants.*

The reader will recall that an individual's membership groups are those societal subgroups into which a person is born. Race, sex, and ethnicity are examples of membership groups. Since other research has demonstrated that race, sex, and ethnicity can influence an individual's thoughts, feelings, and behaviors, it is possible that group development is affected by these member characteristics as well. Individuals choose, to some extent, to belong to reference groups, which include occupation or profession, political groups, religious groups, and the like. These, too, can influence attitudes, feelings, and behaviors. Age and income are other factors that may be influential. Determining participants' membership and reference groups may prove helpful in attempting to understand the findings of research. It may also prove useful in comparing the results of a number of field studies.

Given the current state of group research, laboratory research is not recommended. Field studies that investigate natural groups operating in context are generally more useful. In field studies, researchers make no attempt to control or manipulate what is occurring. They simply attempt to describe group processes or development. Natural field experiments are also useful. Such studies take advantage of naturally occurring events. For example, comparisons among groups with different tasks, contexts, leaders of different sexes, or member compositions could be made if natural groups meeting the experiment's requirements can be found.

This chapter outlines the who, what, and where of group research. The initial phases of the research process have been described. The conceptualization of the research question is the first step. This requires that the researcher become very familiar with the theoretical and research literature that is available. A good research question is one that takes the next step in an area of inquiry. In order to know what that step is, one needs to be familiar with the steps that have been taken in the past. Previous research provides a map for the researcher. It outlines what others have investigated, in what contexts, and who the study participants were. It also offers guidance about blind alleys, pitfalls, and successful paths followed by previous researchers.

The map left by previous researchers and theoreticians is not very easy to read. While there are summaries of previous research that help new researchers to understand what others have done, they are usually not detailed enough. They do offer some guidance and alert the new researcher to issues and concerns in a research area. However, they are not a substitute for reading the actual studies in that area, since these contain much more detail. Ultimately, each researcher or research team creates its own map by reading the previous literature, discussing the meaning of that literature with others, and determining the best way to continue exploration in that area.

The chapter also describes the preliminary considerations that every researcher must address in attempting to clarify a research question. Considerations concerning who should be studied and where the study should be conducted are crucial to the ultimate success of a research project. Given the criticisms that have been leveled at laboratory studies with naïve subjects, the consensus among group researchers is that more field studies with natural groups are needed. This does not mean that experiments cannot be done. Lewin, Lippitt, and White's (1939) classic study is an example of field experimentation. However, studies conducted in the field rather than the lab are considered more fruitful. Field research is more difficult in terms of finding willing groups and determining the member composition, group context, and task. It is also more difficult to understand the findings, since it is not always clear what factors contributed to the results. However, field research is more realistic in that it attempts to study naturally occurring social processes rather than attempting to simulate these processes in the lab.

Previous work also suggests that we study groups in context and whenever possible study a number of groups operating within the same context, since they may influence each other and are influenced by the system as a whole. In addition, researchers are urged to pay more attention to the membership and reference group affiliations of participants, since these may influence the functioning of the groups under study.

Shaw (1981) stated that "significant problems must be attacked even if this means using less than perfect research procedures" (p. 451). This author would add that perfect research procedures when applied to groups may not be perfect at all. Perfect research procedures can only be used with groups created in the lab. Such groups bear little resemblance to real groups operating in our messy and imperfect social world. It is these real groups that we seek to understand. A comparison can be made to the study of the social or group behavior of animals other than human beings. The behavior of zoo or domesticated animals is not always the same as that of animals in their natural habitat. Therefore, naturalists study animals in context. Group researchers need to become naturalists as well. Observation of human groups in their natural environments is called for. Imperfect studies of natural groups will increase our understanding in this area much more than perfect studies of unnatural groups.

11

STUDYING GROUPS: HOW?

The collective judgment of social scientists engaged in group research suggests that natural groups should be studied and that careful attention should be paid to the contexts in which they are operating, their member composition, and their goals and tasks. The question, then, is *how* to study group development or other group processes. What methods are available for the study of group development, for example, and which of these methods are the most promising? This chapter addresses these two main questions. While the focus of the discussion is on methods for the study of group development, similar methods are employed in studying other group processes as well.

If one is interested in studying group developmental patterns, there are a number of possible ways to go about it. For example, one strategy would be to periodically ask group members about their impressions of how the group is operating. One could do this in one-to-one interviews outside the group or by interviewing the whole group at the conclusion of a session. Another possibility would be to ask for the impressions of group leaders or of observers who watch the group but do not participate.

Alternatively, one could distribute questionnaires concerning the group to members periodically or after each session. The researcher could develop questionnaires or design instruments specifically to measure group processes or development. Another method might be to ask participants about themselves by administering instruments designed to determine how they relate to group participation and to see if their responses change over the life of the group. Group development could, theoretically, be inferred from the results. Another possibility might be to ask participants to keep journals in which they record their reactions to the group following every session. Analysis of these journals might offer insights into group developmental patterns.

The researcher could also employ observers who would record behaviors or interactions that occur in the group over time. Finally, the researcher could join the group, and by carefully recording his or her observations and trying to understand the behaviors and feelings of members, attempt to determine group developmental patterns. All of these methods, among others, have been utilized in research on group development. Each research methodology is discussed in the following sections of this chapter.

IMPRESSIONS OF LEADERS AND OBSERVERS

Many theories of group development are based on the impressions and experiences of the individuals who generated the theory (e.g., Bennis & Shepard, 1956; Bion, 1961; Caple, 1978). Typically, the theoretician has had considerable experience as a group leader, therapist, or facilitator. As a result of his or her accumulated experience and personal observations of a number of groups, the theoretician formulates general statements to explain these personal observations. This method is a useful way to generate theories and models. The results of this form of impressionistic research are not proof, but may be used as a guide for future research. Formulations of group development derived in this way are typically investigated by others using more rigorous research methods. For example, Bennis and Shepard's (1956) theory of group development was based on the impressions and observations of its creators. In 1978, Babad and Amir conducted research to test the veracity of the theory. They employed an observer rating system similar to those described later in this chapter. Their findings generally supported the theoretical formulation proposed by Bennis and Shepard. In a similar vein, Runkel and associates (1971) conducted research intended to test Tuckman's (1965) model of group development. Their findings lent support to the Tuckman model and led Tuckman to adapt his model to more adequately reflect the research findings (Tuckman & Jensen, 1977).

Leaders' impressions formed the basic research strategy in a study that examined the final phase of group development (Lewis, 1978). The researcher developed a questionnaire by examining previous literature that described the characteristics of the final phase of group development (Garland, Kolodny & Jones, 1965). The questionnaire served as the basis for interviewing sixteen leaders of groups that were ending. The researchers taped the interviews, analyzed their contents, and compared the results to previous descriptions of the termination phase. Finally, Lewis proposed a new description of this phase.

The use of interviews to discover the impressions and observations of leaders can be helpful in furthering our understanding of group development. It is important to keep in mind, however, that only one member of the group is providing information. That member also has a unique role in the group. Leaders and members do not always have the same impressions and observations of a group. Studies of this type would be stronger if all members were asked for input. Finally, while findings from studies using this methodology are helpful, the information is filtered through the thoughts, feelings, and biases of the interviewees. As such, it may or may not accurately reflect developmental patterns. Studies of this type are considered exploratory, since they help researchers to refine their thinking with regard to the questions under investigation. They may also suggest the direction of future investigations. In and of itself, the evidence that such studies provide is not very strong. However, such studies serve a very useful purpose, especially during the early stages of an investigation.

JOURNALS AND BOOKS

Dunphy's (1968) study of two sections of an undergraduate class provides an example of the use of journals or weekly reports written by participants as a method for conducting research on group development. The two classes were conducted utilizing the T-group model. The task of each group was to study behavior occurring within the group itself. Dunphy chose to collect data by asking participants to write weekly reports about the group in which they were members. The reports were limited to 250 words each. Group members were asked to write about (1) their feelings and their effects on others, (2) the motives of group members, (3) things that the group might be avoiding and speculations as to why avoidance was occurring, (4) connections between current and past group behavior, and (5) concepts or theories that might explain current group behavior (p. 202). The reports were analyzed using a computerized content analysis system that reduced the words and phrases to eighty-three categories related to the theory of group development being studied. Changes in the frequency with which these categories appeared over the life of the group were analyzed and compared to the theoretical model under investigation.

Another kind of written material was analyzed in a study by Farrell (1982). He was interested in determining whether phases of group development occurred in groups of artists. He chose to study the Batignolle group of Impressionist painters who were active during the second half of the nineteenth century. Since the group was no longer in existence, Farrell relied on historical studies of the group that had been conducted by Rewald (1973) and material from the 1886 novel, *The Masterpiece,* written by Emile Zola, who had actually observed the group as it existed. Farrell used additional historical accounts of the artists' group as well.

A similar strategy was used to study the Camp David summit of 1978 (Hare & Naveh, 1984). The researchers were not participants or observers at the summit. The data for the study were drawn from biographies of people who had participated in the summit. Some participants were interviewed as well. The thirteen-day conference was divided into five time periods, which were then analyzed to determine how the events that occurred related to Hare's (1982) theory of group development.

Using written reports, historical studies, and novels as methods to explore group development is quite a creative solution. Of course, there are drawbacks as well. Novels are the subjective perceptions of their authors and are not typically written at the time the group actually exists. The accuracy of the author's recollections becomes an issue, as do his or her biases, feelings, and interpretations. Historical studies attempt to be more scientific and accurate. However, such studies are also removed from the actual event in that the researcher is not typically a participant. Studies based on written reports of participants are much closer to the source. Again, however, observations and perceptions are retrospective, although the time between a group session and report writing may have been short. Written reports are also filtered through the participant's internal processes and are subject to that individual's biases and interpretations. The use of written reports assumes, to some extent, that individuals are capable observers and interpreters of their own experience. Perceptions vary widely among individuals, however. Written reports have utility in that the subjective experience of group members is an important aspect of the study of groups. They offer insights into the thoughts and feelings of members as they experience developmental processes in groups. As such, this methodology is quite valuable and provides us with important information. In conjunction with other types of research methods, it has proved useful in increasing knowledge in this area.

QUESTIONNAIRES AND INDIVIDUAL TESTS

Rugel and Meyer (1984) asked fifty-two members of five groups to rate themselves and other members on a number of dimensions related to group development and the value of the group for each participant. The questionnaire was administered at the last session of each group. Responses were analyzed to determine whether there were clusters of similar responses in the data. That is, did members answer subsets of questions in a similar way? The findings suggest that there were clusters or factors that were similar, and these clusters corresponded well with the models proposed by Bion (1959) and Bennis and Shepard (1956). This study does not directly test group development, since members completed the ratings only once. However, the rating instrument could be used to investigate group development if it were administered a number of times over the life of a group. It does provide an example of one strategy to determine member reactions via the use of a questionnaire. The questionnaire, however, asks members to rate each other, not the group. This may be problematic in that it may not reflect member impressions of the group as a whole. The individual focus addresses group patterns indirectly rather than directly.

INSTRUMENTS DESIGNED TO MEASURE GROUP DEVELOPMENT

Given the difficulties involved in research studies with groups, it would be wonderful to have access to an instrument that accurately measures group development at a given point in time. This would significantly speed up the research process by making it unnecessary to employ more labor-intensive methods, such as systematic observation, in order to determine developmental processes. Instead, a researcher could ask group members to complete an instrument designed to assess the group's current developmental patterns. The instrument could be readministered periodically in order to trace developmental patterns.

Of course, developing such an instrument at this stage in our understanding of group development would be quite difficult, since disagreement still exists concerning what the stages of group development are and what the characteristic behaviors of groups during these stages might be. Surprisingly, however, five instruments were located that attempt to directly or indirectly measure group development.

The Team Development Inventory was developed by Jones and published by University Associates in 1982. It was designed for use with work groups in general. The instrument requires each member to rank all members of a particular group on eight dimensions thought to be associated with teamwork. These dimensions are participation, collaboration, flexibility, sensitivity, risk taking, commitment, facilitation, and openness. While the instrument manual suggests an order to the occurrence of these dimensions, it does not really measure group development, since it only investigates the interpersonal dimension of group functioning. Another problematic issue is that during the course of the instrument's development, no attention was paid to reliability. An instrument is reliable if we trust that individual responses are repeatable. That is, if an individual completed the instrument more than once, his or her responses would be the same each time. In developing an instrument, then, a researcher usually tests its reliability through repeated administrations to the same individuals. If their responses are the same over time, the instrument is considered a reliable measure.

When what one is attempting to measure is fluid or changeable, reliability as defined above is not to be expected. For example, if an individual completes a measure of group development during the first and third weeks of the group's life, his or her answers may be different not because the instrument is unreliable but because the group has changed over time. However, there are other ways to check the reliability of an instrument: by determining whether items within a particular scale of the instrument elicit similar responses from respondents, and by checking to ensure that scales that are assumed to be different do not elicit similar responses. There are other procedures as well. In short, if the reliability of an instrument has not been assessed in any way, it is suspect.

Also, no evidence is provided by the author or the publishers regarding the validity of the Team Development Inventory. An instrument is considered to be valid if it actually measures what it was designed to measure. There are a number of ways to assess the validity of an instrument. For example, in creating an instrument, the developer typically submits items to experts in the area that the instrument is attempting to measure. The experts assess each item and determine whether it is relevant to what the instrument is measuring. Experts may point out areas that have been overlooked and suggest changes in items that might increase their clarity. In addition, the instrument should be based on an accepted theory, in this case of group development. If similar instruments exist that have demonstrated their worth in assessing group functioning or development, the new instrument could be compared with the more established instrument. Also, the results of the instrument might be compared to findings concerning group development that were derived in a different manner. For example, groups could be studied using systematic observation techniques. At the end of a session, members would complete the instrument. Results from these two assessment methods could then be compared. If the instrument is a valid one, results should be similar. There are a number of ways to test the validity of an instrument. The goal of all of these methods is to ensure that an instrument actually works.

No norms are provided with the Team Development Inventory. Typically, as an instrument is employed over time, its creators collect and organize results obtained from different types of groups. In the case of a measure of group development, norms would report what the typical range of scores has been for groups that are functioning productively and those that are not. Norms, or the typical scores, for groups working in a particular industry might be different from groups operating in another industry. This kind of information is generally included as well. Information concerning norms helps those who use the instrument to understand their results in relation to other groups who have used the same measure.

The Team Development Inventory was not developed as a research tool. Its primary purpose is to help group members think about how their group is functioning and to determine ways to improve effectiveness. Jones (1982) stated that reliability, validity, and norms were unnecessary, since the worth of the instrument is determined by whether groups who use it find it helpful in enhancing their team development. However, determining reliability, validity, and norms would strengthen the instrument even if it were used exclusively in applied settings. Trainers and consultants would be more confident that the instrument reflects what is actually occurring in a particular group. In its current form, it may or may not be useful in applied settings. However, as an assessment tool for group research, its utility is very questionable.

The Group Development Assessment (Jones & Bearley, 1986) is published by Organizational Design and Development, Inc. This forty-item instrument attempts to directly assess group development. The instrument is based on Jones' theory of group development that suggests that groups develop along two dimensions. The task dimension includes four phases: orientation, organization, open data flow, and problem solving. The process dimension consists of phases characterized by dependency, conflict, cohesion, and interdependence. According to Jones and Bearley (1986), these dimensions may develop in tandem or unevenly. The proposed theory of group development has much in common with more established theories (e.g., Caple, 1978; Tuckman, 1965; Tuckman

& Jensen, 1977). However, it contains differences as well, and no research has been conducted to test the theory. Also, no evidence of reliability or validity is presented, and norms have not been established.

Group Development Stage Analyses was created by Carew and Parisi-Carew and published by Blanchard Training and Development, Inc., in 1988. This instrument is based on eight characteristics thought to be associated with high-performance teams. These characteristics are productivity, empathy, empowerment, roles and goals, flexibility, open communication, recognition, and morale. Four options are listed under each characteristic, which correspond to a four-stage model of group development. The stages include orientation, dissatisfaction, resolution, and production. The goal of the instrument is to determine a group's stage of development. Again, no reliability, validity, or norms are reported.

The **Reactions to Group Situations Test** is titled to Stock Whitaker and was published by University Associates in 1974. This fifty-item test indicates individual member preferences for certain behaviors in groups. Preferences for work, fight, flight, dependency, and pairing are assessed. The theory underlying this instrument is that of Bion (1959). Stock Whitaker and Thelen (1958) collaborated in developing the initial instrument (Thelen, 1974). This instrument reports findings concerning reliability and validity (Thelen, Hawks & Strattner, 1969). However, the reported results were not very good, and the instrument was not altered to strengthen it. In addition, the instrument appears to have another problem: It asks individuals to assess their preferences rather than to assess the group's functioning. This is problematic, since individual preferences may or may not relate to what is occurring in a particular group at a certain point in time.

The **Group Attitude Scales** (Evans & Jarvis, 1986) is a twenty-item instrument that measures member attraction to a particular group at a certain point in time. While it does not specifically measure group development, the authors suggest that if the instrument is administered several times over the course of a group's life, group development can be inferred, since member attraction to the group is different at different stages of development. This instrument is included here because it does provide good evidence of reliability and validity. The drawback is that it was not designed to measure group development directly.

It appears as though researchers will have to wait for a good measure of group development to be created. A solid instrument that becomes generally accepted will take some time to generate, since more research is necessary to clarify developmental processes in different types of groups. This is not meant to discourage efforts to develop such an instrument, but rather to point out the need for instruments to be based on theories and models of group development that have been subjected to research investigations. The creation of an instrument that accurately depicts phases or patterns of group development would be very useful. It might also shed light on the congruence, or lack of congruence, between subjective member perceptions of group functioning and observationally derived assessments.

ETHNOGRAPHY: A PARTICIPANT-OBSERVATION RESEARCH METHOD

Perhaps the most highly regarded **participant-observation** study was conducted by Whyte (1943a, 1943b, 1943c, 1955). It was a three-year study of a poor neighborhood called Cornerville. In that study, Whyte attempted to gain a picture of the neighborhood as a whole by interacting with individuals and groups and observing how different segments of the community related to each other. In order to accomplish the study, Whyte essentially became part of the community. He attempted to build a description of the structure and culture of Cornerville through intensive examination, observation, and interaction with its people and groups. He asked questions, listened to people, observed interactions among them, and attempted to discover the beliefs, values, norms, and structures that defined the culture of the community as a whole. He also attempted to describe cultural differences among the various groups within the community.

Of course, Whyte did not invent the participant-observation method of research. Anthropologists have employed this strategy for quite some time. What Whyte is noted for are his detailed descriptions of what he referred to as "anthropological methods" (Whyte, 1961, 1969; Whyte & Whyte, 1984). When participant observation is employed to study the cultures of groups, organizations, or societies, this method is referred to as **ethnographic research.** Ethnography requires the researcher to describe in great detail the group or organization under investigation. This approach attempts to see the group through the eyes of its members, and as a result, requires the researcher to get close to those members. Ethnography has a process orientation. That is, studies of this type examine group or organizational processes across time. The observed social system is studied in context, and efforts are made to understand the relationships among the various aspects of the system.

Another characteristic of this method is that the research design is flexible. The researcher enters the system with a rudimentary plan for how the research will be conducted. As the study proceeds, the plan may change in order to accommodate the events and behaviors that are encountered. Other kinds of research methods determine the research plan in advance and stick to that plan in order to ensure the accuracy of the results. In the exploration of certain questions, a predetermined research design can be very useful. However, this strategy may narrow the focus of the study and cause the researcher to overlook important events or issues that emerge during the investigation. Ethnography tries to avoid this pitfall by assuming that the research plan can be altered during the study. In order to compensate for changes in the research plan and to ensure that future researchers will be able to replicate a particular study, ethnographers provide very detailed descriptions of how a study was conducted and what the researcher actually did to obtain the results. Ethnographic research is a qualitative approach to research in that it generally does not employ quantitative research methods such as questionnaires, surveys, tests, coding systems, or other measurement systems. Ethnographers focus instead on gaining an understanding of the group, organization, or society as a whole (Bryman, 1992).

Emerson (1987) developed a set of criteria to evaluate the quality of ethnographic research. First, good ethnographic research should be based on extensive observation of the group or organization being investigated. Brief studies of three or four weeks' duration are, in Emerson's opinion, not long enough to adequately describe the culture under investigation. Emerson also suggests that ethnographic research should have a theoretical focus. That is, the initial research plan should be based on a theory of group or organizational behavior. Without some focus, the investigator might miss certain key aspects of the culture being studied. However, Emerson warns the researcher not to impose the theory on the obtained data. If findings differ from the initial theoretical formulation, this should be noted and other interpretations raised for future study. Finally, Emerson stated that quality ethnographic research provides very detailed descriptions of how the study was conducted, what was observed, and how the researcher interpreted the results.

Participant observation is used extensively in studies of organizational culture (e.g., Jones, 1990; Jones, Moore & Snyder, 1988; Siehl & Martin, 1988; Van Maanen & Schein, 1979). It has also been used to study groups (e.g., Schwartz & Jacobs, 1979; Schwartz & Schwartz, 1955). Ethnographic studies are helpful, especially in studying the complexities of systems such as groups and organizations. They provide very detailed descriptions of the inner workings of these systems and can facilitate the development of theories capable of explaining their intricacies. Whyte (1992) cautions ethnographers, however, to be careful to base their analyses on observations and descriptions as opposed to interpretations. Participant observation can be problematic, since the observer's biases may taint the findings and their interpretation. Whyte believes that ethnography can be a reliable and valid scientific method, but that this kind of research must be carefully conducted. He also advises that ethnographic methods be combined with other methods, such as systematic observation, questionnaires, and other quantitative procedures, in order to strengthen their reliability and validity. Ethnographic studies enable us to learn things that are typically hidden from view. By participating in the group or organization under investigation, the researcher becomes an insider. Insiders can see things and hear things that outsiders cannot. On the other hand, the presence of an additional person, especially a researcher, may change the dynamics of the observed system and lead the researcher to formulate misconceptions. Also, by entering the system, the researcher becomes a participant in the culture that he or she is studying. Over time, the researcher becomes part of the culture and may begin to interpret events in ways that other members of the system do. This is positive in that the researcher begins to see things through the eyes of group and organizational members. However, since many aspects of culture are outside the conscious awareness of members (Schein, 1990), the participant observer may become equally unaware of these hidden aspects of culture.

CLINICAL DESCRIPTION

Schein (1987) advocated the use of a clinical descriptive research method for the study of groups and organizations. This method is employed by consultants while they are helping groups or organizations to resolve problems and increase their effectiveness. Consultants observe the social system, collect information utilizing a variety of means, and make interventions aimed at facilitating positive change in the system. In Chapter 10, the difficulties that researchers encounter in gaining access to groups and organizations were described. A consultant does not encounter the same problems, since the group or organization has asked for the consultant's assistance. Consultants are often supplied with access to information and groups that have been inaccessible to researchers (Schein, 1985, 1987).

Traditionally, it has been difficult to conduct research with the more powerful top-management groups in organizations. Middle-level management groups are easier to gain access to, but powerful groups tend not to make themselves available. Consultants, however, often have access to these groups, since members recognize that it is in their best interest to be open with a consultant (Schein, 1990). The consultant would be of little use to the organization unless he or she were able to develop a clear picture of how various organizational groups function. A number of clinical studies of these powerful organizational groups have been conducted (e.g., Hirschhorn, 1987; Jacques, 1951; Schein, 1983). They have added to our understanding of how culture is created and changed.

The data that consultants collect can also add to our understanding of group and organizational processes and development. This research strategy requires the consultant/researcher to carefully think through, in advance, how information will be collected and recorded. Any consultant has to prepare data collection strategies that he or she will employ when assisting a client system. However, if the consultant also plans to use the opportunity to conduct clinical research, more careful preparation is necessary. For example, audiovisual equipment might be necessary to allow additional data analyses. If the consultant conducts surveys or interviews before and after the consultation, he or she might need to identify responses in some way in order to match the responses of individuals or subgroups. More detailed notes might be required. Most consultants do many of these things anyway, so the amount of work involved in turning a consultation into a research opportunity is minimal.

Clinical observation does not provide the detail and depth of ethnographic studies. It does, however, solve one of the problems associated with ethnography. The consultant does not join the group or organization with which he or she is working. Consultants move in and out of the organization and frequently work with more than one organization at a time. As a result, their objectivity may not be as subject to compromise as that of the ethnographer who becomes immersed in one system. Also, in the course of their work, consultants intervene in the groups and organizations with which they are working. Ethnographers do not. Ethnographers are observers of systems, and their findings describe how systems function naturally. Consultants consciously attempt to change the ways groups and organizations operate. Their results can help us to understand what the effects might be of various strategies designed to change the operations or culture of groups and organizations. Finally, ethnographers attempt to gain a picture of the group or organization as a whole. To the best of their ability, they try to observe all aspects of a system. The scope of clinical research conducted by consultants is usually more limited, since what is to be observed and who the consultant has access to are defined by the group or organization.

The clinical research method has provided insights into many aspects of group and organizational processes and development. Like all research methods, it has strengths and weaknesses. Its utility has been demonstrated, however, in studies of organizations and their member groups.

OBSERVATION

The goal of observation is to watch and record group behaviors, interactions, and events in order to answer research questions or to test hypotheses (Kidder, 1981; Weick, 1985). If group members are aware that they are being observed, this is referred to as **overt observation.** One drawback of overt observation is that the presence of an observer may change the behaviors of members and the dynamics of the group. This change of behavior in the presence of an observer is known as the **Hawthorne effect.** The name of this phenomenon refers to studies conducted by Mayo at the Hawthorne plant. In those studies, characteristics of the physical environment such as room changes, brighter lights, and more rest periods were varied to determine their effects on productivity. Mayo and his colleagues were surprised to find out that everything they tried increased productivity. In fact, the physical changes were not responsible for the increases in productivity. The plant workers were aware that they were being observed and took this to mean that the company was taking a special interest in their area. As a result, they worked harder (Landsberger, 1958; Mayo, 1945; Roethlisberger & Dickson, 1939). Since then, other studies have confirmed that group members behave differently when they are aware that they are being observed by others (Barnard, 1938; McGregor, 1960).

Covert observation refers to situations in which group members are not aware of being observed. From an ethical standpoint, covert observation is problematic, since it violates individual and group privacy (Cook, 1981; Douglas, 1976; Reynolds, 1979). In order to gain more accurate observations, then, researchers attempt to conduct unobtrusive observations. **Unobtrusive observation** refers to situations in which group members are aware of being observed. However, the researcher has taken steps to ensure that the observation process is as inconspicuous as possible. For example, concealed videotapes or audiotapes are less disturbing than visible observers. One-way mirrors are considered unobtrusive as well, since group members cannot see or hear the observers. The goal of unobtrusive observation methods is to increase the likelihood that observed behaviors would be the same whether observation was occurring or not. Another strategy is to observe for long periods of time. Over time, group members become used to the observation process and behaviors tend to normalize. The extensive use of audio and video equipment in the society at large may prove helpful to researchers. These days, people are videotaped at family gatherings and parties, in school, and at the office. This may reduce our tendency to alter our behavior for the cameras or the tape recorder.

If a researcher were interested in observing a rare species of animal that was recently discovered on a remote island, what should he or she observe? Would it be best to go in and just watch for a while or to determine what to look for beforehand? In this case, the researcher would most likely choose to just watch for a period of time. This form of observation is referred to as **open observation** and is very useful, especially in new areas of study. It is also useful in areas in which we know more but are interested in studying something that cannot, at least at this point, be predicted in advance.

For example, this author and an associate (Wheelan & Krasick, 1993) were interested in asking some group-process questions whose answers could not be predicted in advance. One such question is: How do themes or topics of conversation emerge, travel, and gain acceptance in a set of interacting groups? Do individuals or subgroups introduce topics and continue to push for their acceptance in subsequent groups, or are topics the product of the total organization? In order to study this question, we had to identify the topics that gained acceptance in the organization and trace their emergence through groups in the organization. Since it was not possible for us to determine the topics in advance, we employed open observation. We audiotaped and transcribed all group sessions. Next, we assessed the transcripts, utilizing a content analysis system. **Content analysis** is a research technique used to determine the unmistakable content of communication (Holsti, 1969). Researchers observe the content of communication (in this case, simultaneously listening to and reading) and ultimately place it into conceptual categories (Glaser & Strauss, 1967). As words and phrases occur in the discussion, they become associated with each other, and categories or themes emerge. Thus, the categories or themes arise from the data rather than being developed in advance by the researcher (Spradley, 1979). It is customary for two researchers to separately perform content analysis. They then compare their findings to ensure that the results are reliable. In this case, assuming beforehand what the topics might be could narrow the scope of observation and cause the researchers to draw erroneous conclusions. Therefore, we employed open observation in the form of content analysis.

If a researcher were interested in testing the validity of a particular theory or theories of group development, open observation would not be as useful. In this kind of research, systematic observation would be more appropriate. **Systematic observation** requires the researcher to determine before the study is conducted what behaviors will be observed. For example, in a recent study of developmental processes in same-sex and mixed-sex groups, the researchers were interested in whether developmental patterns in all-female, all-male, and mixed-sex groups were similar or different (Verdi & Wheelan, 1992). An observation system was developed, based on the work of Bion (1961) and extended by Thelen (1954) and Stock Whitaker and Thelen (1958). The seven categories represent the types of verbal statements associated with the various stages of group development outlined in the research literature.

Dependency statements are those that show the inclination to conform with the dominant mood of the group, to follow suggestions made by the leader, and generally, to demonstrate a desire for direction from others. **Counterdependency statements** are those that assert independence from and rejection of leadership, authority, or member attempts to lead. **Fight statements** are those that convey participation in a struggle to overcome someone or something; they imply argumentativeness, criticism, or aggression. **Flight statements** are those that indicate avoidance of task and confrontation. **Pairing statements** are those that include expressions of warmth, friendship, support, or intimacy with others. Pairing statements are similar to positive maintenance statements as outlined in Bales's (1950) observation system. **Counterpairing statements** are those that indicate an avoidance of intimacy and connection and a desire to keep the discussion distant and intellectual. **Work statements** are those that represent purposeful, goal-directed activity and task-oriented efforts.

As in the previous example, the researchers audiotaped and transcribed a number of groups. Instead of using a content analysis system, however, the researchers analyzed each complete thought and placed it in one of these seven categories. If a complete thought did not fit the definition of any category, it was placed in a category entitled *unscoreable.*

In this sample study, a statement or unit was defined as a complete thought. This strategy has been used in other studies (e.g., Mills, 1964). Various units have been used in research on groups, ranging from single words (Dunphy, 1968; Stone, Dunphy, Smith & Ogilvie, 1966), to bits of verbal behavior (Bales, 1950). Direct or symbolic acts that varied in length but always referred to the activity of one member were used by Mann (1966). Stock Whitaker and Thelen (1958) used natural units that varied in length, but were homogeneous with respect to theme and subgroup. Farrell (1976) analyzed twenty-minute units. Babad and Melnick (1976) used whole sessions as the unit of analysis.

Choosing the size of the unit is an important decision. Shorter units tend to produce higher reliability among observers (Babad & Amir, 1978). It is easier to agree on how to categorize one complete thought or simple sentence than it is to agree on a whole conversation. Using the coding system described above, a statement such as "Don't listen to the boss" would be classified as counterdependent. "That's a great idea, Sarah" would be classified as pairing. If the unit of analysis were longer and these sentences were embedded in other statements and conversation, the larger unit might be more difficult for observers to classify, since the discussion might contain a number of categories. Smaller units, then, are more reliable. However, they are more numerous and take more time, and some statements may be lost if the equipment used for recording is not of high quality. Early researchers often resorted to larger units of analysis for these reasons. For example, Stock Whitaker and Thelen (1958) reported that when a smaller unit was used, up to 30 percent of the statements were lost or unscoreable. This is less of a concern with larger units, since the unit can still be classified even if it contains a missing sentence or two.

Another reason why some researchers chose larger units is to reduce the amount of data generated in the analysis. The average small group produces about 1100 complete thoughts or simple sentences in one-and-a-half hours. The Verdi and Wheelan (1992) study, for example, investigated ten group sessions. Each session lasted one-and-a-half hours. The total number of units was 11,698. Fortunately, advances in computer technology have eased the strain of managing the mass of data generated in group research.

Category coding systems such as the one described earlier (Verdi & Wheelan, 1992) are often referred to as **process analysis systems.** In contrast to content analysis, process analysis is less concerned with what is said and more concerned with how things are said, the dynamics underlying communications, and the patterns and sequence associated with these dynamics. This makes such systems applicable to group development studies that are intent on discovering patterns and sequences.

The most famous and most widely used process analysis system was developed by Bales in 1950. The system, **Interaction Process Analysis,** classifies each unit of behavior into one of twelve categories. Six of the categories relate to the maintenance or socio-emotional dimension of the group. A unit is coded as seeming friendly, dramatic, agreeing, unfriendly, showing tension, or disagreeing. The remaining six categories are related to the group's task. A unit is coded as giving suggestions, opinions, or information or asking for suggestions, opinions, or information (Bales, 1970).

In 1980, Bales, Cohen, and Williamson developed another system called System for the Multiple Level Observation of Groups, or SYMLOG. Interaction Process Analysis was designed to investigate role structures in groups. It is based on the underlying assumption that there are similarities in the roles that are performed in groups. SMYLOG was designed to investigate role structures, status, and attraction in groups. Both these systems have been used to investigate a variety of processes that occur in groups. It is important to notice that neither of these observation systems is specifically designed to observe group development as it is generally described in the literature. They have been used for this purpose, however.

Bales (1965) utilized Interaction Process Analysis to test his equilibrium model of group development. The model states that groups attempt to keep a balance between task and socio-emotional activity and move back and forth between these two dimensions across the life of a group (Bales, Cohen & Williamson, 1980). Accepted theories of group development do suggest that different amounts of task and positive or negative emotional expression would occur at different phases of group development. For example, one would expect to see high levels of positive socio-emotional expression during the forming stage and negative emotional expression during the storming period, as described by Tuckman (1965). Task behavior would be high during the work or performing stage. Bales's observation systems, then, can be used to confirm or disconfirm these expectations in different types of groups. However, neither system is directly designed to capture the range of behaviors generally associated with the various stages of group development.

Another system that has been used to investigate group development is the **Process Analysis Scoring System (PASS)**. It was originally designed to classify member-leader interactions (Mann, 1966; Mann et al., 1967). Hartman (1979) expanded the system to include member-member interactions. Each interaction or unit is defined by the speaker and the person receiving the interaction. Next, units are classified into one of eighteen categories that represent five types of interpersonal behavior. The area of **hostility** is described as (1) moving against, (2) disagreeing, (3) withdrawing or expressing indifference, and (4) attempting to induce guilt. **Affection** includes (5) making reparations, (6) identifying with the other, (7) agreeing, and (8) expressing personal affection. **Power relations** are defined by (9) showing submission, (10) showing equality, and (11) showing dominance. **Ego states** include (12) expressing anxiety, (13) denying anxiety, (14) expressing depression, (15) denying depression, (16) expressing guilt, (17) denying guilt, and (18) expressing self-esteem. An act or unit could receive more than one code in this system.

This observation system has been used to study self-analytic groups (e.g., Mann et al., 1967) and psychotherapy groups (e.g., Brower, 1986). The PASS system is capable of delineating phases of group development. For example, Brower (1986) was able to identify phases in two therapy groups. The phases were distinct from each other in that different amounts of the PASS categories occurred in the identified phases. The PASS system is well suited for studies of groups in which the task is intrapsychic or interpersonal. Its utility with workplace groups and other groups with an externally oriented task, however, seems limited. The system is able to describe the work phase in a therapy group. Work on personal and interpersonal issues would be associated with increases in self-expression and openness. It would be difficult for the PASS system to categorize work as it is generally understood when group tasks consist of such things as setting production goals and establishing strategies to meet those goals, for example. While some PASS categories might increase or decrease during the work phase in this type of group, many types of behaviors would likely be missed by this system. The task dimension categories of Bales's Interaction Process Analysis System might be more useful. However, as was stated previously, while Bales's systems are more capable of delineating the work phase, they are less useful in discerning other phases of group development. The PASS system is better able to discern dependency, flight, fight, and other modes of behavior associated with group development.

Researchers have employed a number of structured observation systems in the study of group processes and development (e.g., Babad & Amir, 1978; Hill,

1977; Lundgren, 1971; Mills, 1964). Trujillo (1986) has developed a classification system to describe group observation systems. However, problems still remain for the researcher interested in group research, especially studies of group development. First, most available systems were not designed directly to study group development. As a result, phases of group development have to be inferred from the obtained behaviors. Second, as in the previous example, observation systems are typically designed for use in groups with a specific kind of task. Their utility in groups with a different task is often questionable. The PASS system (Mann, 1966), for example, is useful in therapy or self-analytic groups such as T-groups. However, it is not well suited for studies of workplace groups. Thus, a researcher interested in similarities and differences between groups with different tasks would be hard pressed to choose an observational system capable of accurately observing both types of groups. Third, detailed descriptions of available systems are difficult to find. For example, Babad and Amir (1978) briefly described a coding system that appears to be similar to that developed for use in the Verdi and Wheelan (1992) study described earlier. However, a detailed description of Babad and Amir's (1978) system is unavailable. Therefore, creation of a new system was necessary.

There is a fourth difficulty. The lack of standard systems used in a number of studies and capable of directly recording behaviors associated with group development impedes progress in this field of study. Given the fact that research on group development is time consuming and labor intensive, knowledge in the area would be greatly enhanced if standard observation systems were employed by collaborating researchers. For a single researcher or research team, it would take years to investigate a sufficient number of groups to even begin to answer some of the basic questions concerning group development. However, if many researchers and teams utilized standard research designs and observation systems, information would be accumulated more expeditiously.

Structured observation is one of the strongest research methods available to group researchers. Well-constructed systems produce reliable and valid information about group dynamics and development. Of course, the quality of the obtained information depends on how well the system can test theories of group development. The more directly categories are related to theory and previous research, the more useful they are. Structured observation limits the number of variables or factors that the observer looks for in a group. This is a plus, since it increases reliability and objectivity in viewing a group. If categories are defined in sufficient detail, observers will see similar things. However, if the categories guide the researcher to look for the wrong things, or for behaviors that are not related to group development, they are of little use. While no research method in the social sciences is perfect, structured observation is a very good research tool. If they are well conceived and well designed, observational systems may help us to answer some of the critical questions in this area. However, other methods described in this chapter are useful as well. Structured observation does not provide the breadth and depth, for example, that ethnographic research delivers. Also, structured observation does not take into account the experiences and reactions of group members. Interviews, questionnaires, and the like are needed to yield a balanced picture of group functioning.

COMBINING METHODS

Reliance on one method for conducting group research does not seem advantageous at this point. Researchers are well advised to incorporate a number of strategies into their research designs. Each strategy adds a different dimension and increases our ability to more fully understand group processes. Brower (1986) conducted a study of two therapy groups utilizing Mann's (1966) structured observation system. Drawing on the findings of this quantitative analysis, he described the developmental patterns in the two groups. Near the end of the article, Brower stated that "one has to wonder whether these descriptions bear any resemblance to what actually transpired in the groups" (p. 182). He seems to be expressing concern about the adequacy of quantitative observational methods to capture the human social experiences that occur in groups.

Human beings experience things on a variety of levels, and no single research methodology is capable of adequate description of these multiple levels. For example, the author and several colleagues have been engaged for a number of years in a series of studies of group and organizational behavior. One of the many things that we have noticed is that the subjective experience of members is often radically different from what one would expect based on the results of systematic observation. Subjective experience is unknowable through systematic observation alone. For example, a minor increase in the percentage of fight statements, from 6 percent to 10 percent of the total statements made, can signal a dramatic change in the emotional reactions of members. The lower percentage may be associated with feelings of security and comfort. An increase of only 4 percentage points in the amount of expressed conflict may be associated with feelings of anxiety and discomfort. From a quantitative perspective, such an increase is inconsequential. From a qualitative perspective, the increase has significant, perhaps dramatic, effects on members.

The study of human social systems requires methods that can objectively describe their dynamics and development and can also discover subjective human reactions to these processes. Subjective experience should not be sacrificed for the sake of objectivity, or vice versa. Only when we view social systems from both perspectives will we obtain a fuller understanding of their operations and the mutual influences among individuals, groups, organizations, and societies.

12

THERAPY, COUNSELING, AND PERSONAL-GROWTH GROUPS

The readers of this book may be members, or aspiring members, of a number of professions. It is likely that current or potential psychologists, social workers, managers, educators, counselors, nurses, recreation specialists, and many other professionals are among the readership. The application of the information contained in this book to real-world situations, then, is likely to be a high priority, since working with groups is an integral part of many professional roles. To that end, this chapter discusses the relevance of group theories and research to therapy, counseling, and personal-growth groups. Subsequent chapters focus on educational skills training and work groups.

Given the complexities of modern work roles, individuals from a variety of professions may be called upon to lead or participate in a number of different kinds of groups. For example, a manager leads his or her team. That manager may also be required to train employees in new approaches or to teach in certain content areas. Psychologists, social workers, and counselors may conduct counseling or skills training groups and facilitate meetings and may also be team leaders. Most people will be students, participants in training groups, and team members, and quite a number will choose to participate in counseling or personal-growth groups. Consequently, knowledge of the workings of different types of groups may prove useful in a variety of roles.

Each of these group approaches is discussed in light of what is known about group dynamics and development. Typically, such discussions focus solely on the leader's role and tasks in different kinds of groups. However, the role of member is discussed here as well, since from a group perspective, effective membership is as important as effective leadership.

GROUP APPROACHES TO INDIVIDUAL CHANGE

Definitions and Distinctions

While there is some lingering disagreement concerning the definitions of thera-py, counseling, and personal-growth groups, there is considerable consensus that the differences among them are related to the population that each approach is designed to serve. These distinctions are evident in dictionary defin-itions of the terms *therapy, counseling,* and *growth. Webster's Dictionary* (1989) defines therapy as "a remedial treatment designed or serving to bring about social adjustment" (p. 1223). Counseling is defined as "professional guidance of the individual" (p. 296). Growth is defined as "progressive development" (p. 540). These definitions are very similar to those of Corey and Corey (1992), which are provided below.

> *Group therapy is a group "designed to assist individuals to alleviate specific symp-toms or psychological problems." (p. 10)*

> *Group counseling "deals with conscious problems, is not aimed at major personality changes, is generally oriented toward the resolution of specific and short term issues, and is not concerned with treatment of the more severe psychological and behavioral disorders." (pp. 10–11)*

> *Personal-growth groups are "intended to help relatively healthy people function bet-ter on an interpersonal level. . . . Such groups are developmental, in that they explore personal issues that most people struggle with at the various transition peri-ods in life." (p. 12)*

All of these definitions emphasize that therapy remediates, counseling guides, and personal growth enhances or augments. Thus, an individual with a history of depression that interferes with daily functioning would potentially benefit from group therapy. An individual experiencing a divorce might be an appropriate candidate for group counseling, assuming that there is no evidence of serious emotional problems. Finally, a well-functioning individual who is not currently experiencing a life problem and is interested in self- and interpersonal development might benefit from participation in a personal-growth group.

Two other distinctions among these models are often made. Therapy groups tend to be held in clinical settings and meet for extended or indefinite periods of time. Counseling groups are held in educational, work, and private practice environments and meet for a predetermined, limited amount of time. Personal-growth groups are held in a wide variety of contexts and typically meet for less time than the other two models (Shaffer & Galinsky, 1989).

Finally, the knowledge and skills required of leaders of these different groups have both similarities and differences. All leaders need to be knowledgeable about human behavior, individual development, change and learning strategies, facilitation and intervention strategies, and group development. They also need to be able to identify individuals with serious psychological problems. In the case of counseling and personal-growth groups, the identification of individuals with serious problems is important in order to screen potential members and to refer individuals for more appropriate treatment. Group therapists require the ability both to identify and to treat individuals with psychological disorders. The education and training for leadership roles in such groups are similar in many ways. However, more extensive training is required of those who work with individuals experiencing severe psychological problems.

Goals and Theories of Individual Change

In all three models, the primary goal is to facilitate change and learning in individuals. Group therapy attempts to remediate psychological problems that seriously interfere with the ability of individuals to function in work, social, or familial roles. Group counseling seeks to help individuals to resolve specific, short-term issues or problems, and personal-growth groups work to assist individuals to achieve further growth or development in self-acceptance, self-directedness, and self-awareness. In order to accomplish these goals, the leader and, ultimately, the members require a shared view of how change and learning occur in individuals. Psychology, the discipline most associated with the study of change and learning in the individual, has produced not one theory of these processes, but several. While a complete explication of the various theories of the change/learning process is well beyond the scope of this book, a brief overview will be provided.

How do individuals change? If an individual is troubled by thoughts, feelings, or behaviors that interfere with daily functioning and quality of life, how can that individual become more functional and content? How can relatively healthy individuals continue positive self-development? These questions are of paramount importance to those who lead therapy, counseling, and growth groups and to those who participate in them. The answer determines the tasks and activities that such groups will undertake in order to help individual members change or grow and to accomplish their respective goals.

Essentially, individual thoughts, feelings, and behaviors are the targets of change and learning strategies. For example, if an individual is experiencing bouts of depression, some would argue that the individual's negative or self-deprecating thoughts must be altered in order to eradicate the depression. Others would focus on reducing feelings of isolation, anxiety, sadness, or hopelessness. Still others would attempt to change behavior patterns by increasing the individual's activity level and by helping the individual to learn more effective social skills. Since thoughts, feelings, and behaviors are interdependent parts of the person, each approach has validity, and change in one of these areas is likely to produce change in the others as well.

The view that one holds, however, does determine the tasks and activities of therapy, counseling, or personal-growth groups and provides the framework for understanding individual behavior and strategies to facilitate change and learning in individuals. For example, if thought patterns are the focus of change efforts, then the group leader and members will spend considerable time discussing member thoughts, attitudes, and beliefs and giving feedback to each other about them. The hope would be to correct certain cognitive errors or dysfunctional thoughts in order to effect changes in individual cognition.

If, however, the focus of change efforts is the emotional responses of an individual, a group might spend considerable time discussing painful experiences in order to allow an individual to fully express them. The hope is that reexperiencing painful emotions in a safe environment will rid the person of these disruptive feelings. Finally, when behaviors are the focus of change efforts, a group will spend considerable time attempting to develop new behavioral responses to situations in the hope of changing the ways individuals react to situations. In each instance, the assumption is that change in one area will effect changes in other areas as well.

The previous discussion is, of course, overly simplistic, since there are many other factors that influence the change process. For example, individuals are not always conscious of their thoughts, feelings, or behaviors. Some thoughts and feelings are repressed or forgotten, and individuals are often unaware of how they behave or of the effect of their behavior on others. Therefore, regardless of the focus of intervention, it is usually necessary for the leader and members to help each other to become increasingly aware of their cognitive, behavioral, and emotional patterns.

Individuals, however, typically resist efforts to increase their awareness or to facilitate changes in habitual response patterns. Increased awareness and suggestions for change can produce considerable anxiety in people. Our consistent sense of self is threatened by such efforts. Change may also pose a threat to current relationships, since individuals seem to intuitively recognize that individual change may not be appreciated by the significant persons in their lives. Therefore, resistance must be overcome if change is to be initiated and maintained outside the group experience.

Shaffer and Galinsky (1989) describe in detail twelve models of group therapy and personal growth. Some models focus primarily on effecting change in thoughts or feelings or behaviors, and some pay attention to two or more of these factors. Their book is recommended for those interested in a more complete discussion of how different group models view individual change and what strategies are employed to facilitate the change process. For our purposes, suffice it to say that since the group approaches described in this chapter have as their goal individual change or growth, a theory of individual change and learning is essential to goal achievement. The chosen theory will provide a lens through which to view, understand, and interpret individual responses. It will also offer guidance to the group about how to facilitate individual change or learning.

If individual change is undertaken in a group context, however, the dynamics of the group will influence the effectiveness of any change/learning approach. Therefore, leaders and members also require a framework that will equip them to understand and to manage group-level events. The following sections describe this group-level framework. Regardless of the individual change or learning framework being employed, knowledge and skills related to group functioning can significantly increase the likelihood of individual goal achievement.

The Group Approach to Individual Change

Since the goal of these three approaches is personal change, one might wonder why work on this goal is conducted in groups. Wouldn't individual approaches to therapy, counseling, or personal growth be more effective? In certain circumstances, the answer to this question is yes. For some individuals and some types of problems, individual approaches are more helpful. However, for many people, individual change and personal development are best accomplished in a group setting.

Yalom (1970) outlined ten factors that occur in groups that facilitate individual change and personal development. He noted that groups provide considerable information about how other people think, feel, and behave. Differences in the way members and leaders respond to situations can provide alternatives to members. Groups instill hope in people as well, since individuals interact with others who are actively trying to change. Many people feel that they are the only ones who struggle with issues and problems. However, the universality of problems and concerns becomes apparent in the group context. Groups also encourage altruistic behavior in individuals, since they afford the opportunity not only to be helped but to help others. This can positively affect self-esteem.

Group settings allow for what Yalom refers to as the "corrective recapitulation of the primary family" (p. 5). Many personal problems and concerns are the result of an individual's membership in a dysfunctional family. Therefore, membership in a functional group can undo some of the hurts and response patterns created in the original family group by providing a caring, healthy alternative family setting. Groups afford individuals the opportunity to hone their social skills, since they interact with a number of different people in the group context. They may imitate others and acquire new ways of thinking, feeling, and behaving as a result. Groups also provide the opportunity for exploring and improving interpersonal relationships, and the cohesion that develops in groups facilitates exploration in a supportive environment. Finally, the group provides the opportunity for catharsis or the open expression of feelings that individuals typically do not communicate to others (pp. 5–55).

From the perspective of group theories and research, there is an additional benefit to group approaches. That is, the group environment changes individuals in and of itself. The saying "by the crowd they have been broken; by the crowd shall they be healed" (Marsh, 1931, p. 329) reflects this view. Individual thoughts, feelings, and behaviors are continuously being shaped by the groups in a person's environment. Individual problems, therefore, are the result, in part, of group participation. It seems reasonable to assume that participation in a functional group would ameliorate such problems. In fact, there is evidence that this is the case. Membership in a well-functioning group can reduce individual stress and the occurrence of psychological problems and can improve self-concept (Barrera, 1986; Bednar & Kaul, 1978, 1979; Bednar & Lawlis, 1971; Cohen & Wills, 1985; Dalgard et al., 1990; Kaul & Bednar, 1986; Lieberman, 1980; Yalom, 1975, 1985).

Research on the effectiveness of group therapy and personal-growth groups for the achievement of individual goals, however, has produced mixed results. Smith, Wood, and Smale (1980), for example, conducted an extensive review of group therapy outcomes. They concluded that there is considerable evidence to support the use of group therapy as a method of treatment. However, it does not work in all cases and may not be helpful for all populations. Severely disturbed individuals, for example, do not seem to benefit from intensive, verbal group therapies. However, they may benefit from groups that stress the development of social skills. Different models of group therapy and differences in leadership style also influence outcomes.

Personal-growth groups also do not always produce positive changes in their members. In a review of 177 tests (reported in ninety-one studies) of the immediate effects of such groups, 54 percent reported positive changes in members. Only twenty-eight studies did follow-up and, of these only 33 percent found that positive changes endured over time (Smith, 1975, 1980). This leads to the conclusion that there is evidence that positive change can occur in such groups. However, many of these changes tend to fade out with time.

There are a number of reasons why studies of therapy and personal-growth groups produce mixed results. Differences in the way studies are conducted and weaknesses in study designs account for some of the variability in results. The fact that different models and theories of change are used by group leaders also makes comparisons difficult. Also, groups are led by human beings who vary in their skill and competence to facilitate positive change. Finally, many leaders and members are unaware of or do not attend to group processes and development. As a result, a well-functioning group, more capable of supporting member goals, does not develop.

Regardless of leader or member views concerning individual change or learning, this process is enhanced by participation in a well-functioning group. Therefore, a primary task of group leaders and members is to create an effective group environment. This will require knowledge of groups and the skills necessary to facilitate group development. As Agazarian and Peters (1981) stated, "group dynamics can tell us what sorts of conflicts and problems to expect during the various developmental stages of the group. . . . whose resolution is absolutely essential to the effective functioning of the therapy group" (p. 16). This is equally true of personal-growth groups as well. During each stage of group life, member and leader actions can inhibit or enhance positive group development. How this occurs is described next.

PREGROUP PREPARATION

In the past, most discussions of group approaches that focus on individual change have centered on the knowledge and skills required of leaders. It was assumed that leader personality traits, style, and expertise were central to effecting change in individual participants. While skillful leadership is very important, members also play a vital role in creating an effective group culture and social structure. Group therapy, counseling, or personal growth are not like surgery, in which an expert operates on a passive and in most cases unconscious person. Individual psychological change or learning requires the active participation of that individual. In the group context this is even more true, since members and leaders must work together to create a positive group environment in which to achieve individual goals. If the leader is the sole participant with knowledge of groups and the skills to facilitate group development, the chances of success are diminished. Members require this knowledge and skill as well.

The realization that members are participants in the change/learning process has led many to advocate an orientation session prior to the start of group therapy and counseling. While this is far less commonly done with personal-growth group participants, an orientation would undoubtedly prove useful in this context as well. The pregroup session provides the opportunity for potential group members to discuss their goals and expectations. The leader typically discusses his or her goals and expectations as well. Group guidelines are established at this time. Meeting times, confidentiality, and general rules are also established during the orientation.

The pregroup session has a teaching function as well. The leader typically outlines the benefits and risks of group participation and discusses the phases of group development with participants. Such information tends to reduce apprehensiveness on the part of members and provides them with a framework for understanding what will occur during the group.

Pregroup orientation sessions have been found to increase the likelihood of individual goal achievement (Bednar, Melnick & Kaul, 1974; Borgers & Tyndall, 1982; Burlingame & Fuhriman, 1990; Fuhriman & Burlingame, 1990). Piper and Perrault (1989), however, reviewed twenty studies of the effect of a pregroup session on outcomes. They concluded that pregroup sessions positively influenced attendance and reduced the likelihood that members would drop out. However, they did not find that pregroup sessions increased the likelihood of individual goal achievement. Since there are many other factors that influence goal achievement, it is not surprising that an isolated factor does not consistently predict success. This should not discourage practitioners from conducting pregroup orientations, however. Regular attendance and retention are important enough outcomes to support the use of pregroup sessions.

The influence of pregroup sessions might be enhanced if member tasks were more clearly outlined. That is, more time could be devoted to educating people about effective group membership. For example, reading material might be provided to potential members to increase their awareness of group processes and their role in facilitating group effectiveness. Education about groups, group approaches to individual change, and leader and member roles in facilitating positive outcomes could be discussed as well. Pregroup sessions with an expanded educational component are likely to more adequately prepare individuals for group participation. Perhaps most important, preparation empowers individuals by giving them a role in the change/learning process. Instead of perceiving themselves as dependent on the therapist or facilitator, individuals come to see themselves as active participants in their own goal achievement and that of others.

STAGE ONE: DEPENDENCY AND INCLUSION

The initial meetings of any group are typically a bit uncomfortable. This is even more true in therapy and personal-growth groups. In therapy and counseling groups, members join to work on personal problems that are difficult to talk about even with intimates. They may be ashamed of or embarrassed by their problems or by being identified as in need of help. Members know that they will be called upon to discuss personal issues in the group and will naturally be anxious about doing so. In personal-growth groups, members will also be anxious about sharing personal information and concerned about how others will react to them.

In any group, members are concerned about personal safety and anxious about possible rejection by others. However, in groups focused on individual change and learning, these concerns are exacerbated. The wish for strong, dependable leadership is more intensely felt, and resistance to working on personal goals is high. Leader tasks during this early period are described next.

The Tasks of the Group Leader at Stage One

The basic tasks of a stage-one group are to create an environment in which individuals feel progressively safer and more connected to the group. During this stage then, the leader's task, on the group level, is to facilitate feelings of safety and inclusion. On the individual level, the therapist's task is to observe how individuals respond to this new situation. As a result of individual interviews and the pregroup session, the leader has some information about the problems or personal goals of each member, but there is a vast difference between hearing about and actually witnessing the responses of another.

For example, Mary may have described herself as shy and awkward in social situations. However, during the first session the leader notices that Mary was the first to speak and was generously asking others about themselves in an apparent attempt to make others feel more comfortable. This discrepancy between Mary's self perception and her actions is noted by the leader for possible use at a later point. Typically, it is not wise for the leader to begin making verbal observations or interpretations of member behavior too quickly. On the individual level, one event does not constitute a response pattern. It is usually better to watch and observe more incidents before commenting on an individual's behavior. On the group level, singling out an individual at this early time may cause divisiveness or competitiveness among members.

The primary leader task at this stage is the facilitation of inclusion and safety. An intervention that praises Mary for her efforts to comfort others might cause members to feel competitive and to exclude her. An intervention that points out the discrepancy between Mary's self-perception and her current group behavior might be perceived by Mary, and others, as confrontational. This could make members feel even less safe than they did prior to the intervention.

What leaders say at this stage of the group is of critical importance, and it is often better to say less rather than more for two important reasons. First, anything that a leader says will be taken as directive by group members. If the leader praises Mary for attempting to make others feel more comfortable, other members may feel chastised for not doing the same. If the leader gently points out the discrepancy between her perception of herself as shy and her assertive initiation of conversation in the group, it may be perceived as criticism despite its intent. This can lead others to be less comfortable initiating conversation.

Second, if the leader speaks frequently at this stage, he or she may inadvertently contribute to the establishment of a centralized communication network in which discussion flows to and from the leader. This would contribute to the creation of a status hierarchy with the leader at the top. Leader centrality reduces the likelihood of individual goal achievement by exacerbating member dependency on the leader, limiting input, and inhibiting the development of cohesion among members. The net effect of excessive leader input can be to interfere with group development, which in turn limits the natural healing power of the group.

It becomes apparent that the leader's actions during the dependency and inclusion stage of group development are very important. Regardless of the model of group therapy, counseling, or personal growth and the theory of personal change being employed, their effectiveness is enhanced or diminished by the group's dynamics. The leader's role is critical, since that role is the most clearly defined at this early stage. As a result, each leader action, whether directed to an individual or the group, must be examined prior to implementation to ensure that it will support the following objectives:

- The development of a safe, inclusive, and accepting group environment;
- The creation of a decentralized, nonhierarchical, open communication system;
- The establishment of norms that support individual disclosure, experimentation, and work.

To accomplish these objectives, leaders are advised not to be too active during this phase. When they do intervene, it should be with actions that support these objectives. Group-level interventions are often more effective at this time than comments directed at individuals. For example, if the leader wished to comment on the event described earlier, in which Mary facilitated conversation in an attempt to make others feel more comfortable, a statement like "Members are working hard to help each other feel more comfortable" might be helpful. Such an intervention compliments and encourages the development of a supportive climate, reminds members that they have a role to play in creating an effective group, and praises Mary without distinguishing her from others. Positive feedback from the leader early in the group has been shown to contribute to group and individual success (Dies, 1983; Stockton & Morran, 1981).

Dies (1983) noted that leaders who encourage the establishment of enabling norms, trust, direct communication, and a work orientation during this early phase are more successful. This can be accomplished by giving positive feedback to group members when their actions contribute to group development. Leaders can also intervene at strategic moments to prevent the establishment of restrictive norms (Whitaker & Lieberman, 1964) by simply encouraging members to continue to discuss proposed norms. A statement like "How will this decision help you reach your goals?" may be sufficient to cause people to rethink a proposed rule.

Since some group decisions occur without awareness, an important leadership task is to continuously assess member actions for their impact on group dynamics. Leaders are in a better position than members to do this, since their role and training make it easier for them to identify and understand group processes. When members are anxious, it is more difficult for them to see the big picture. A leader might say, "The group seems to have decided not to share personal information," if this is the case. Leaders can use interventions to teach as well. For example, a statement like "Beginning groups usually find it difficult to focus on their goals" can encourage members to discuss personal and group goals without blaming them for not doing so. It also helps members to understand their collective actions, which may help them to be more self-reflective as well. Providing members with ways to understand their personal and collective behavior is important to eventual goal achievement (Lieberman, Yalom & Miles, 1973).

The Tasks of Group Members at Stage One

Members can help during this early period by attempting to get to know one another. Since everyone is a bit anxious and uncomfortable in a new situation, it can be difficult for individuals to initiate conversation or to ask about each other. However, doing so increases feelings of safety and inclusion. Individuals can also contribute to the process by asking questions of each other and of the leader and by sharing information about their personal goals. It is important to try to include everyone in the conversation and not to dominate the discussion, since this may inadvertently create resentments and increased anxiety.

When asking others about themselves, it is helpful not to ask questions that are too personal or that might be perceived as threatening. At this stage, no one feels safe enough to share in an intimate way. When leaders and group members do not insist that people reveal themselves at this early date, they increase the chances that people will do so eventually. If members do not pressure each other to share, individuals will feel safe and accepted by the group. These feelings of safety will encourage individuals to share as they feel ready.

Members can also facilitate group and individual success by focusing on their own goals. Sharing with others what led an individual to join the group and what he or she hopes to accomplish will help the group to develop a work orientation, which is essential to its ultimate success. Finally, sharing personal thoughts, feelings, and reactions to events that occur in the group will aid the creation of an effective group. These individual actions contribute to the group's development and are helpful to individuals as well. They provide people with the opportunity to hone their social skills and increase their sensitivity and responsiveness to others. Undoubtedly, this will have a positive effect on personal goal achievement and development as well.

STAGE TWO: COUNTERDEPENDENCY AND FIGHT

The Tasks of the Leader at Stage Two

The goal of a stage-two group is to forge agreements about beliefs and values. In a group focused on individual change, this is a very important time. Individual problems or concerns are often the result of misconceptions about the nature of human beings, social relationships, and working relationships. These misconceptions can be the result of limited exposure to diverse perspectives. Typically, individuals are raised in one family and one neighborhood and attend a limited number of schools. People tend to adopt the beliefs, attitudes, and values of others in their social spheres. As a result, we may come to adulthood with beliefs and values that help or do not help us to manage our lives effectively. Groups provide individuals with the opportunity to examine their beliefs and values in relation to those of other people with different life experiences. This reassessment process is a major benefit of group approaches to personal change or development.

For example, a female participant in a therapy group was discussing her attraction to a man with whom she worked. She told the group that she often wished that she could have lunch with him in the cafeteria, but it had not happened yet, since he had not asked her to join him. Other members asked why she did not invite him to join her. She responded by saying that women do not ask men to have lunch with them. This was said with certainty, as if it were a universal social law. Several women in the group told her that they often invite male colleagues to lunch. This led to a discussion and eventually to a change in the belief system of the woman in question. Subsequently, she asked her colleague to lunch and, to her amazement, he accepted.

During the second stage of group development, participants have the opportunity to assess their beliefs and values about authority, how they respond to people with different views or ways of behaving, and how they believe the group should function. Members at this stage begin to feel safer about expressing their opinions and disagreeing with those of others. This conflict is an inherent part of group development and provides a wealth of information to members about how others think, feel, and behave. In addition to creating a unified group culture, then, individuals gain useful insights into the utility of their own beliefs and values. Assessment and alteration, if necessary, of these beliefs are made possible as a result.

The task of the group leader, then, is to help the group forge a unified set of beliefs and values and to encourage exploration of individual beliefs and values as well. This requires considerable fortitude on the leader's part, since member conflicts with authority figures are typically explored in relation to the leader. Members may express their negative feelings toward authority figures by reacting with hostility toward the leader. Of course, all groups experience a period of conflict with the leader. This conflict is necessary in order to reduce the centrality of the leader and to redistribute power and influence more equitably among group participants. However, it takes on special meaning in therapeutic or growth groups, since for some members, issues with parents, bosses, and other authorities may be a central component of the problems or concerns that they wish to explore in the group. Simply put, the task of the group leader is to allow himself or herself to be used as a symbol of authority and to allow members to explore their relationships to authority by examining their reactions to him or her.

Most leaders have the impulse to correct misperceptions of their intentions or behaviors and to encourage members to see them as the kind and democratic people that they really are. In fact, this is an appropriate goal in that it is useful for members to distinguish among authority figures and to learn that not all authority figures are the same. However, this is not accomplished by discouraging members from expressing their reactions to the leader. Encouraging members to share their feelings and to discuss their reactions is much more likely to produce a positive relationship between members and the leader.

Good relationships between group members and the leader are associated with individual goal achievement (Fuhriman & Burlingame, 1990). Continuing tension between the leader and members has negative effects on group and individual success (Lieberman et al., 1973). Therefore, the leader is advised to work to create positive relations with members. This task is accomplished by accepting the changes that occur in member feelings toward the leader. It is also accomplished by accepting the shift in leader power and influence that inevitably accompanies this phase.

Effective leaders encourage members to express their views regarding leader-member and member-member relations. They also intervene in ways that model compromise, tolerance, and the value of conflict resolution. For example, if a member challenges the leader's skills, an appropriate response might be to ask the member for suggestions, rather than to debate the validity of the challenge or to suggest that the individual probably has trouble with all authority figures. When two members are fighting with each other over perceived differences in beliefs, an appropriate intervention might be to point out that the disagreement is a wonderful opportunity to learn about each other, rather than to try to stop the exchange. The leader's task is to help the group develop a unified culture without sacrificing individuality. In so doing, he or she also encourages individual self-awareness and assessment that may prove critical to ultimate goal achievement.

Member Tasks at Stage Two

Individual members play a significant role in helping the group to successfully resolve the conflicts that inevitably arise during stage two. Members are advised to expect conflict to occur in the group and to view it as a sign of progress rather than a negative occurrence. If members view conflict among participants as opportunities for self-exploration and group building, the conflict is less likely to escalate to levels that will impede the group's effectiveness. This view of conflict also reduces the likelihood that members will personalize conflicts by attacking people rather than disagreeing with their ideas. The most important way that members can help the group to manage conflict is to encourage each other to use effective conflict management strategies. (See Chapter 5 for further discussion of this issue.)

STAGE THREE: TRUST AND STRUCTURE

The Tasks of the Leader at Stage Three

If the group manages to resolve key conflicts at stage two, feelings of trust, cohesion, and cooperation increase. Such feelings will make it possible for members to share more personally and to more readily accept and utilize feedback from each other and the leader. The quality of feedback tends to improve later in a group (Morran, Robison & Stockton, 1985). That is, members are more able to phrase their feedback to each other in descriptive rather than judgmental ways. Descriptive feedback has been found to be more effective than judgmental feedback in helping people to learn about themselves (Stockton & Morran, 1980). Judgmental feedback tends to classify the person in some way. A statement like "You seem distant and remote" is judgmental, whereas "John, I've noticed that you seem quiet and less involved today" is descriptive.

The growing sense of trust and cooperation during this period creates a context in which members can be more open with others and with themselves. Sharing thoughts, feelings, problems, and concerns, which is so essential in groups focused on individual change, occurs more easily at this time. In a work group, the third stage of group development can be quite brief, since the feeling of trust is sufficient to move the group into preparation for work and work itself.

In therapy and growth groups, however, this phase tends to be longer in duration, since personal sharing, feedback, and the exploration of interpersonal relations is part of the group's work.

Self-disclosure and the reactions of others to those disclosures are considered essential to increasing individual awareness. The exploration of interpersonal relationships that develop among members is also a key element in facilitating individual change or development. At this point, leader interventions can focus more directly on individuals and will be more likely to be heard by those individuals, since the heightened trust level extends to the leader as well. Member attitudes toward the leader are generally positive by this time. He or she is no longer perceived as a savior or a dictator. Instead, the leader tends to be viewed as a member who has special expertise that may be of use to members. What the leader says is often seen as valuable and helpful.

Leaders at this point can focus more on helping individuals work on their goals by intervening in ways that heighten member awareness. Depending on the theory of change or learning being employed, the leader will address interventions to individuals and will describe and interpret individual actions as they occur. Leaders may focus on individual thoughts, feelings, or behaviors, or some combination of the three, in order to help individuals to discover more about themselves. Increasing awareness is important in all theories of change and learning.

Member resistance to feedback or suggestions for change tends to lessen as the group environment becomes more trusting and cooperative. This facilitates the change process by creating an atmosphere in which people are more willing to engage in self-exploration, accept feedback on their response patterns, and try out new ways of responding.

The feelings of closeness and trust that develop among members at this stage are very influential in facilitating member goal achievement. However, it is possible that members will find this period so rewarding and comfortable that they may ignore the equally important task of creating structures that will facilitate goal achievement. Self-awareness and the exploration of interpersonal relationships are necessary but not sufficient elements of the change process. New ways of thinking, feeling, and behaving must ultimately be exported into the daily lives of individuals, and this is no easy task. The sequence of individual change includes increased awareness of current response patterns, a willingness to experiment with new ways of acting, the acquisition of the skills necessary to act in these new ways, and the ability to do so in one's daily life. Stage three provides members the opportunity for increased awareness and exploration of alternative ways of responding. However, it must also focus on individual and group planning. That is, members must determine how they will acquire the skills necessary to act in new ways and how they will integrate new ways of acting into their ongoing lives.

Some theories of individual change assume that once people become aware of how they typically act and what actions would be more effective, they will simply begin acting in these new ways. However, people don't automatically know how to respond differently. For example, lonely people do not always know how to meet people or how to maintain friendships. Meek people do not always know how to be assertive. Therefore, group members need to plan ways to acquire the skills necessary to achieve their goals. They also need to discuss ways to utilize these skills in their daily lives, where people are likely to be less supportive than other group members.

Leaders at this stage can help members to plan by raising the issue of planning with individuals and the group. A statement like "You seem to know what you want to change. What can we do to help you to do this outside the group?" calls attention to the need for planning. Personal-growth leaders and some therapists initiate structured activities to assist the planning process. For example, leaders may describe factors that inhibit the change process and then ask subgroups to meet to discuss their change goals and to help each other plan ways to accomplish these goals outside the group.

It is relatively easy for individuals to behave in new ways in the safe and supportive group environment. Sustaining these changes in the ongoing groups that constitute their social world, however, can be very difficult. Changes in individual behavior may be perceived as threatening or disruptive to the established patterns and roles in the groups to which individuals belong. Therefore, members need to develop strategies to overcome the natural resistance of others to their change. Not to do so reduces the likelihood that changes will be maintained in daily life.

Member Tasks at Stage Three

The trust and structure stage of group development is typically an exciting and stimulating time for group members. It is exhilarating to feel close to and supported by others. Some members find themselves wishing that the rest of the people in their lives were so accepting and supportive. People who have not had many opportunities to express themselves or to share their inner thoughts and feelings with others will find this phase of group life very special and satisfying. These feelings are normal and necessary. However, they may cause individuals to lose sight of their goal, which is to effect changes in their ongoing lives outside the group. Members, then, can help themselves and the group by maintaining their focus on real-world change.

Individuals can also facilitate group development and personal goal achievement by being open to new ideas and ways of reacting. Giving and receiving feedback is perhaps the most important task of all members at this time. Helping oneself and others to gain awareness and to experiment with new ways of responding is important as well. Finally, participating in individual and group planning focused on transferring group-initiated changes to real world contexts is crucial.

STAGE FOUR: WORK

Leader Tasks at Stage Four

The work phase of a therapy or growth group addresses skill acquisition and the transfer of learning to the real world. By this time, members have decided what changes they wish to make and what they need to do to make them. Now it is time to do it. Doing it means practicing new ways of responding and behaving in the group in order to prepare to do the same outside the group. Sometimes the practice is informal. For example, an individual who is working on becoming more sensitive to others will find ample opportunities to practice in the group. When others express feelings of vulnerability, the individual can try to react in a more supportive way. Since others know that he or she is working on being more responsive, they have the chance to acknowledge his or her efforts and to suggest ways to improve his or her skills.

In some cases, role playing and behavior rehearsal can be employed to help an individual or the group as a whole to work on specific skills. Communication and assertion are examples of skills that can be enhanced through the use of these techniques. The aim is to translate general goals into specific skills that will equip members to act in new ways after the group is over.

Another important part of the work stage is to begin the export process. Some of this happens informally as well. For example, if a member has as a goal the development of a better relationship with her daughter, she may begin to try to change that relationship. She may ask her daughter to go with her to the movies or to dinner. She may then bring this up at the next group session and describe what transpired. This provides the group with a chance to support her efforts, to give her feedback about how she handled the situation, and to make suggestions about ways improve her effectiveness in the future.

Formal, more structured methods to transfer new ways of thinking, feeling, and behaving can also be undertaken by the group. For example, all members can identify some small action that they will implement during the week. Pairs may be formed who will call each other during the week to encourage each other and offer advice. One member may decide to approach her boss about a raise and another may decide to call his estranged brother. These two people would phone each other to see how things are going and to offer support. Whether formal or informal, these activities are essential, since they increase the likelihood that changes will be incorporated into daily life.

Leaders at this stage need to encourage independence and confidence in members. If leaders do this, members internalize what they have learned and changes they have made and do not rely as much on the leader or the group for support and encouragement. To accomplish these objectives, leaders become increasingly less directive over the course of the group. For example, questions directed at the leader can be referred back to the members for discussion and resolution. Problem solving and decision making are left to individuals or to the members. The leader's role becomes increasingly peripheral with the passage of time.

Member Tasks at Stage Four

Members can facilitate the work stage of group development by assuming more personal responsibility as they feel able to do so. Their role is to work to consolidate the gains they have made in the group, to practice new ways of acting, to export their learning and skills to their daily environment, and to help others do the same. While the group has become a safe haven for individuals, it will end. The group was not meant to replace other contexts. Rather, it served as a temporary training ground to prepare individuals for more effective membership in the ongoing groups of daily life. Therefore, the task for members at this stage is to work to incorporate new ways of thinking, feeling, and acting into everyday life.

STAGE FIVE: TERMINATION

Leader and Member Tasks at Stage Five

When a meaningful and helpful experience nears its end, it is normal to want to forestall that ending. Members and leaders may feel a sense of loss and may even attempt to continue meeting beyond the agreed-upon time frame. In groups that do not have a designated end, individuals who are ready to terminate may have difficulty doing so, and other members may want these individuals to remain in the group as well. Termination can be an emotional time for members and leaders alike.

Leaders and members can help each other during this final stage by reminding each other that goal achievement is not accomplished inside the group, but outside. The group was intended to help individuals to function more effectively in their daily lives. Continuing the group for longer than necessary may actually interfere with this objective, since it delays full integration of changes and new skills into the daily experience of individuals.

Perhaps the best outcome of a therapy, counseling, or personal-growth group occurs when the group is internalized by individuals and becomes a functional and supportive reference group in the minds and memories of its members. It becomes one of the groups in our heads that we look to for ongoing guidance and support as we make choices in everyday situations. In this way, the actual group ends but its ongoing influence and support continue in its members' everyday lives.

13

SKILLS TRAINING GROUPS

One of the most exciting developments in modern psychology and education is the creation of group-based methods to teach people the skills necessary to function more effectively and happily at work, at home, and in other social contexts. These methods represent the first systematic effort to prevent, rather than to remediate, individual psychological and social problems. In the last thirty years, methods to teach individuals how to communicate, listen, make decisions, manage relationships, supervise employees, raise children more effectively, and the like have been designed and implemented.

The significance of this development cannot be overestimated. Prior to the availability of such approaches, individuals acquired life skills in the process of daily living. Observation, imitation, and the tutelage of parents and other significant adults were the primary means through which people learned how to cope with life problems and how to interact with others. While these time-honored, natural methods of socialization have produced great numbers of competent and capable people throughout human history, not everyone has fared so well. Some people, for example, have not had a sufficient number of positive, capable role models to pattern themselves after. Instead, they learned inadequate or psychologically damaging ways of dealing with life situations. Until the advent of skills training groups, the only recourse for these individuals was psychotherapy, which was not specifically designed to teach life skills. In general, psychotherapy was designed to overcome blocks to interacting effectively, but not to instruct clients in interaction skills. Some therapeutic approaches have incorporated skills training into treatment, but this is a relatively recent phenomenon and is not universally employed.

Even individuals who had excellent role models often feel the need to learn better ways of dealing with an increasingly complex and problematic social world. Coping strategies that were effective in the past are often insufficient to manage mounting stress, the pressures of dual-career relationships or raising children alone, the maintenance of friendships in fast-paced and alienating urban settings, or increasing career demands. The methods of previous generations may not be as useful in our complicated and sometimes chaotic social world. We interact with more diverse people in more varied social settings, and many of us feel ill equipped to do so. Changes in the U.S. economy from a production to a service orientation have increased the demand for employees with better social skills. Technical competence alone no longer ensures career advancement. Therefore, skills training groups can be helpful in augmenting the abilities of people who are already functioning quite well.

In addition, social and psychological research have gained a much better understanding of factors that influence positive social and psychological development. There is increased awareness of how effective parents, teachers, managers, and the like behave and what distinguishes them from their less effective counterparts. This understanding makes it possible to teach people how to interact more effectively in a number of contexts and social roles. Skills training groups share this information directly with people from all walks of life. Research findings are being translated into understandable and practical prescriptions for improving the quality of individual human life. While more research is needed, and caution is always warranted when making suggestions to people about how to live, sharing what is known about people with people is perhaps the most significant advance in the social sciences in this century. It makes it possible to arm individuals with the skills necessary to prevent some serious psychological problems and empowers them to take more control over their own lives.

DEFINING TRAINING GROUPS

A skills training group is "a group established to teach such human relations skills as assertion, communication, management, or leadership in order to enhance personal and professional effectiveness" (Wheelan, 1990, p. 49). Nelson-Jones (1992) defines skills training groups as

> *time-limited structured groups in which one or more leaders use a repertoire of didactic and facilitative skills to help participants develop and maintain one or more specific lifeskills. Important features of training groups include: no assumption of psychological disturbance, systematic instruction, experiential learning-by-doing, and a high degree of participant involvement. (p. 6)*

Terms other than *skills training* have been used to identify groups of this type. For example, Carkhuff (1971) used the term *human resource development*. Mosher and Sprinthall (1970, 1971) refer to such groups as *deliberate psychological education*. *Psychoeducation* (Ivey, 1976), *lifeskill training* (Gazda, 1989), and *developmental education* (Nelson-Jones, 1988) are other terms used to describe these groups. Skills training groups have also been used with psychiatric patients to increase life skills and coping (e.g., Gazda, Childers & Brooks, 1987). Regardless of their title or the population served, however, the goal is to provide participants with "increased awareness of some life problem and tools to better cope with it" (Corey & Corey, 1992, p. 13).

What are the skills that training groups attempt to teach? According to Nelson-Jones (1992), "life skills are personally responsible sequences of choices in specific psychological skill areas conducive to mental wellness" (p. 15). People of different ages, in different roles, and faced with different problems require specific sets of skills in order to adequately cope with the challenges and tasks of their particular life circumstances. For example, adolescence is a period in which young people are learning to build and sustain personal relationships. Some of the skills associated with developing relationships include empathy, active listening, and the appropriate expression of anger. Skills training groups have been designed to assist teenagers in acquiring these skills (e.g., Hatch & Guerney, 1975; Huey & Rank, 1984; Sprinthall, 1980).

When people have children, they need to learn how to be effective parents. Some of the skills associated with effective parenting include discipline strategies, assertive communication with children, limit setting, empathy, and strategies to support and encourage children to achieve their potential. A number of training programs have been developed to help individuals to acquire these skills (e.g., Gordon, 1970; Silberman & Wheelan, 1980).

Stress accompanies many of life's tasks and problems. Skills that increase an individual's ability to manage stress include relaxation, time management, goal setting, and modifying our thinking with regard to potentially stressful situations. A variety of training groups have been designed to teach these and other stress-reduction skills (e.g., Bruning & Frew, 1987; Murphy & Hurrell, 1987).

Individuals who assume management roles require leadership, communication, and decision-making skills. The management role also requires the abilities to facilitate team development, to motivate employees, and to organize materials, schedules, and personnel. Even this list does not begin to exhaust the set of skills required of managers in an increasingly competitive, diverse, and complex work environment. Management and employee training groups have proliferated rapidly in both private and public sector organizations. They have become an integral part of workplace practices and are the focus of significant research investigations to increase their effectiveness (e.g., Campbell & Campbell, 1988; Latham, 1988; Offermann & Gowing, 1990).

GOALS

The goals of skills training groups are the same regardless of content. First, skills training groups are designed to educate individuals about specific life situations and strategies to manage these situations more effectively. Second, they facilitate the acquisition of the skills necessary to cope in particular situations. The first goal is similar to many other educational designs in that training groups attempt to increase knowledge in a particular content area. They are different from some other educational designs in that training groups also have performance as a goal.

A history professor, for example, is successful if a significant number of students become more knowledgeable concerning historical events. However, a skills trainer is successful if participants become more knowledgeable about communication and more able to communicate effectively. In that sense, there are many skills training courses in traditional educational settings. For example, as part of their professional preparation, counselors take courses that increase their knowledge of counseling theory and their skills in actual counseling situations. Skills training designs are part of the educational process in a wide variety of disciplines. They are distinguished from other educational designs in that knowledge and performance are addressed.

THE CHANGE/LEARNING FRAMEWORK

The following formula represents the learning framework in skills training groups:

Learning + modeling + practice + support = skill acquisition
(Wheelan, 1990, p. 97)

The fundamental assumption underlying skills training groups is that human behavior is learned. Miller and Dollard (1941) stated that imitation is the basic learning mechanism employed by human beings to acquire what have become known as life skills. By observing the behavior of others, we internalize that behavior which is stored in our memories. In a similar situation, we can reproduce that behavior if we believe that it is in our best interest to do so (Bandura, 1977). A number of factors influence the acquisition of social skills through observation. First, the the amount of attention that an individual pays to someone who is modeling a response affects learning. Learning is enhanced when the modeled behavior is distinctive, noticeable, complex, and novel. Learning is also enhanced when the observer has a positive emotional response to the model and views the model as attractive, powerful, and supportive or rewarding. A motivated, interested, and receptive observer is more likely to acquire the modeled skills (Bandura, 1977). Motivation and receptivity are increased by exploration and discussion of individual attitudes and perceptions concerning the target skills and by changing thought patterns that may interfere with skill acquisition and performance (Beck, 1976; Lazarus, 1977).

Individuals retain what they have observed more effectively if they mentally rehearse the observed skills and use words to describe or label those skills. Practicing or overtly rehearsing the skills also facilitates performance, as does accurate feedback from others and from the individual about his or her performance. Finally, an individual is likely to perform the skills well if he or she is rewarded or supported for doing so (Bandura, 1966, 1971, 1977).

Skills training groups, then, assume that individuals acquire life skills by

- learning about these skills and how they can increase one's ability to function effectively in specific social contexts;
- learning to differentiate between when and when not to use specific skills;
- developing attitudes and beliefs that support skill acquisition;
- observing competent individuals demonstrating the skills in clear, interesting, and unique ways;
- developing positive emotional attachments to those models;
- mentally practicing the skills;
- discussing and verbally labeling the skills;
- overtly practicing the skills;
- personally assessing their performance;
- receiving feedback from others about their performance; and
- receiving praise, encouragement, and support for their performance.

The Group Context

Skills training can be, and sometimes is, conducted on an individual basis. However, in the vast majority of cases, training occurs in a group setting. One reason for this is that it is more practical. More people can be trained in less time, for less cost, than would be the case with individual instruction. The primary reason for conducting skills training in groups, however, is that the group context can positively affect learning, skill acquisition, and performance. It is often easier to change attitudes and behaviors in a group than in a one-to-one situation (Lewin, 1943). Well-functioning groups strengthen the bonds between leaders and members. Since leaders are the primary models in skills training groups, these bonds increase learning by generating positive feelings toward the models. Unity and cohesion contribute to feelings of safety and support and increase the likelihood that attitudes toward learning will be positive. Groups also offer the opportunity for more feedback and suggestions about performance and to experience more support and reward.

The key to successful skills training, then, is a well-functioning group. In groups that do not meet this criterion, learning is often diminished regardless of the expertise of the trainer or the elegance of the training design. For example, if group members are not able to resolve their hostile feelings toward the leader, they will not develop the positive affective ties that support observational learning. If members disagree about the utility of training, then cohesion and support are undermined. Members may also join together to resist learning as a result of unresolved conflicts with authority. All of these situations reduce the probability of learning, retaining, and eventually using the skills being taught. If group conditions are not conducive to learning, successful skill acquisition is very unlikely. However, when groups are functioning well, skill acquisition is almost assured.

PRETRAINING ASSESSMENT

There are a number of good sources of information about designing curricula for skills training groups (e.g., Goad, 1982; Mayo & DuBois, 1987; Nelson-Jones, 1992; Silberman, 1990). However, it is important to remember that standard training designs do not always fit the needs of every group. Each set of participants has different needs, and each group may vary with regard to its developmental level. Therefore, it is always advisable to gain as much information as possible about the potential participants, their needs, and their current circumstances prior to designing or initiating a training program. Key assessment questions include:

1. Who are the participants? (Age, roles, sex, job, ethnicity, and so on)
2. What are their specific training needs?
3. What do they believe their training needs are?
4. Have individuals had previous training experiences?
5. Are they volunteers, or are they required to attend?
6. Are participants members of an ongoing group within an organization, different groups within the same organization, or individuals from diverse organizations or contexts?
7. If participants are from the same group or organization, what are the current developmental issues in that group and organization?
8. If participants are from the same group or organization, is the environment supportive of training, and will participants be encouraged or discouraged from using new skills in this environment?

Trainers may conduct interviews, use questionnaires, or apply other methods to answer these questions. The answers help the trainer to determine whether skills training is appropriate, how to design the training, and what group-level issues to expect during the training. For example, if the personal characteristics of individuals are similar, designing the training is easier in many cases. Thus, designing training for a group of middle-aged white male electrical engineers, recently promoted to managerial roles, with no prior training experience, who desire to learn how to communicate more effectively with employees, is a relatively simple task. However, if they are required to attend and do not actually believe that management skills can be learned, the design and implementation of training become more difficult.

If participants are from the same company, and that company has had recent layoffs, and there are rumors that more managers will be laid off, the job will be much more difficult. In this case, participants are likely to be hostile and threatened by the training process. They may even see the trainer as a company spy who will report their actions to upper management. Such conditions make it much more difficult to create a training environment that is conducive to learning.

If the same individuals, with the same characteristics, want training in how to deal with females or employees from diverse racial or ethnic backgrounds, the difficulty in designing and conducting the training increases. This author was faced with a similar situation. The task was to develop skills for dealing with female and ethnically diverse employees. Participants were approximately 98 percent white male managers. Participants were required to attend. The company's upper management was invested in the training outcomes, since they had been cited by the government for not hiring enough minorities and women.

Such conditions increase the difficulty of designing an effective training program, due to the lack of diversity among participants. If they were more diverse, activities could be designed that utilize differences among participants as a source of information about sexual, racial, and ethnic issues in the workplace. Lacking those differences, other less potent sources of information would be required. Films, reading material, and handouts could be used. However, these are much less effective than actual human beings who are willing to share their own experiences.

Group conditions were not the best in this case either, since the participants felt that upper-level management blamed them for not hiring enough women and minorities. They saw the training as a kind of punishment and the trainer as a potential informant concerning their attitudes and skill levels in this area. In essence, the training began with the participants in the conflict and fight stage of group development, and unless this condition could be altered, training would not be effective.

Sometimes assessment reveals that training has been mandated by higher-ups in order to deflect blame for a problem onto a subgroup of the organization. Unfortunately, this is a common occurrence in schools. Declining test scores, grades, and pupil attendance are perceived to be the results of ineffective teachers. Training in student motivation, empathic listening, or disciplinary strategies may be mandated by the school board and administrators or demanded by parents. These three groups, however, usually do not attend. If a pretraining assessment reveals this kind of situation, it is often best to decline the training assignment and to suggest that a school-based organizational assessment and intervention project would be more appropriate. Training teachers, in this case, is likely to exacerbate the school's problems, since it may increase conflict and resentment between teachers and other school groups and does not involve all constituent groups in addressing and remediating problems. Dealing with the school as a whole is a much more effective strategy (Wheelan & Conway, 1991).

Pretraining assessment provides critical information to a trainer. The information may lead the trainer to accept or decline a training assignment. It alerts the trainer to group and organizational issues that may influence the learning process. It reveals characteristics of the trainees, which aids in the design process, and it may suggest alternatives to training that might be more effective in a particular situation.

Designing Training

While a complete explication of the design process in training is beyond the scope of this book, some central elements are discussed and critical issues are highlighted. The reader is referred to the authors cited in the previous section for more in-depth descriptions of the design process.

Imagine, if you will, that you have been asked to conduct a two-day training session for physicians. The topic is effective communication with patients. As a result of a needs assessment, you learn the following:

- The training is being offered to physicians who have been successfully sued by patients more than once. Research suggests that suits are not always the result of incompetence, but can be the result of ineffective communication with patients. Therefore, a state medical board is offering training to doctors with a history of suits.
- The physicians do not have to attend. They are volunteers. Most participants are white male surgeons or obstetricians between 40 and 50 years old. They want to learn to communicate more effectively with patients. However, they are a bit embarrassed to attend a training in remedial bedside manner and worry that spending a lot of extra time with patients will interfere with the important parts of the job, such as reviewing test results, planning with nurses and residents, and performing technical procedures. They worry that they will be reprimanded by hospital administrators if they see fewer patients per day, since that would affect hospital finances.
- Participants from a number of hospitals will participate in the training. They are from all over the United States and, in general, do not know each other.

The needs assessment alerts you to a number of design issues. First, training in assertive communication will be of use to the physicians. Second, the shame and embarrassment that participants are experiencing may interfere with learning. Therefore, strategies to reduce negative self-image and self-blame must be incorporated into the training from the outset. Third, extensive and time-consuming communication skills will be resisted, since the physicians are concerned about maintaining schedules and the quality of technical services to patients. Fourth, the physicians perceive themselves as scientists first and foremost. Therefore, including research evidence supporting the effectiveness of the skills being taught will be necessary. Fifth, the two-day format does not provide sufficient time for group development to occur at a natural pace. Consequently, the design must be structured to create safety and cooperation more rapidly. Sixth, since participants are from different places, there will be no opportunity for them to support each other in utilizing learned skills after the group is over. Therefore, the design must include a time for individuals to plan ways to gain support for personal style changes in their particular work settings.

The training design for this population would include:

1. An introductory lecture in which the trainer makes the following points:
   - medical education emphasizes technical skills but does not usually adequately prepare physicians to communicate effectively with patients;
   - communication skills are learned;
   - communication with patients is more difficult due to the stress of illness;
   - effective doctor-patient communication does not need to be time consuming;
   - the acquisition of a limited set of communication skills can increase a physician's effectiveness as a communicator;
   - there is significant research that shows that assertive communication skills facilitate positive relationships, decrease misunderstandings, and create an atmosphere of mutual respect (Fensterheim & Glazer, 1983; Wheelan & Bastas, 1979).
2. An activity in which participants introduce themselves in an assertive, nonassertive, or aggressive manner and state what they hope to learn from the workshop.
3. A discussion of the nonverbal and verbal components of these three communication styles.
4. Group discussions of the likely outcomes of using the different styles.
5. Video examples of physicians employing the three styles in interactions with patients.
6. Group discussion of the key behaviors employed in the video demonstrations of the three styles.
7. Trainer demonstration of active listening skills.
8. Group covert and overt practice of these skills, utilizing case examples of doctor-patient interactions provided by the trainer.
9. Trainer feedback to participants on their performance.
10. Trainer demonstration of two basic assertive techniques: broken record and fogging.
11. Group covert and overt practice of these skills, utilizing cases generated by participants themselves based on their experiences with patients.
12. Trainer and member feedback on individual performance.
13. Trainer demonstration of negative and positive assertion, negative and positive inquiry, free information, and self-disclosure techniques.
14. Group covert and overt practice of these skills.
15. Trainer and member feedback to individuals on their performance.
16. Individual and group planning sessions focused on implementing these skills in their practice and ways to gain support from others for utilizing assertive skills with patients.
17. Discussion of participants' reactions to the training.
18. Formal evaluation of the training experience.

A number of detailed descriptions of assertion training designs exist in the literature (e.g., Alberti & Emmons, 1974; Butler, 1981; Lange & Jakubowski, 1976; Silberman & Wheelan, 1980; Wheelan, 1978; Wheelan & Bastas, 1979). All teach a set of assertive communication skills through the use of modeling, role play, and covert and overt behavior rehearsal. They also advocate the adoption of attitudes and beliefs that support an assertive communication style. Finally, all assertiveness training designs emphasize support, encouragement, and reward as essential to learning. What is not addressed in much detail, however, are methods to deal with group-level events that may either enhance or diminish participant learning. This is true of most published material on training designs in all skill areas. In the previous example, success will be based not only on the adequacy of the design but also on the leader's and members' actions during the training. These issues are addressed next.

The Role of the Leader as Training Begins

Unlike therapy and personal-growth groups, training groups do not always begin at the beginning. If participants are volunteers, from diverse organizations and contexts, and unknown to each other, the group will begin, as all new groups do, in the dependency and inclusion stage of group development. However, if the participants are members of a longstanding group or are from the same organization, the training group may begin at any stage of group development. The dynamics of the ongoing group or organization are not left at the door of the training room. These preexisting dynamics will influence the training, for good or for ill, from its inception.

For example, a training group may begin at the conflict and fight stage. This is frequently the case with intact groups when the training topic is team building. The identified need for team building is often the result of a group's inability to resolve conflicts with authority or with each other. Other groups may begin training with a high level of trust. Still others may be very well functioning and productive. The fact that beginning training groups may vary with regard to their developmental level highlights the need for pretraining assessment. Trainers who are unaware of preexisting conditions can inadvertently disrupt a positive group culture or exacerbate negative group conditions. For example, if a trainer assumes that a new training group is at the dependency stage of group development when it is, in fact, a mature group, participants may resent trainer attempts to create safety and a supportive atmosphere, since one already exists. Introductory activities, designed to introduce members to each other and to reduce anxiety, may be seen as too elementary or silly. The trainer may be perceived as incompetent, since he or she is unaware of the group's history. The group may begin to perceive the trainer as an interloper and may revert to the conflict stage as a result. Both of these situations reduce the likelihood that learning and skill acquisition will occur.

Perhaps the most unnerving situation for a trainer is to walk into a training group that is in the conflict stage of group development. In this situation, the trainer is frequently granted no grace period. Instead, unresolved conflicts with group or organizational authority figures are immediately transferred to the trainer, who is attacked and challenged from the beginning. Foreknowledge of group conditions is extremely helpful in such cases, since training designs and trainer styles must be geared to group developmental conditions.

If the training group is new or in the dependency and inclusion stage of group development, the trainer works to create safety. Participants in training groups are asked to practice skills, participate in role plays, and share information about their level of skill in particular areas. Most of us have been in situations in which we have been asked to try a new behavior in a public setting. Band practice, athletic practices, dancing classes, school plays, and the like are examples of such situations. For most people, these experiences arouse feelings of anxiety and embarrassment. The skills training group does as well. Therefore, trainers who act in supportive, nonjudgmental ways in the beginning will facilitate the development of these same characteristics in the group as a whole. Trainers are also advised to be directive and to present themselves as capable and trustworthy at this stage. Natural feelings of dependency associated with this group stage will aid the trainer in this regard. Individuals will typically go along with activities and can be encouraged to try new things early on. This sets a norm for experimentation and risk taking that may continue throughout the training.

Members of groups in the first stage of group development should not be asked to share very personal things or to engage in overt practice sessions. Instead, group-building activities are the initial focus. Group-building activities focus on increasing member safety and inclusion by providing opportunities to talk and become comfortable with the trainer and each other. Once this is accomplished, practice sessions are more easily initiated.

If a training group begins at the second stage of development, the trainer's task is to help the group to change this situation. It is important for the trainer to accept group hostility directed at him or her and to differentiate him- or herself from other authority figures with whom the group is in conflict. For example, the author was asked to provide training for child care workers in a large city. The participants were often required to go into dangerous sections of the city in order to investigate allegations of child abuse. The goal of the training was to provide participants with communication skills that would reduce the risk of violence or other forms of aggression in these potentially volatile situations. The child care workers felt that communication skills were insufficient protection and were angry at their superiors about the training.

The group was initially hostile toward the trainer. In order to gain the group's confidence, the trainer joined with the group's belief that communication skills would not provide sufficient protection to child care workers in all situations. Communication skills were not presented as the answer, but as tools that would help in certain circumstances. In more dangerous situations, other strategies, such as police protection, would be necessary. The trainer presented her views with humor and down-to-earth examples, much to the delight of the participants. The initial hostility decreased and the members became more receptive to the trainer and the learning process.

If a training group is functioning well and norms for cooperation and productivity already exist, the trainer's task is not to interfere with these dynamics. The presence of the trainer can disrupt the group's processes, since he or she is a new element. Initially, close-knit, mature groups will resist new people, especially those in leadership roles. It is important to remember that intact groups already have a defined and, in this case, functional leadership structure. The trainer's presence, then, can be perceived as threatening to the positive climate that has been previously established. In this case, the trainer must take care not to be seen as competing with preexisting leaders. At the same time, the trainer must establish him- or herself as a leader figure in order to set the stage for observational learning. As was previously mentioned, individuals learn best from models who are perceived as powerful, supportive, and rewarding.

Establishing trainer authority without replacing existing leaders can be accomplished by complimenting the group and its leaders on how well they work together. It is helpful to praise the group for being able to identify areas in which they would benefit from further training and to point out that this is a major sign of a well-functioning team. The trainer is advised to remind the group that they are the content experts with regard to their roles. What the trainer adds is expertise in a particular set of skills. This kind of discussion reduces resistance to the trainer as outsider by differentiating between types of authority. Ongoing leaders remain the legitimate authorities, and the trainer is established as an expert in a particular skill area.

Member Tasks in the Beginning

Members can facilitate successful outcomes in training groups by remaining open to learning new things and helping others to do the same. This is relatively simple when people are involved in training sessions in areas in which they are not expected to have expertise. For example, new parents are not expected to be familiar with the intricacies of the parenting role. Participants in training for new parents, then, find it easy to be open to learning, to share their concerns about the parenting role, and to practice new skills. For participants in professional training groups, however, the stakes are higher. Skills training groups require that individuals identify personal areas that need improvement, practice new skills, and receive feedback from others. This can be very threatening, especially for participants who work together on a daily basis or who are members of the same profession. It can seem very risky to share areas of vulnerability in the presence of peers.

It is useful to remember that everyone has areas that would benefit from further development. Individuals want to learn more effective ways to manage job-related situations, and training provides the opportunity to learn from peers as well as from the trainer. Being open to learning and to sharing strategies that have worked personally as well is key to creating a successful learning environment.

Participants who share vulnerabilities are typically seen as courageous and strong by their peers.

Leader Tasks in Middle Sessions

Once a sense of safety and support has been created and the trainer has established him- or herself as a positive role model, work on skill acquisition can begin in earnest. The first step in the learning process is to increase member awareness of particular problems and skills to handle those problems more effectively. For example, new parents may need to know more about the physical, psychological, and social needs of children at various ages before specific parenting skills are taught. Similarly, managers may need to learn more about what motivates individuals before motivation techniques are taught.

Traditional views of education might suggest that the best way to raise awareness would be to give a lecture on child development or human motivational factors. However, people, and especially adults, already have information about these issues. The process of living teaches us a great deal about a great many things. Therefore, trainers typically involve participants in the process by asking them to share their views on the training topic. Once participants' views have been elicited, they can be compared with the views and research findings of social scientists. This more interactive teaching strategy is employed for at least two reasons. First, experiential education is generally more effective, since it engages people in the process of learning. To share personal views on a subject, individuals have to organize and communicate their thoughts. During a lecture, individuals may or may not compare their views with those that are presented. Mentally interacting with the ideas that are presented enhances the learning process. Second, member discussions facilitate group development and increase the likelihood that individuals will adopt the views that are ultimately accepted by the group. Both these results are conducive to learning and to skill acquisition.

The second trainer task during this period is to teach skills. This task demands that the trainer be capable of demonstrating the skills highlighted in the training design. Considerable preparation is required to do this well. Unfortunately, many trainers believe that they can teach almost any set of skills. In traditional educational formats, this might be the case. However, the skills training format requires the trainer to be able to verbally describe the skills in question and to provide competent demonstrations of those skills as well. Thus, assertion trainers must be expert in assertive communication. Management trainers must be thoroughly familiar with and able to perform management techniques. Empathy training requires an empathic trainer, and relaxation training requires a trainer capable of relaxing. Not all trainers possess the skills necessary to conduct particular training sessions. Usually, trainers become expert in certain types of training, since expertise in all forms of training would be difficult if not impossible to develop. Some trainers rely on videotaped demonstrations of particular skills. However, this tends to dilute observational learning, since participants are not emotionally connected to the actors on the screen.

Films can be helpful as supplementary teaching aids. However, there is no substitute for live demonstrations.

The third major task during this period is to provide opportunities for participants to practice the new skills. In general, people are reluctant to role play. However, there is no substitute for practice. Music theory courses do not create good pianists. Practice does. In the same way, while watching others behave in new ways may help participants to learn new skills, performing those skills in daily life is enhanced by prior practice and feedback on one's performance.

Teaching, modeling, and facilitating practice sessions are the major trainer tasks during this period. These tasks are essential to group success. How they are done and how the trainer manages group-level events that occur during work on these tasks, however, is also of vital importance. What trainers say, how they respond to member questions, challenges, and concerns, and how they deal with group dynamic processes that emerge have significant impact on the learning process (Wheelan, 1990).

Member Tasks in Middle Sessions

The goal of participants in training groups is skill acquisition. They can help themselves and others to accomplish this goal by listening, watching, practicing, and asking for feedback on their performance. Of course, this is easier said than done. Old ways of doing things are familiar. New ways are strange and uncomfortable, especially at first. It is only natural to resist change in some way. For example, members may find themselves more eager to talk about situations than to practice alternative ways of responding to those situations. While this is more comfortable, it inhibits learning by reducing practice time. A work orientation on the part of members is very important.

Practice sessions are not always fun. Participants and even some trainers assume that good training must always be entertaining and absorbing. While training should be engaging and interesting, good training, like a good workout at the gym, requires periods of repetition, attention to detail, and discipline. Participants need time to hone their skills in order to securely anchor them in their behavioral repertoire.

Finally, participants can help themselves and others to acquire and tune their new skills by giving and receiving feedback in generous and helpful ways. When an individual practices a new skill, direct, specific feedback is very useful in improving performance. Feedback that is specific and nonjudgmental is best. Praise, encouragement, and supportive comments from other members are as important as, if not more important than, support from trainers. Support from members to members is an essential ingredient in the learning process and creates a healthy group environment as well.

Leader and Member Tasks in Ending Sessions

Learning skills does not automatically mean that those skills will become part of the daily actions of individuals. As was stated in Chapter 12, integrating new ways of behaving into one's daily life can be a daunting task. Therefore, the primary task of the trainer and members at this period is to discuss and plan ways to utilize newly acquired skills in day-to-day life. For example, participants can identify individuals who are likely to support their efforts and then plan ways to elicit that support. They may also plan a follow-up session a month or two in the future, when participants will reconvene to discuss their experiences in applying skills and offer suggestions and support to each other. Participants may also spend time identifying situations in which the new skills would be helpful and others in which they would not be helpful. No set of skills is appropriate in every situation. Such a discussion can be very useful in teaching individuals to exercise judgment concerning appropriate and inappropriate responses in particular situations. The leader creates time for discussions regarding the transfer of learning to real environments. He or she may also offer suggestions. However, the trainer should not be central in this discussion, since the goal is to foster the participants' independence of the training process.

The development of methods to teach individuals the skills necessary to cope more effectively with life situations is a major step forward in preventing psychological problems and creating more socially competent and self-assured persons. There are a growing number of training designs and educational programs to prepare competent skills trainers. In general, however, both the training designs and the education of trainers fail to consider the influence of group processes on learning and skill acquisition. More research is needed in this area, and more emphasis on group facilitation skills is essential in programs that prepare trainers. Skills training is a powerful new technology. To undermine that power by ignoring the effect of the group context in which learning occurs is ill advised. The dynamics of learning groups are critical to skills training success.

14

WORK GROUPS

Organizations have recently rediscovered the work group or team. Books, articles, and research studies that attempt to describe the characteristics of high-performance work teams have proliferated over the last decade (e.g., Cummings, 1981; Dyer 1984; Friedlander, 1987; Hackman 1989; Larson & LaFasto, 1989; Sundstrom et al., 1990). The focus on the importance of work groups in increasing organizational productivity has been alternately described as a "management transformation" (Walton, 1985) or a "corporate renaissance" (Kanter, 1983). The term *transformation* implies a change or shift in emphasis from individual to group effectiveness as the key to productivity. The term *renaissance*, however, suggests a rebirth or revival of interest in a traditional method of accomplishing tasks.

In fact, people have formed groups in order to achieve goals and tasks since the beginning of human history. The small group of persons working collaboratively for their mutual benefit or survival is the oldest form of social organization (Hogan, 1975). The vast majority of people participate in groups or teams on a daily basis at work and in other task-oriented contexts in their communities. However, this fact of human experience has been overshadowed and pushed from view in modern times by the dominance of individualistic thinking. For years, finding the right individual for the job was considered the key to goal achievement and productivity. The context in which that individual would func tion was not considered to be an important factor. And yet, even the most capable and talented person cannot be effective if he or she is a member of a group mired in conflict or preoccupied by external factors that inhibit its ability to function. Recently, the role of groups in facilitating or blocking individual and organizational effectiveness has reentered human consciousness. Fueled in part by the need to find new methods to compete in a global economy, we have turned our attention to the most ancient method of all. After years of neglect, the current task is to understand how work groups function and what can be done to facilitate their effectiveness.

EFFECTIVE WORK GROUPS

A work group or team "has two or more people; it has a specific objective or recognizable goal to be attained; and coordination among the members of the team is required for the attainment of the team goal or objective" (Larson & LaFasto, 1989, p. 19). Work teams are "small groups of interdependent individuals who share responsibility for outcomes for their organizations" (Sundstrom et al., 1990, p. 120). Team goals and tasks may relate directly to production or service. Groups may also be employed in planning, decision making, policy setting, and other activities related to organizational goals.

Research investigations have provided us with a reasonably consistent description of the characteristics of effective teams. For example, Larson and LaFasto (1989) found that effective teams shared the following characteristics:

- a clear, elevating goal
- a collaborative climate
- a results-driven structure
- standards of excellence
- competent team members
- external support and recognition
- unified commitment
- principled leadership (p. 8).

In a recent review on work-team effectiveness, Sundstrom, DeMeuse, and Futrell (1990) found evidence to support the validity of the characteristics outlined by Larson and LaFasto. In addition, they noted that effective work groups are commonly found in organizations that support innovation and excellence. Such groups have the technical, training, and consulting resources necessary to do their jobs and sufficient autonomy to regulate and manage their own activities.

The foregoing descriptions are generally supported by an extensive body of research (see Chapter 7). We know with some degree of certainty the characteristics of effective work groups. However, there are very few practical prescriptions about what leaders and members can do to create effective teams. We know the desired ends, but the means to those ends have been less clearly articulated. The remainder of this chapter attempts to offer some concrete suggestions to members and leaders about ways to facilitate the effectiveness of the task-oriented groups to which they belong.

Before deciding where to go, it is important to know where you are. A clear picture of the current dynamics of a group helps members and leaders to determine what steps to take in order to create or sustain group effectiveness and performance. Consider the following two scenarios.

Cases

Scenario 1   Everyone enjoys working for Joe, who is the manager of a twelve-person team of engineers. Joe is terrific. When a team member has a problem with one of the computer programs, Joe is right there. He just comes to your office and gets the bugs out of the program himself. The guy is brilliant. Rumor has it that he sleeps with a computer by his bed in case he gets an idea about how to solve a problem during the night. He's tough but he's fair. No one wants to get on his bad side. In fact, people try to get on his good side. Whatever Joe wants, he gets. If he says, "Jump," we say, "How high?" People would do anything for Joe.

We don't have meetings, really. Oh, we do get together with Joe once a month and he tells us what he wants each of us to do. Everybody is pretty agreeable. We never fight about things. We don't need to, since Joe always makes everything clear. He's great that way. We'd be lost without him. One time, when he took a few days off, we had some problems. No one knew the specifics of the project we were working on. Fortunately, Joe's a workhorse. He says we need him around. In the last few years, Joe's only taken a few days off at a time. He even helps some of the younger guys sort out their family problems. Some of them actually call him at home.

Scenario 2   I wish that I could make more decisions on my own, but Rita likes to be in on everything. After all, it's her nickel, so to speak. She started the company from scratch. She's a real visionary. Rita knew that the demand for information services was going to increase dramatically, and she jumped in ahead of the rest. That took guts and a lot of start-up money. Why shouldn't she know how people are spending that money? She's a stickler for detail. It drives me crazy sometimes, but how can you get mad at somebody who's doing it right?

This company has grown from five employees to thirty in just four years. I was one of the initial five. We're the management team. I never thought that I'd be keeping the books for a company this large. Sometimes it scares me a little, since procedures get more complicated as the company expands. But Rita seems to be on top of things, although it's getting harder to pop into her office with a question. As we've gotten bigger, there are more people with more questions.

The new people don't have the same feelings about the company or Rita. They like their jobs all right, but they seem eager to take on more responsibility for their own areas. They just don't understand that this company is Rita's baby. I told her not to hire people with delusions of grandeur. They expect to get promoted and to be in charge of things someday, but Rita's in charge and always will be. Rita said she hired them because she needed highly qualified people in order to keep expanding. But they rock the boat. Even she is getting tired of their enthusiasm and new ideas.

Assessing Group Processes and Development: Scenarios 1 and 2

Both of these scenarios describe groups in the dependency stage of group development. In Chapter 4, a list of twenty-one characteristics common to groups at this stage was provided. That list is repeated below in order to provide the reader with an opportunity to assess Joe's team and Rita's five-person management team.

Identifying a Stage-One Group

1. Members are concerned with personal safety in the group.
2. Members are concerned with acceptance and inclusion.
3. Members fear group rejection.
4. Members communicate in a tentative and very polite manner.
5. The members behave in ways that suggest a need for dependable and directive leadership.
6. The leader is seen as benevolent and and competent.
7. The leader is expected and encouraged to provide members with direction and personal safety.
8. The leader is very rarely challenged.
9. Goals are not clear to members, but clarity is not sought.
10. Members rarely express disagreement with initial group goals.
11. The group assumes that consensus about goals exists.
12. Role assignments tend to be based on external status, first impressions, and initial self-presentation of members, rather than on matching member competencies with goal and task requirements.
13. Member compliance is high.
14. Communication tends to be centralized.
15. Participation is generally limited to a few vocal individuals.
16. Overt conflict is minimal.
17. Conformity is high.
18. A lack of group structure and organization is evident.
19. Member deviation from emerging norms is rare.
20. Cohesion and commitment to the group are based on identification with the leader rather than other factors.
21. Subgroups and coalitions are rare at this stage.

Many of these characteristics describe the groups in question. In the case of Rita's company, however, the newer employees do not fit the profile of a stage-one group as readily. While the newer group has not actively rebelled yet, it is apparent that conflict will erupt soon. If conflict does become overt, this may actually be useful to the company as a whole, since it would provide the total group with the opportunity to resolve issues and to plan ways to operate more effectively. On the other hand, Joe's team appears content with the current situation. This decreases the likelihood that Joe or the team will initiate changes. In this case, outside pressures could precipitate changes within the group. Barring that, however, the status quo will most likely be maintained.

Development is usually preceded by feelings of discomfort and constraint. Such feelings are evident in varying degrees in Rita, her management team, and the newer employees. They are poised on the brink of change. This scenario presents a more positive picture, even though problems are evident. For example, Rita is described as a stickler for detail, intrusive, and autocratic. A rift is developing between older and newer employees, and there is some concern among managers about their competence to handle the increasing complexity of a larger system. This system appears, at first glance, to be experiencing more problems than Joe's engineering team. However, much of what is occurring is a normal part of group development, and while things could go awry, these growing pains are a good sign.

Joe's group seems fairly happy and content. In fact, in times past Joe would have been considered an ideal manager. He is tough but fair, competent, concerned about his employees, and well liked by them in return. There are problems in the group, but they are not recognized as such. The primary problem is the dependency of team members on their leader. They do not function well without him, and they do not have sufficient information or competence to do so. The leader is so central to the task that work cannot proceed without him. Another key problem in this scenario is that all decisions are made by one person. Other members simply carry them out. Given the nature of engineering tasks, reliance on one individual to generate ideas and solve problems is not likely to be effective in the long run. While no information about the group's products is supplied, it is reasonable to assume that the lack of staff input negatively affects outcomes. Finally, the group has remained dependent for quite some time. Growth and change have not occurred, and the need for change is not apparent to team members. This scenario presents conditions that are less amenable to change.

Leader Role in Facilitating Group Development: Scenario 1   In the first stage of group development, leaders play an important role in facilitating group growth. This is so because leaders have the most clearly defined role during this period. Since development is progressive, the task of a leader at stage one is to facilitate movement to the next developmental phase. That is, the leader's task is to act in ways that will precipitate open discussion of values, goals, tasks, and leadership, so that differences of opinion regarding these elements of group life can be resolved. While general guidelines could be provided to help leaders to determine what actions might influence a group to discuss and resolve conflicts, each group situation is different to some extent.

The first step for Joe is to become aware of the need for change in the functioning of his team. This might occur in a number of ways. Forces external to the group could lead Joe to change his perspective of himself and the team. For example, upper management might express concern about team productivity or the members' excessive reliance on Joe for direction. Joe's awareness could also be raised by his own internal feelings of fatigue, resentment over the long hours that he puts in, or over member intrusions into his personal life. Team members may become uncomfortable with the situation and voice their concerns to Joe. Finally, Joe may realize that change is needed as a result of management training or other educational activities. Without awareness of the need for change on Joe's part, change that includes Joe is unlikely. Upper management could precipitate change by transferring Joe. However, Joe's removal would most likely have a negative effect on the rest of the team because of their loyalty and respect for him. Change that includes Joe will be best for the team, the company, and Joe.

Once Joe becomes aware that he must change his management style, he will need to carefully consider current circumstances before initiating any change. For example, the team has been in the dependency stage for quite a long time. Therefore, an abrupt change in leadership style might precipitate a very negative reaction from team members. This would move the group into the conflict and fight stage, but might make it extremely difficult for the group to resolve those conflicts. Members have become used to depending on Joe for direction. Removing that direction too quickly could have serious ramifications. In addition, team members are unprepared to participate in directing their own affairs. Joe has not provided them with enough information about goals and tasks for them to make informed decisions. Team members are not confident about their abilities to solve problems and complete tasks competently. Also, their dependence on Joe and lack of connection with each other make it unlikely that they will be able to engage in open discussions.

Given these circumstances, Joe would be wise to begin by ensuring the task competence of each member. Rather than solving technical problems for the team, he would begin to teach them the skills necessary to solve their own problems. When individuals come to him for solutions, he might ask them what they think rather than telling them what to do. He might refer them to another team member for advice. He might also provide seminars or technical training in order to enhance their skills. When they act in more independent ways and perform well, Joe is advised to praise their efforts and reward their initiative.

It would also be helpful for Joe to hold more team meetings and to restructure those meetings. Setting agendas in advance and designating individuals to take responsibility to report on issues and make suggestions about how to deal with those issues would be a helpful strategy. Getting feedback from all team members would be important as well. Finally, it would be beneficial to both Joe and the team if Joe began to slowly increase the amount of vacation time that he takes.

The change in leadership style and group procedures is likely to be met with resistance from team members and from Joe himself. Members may try to influence Joe to return to his original style because they are uncomfortable with new responsibilities. Some will undoubtedly become angry with their leader. Given that Joe is used to being liked and admired by employees, he may find it difficult to deal with being less popular and less central in the lives of team members. If Joe perseveres, however, team members will gradually feel more able to participate in discussions about group functioning. Essentially, the plan alters group patterns, disrupts dependency, increases member competence, and creates sufficient discontent to stimulate more open discussion of group issues.

Member Roles in Facilitating Group Development: Scenario 1 Members, too, play a part in encouraging group development. In this case, the members of Joe's team can help Joe become aware of the need for change by asking for more information about total project goals rather than confining their inquiries to their specific tasks. They can raise concerns they might have about their abilities to handle tasks and ask for more training in specific areas. Members can encourage Joe to be less directive by consulting other team members about problems rather than turning to Joe for solutions. Going to Joe with solutions rather than questions may increase his confidence in the staff's ability. Finally, Joe will need support for his efforts to change, and members will require reassurance that this shift in the group will produce positive outcomes in the long run. Members can help, therefore, by encouraging each other and Joe to persist with efforts to facilitate group growth. In essence, both the members and the leader have the same task, which is to create the conditions that make discussion, disagreement, and debate an acceptable part of group life.

The Leader's Role in Facilitating Group Development: Scenario 2 The circumstances in the second scenario are somewhat different. As a result of the company's growth, Rita now has two distinct groups to deal with, each operating at different developmental levels. The management team is operating at the dependency stage. With this group, Rita could implement many of the suggestions for a change in leadership style outlined in the first scenario. The management team needs to gain confidence in their ability to handle increasing task demands. They also need to gain confidence in themselves as managers. Rita is advised to delegate responsibilities and more authority to the management team. If management or technical training would be helpful to the management team, it should be provided. Rita should set the standards for performance, delegate responsibilities to the management team, and then allow them to interact directly with the newer employees. Rather than meeting with individual staff, Rita should attempt to redirect the flow of communication so that the management team and the staff are interacting with each other rather than through her. Rita is also advised not to appear to favor either group's views and to encourage open discussion of problems by holding meetings at which all managers and staff are present.

The newer employees, or staff group, are not solidly in the dependency stage. They appear to be ready to enter the second stage of group development, since they are making suggestions and beginning to question traditional ways of doing things. Rita's response to this group is critical. If she reprimands them or conveys a negative reaction to their efforts to have more input, they may slide back into dependency. If she encourages them without addressing the concerns of the management group, she may exacerbate the conflict between these two groups and make it more difficult for differences to be resolved. An alternative might be to encourage the staff to bring their suggestions and challenges directly to the managers rather than to her.

These changes in Rita's behavior will be disconcerting to the management group. Rita will need to reassure them by supporting their efforts to be leaders in their own right. In the scenario, it is apparent that the management group is a bit uncomfortable with Rita's intrusive leadership style and want more autonomy, even though they fear the added responsibility. By allowing managers more autonomy to manage their own teams, Rita will help them to feel supported and encouraged to take more responsibility. There will undoubtedly be some discomfort and anger expressed by managers about the shift in Rita's style. She is advised to see this as positive and to convey that view to managers and staff.

Member Roles in Facilitating Group Development: Scenario 2   The management group can support efforts to change by accepting the increased responsibility and authority to act as leaders in their own right. As this change occurs, it is likely that the managers' roles and tasks will be unclear. It will be important for managers to ask for clarification from Rita and each other if the organization is to grow in positive ways. Developing a sense of team between individual managers and their staff groups will be key as well. This should be a primary focus of each manager's efforts. The newer staff can be helpful by supporting the structural changes that are occurring. This means going to their designated manager with problems or suggestions. The structural changes will be confusing initially. Therefore, asking for clarification about goals, roles, and tasks will be important to each team and the organization as a whole.

Summary   Some general principles emerge from these examples. These are:

1. The leader's task during the first stage of group development is to act in ways that will precipitate open discussion of values, goals, tasks, and leadership so that differences of opinion regarding these elements of group life can be resolved.
2. Members have the same task.
3. For open discussion to occur, team members must feel safe enough to express their opinions.
4. Members must feel competent in relation to group tasks.
5. Leaders facilitate feelings of safety by rewarding and encouraging member input.
6. Leaders facilitate feelings of competence by providing supervision, training, and education in task-related activities.
7. Leaders set high performance standards and provide guidance as needed.
8. Leaders gradually decrease direct supervision and increase independent and collaborative problem solving among members.

9. Members ask constructive questions regarding goals, tasks, roles, and leadership style.
10. Members accept more responsibility and authority as they feel able.
11. Members redirect their focus from the leader to the group as a whole.

Cases

Scenario 3   Dr. Smith was the third dean to be hired to lead the college faculty in three years. This is an unusual situation, since the typical tenure of deans ranges from five to fifteen years. The two previous deans were dismissed after one and two years respectively, and reasons for the dismissals were similar in both cases. Lack of initiative, an inability to communicate with the faculty, and a lack of leadership were cited in both cases. The new dean took the job with some trepidation. He did not know what to expect, but he did believe that his open and collaborative leadership style would work to his advantage.

The new dean immediately initiated a series of meetings with the chairpersons of the various college departments. Of the twelve department heads, only five attended the first meeting. Those who did attend spent considerable time telling the dean whom to watch out for among those who were not present. The dean explained that he intended to have an open-door policy and to include the chairs in decision making. The five attendees told the dean that this would not work, since the absent chairpersons disagreed with everything.

Over the course of several meetings, attendance at meetings increased, and so did the tension. Many of the chairs did disagree about most things. Fights erupted frequently between department heads, and decisions did not get made. Arguments centered around the appropriate focus on teaching versus research, admissions procedures, and many other issues. The dean was attacked by some for being too passive and by others for moving too quickly. Finally, he created three assistant dean positions and chose individuals he perceived as allies to fill those roles. This small group met and spent time planning ways to gain cooperation from the others. These strategy sessions identified chairs who were resistant to change and planned ways to overcome that resistance. Meanwhile, the resistance grew in intensity. The remaining chairs perceived the dean's inner circle of supporters as spies and as threats to the autonomy they had enjoyed in the past. By this time, the dean was feeling hurt by the constant barrage of criticism and began retaliating in subtle ways by rejecting conference travel or supply requests from chairs in the enemy camp.

Scenario 4   The management group of the county mental health center was in an uproar. Unilateral decisions were being made that were antithetical to their belief system. Previously, if an individual could not pay for therapy at the center, he or she was seen anyway. Now, a nonpaying client could be seen for four sessions only. After that, services could not be provided unless the client paid or an alternate source of funding could be located. But grants and county, city, or state funding had been decreasing for years. Therefore, the new policy effectively denied services to people who were often most in need of those services. This was intolerable to the managers, who were social workers and psychologists in the main. They worked at the center for considerably less than they could have made in private practice, and they did so because of their commitment to social justice and to the poor.

Productivity had become the watchword at the center. Staff had to keep track of their billable hours and were required to discuss payment schedules or delinquency with their clients. The clinical staff believed that this interfered with the client-therapist relationship and could compromise treatment outcomes. All of these changes, in the opinion of both managers and staff, had been initiated by the director of the center without consultation.

The director of the center was under enormous pressure from the board to make the center more financially sound. The board was comprised primarily of people from the business sector who saw board service as a community responsibility. The board was responsible for the finances of the center and was worried about possible layoffs or significant program cuts if the center's financial picture did not improve. The board did not want to cut services to individuals who could not pay, but the center could not help every person who had psychological problems and no financial resources. This is not a perfect world. If center finances deteriorated further, no clients would be served, since the center would not survive. It is better to provide some service than none at all.

The director was caught in the middle. He, too, was committed to social justice and to providing services to those with little means. However, he felt obligated to implement board policies and saw no alternatives that would change things. He did not consult the staff, since he knew their opinions and believed that nothing would change the board's position. He had enjoyed a cordial relationship with managers and staff prior to these changes. His manner was a bit more formal and distant than that of most of the staff, but he was honest, direct, and committed to client service. He was also, in his own view, more respectful of authority and more realistic than his staff about what was and was not possible for the center to achieve. When the staff responded to these changes with anger and hostility directed toward him, he was dumbfounded. Didn't they see that there was no other alternative? Didn't they understand that he was working to save jobs and services?

Assessing Group Processes and Development: Scenarios 3 and 4

Both of these scenarios describe groups in the conflict and fight stage of group development. The reader is invited to compare the characteristics of stage-two groups with those of each group described.

Identifying a Stage-Two Group

1. Conflicts about values surface.
2. Disagreements about goals and tasks emerge.

3. Increased feelings of safety allow dissent to occur.
4. Dissatisfaction with roles may surface.
5. Clarification of goals begins.
6. Role clarification also begins.
7. Members challenge the leader.
8. Subgroups and coalitions form.
9. Group intolerance of subgroups and coalitions is manifest.
10. Increased member participation is evident.
11. Decreased conformity begins.
12. Deviation from emerging group norms occurs.
13. Attempts at conflict management are evident.
14. If efforts to resolve conflicts are successful, increased consensus about group goals and culture become evident near the end of this stage.
15. Conflict resolution, if successful, increases trust and cohesion.

The reader will note that neither group has every characteristic on the list. Development is a process, and the scenarios provide a view of one point in that process. The third scenario presents an example of a group that has been in conflict for an extended period of time. Differences of opinion about values and goals have not been resolved, and the group has split into warring camps. Battles have produced casualties in that two previous leaders have been defeated. When the conflict stage of group development produces casualties, conflict resolution becomes extraordinarily difficult. Feelings of safety are nonexistent in the group as a whole. Therefore, members seek safety in subgroups that fight each other for control. Essentially, this situation is akin to a state of war, and it is common in protracted wars to forget the initial reasons for the conflict. War is sustained by the continuing casualties, which increase desires for revenge and retaliation. The new dean hoped to alter this situation, but he, too, became a casualty and as a result formed his own army for protection and retaliation. The situation described in this scenario is all too common, and the prognosis for change is poor. Once conflicts become entrenched, it is difficult for a group to extricate itself from battle.

The group described in the fourth scenario is also experiencing major conflicts. Different world views, roles, and responsibilities are generating serious disagreements and communication blocks. However, all the parties involved share a common concern for and commitment to client service. This may make it easier to resolve the existing conflicts. Also, the conflict surfaced only recently and has not yet become entrenched. This, too, may make resolution easier.

The Leader's Role in Facilitating Group Development: Scenario 3   The leader's task during the conflict and fight stage of group development is to act in ways that will facilitate open discussion and resolution of conflicts regarding values, goals, and leadership. Resolution of these conflicts increases group cohesion and trust, which makes it possible for the group to focus on strategies to achieve shared goals. How leaders accomplish this task will vary in different situations. Dr. Smith and the director of the mental health center, for example, will need to focus on somewhat different issues in order to facilitate conflict resolution.

Unfortunately, Dr. Smith has been caught up in the conflict dynamics of the college chairs. His initial good intentions were diverted by the hostility that was directed at him by the department heads. He felt personally attacked and maligned by the staff and acted to protect himself by establishing his allies in the role of assistant deans. This new group was perceived, and perceived itself to some extent, as operatives in the ongoing war within the college. Winning the war had become more important to all subgroups than the education of students or research endeavors.

Dr. Smith realized that he had made mistakes in his efforts to create a cooperative and productive group, but he was at a loss as to how to correct his miscalculations. He decided to seek the advice of an organizational consultant. In difficult group situations, it is common and prudent to seek help from outside experts, especially when the leader has become enmeshed in the dynamics of the system. The objectivity of an outsider is often necessary to provide new perspectives to a group entrenched in conflict.

The consultant met with the dean and was individually introduced to each chairperson. The consultant's role was discussed and agreement to work to resolve conflicts was sought from every department head. The consultant advised meeting with people individually first to sidestep the counterdependency of the group as a whole. After individuals agreed to participate in efforts to resolve conflicts, a meeting of the entire group was held. The dean addressed the group and expressed his desire for the group to resolve its conflicts. He also stated that he had made some initial mistakes and consequently was altering direction. The consultant was introduced to the group, and a discussion of the steps in the consulting process ensued.

Next, the consultant interviewed each department head individually. The chairs were also asked to complete some questionnaires. The consultant compiled a group profile with the obtained information and scheduled a meeting with the dean to go over the results. No individual response was identified. Instead, general trends and concerns were presented. The consultant suggested that the dean call a meeting to review the results with the chairs and to begin the process of addressing their concerns. The dean was also advised that in order to resolve conflicts, all group members must be involved in the process and decisions reached by the group could not be countermanded by the dean. He agreed.

During the feedback session, the group prioritized the issues that emerged during the assessment phase, and small task groups were formed to work on these issues and make proposals to the entire group concerning their resolution. The task groups contained individuals who represented different views and opinions. The consultant met with each group periodically to assist them in resolving disputes or to offer suggestions about how to proceed. Task groups met over a four-month period. During that time, training in group and organization dynamics, communication, problem solving, and conflict resolution was provided to the staff. Once a month the entire group convened to review task-group progress and to discuss the task-group proposals that were presented.

During the process, new alliances were formed. The dynamics of the group as a whole were disrupted, and a more cooperative spirit began to emerge. Tensions between individuals and subgroups subsided, and things were proceeding quite well. The dean was beginning to implement recommended changes, and perceptions of him were changing as a result.

The reader, at this point, is probably envisioning a happy ending to this story. In reality, however, this was not to be. An anonymous letter was sent to the university president denouncing the dean and his change strategy. When the dean learned of this, he became very angry and brought this up to the whole group. He did not discuss this with the consultant prior to venting his anger on the group. The letter reignited the dean's search for enemies and curtailed his efforts to institute recommended changes. The dean's discussion with the chairs about the letter led to renewed feelings of paranoia about the dean's intentions and anger at his perceived accusations. The fragile truce was violated and open conflicts began again.

Member Roles in Facilitating Group Development: Scenario 3   Members also have the task of acting in ways that will facilitate open discussion and resolution of conflicts regarding values, goals, and leadership during periods of conflict. In the preceding example, members were initially able to do this. They expressed a willingness to seek conflict resolution and were able to put aside hostile feelings for the good of the group. Members began to work to resolve conflicts and sought ways to negotiate agreements. The letter incident and the dean's reaction to that incident, however, returned the group to old patterns of response. Had members been able to help the dean regain perspective by showing support for him at that moment and encouraging him to continue efforts to resolve conflicts, the ending might have been more positive. Members have the same responsibility for group outcomes as leaders. Their actions at this stage are critical to the resolution of conflicts and the establishment of a more trusting and cooperative group climate.

Leader and Member Roles in Facilitating Group Development: Scenario 4   The director of the mental health center described in the fourth scenario also made some mistakes that inadvertently precipitated a serious conflict. Directors of organizations are members of a number of groups. In this case, the director is a member of the board group, the management group, and the entire staff group. He also has different roles in these groups. For example, he is a less powerful member of the board group and leader of the management team and the staff as a whole. Each group has different world views and role responsibilities. This state of affairs can be confusing for the individual who is a member of a number of groups. He shares the board's responsibility for fiscal management and the staff's commitment to provide services to clients regardless of their ability to pay for those services.

The director's decision to change policies and procedures without input from the management group reflects his attempt to be loyal to the board group and to protect managers from deliberating about changes that he perceived as inevitable. He also believed that the new policies would protect the entire staff from the threat of layoffs or program cuts. This is truly a man in the middle.

In order to reestablish cooperation and productivity, the director also engaged the services of an outside consultant. A process similar to that described in the third scenario was undertaken, in which interviews with managers, staff, and the director were conducted. Board members were also interviewed. The entire organization of approximately ninety-five people attended a series of meetings designed to identify and address problems and conflicts.

During the first session, differences in world views among the various groups became very apparent. The board members emphasized economic concerns. Managers and clinical staff emphasized commitment to clients. Support and clerical staff expressed concerns about procedures and work flow. The director expressed his concern over the lack of a shared vision among the various groups. Eventually, with the help of the consultant, participants began to realize that all of these concerns were legitimate and that each group was correct in championing its particular concerns. They also began to see the interconnectedness of these issues and that overall success was dependent on the organization's ability to work together to address these concerns.

This realization almost instantly reduced tensions and hostilities among participants. The conflicts were no longer perceived as such. Rather, they became problems to solve. As in the previous case, task groups were formed. Each task force contained at least one board, one management, and one staff representative. Recommendations were proposed to the group as a whole, and those that met with approval were enacted. New ideas were presented about how to generate additional sources of revenue to fund services for the poor. Compromises were negotiated and a shared sense of mission took shape.

Both the director and members of the various subgroups within the organization played significant roles in achieving these positive outcomes. The director identified a problem and provided a structure designed to facilitate problem solving and conflict resolution. Members of the board, management, and staff participated in that process in constructive and task-oriented ways. These actions were critical to successful resolution of value conflicts and to the establishment of a shared organizational mission. People managed to focus on their collective mission and to respect the different roles necessary to accomplish that mission. There was still work to be done, of course. Shared goals would need to be operationalized, and strategies to achieve them were required. Undoubtedly there would be disagreements about how to proceed, but their new spirit of cooperation would see them through.

Cases

Scenario 5   This small private elementary school was perceived as a wonderful place for children. The teachers were caring and invested in the personal development of the children. Teachers and parents formed a supportive team. Many of the teachers' own children were students at the school, and parents, teachers, and children socialized together outside of school hours regularly. Potluck dinners, barbecues, camping trips, and educational excursions were well attended. Many personal friendships existed among teachers, parents, the principal, and the children in various combinations.

Everyone loved the school environment, where cooperation and friendship were the norm. People even dressed alike to a certain extent: The students, staff, and parents all seemed to prefer the casual outdoor look typical of L. L. Bean or Oshkosh fashions. Feelings always took precedence over work or lessons at the school. All decisions were made consensually, which took quite a bit of time. As a result, some things were not addressed in a timely manner, and this was beginning to concern some people, especially the principal, who worried most about how all the work would get done. She was especially concerned about the quality of the school's curriculum and its academic standards. Some parents were worried as well.

Scenario 6   The staff of a small consulting firm had been through some difficult times. People's views about the direction of the company had been quite divergent for some time. Some individuals believed that human resource skills training should be the focus. There was plenty of work in that area and the firm had established a good reputation for providing quality training. Why tamper with success? Other people, however, were frustrated with the limitations of training. They argued that some organizations ask for training when what is really needed is an organizational intervention. Training cannot be effective when the organization is in conflict. In fact, it was not ethical, in their view, to provide the wrong service.

To the relief of everyone, this disagreement had been resolved recently. The whole staff had participated in a series of planning meetings. The meetings gave people time to discuss their opinions about the future of the firm and to listen to each other. Finally, they came up with a more unified perspective on the future. The staff decided to begin to slowly integrate consulting into the services they provided. Those individuals with expertise and interest in that area would take a lead role in developing the consulting area and establishing a client base. They would also act as mentors to staff interested in learning about organizational consultation. In the meantime, training would continue to be the primary focus of the firm. If the training staff thought that an organization might benefit from consulting services, they would refer that organization to the group providing that service. Also, since consulting often reveals training needs, the consultant group would refer to the training group.

The staff was pleased with these decisions, and feelings of cooperation and trust increased. The next step was to figure out how to implement the plan. Decisions about who would constitute the training and consulting staff needed to be made. Marketing strategies would have to be altered to incorporate the new services. The staff began meeting to make these decisions. While there were differences of opinion about how to accomplish the new goal, these disagreements were not disruptive. People felt free to express themselves and were more willing to compromise when necessary.

Assessing Group Processes and Development: Scenarios 5 and 6

Identifying a Stage-Three Group

1. Increased goal clarity and consensus are evident.
2. Roles and tasks are adjusted to increase the likelihood of goal achievement.
3. The leader's role becomes less directive and more consultative.
4. The communication structure appears to be more flexible.
5. The content of communication becomes more task oriented.
6. Pressures to conform increase again.
7. Helpful deviation is tolerated.
8. Coalitions and subgroups continue to form.
9. Increased tolerance of subgroups and coalitions is evident.
10. Cohesion and trust increase.
11. Member satisfaction also increases.
12. Cooperation is more in evidence.
13. Individual commitment to group goals and tasks is high.
14. Greater division of labor occurs.
15. Conflict continues to occur.
16. Conflict management strategies are more effective.
17. The group works to clarify and build a group structure that will facilitate goal achievement and productivity.

The dynamics described in the fifth and sixth scenarios are representative of the trust and structure stage of development. The school community appears to have attained a reasonable level of trust and cooperation. Conformity, cohesion, satisfaction, and commitment to the group are all in evidence. However, structural issues have not been adequately addressed. The school may be in what Bennis and Shepard (1956) referred to as the *enchantment phase,* in which agreement, similarity, and cohesion are so highly valued that potentially conflictual issues are avoided.

Schools have two primary tasks. First, schools strive to provide students with the cognitive knowledge and skills necessary for productive participation in society. Second, schools attempt to facilitate the development in students of self-esteem and interpersonal competence necessary for learning and effective interaction in the adult world. This particular school emphasized the second goal more than the first. Psychological and social development is more consistent with the school's developmental level, in that attention to relational issues in students fits the needs of the system at the moment. Addressing more task-oriented issues, such as the quality of the curriculum or the academic achievement of students, might create disagreement and damage the positive interpersonal climate that had been established.

This situation is not an unusual one, in that groups are often reluctant to deal with structural and procedural issues that may disrupt cohesion and renew conflicts. No one is eager to disturb the sense of camaraderie and connection that exists. While groups at this stage typically have the skills and experience to tackle structural issues, some groups are unsure of their abilities to organize effectively or to accomplish certain goals. This may be especially true of this school community, since relationships seem to be valued more than task accomplishment and educational achievement. Addressing task issues could precipitate principled or ideological conflicts, which are more difficult to resolve than structural or procedural disagreements.

The consulting group described in the sixth scenario has taken this step, however. They have achieved consensus on goals, and a spirit of trust and cooperation has been established. Now they are attempting to determine the best methods to achieve those goals. The group appears to be aware that differences of opinion regarding structural issues exist and will have to be worked through. However, they seem confident that they can reach agreements about how to proceed.

Leader and Member Roles in Facilitating Group Development: Scenarios 5 and 6

The task of both leaders and members of stage-three groups are the same. By this time, the power differential between leaders and followers has been reduced, and participants are operating in more egalitarian ways. All participants share responsibility for and commitment to the group. Their shared task is to consolidate gains in trust and cohesion and to organize themselves in ways that will ensure group productivity.

The consulting group described earlier seems to be working quite effectively on this task. Roles and tasks are being redefined to maximize the probability of goal achievement. Subgroups are forming to work on specific aspects of the task. Issues related to goal achievement are being discussed openly, and task-related disagreements are likely to be resolved in constructive ways. Finally, the group appears to be maintaining and enhancing cooperation and cohesion as it prepares itself for directly working on its goals.

The elementary school, on the other hand, appears to be consolidating trust and cohesion at the expense of working on structural issues. Roles and tasks are not clear. Task-oriented subgroups are not in evidence, and conflict has not surfaced. The group is in danger of becoming stuck in the enjoyable but evasive dynamics of enchantment. Members and leaders of this group can help the group to begin to address structural concerns by raising these issues in meetings and in their daily interactions. How issues are raised, however, will be important. For example, statements like "We don't seem to be able to make changes in the curriculum" will not be very helpful, since the group lacks confidence in its abilities already. An alternative might be "We're working so well together that I think we could easily begin to make changes in the curriculum." Such a statement emphasizes group strengths and raises members' confidence in their abilities to face challenges.

Members and leaders could also make suggestions about how the group might address structural issues. Planning processes and decision-making strategies will be necessary if the group is to organize itself effectively. Also, introducing strategies to address organizational issues helps the idea of structure to become more salient in the minds of members. This may help to overcome resistance to working on organizational issues by providing models of how to proceed.

Cases

Scenario 7   Everybody in the emergency room knew his or her job and performed it well. They had to make split-second decisions about what actions to take when a patient came through the door. Technicians, nurses, doctors, social workers, and clerks worked together extremely well. Sometimes people yelled or got tense when a patient was in trouble, but no one took those things personally. After all, someone's life was on the line, and that makes everyone anxious.

The staff spent time practicing their responses to particular emergency situations so that they would know what to do when they occurred in reality. They gave each other advice and feedback about their performance. Everybody knew his or her job, but people were not territorial about things. If something needed to be done, the person available did it. The director would jump in if an extra pair of hands was needed. She did not stand on ceremony. No one did. The patient was important, not titles or job descriptions.

Even though this was a tense job, the staff had fun at work. They goofed around a lot and jokes flew back and forth among people, especially when things got rough. Comic relief was important and kept folks from burning out. People liked each other and valued each individual's contribution. They talked openly and frankly at meetings, during breaks, and on the job.

It had not always been this way. Less than a year ago, things had been grim, and some people had actually threatened to quit. They had been short staffed at the time, and mistakes were made as a result. The hospital's budget crunch was causing strain and conflict. Like many other groups in similar circumstances, they had taken their frustrations out on each other. Conflicts were affecting their ability to work together. Finally, one of the nurses suggested that the staff needed to get its act together. At first some folks resisted, but eventually they all sat down together to figure out what was going wrong and what they could do to fix it.

The director asked someone from human resources to facilitate their meetings. This helped the staff to focus and to get beyond some of their negative feelings. Over time, they were able to get at some of the root problems. They discovered that much of what was occurring had little to do with individuals. Conditions in the hospital were causing some of the problems. They also realized that they needed additional training in certain areas. The director managed to persuade the hospital administration to underwrite the cost of a training seminar.

In exchange, she and the staff promised to find ways to reduce costs in some areas. People began to pull together, and things improved after that. People know that things cannot stay this good forever. Problems will inevitably crop up. But the next time, they will know what to do about it. At least they hope they will.

Scenario 8   Trouble was brewing in the neighborhood. Jim, the block captain on Elm Street, was worried. The Elm Street Block Association had accomplished so much over the years, and now those accomplishments were being threatened by the encroaching drug sales and violence occurring on neighboring streets. The Elm Street Block Association was a tight-knight group. They looked out for each other. The block was clean. People knew each other and helped each other out. All the adults watched out for everybody's kids. The kids ran errands for elderly neighbors. People patrolled the block, watching out for crime or other signs of trouble. They met with a police representative periodically to discuss problems and concerns. Surrounding blocks had not fared as well, however. The crime rate was increasing, and people were afraid to let their kids play outside. Most of these blocks were not organized, and this troubled Jim, since it would make it more difficult for the people of Elm Street.

At the next meeting of the block association, the residents of Elm Street discussed this issue in great detail. Some people felt that it would be best to keep their own house in order. They thought that their block association was cohesive and worked well. They were not in favor of expanding their focus to work with other neighborhood streets because that might take energy away from their own tasks. Others felt that there was no choice. Unless other blocks became active, the residents of Elm Street would not be able to keep their street safe. While they worked well together, they could not sustain that effort unless they reached out to other neighborhoods.

The discussion was long, and issues were passionately debated. Eventually, everyone was persuaded that it was best to offer to help other blocks to organize. They decided to call the city streets department, which had a section devoted to helping blocks to organize. The Elm Street group asked that a staff person from that section attend their next meeting to help them plan ways to interest residents of other streets in forming block associations. They also invited some residents of neighboring streets to attend that meeting.

Assessing Group Processes and Development: Scenarios 7 and 8

Identifying a Stage-Four Group

1. Members are clear about group goals.
2. Members agree with the group's goals.
3. Tasks are appropriate to group versus individual solution.
4. Members are clear about their roles.
5. Members accept their roles and status.

6. Role assignments match member abilities.
7. The leadership style matches the group's developmental level.
8. During the work stage, delegation, or unleadership, is the prevailing leadership style.
9. The group's communication structure matches the demands of the task.
10. The group has an open communication structure in which all members participate and are heard.
11. The group has an appropriate ratio of task and socio-emotional statements.
12. The group gets, gives, and utilizes feedback about its effectiveness and productivity.
13. The group spends time defining problems it must solve or decisions it must make.
14. The group spends time planning how it will solve problems and make decisions.
15. The group spends enough time discussing the problems and decisions it faces.
16. The group chooses participatory decision-making methods.
17. The group implements and evaluates its solutions and decisions.
18. Voluntary conformity is high.
19. Task-related deviance is tolerated.
20. The group norms encourage high performance and quality.
21. The group expects to be successful.
22. The group encourages innovation.
23. The group pays attention to the details of its work.
24. The group accepts coalition and subgroup formation.
25. Subgroups are integrated into the group-as-a-whole.
26. Subgroups work on important tasks.
27. Tasks contain variety and challenge.
28. Subgroups work on a total product or project.
29. The group contains the smallest number of members necessary to accomplish its goal or goals.
30. The group has access to the technical and people resources necessary to accomplish its task.
31. The group has access to technical or interpersonal consulation as needed.
32. The group has access to technical or human relations training as needed.
33. The group has a defined work territory.
34. The group is allotted sufficient time to develop a mature working unit and to accomplish its goals.
35. Subgroups are recognized and rewarded by the group.
36. The group is highly cohesive.
37. Interpersonal attraction among members is high.
38. Members are cooperative.

39. Periods of conflict are frequent but brief.
40. The group has effective conflict-management strategies.

Both of these scenarios describe groups that are currently functioning at the work stage of group development. Both have many of the characteristics of high-performance teams described above. Group development has proceeded to the point where these groups can work effectively. The developmental processes that have preceded this stage have been difficult, but both groups have achieved a level of maturity that enables them to accomplish tasks and achieve goals.

It seems unnecessary to reiterate the characteristics of work groups here. However, it is important to note that a working group deals not only with its internal dynamics but also with the external context in which it is operating. If the emergency room team, for example, did not address the problems and concerns of the hospital context, its ability to function productively would be short lived. This is equally true of the Elm Street Block Association. Events occurring outside a group's boundaries dramatically influence that group's viability. Internal solidarity, organization, and work are not enough. Mature groups look inward and outward. They work to facilitate their own dynamics and those of the groups, organizations, and societies that surround them.

Leader and Member Roles in Maintaining Group Development: Scenarios 7 and 8   Reaching the work stage of group development does not ensure that a group will maintain that level of functioning. Developmental processes are not linear in the sense that groups progress to a specific plateau and remain there. Developmental processes are cyclical, and mature groups can expect regressions and diversions throughout their life. An analogy can be drawn between individual and group development. Mature adults do not cease to experience feelings of dependency, competition, fear, anger at authority figures, and other emotions that are generally associated with childhood or adolescence. Adults, too, grapple with these feelings. Generally, however, their life skills and experience help adults to address and manage these feelings more readily. Mature groups can expect to experience frequent periods of dependency, conflict, fight, and other dynamics that can divert attention from work. Their previous success in dealing with these dynamics, however, will make it easier to regain a work focus.

Each time a member leaves, a leader is replaced, or external conditions change, for example, group dynamics are affected. In each of these circumstances, the group will experience disruptions, and adjustments will be required to regain former levels of cohesion and productivity. Awareness and discussion of this fact of group life on the part of members is essential. Members can also help to maintain group effectiveness by periodically assessing the group and identifying issues that need to be addressed. In this way, a group can continually monitor its functioning and make the necessary adjustments. No group or individual sustains high levels of productivity for long periods of time. People and groups require periods of rest, relaxation, flight, grumpiness, and fun.

Unrealistic expectations of our human capacities may be the biggest threat to individual and group effectiveness.

All the scenarios described above are real examples of groups struggling to enhance or maintain group development. This chapter is not meant to outline all the possible ways in which members and leaders can help to facilitate group development. Rather, it is designed to facilitate thinking about the issues involved and possible strategies to employ in particular circumstances. Determining what to do to encourage group development requires good observation skills and the ability to interpret those observations. Acting in a facilitative manner is difficult as well. It requires good communication and social skills, empathy, and timing. Finally, it is not easy for individual members or leaders to maintain a helpful stance in groups. Attempts to be helpful can be misinterpreted or rejected. It can be risky at times to intervene in ongoing dynamics. However, members and leaders share responsibility for group outcomes. Without guidance from all members, the group may run aground.

A FINAL THOUGHT

Creating healthy and effective groups capable of responding to new challenges is perhaps the most important task facing the human community of today. Living in peace—in fact, living at all—depends on our ability to live and work together effectively. No system is exempt from the dynamics described in this book. Senate subcommittees, research teams, sports teams, church groups, work teams, and larger social systems are all affected by these natural processes. Our social world is made up of millions of groups struggling to interact effectively, and these millions of groups are interdependent. No one individual, group, institution, or nation is responsible for creating a habitable social environment. They all are. We need to increase our understanding of the dynamics of the systems in which we live and our efforts to apply what we already know in the groups of our everyday lives. Our very lives may depend on it. Good luck to us all.

REFERENCES

Adams, J. S. (1980). Interorganizational processes and organization boundary activities. In B. Staw & L. Cummings (Eds.), *Research in Organizational Behavior* (Vol. 2, pp. 321–355). Greenwich, CT: JAI Press.

Adams, S. (1952). Effect of equalitarian atmospheres upon the performance of bomber crews. *American Psychologist, 7*, 398.

Adelson, J. P. (1975). Feedback and group development. *Small Group Behavior, 6* (4), 389–401.

Agazarian, Y. & Peters, R. P. (1981). *The Visible and Invisible Group.* London: Routledge and Kegan Paul.

Alberti, R. & Emmons, M. (1974). *Your Perfect Right.* San Luis Obispo, CA: Impact Press.

Alderfer, C. P. (1987). An intergroup perspective on group dynamics. In J. Lorsch (Ed.), *Handbook of Organizational Behavior* (pp. 190–222). Englewood Cliffs, NJ: Prentice Hall.

Allison, S. T. & Messick, D. M. (1985a). Effects of experience on performance in a replenishable resource trap. *Journal of Personality and Social Psychology, 49*, 943–948.

Allison, S. T. & Messick, D. M. (1985b). The group attribution error. *Journal of Experimental Social Psychology, 21*, 563–579.

Allison, S. T. & Messick, D. M. (1987). From individual inputs to group outputs, and back again: Group processes and inferences about members. In C. Hendrick (Ed.), *Group Processes* (pp. 111–143). Newbury Park, CA: Sage.

Allport, F. H. (1920). The influence of the group upon association and thought. *Journal of Experimental Psychology, 3*, 159–182.

Allport, F. H. (1924). *Social Psychology.* Boston: Houghton Mifflin.

Allport, G. (1968). The historical background of modern social psychology. In G. Lindzey and E. Aronson (Eds.), *The Handbook of Social Psychology* (Vol. 1, pp. 1–80). Reading, MA: Addison-Wesley.

Altman, L. S. & Plunkett, J. J. (1984). Group treatment of adult substance abusers. *Journal for Specialists in Group Work, 9* (1), 26–31.

Ames, R. (1975). Teachers' attributions of responsibility: Some unexpected counter-defensive effects. *Journal of Educational Psychology, 67*, 668–676.

Amir, Y. (1976). The role of intergroup contact in change of prejudice and ethnic relations. In P. Katz (Ed.), *Towards the Elimination of Racism* (pp. 245–308). New York: Pergamon.

Ancona, D. G. (1987). Groups in organizations: Extending laboratory models. In C. Hendrick (Ed.), *Group and Intergroup Processes* (pp. 207–230). Beverly Hills, CA: Sage.

Anderson, A. B. (1975). Combined effects of interpersonal attraction and goal-path clarity on the cohesiveness of task-oriented groups. *Journal of Personality and Social Psychology, 31,* 68–75.

Anderson, R. C. (1959). Learning in discussion—a review of the authoritarian-democratic studies. *Harvard Educational Review, 29,* 201–215.

Argyle, M., Gardner, G. & Ciofi, F. (1958). Supervisory methods related to productivity, absenteeism, and labour turnover. *Human Relations, 11,* 23–40.

Argyris, C. (1957). *Personality and Organization: The Conflict Between the System and the Individual.* New York: Harper and Row.

Argyris, C. (1964). *Integrating the Individual and the Organization.* New York: John Wiley and Sons.

Aries, E. (1976). Interaction patterns and themes of male, female, and mixed groups. *Small Group Behavior, 7* (1), 7–18.

Aronson, E., Stephan, C. W., Sikes, J., Blaney, N. & Snapp, M. (1978) *The Jigsaw Classroom.* Beverly Hills, CA: Sage.

Asch, S. E. (1951). Effects of group pressure upon the modification and distortion of judgements. In H. Guetzkow (Ed.), *Groups, Leadership and Men* (pp. 177–190). Pittsburgh: Carnegie Press.

Asch, S. E. (1952). *Social Psychology.* Englewood Cliffs, NJ: Prentice Hall.

Asch, S. E. (1955). Opinions and social pressures. *Scientific American, 193* (5), 31–35.

Astley, W. G. & Van de Ven, A. H. (1983). Central perspectives and debates in organization theory. *Administrative Science Quarterly, 28,* 245–273.

Axelrod, R. & Hamilton, W. D. (1981). The evolution of cooperation. *Science, 211,* 1390–1396.

Babad, E. Y. & Amir, L. (1978). Bennis and Shepard's theory of group development: An empirical examination. *Small Group Behavior, 9* (4), 477–492.

Babad, E. Y., Birnbaum, M. & Benne, K. D. (1983). *The Social Self: Group Influences on Personal Identity.* Newbury Park, CA: Sage.

Babad, E. Y. & Melnick, I. (1976). Effects of a T-group as a function of trainers' liking and members' participation, involvement, quan-

tity and quality of received feedback. *Journal of Applied Behavioral Science, 12,* 543–562.

Back, K. W. (1951). Influence through social communication. *Journal of Abnormal and Social Psychology, 46,* 9–23.

Back, K. W. (1979). What's happened to small group research? *Journal of Applied Behavioral Science, 15,* 265–432.

Back, K. W. (1990). Woe unto you that are a grandchild. In S. Wheelan, E. Pepitone & V. Abt, (Eds.), *Advances in Field Theory* (pp. 27–37). Newbury Park, CA: Sage.

Back, K. W., Bunker, S. & Dunnagan, C. (1972). Barriers to communication and measurement of semantic space. *Sociometry, 35,* 347–356.

Bales, R. F. (1950). *Interaction Process Analysis: A Method for the Study of Small Groups.* Cambridge, MA: Addison-Wesley.

Bales, R. F. (1965). The equilibrium problem in small groups. In A. P. Hare, E. F. Borgatta & R. F. Bales (Eds.), *Small Groups: Studies in Social Interaction.* New York: Knopf.

Bales, R. F. (1970). *Personality and Interpersonal Behavior.* New York: Holt, Rinehart and Winston.

Bales, R. F., Cohen, S. P. & Williamson, S. A. (1980). *SYMLOG: A System for the Multiple Level Observation of Groups.* New York: Free Press.

Bales, R. F. & Strodtbeck, F. L. (1951). Phases in group problem solving. *Journal of Abnormal and Social Psychology, 46,* 485–495.

Banas, P. A. (1988). Employee involvement: A sustained labor/management initiative at the Ford Motor Company. In J. P. Campbell & R. J. Campbell (Eds.), *Productivity in Organizations* (pp. 388–416). San Francisco: Jossey-Bass.

Bandura, A. (1966). Vicarious processes: A case of no-trial learning. In L. Berkowitz (Ed.), *Advances in Experimental Social Psychology* (Vol. 2, pp. 1–55). New York: Academic Press.

Bandura, A. (1971). Analysis of modeling processes. In A. Bandura (Ed.), *Psychological Modeling.* Chicago: Aldine-Atherton.

Bandura, A. (1977). *Social Learning Theory.* Englewood Cliffs, NJ: Prentice Hall.

Barnard, C. I. (1938). *The Functions of the Executive.* Cambridge, MA: Harvard University Press.

Baron, R. M. & Boudreau, L. A. (1987). An ecological perspective on integrating personality and social psychology. *Journal of Personality and Social Psychology, 53* (6), 1222–1228.

Barrera, M., Jr. (1986). Distinctions between social support concepts, measures, and models. *American Journal of Community Psychology, 14,* 413–422.

Bartol, K. M. & Butterfield, D. A. (1976). Sex effects in evaluating leaders. *Journal of Applied Psychology, 61,* 446–454.

Bass, B. M. (1960). *Leadership, Psychology, and Organizational Behavior.* New York: Harper and Row.

Bass, B. M., McGehee, C. R., Hawkins, W.vC., Young, P. C. & Gebel, A.S. (1953). Personality variables related to leaderless group discussion. *Journal of Abnormal and Social Psychology, 48,* 120–128.

Bass, B. M., Wurster, C. R., Doll, P. A. & Clair, D. J. (1953). Situational and personality factors in leadership among sorority women. *Psychological Monographs, 67,* 16.

Bassin, M. (1988). Teamwork at General Foods: New and improved. *Personnel Journal, 65* (5), 62–70.

Bavelas, A. (1948). A mathematical model for group structure. *Applied Anthropology, 7,* 16–30.

Bavelas, A. (1950). Communication patterns in task-oriented groups. *Journal of the Acoustical Society of America, 22,* 725–730.

Beck, A. T. (1976). *Cognitive Therapy and the Emotional Disorders.* New York: International Universities Press.

Beckman, L. J. (1970). Effects of students' performance on teachers' and observers' attributions of causality. *Journal of Educational Psychology, 61,* 76–82.

Beckman, L. J. (1973). Teachers' and observers' perceptions of causality for a child's performance. *Journal of Educational Psychology, 65,* 198–204.

Bednar, R. L. & Kaul, T. (1978). Experiential group research: Current perspectives. In S. Garfield & A. Bergin (Eds.), *Handbook of Psychotherapy and Behavior Change* (2d ed., pp. 769–815). New York: Wiley.

Bednar, R. L. & Kaul, T. (1979). Experiential group research: What never happened. *Journal of Applied Behavioral Science, 11,* 311–319.

Bednar, R. L. & Lawlis, F. (1971). Empirical research in group psychotherapy. In A. E. Bergin & S. L. Garfield (Eds.), *Handbook for Psychotherapy and Behavior Change* (pp. 812–838). New York: Wiley.

Bednar, R. L., Melnick, J. & Kaul, T. (1974). Risk, responsibility, and structure: A conceptual framework for initiating group counseling and psychotherapy. *Journal of Counseling Psychology, 21,* 31–37.

Bell, M. A. (1982). Phases in group problem solving. *Small Group Behavior, 13* (4), 475–495.

Bellah, R., Madsen, R., Sullivan, W. M., Swidler, A. & Tipton, S. M. (1985). *Habits of the Heart: Individualism and Commitment in American Life.* New York: Harper and Row.

Bennis, W. G. & Shepard, H. A. (1956). A theory of group development. *Human Relations, 9,* 415–437.

Berger, P. L. & Hansfried, K. (1981). *Sociology Reinterpreted: An Essay on Method and Vocation.* Garden City, NY: Doubleday / Anchor.

Berkowitz, L. (1954). Group standards, cohesiveness, and productivity. *Human Relations, 7,* 509–519.

Berkowitz, L. & Daniels, L. R. (1963). Responsibility and dependency. *Journal of Abnormal and Social Psychology, 66,* 429–436.

Bion, W. R. (1959). *Experiences in Groups.* New York: Basic Books.

Bion, W. R. (1961). *Experiences in Groups.* New York: Basic Books.

Blake, R. R. & Mouton, J. S. (1964). *The Managerial Grid.* Houston, TX: Gulf.

Blake, R. R. & Mouton, J. S. (1978). *The New Managerial Grid.* Houston, TX: Gulf.

Blake, R. R. & Mouton, J. S. (1980). *The Versatile Manager: A Grid Profile.* Homewood, IL: Dow Jones-Irwin.

Blake, R. R. and Mouton, J. S. (1982). How to choose a leadership style. *Training and Development Journal, 36,* 39–46.

Blanchard, F. A. & Cook, S. W. (1976). Effects of helping a less competent member of a cooperating interracial group on the development of interpersonal attraction. *Journal of Personality and Social Psychology, 34,* 1245–1255.

Blanchard, K. & Johnson, S. (1981). *The One Minute Manager.* New York: Berkley Books.

Blau, P. M. (1954). Cooperation and competition in a bureaucracy. *American Journal of Sociology, 59*, 530–535.

Blau, P. M. & Scott, W. R. (1962). *Formal Organizations: A Comparative Approach.* San Francisco: Chandler.

Blumer, H. (1973). Fashion: From class differentiation to collective selection. In G. Wills & D. Midgley (Eds.), *Fashion Marketing.* London: Allen & Unwin.

Bond, C. F. & Titus, L. J. (1983). Social facilitation: A meta-analysis of 241 studies. *Psychological Bulletin, 94*, 265–292.

Bond, J. R. & Vinacke, W. E. (1961). Coalitions in mixed-sex triads. *Sociometry, 24*, 61–75.

Borg, W. R. (1960). Prediction of small group role behavior from personality variables. *Journal of Abnormal and Social Psychology, 60*, 112–116.

Borgatta, E. F. & Bales, R. F. (1953). Task and accumulation of experience as factors in the interaction of small groups. *Sociometry, 16*, 239–252.

Borgatta, M. L. (1961). Power structure and coalitions in three-person groups. *Journal of Social Psychology, 55*, 287–300.

Borgers, S. B. & Tyndall, L. W. (1982). Setting expectations for groups. *Journal for Specialists in Group Work, 7* (2), 109–111.

Bormann, E. G. (1975). *Discussion and Group Methods: Theory and Practices* (2d ed.). New York: Harper and Row.

Bovard, E. W. (1951). Group structure and perception. *Journal of Abnormal and Social Psychology, 46*, 398–405.

Bovard, E. W. (1953). Conformity to social norms and attraction to the group. *Science, 118*, 598–599.

Bowers, D. G. & Seashore, S. E. (1966). Predicting organizational effectiveness with a four-factor theory of leadership. *Administrative Science Quarterly, 11*, 238–263.

Braaten, L. J. (1974/1975). Developmental phases of encounter groups: A critical review of models and a new proposal. *Interpersonal Development, 75*, 112–129.

Bradley, P. H. (1978). Power, status, and upward communication in small decision-making groups. *Communication Monographs, 45*, 33–43.

Bray, R. M., Kerr, N. L. & Atkin, R. S. (1978). Effects of group size, problem difficulty, and sex on group performance and member reactions. *Journal of Personality and Social Psychology, 36*, 1224–1240.

Brett, J. M. & Goldberg, S. B. (1983). Grievance mediation in the coal industry: A field experiment. *Industrial and Labor Relations Review, 37*, 49–69.

Brett, J. M., Goldberg, S. B. & Ury, W. L. (1990). Designing systems for resolving disputes in organizations. *American Psychologist, 45* (2), 162–170.

Brett, J. M. & Rognes, J. K. (1986). Intergroup relations in organizations: A negotiations perspective. In P. Goodman (Ed.), *Designing Effective Work Groups* (pp. 202–236). San Francisco, CA: Jossey-Bass.

Brewer, M. B. & Kramer, R. M. (1985). The psychology of intergroup attitudes and behavior. *Annual Review of Psychology, 36*, 219–243.

Brewer, M. B. & Miller, N. (1983). Social categorization and intergroup acceptance. Paper presented to the Society of Experimental Social Psychologists, Pittsburgh, PA.

Brickman, P., Becker, L. J. & Castel, S. (1979). Making trust easier and harder through two forms of sequential interaction. *Journal of Personality and Social Psychology, 37*, 515–521.

Brickner, M. A., Harkins, S. G. & Ostrom, T. M. (1986). Effects of personal involvement: Thought-provoking implications for social loafing. *Journal of Personality and Social Psychology, 51*, 763–770.

Brower, A. M. (1986). Behavior changes in psychotherapy groups: A study using an empirically based statistical method. *Small Group Behavior, 17* (2), 164–185.

Browning, L. (1978). A grounded organizational communication theory derived from qualitative data. *Communication Monographs, 45*, 93–109.

Bruning, N. S. & Frew, D. R. (1987). Effects of exercise, relaxation, and management skills training on physiological stress indicators: A field experiment. *Journal of Applied Psychology, 72,* 515–521.

Bryman, A. (1992). *Street Corner Society* as a model for research into organizational culture. In P. J. Frost, F. Moore, M. R. Louis, C. C. Lundberg, & J. Martin (Eds.), *Reframing Organizational Culture* (pp. 205–214). Newbury Park, CA: Sage.

Buck, R., Miller, R. E. & Caul, W. F. (1974). Sex, personality, and physiological variables in the communication of affect via facial expression. *Journal of Personality and Social Psychology, 30,* 587–596.

Burke, R. J. (1970). Methods of resolving superior-subordinate conflict: The constructive use of subordinate differences and disagreements. *Organizational Behavior and Human Performance, 5,* 393–411.

Burke, W. B. (1982). *Organizational Development.* Boston: Little, Brown & Company.

Burlingame, G. M. & Fuhriman, A. (1990). Time-limited group therapy. *The Counseling Psychologist, 18* (1), 93–118.

Burns, T. (1977). *The BBC: Public Institution and Private World.* London: Macmillan.

Burwitz, L. & Newell, K. M. (1972). The effects of the mere presence of coactors on learning a motor skill. *Journal of Motor Behavior, 4,* 99–102.

Bushe, G. R. (1986). Managing groups from the outside: A model of cognitive task-group types. Paper presented at the Annual Meeting of the Western Academy.

Buss, D. M. (1985). The temporal stability of acts, trends, and patterns. In C. Speilberger & J. N. Butcher (Eds.), *Advances in Personality Assessment* (Vol. 5, pp. 165–196). Hillsdale, NJ: Erlbaum.

Buss, D. M. (1987). Selection, evocation and manipulation. *Journal of Personality and Social Psychology, 53* (6), 1214–1221.

Butler, P. E. (1981). *Self-Assertion for Women.* New York: Harper & Row.

Byrne, D. (1961). Interpersonal attraction and attitude similarity. *Journal of Abnormal and Social Psychology, 62,* 713–715.

Byrne, D., Clore, J. L. & Worchel, P. (1966). Effect of economic similarity-dissimilarity on interpersonal attraction. *Journal of Personality and Social Psychology, 4,* 220–224.

Byrne, D. & Griffitt, W. A. (1966). A developmental investigation of the law of attraction. *Journal of Personality and Social Psychology, 4,* 699–702.

Byrne, D., Griffitt, W. & Stefaniak, D. (1967). Attraction and similarity of personality characteristics. *Journal of Personality and Social Psychology, 5,* 82–90.

Byrne, D. & Nelson, D. (1964). Attraction as a function of attitude similarity-dissimilarity: The effect of topic importance. *Psychonomic Science, 1,* 93–94.

Byrne, D. & Nelson, D. (1965a). Attraction as a linear function of proportion of positive reinforcements. *Journal of Personality and Social Psychology, 1,* 659–663.

Byrne, D. & Nelson, D. (1965b). The effect of topic importance and attitude similarity-dissimilarity on attraction in a multi-stranger design. *Psychonomic Science, 3,* 449–450.

Cahoone, L. E. (1988). *The Dilemma of Modernity: Philosophy, Culture and Anti-Culture.* Albany, NY: University of New York Press.

Caine, B. T. & Schlenker, B. R. (1979). Role position and group performance as determinants of egotistical perceptions in cooperative groups. *Journal of Psychology, 101,* 149–156.

Callaway, M. R., Marriott, R. G. & Esser, J. K. (1985). Effects of dominance on group decision making: Toward a stress-reduction explanation of groupthink. *Journal of Personality and Social Psychology, 49,* 949–952.

Campbell, D. T. (1958). Common fate, similarity, and other indices of the status of aggregates of persons as social entities. *Behavioral Science, 3,* 14–25.

Campbell, J. P. & Campbell, R. J. & Associates. (1988). *Productivity in Organizations.* San Francisco, CA: Jossey-Bass.

Caple, R. B. (1978). The sequential stages of group development. *Small Group Behavior, 9,* 470–476.

Caplow, T. (1959). Further development of a theory of coalitions in the triad. *American Journal of Sociology, 64,* 488–493.

Caplow, T. (1983). *Managing an Organization*. New York: Holt, Rinehart & Winston.

Carew, D. K. & Parisi-Carew, E. (1988). *Group Development Stage Analysis: Matching Leader Behaviors with Team Development*. (Blanchard Training and Development, Inc., 125 State Place, Escondido, CA, 92025).

Carkhuff, R. R. (1971). *The Development of Human Resources: Education, Psychology, and Social Change*. New York: Holt, Rinehart & Winston.

Carment, D. W. (1970). Rate of simple motor responding as a function of coaction, competition, and sex of the participants. *Psychonomic Science, 19*, 340–341.

Carnevale, P. J. D. (1986). Mediating disputes and decisions in organizations. In R. J. Lewicki, B. H. Sheppard & M. H. Bazerman (Eds.), *Research on Negotiation in Organizations* (Vol. 1, pp. 251–269). Greenwich, CT: JAI Press.

Carr, S. J. & Dabbs, J. M. (1974). The effects of lighting, distance and intimacy of topic on verbal and visual behavior. *Sociometry, 37*, 592–600.

Carter, L. F. (1954). Recording and evaluating the performance of individuals as members of small groups. *Personnel Psychology, 7*, 477–484.

Cartwright, D. & Zander, A. (Eds.). (1953). *Group Dynamics: Research and Theory*. Evanston, IL: Row, Peterson.

Cartwright, D. & Zander, A. (Eds.). (1968). *Group Dynamics: Research and Theory*. (3d ed.). New York: Harper and Row.

Cartwright, J. A. (1978). A laboratory investigation of groupthink. *Communication monographs, 45*, 229–246.

Caspi, A. (1987). Personality in the life course. *Journal of Personality and Social Psychology, 53* (6), 1203–1213.

Cassirer, E. (1953–1957). *The Philosophy of Symbolic Forms* (Vols. 1–3). New Haven, CT: Yale University Press.

Cattell, R. B. (1951). New concepts for measuring leadership in terms of group syntality. *Human Relations, 4*, 161–184.

Chapman, J. B. (1975). Comparison of male and female leadership styles. *Academy of Management Journal, 18* (3), 645–650.

Cissna, K. (1984). Phases in group development. *Small Group Behavior, 15* (1), 3–32.

Coates, J. (1987). *Armed and Dangerous: The Rise of the Survivalist Right*. New York: Hill and Wang.

Cohen, A. M. (1961). Changing small group communication networks. *Journal of Communication, 11*, 116–124, 128.

Cohen, A. M. (1962). Changing small group communication networks. *Administrative Science Quarterly, 6*, 443–462.

Cohen, A. M. & Bennis, W. G. (1962). Predicting organization in changed communication networks. *Journal of Psychology, 54*, 391–416.

Cohen, A. R. (1959). Situational structure, self-esteem, and threat-oriented reactions to power. In D. Cartwright (Ed.), *Studies in Social Power*. Ann Arbor, MI: Institute for Social Research.

Cohen, E. G. (1982). Expectation states and interracial interaction in school settings. *Annual Review of Sociology, 8*, 209–235.

Cohen, E. G. (1984). The desegregated school: Problems in status, power and interethnic climate. In N. Miller & M. B. Brewer (Eds.), *Groups in Contact: The Psychology of Desegregation* (pp. 77–96). New York: Academic Press.

Cohen, E. G. & Roper, S. (1972). Modification of interracial interaction disability: An application of status characteristics theory. *American Sociological Review, 37*, 643–655.

Cohen, S. & Wills, T. A. (1985). Stress, social support, and the buffering hypothesis. *Psychological Bulletin, 98*, 310–357.

Collins, E. B. & Guetzkow, H. A. (1964). *A Social Psychology of Group Processes for Decision-Making*. New York: Wiley.

Comte, A. (1855). *The Positive Philosophy of Auguste Comte*. Trans. Harriet Martineau. New York: Calvin Blanchard.

Cook, S. W. (1969). Motives in a conceptual analysis of attitude-related behavior. In W. J. Arnold & D. Levine (Eds.), *Nebraska Symposium on Motivation* (Vol. 18, pp. 179–236). Lincoln, NE: University of Nebraska Press.

Cook, S. W. (1978). Interpersonal and attitudinal outcomes in cooperating interracial groups. *Journal of Research in Developmental Education, 12*, 97–113.

Cook, S. W. (1981). Ethical implications. In L. H. Kidder (Ed.), *Research Methods in Social Relations* (4th ed.). New York: Holt, Rinehart & Winston.

Cook, S. W. (1984). Cooperative interaction in multiethnic contexts. In N. Miller & M. Brewer (Eds.), *Groups in Contact: The Psychology of Desegregation* (pp. 156–186). New York: Academic Press.

Cooley, C. H. (1902). *Human Nature and the Social Order.* New York: Scribner.

Cooley, C. H. (1909). *Social Organization.* New York: Scribner.

Cooper, C. & Marshall, J. (1976). Occupational sources of stress: A review of the literature relating to coronary heart disease and mental ill health. *Journal of Occupational Psychology,* March, 11–28.

Cooper, L. D., Johnson, R. & Wilderson, F. (1980). The effects of cooperative, competitive and individualistic experiences on interpersonal attraction among heterogeneous peers. *Journal of Social Psychology, 111,* 243–252.

Copeland, L. (1988). Learning to manage a multicultural workforce. *Training Magazine,* May, 49–56.

Corey, M. S. & Corey, G. (1992). *Group Process and Practice* (4th ed.). Pacific Grove, CA: Brooks/Cole.

Coser, L. (1956). *The Functions of Social Conflict.* New York: Free Press.

Costanzo, P. R. (1970). Conformity development as a function of self-blame. *Journal of Personality and Social Psychology, 14,* 366–374.

Crosbie, P. V. (1975). *Interaction in Small Groups.* New York: Macmillan.

Crosbie, P. V. (1979). Effects of status inconsistency: Negative evidence from small groups. *Social Science Quarterly, 42,* 110–125.

Cross, J. G. & Guyer, M. J. (1980). *Social Traps.* Ann Arbor, MI: University of Michigan Press.

Crutchfield, R. S. (1955). Conformity and character. *American Psychologist, 10,* 191–198.

Cummings, T. G. (1981). Designing effective work-groups. In P. C. Nystrom & W. Starbuck (Eds.), *Handbook of Organizational Design* (Vol. 2, pp. 250–271). Oxford: Oxford University Press.

Cyert, R. M. and March, J. (1963). *A Behavioral Theory of the Firm.* Englewood Cliffs, NJ: Prentice Hall.

Czarniawska, B. (1986). The management of meaning in Polish crisis. *Journal of Management Studies, 23* (3), 313–331.

Czarniawska-Joerges, B. (1991). Culture is the medium of life. In P. J. Frost, L. F. Moore, M. R. Louis, C. C. Lundberg & J. Martin. *Reframing Organizational Culture* (pp. 285–297). Newbury Park, CA: Sage.

Dalgard, O. S., Anstorp, T., Benum, K., Sorensen, T. & Moum, T. (1990). Social psychiatric field studies in Oslo. In S. Wheelan, E. Pepitone & V. Abt (Eds.), *Advances in Field Theory* (pp. 230–243). Newbury Park, CA: Sage.

Dashiell, J. F. (1930). An experimental analysis of some group effects. *Journal of Abnormal and Social Psychology, 25,* 190–199.

Davis, J. H. (1973). Group decision and social interaction: A theory of social decision schemes. *Psychological Review, 80,* 97–125.

Davis, J. H. (1982). Social interaction as a combinatorial process in group decision. In H. Brandstatter, J. H. Davis & G. Stocker-Kreichgauer (Eds.), *Group Decision Making* (pp. 27–58). London: Academic Press.

Deutsch, M. (1949a). An experimental study of the effect of cooperation and competition upon group process. *Human Relations, 2,* 199–231.

Deutsch, M. (1949b). A theory of cooperation and competition. *Human Relations, 2,* 129–152.

Deutsch, M. (1959). Some factors affecting membership motivation and achievement motivation in a group. *Human Relations, 12,* 81–95.

Deutsch, M. (1969). Socially relevant science: Reflections on some studies of interpersonal conflict. *American Psychologist, 24,* 1076–1092.

Deutsch, M. (1971). Toward an understanding of conflict. *International Journal of Group Tensions, 1,* 42–54.

Deutsch, M. (1973). *The Resolution of Social Conflict.* New Haven, CT: Yale University Press.

Deutsch, M. (1985). *Distributive Justice: A Social-Psychological Perspective.* New Haven, CT: Yale University Press.

Deutsch, M. (1990a). Cooperation, conflict and justice. In S. Wheelan, E. Pepitone & V. Abt (Eds.), *Advances in Field Theory* (pp. 149–164). Newbury Park, CA: Sage.

Deutsch, M. (1990b). Forms of social organization: Psychological consequences. In H. T. Himmelweit & G. Gaskell (Eds.), *Societal Psychology* (pp. 157–176). Newbury Park, CA: Sage.

Dies, R. R. (1983). Clinical implications of research on leadership in short-term group psychotherapy. In R. R. Dies & R. MacKenzie (Eds.), *Advances in Group Psychotherapy: Integrating Research and Practice* (American Group Psychotherapy Association Monograph Series) (pp. 27–28). New York: International Universities Press.

Dion, K. L., Miller, N. & Magnan, M. A. (1971). Cohesiveness and social responsibility as determinants of group risk taking. *Journal of Personality and Social Psychology, 20,* 400–406.

Douglas, J. D. (1976). *Investigative Social Research.* Newbury Park, CA: Sage.

Douglas, M. (1986). *How Institutions Think.* Syracuse, NY: Syracuse University Press.

Druckman, D. (Ed.). (1977). *Negotiations.* Newbury Park, CA: Sage.

Druckman, D. (1987). New directions for a social psychology of conflict. In D. J. D. Sandole & I. Sandole-Staroste (Eds.), *Conflict Management and Problem-Solving: Interpersonal to International Applications* (pp. 55–56). London: Frances Pinter.

Dunphy, D. C. (1964). Social change in self-analytic groups. In P. J. Stone, D. C. Dunphy, M. S. Smith & D. M. Ogilvie. (Eds.), *The General Inquirer: A Computer Approach to Content Analysis.* Cambridge, MA: MIT Press.

Dunphy, D. C. (1968). Phases, roles, and myths in self-analytic groups. *The Journal of Applied Behavioral Science, 4* (2), 195–225.

Dunphy, D. C. (1974). The function of fantasy in groups. In G. S. Gibbard, J. J. Hartman & R. D. Mann (Eds.), *Analysis of Groups.* San Francisco: Jossey-Bass.

Durkheim, E. (1895). *Les regles de la methode sociologique.* Paris: F. Alcan. Reprint, *The Rules of Sociological Method.* New York: The Free Press, 1938.

Durkheim, E. (1897). *Le Suicide.* Paris: F. Alcan. Translation (1951), Glencoe, IL: The Free Press.

Durkin, J. E. (Ed.). (1981). *Living Groups: Group Psychotherapy and General Systems Theory.* New York: Brunner/Mazel.

Dyer, J. L. (1984). Team research and team training: A state-of-the-art review. In F. A. Muckler (Ed.), *Human Factors Review* (pp. 285–323). Santa Monica, CA: Human Factors Society.

Eagly, A. H. (1983). Gender and social influence: A social psychological analysis. *American Psychologist, 38,* 971–983.

Eagly, A. H. & Wood, W. (1982). Inferred sex differences in status as a determinant of gender stereotypes about social influence. *Journal of Personality and Social Psychology, 43* (5), 915–928.

Emerson, R. M. (1987). Four ways to improve the craft of fieldwork. *Journal of Contemporary Ethnography, 16,* 69–89.

Emery, F. (1990). On the nature of the next generation of issues. In S. Wheelan, E. Pepitone & V. Abt (Eds.), *Advances in Field Theory* (pp. 96–108). Newbury Park, CA: Sage.

Erez, M., Rim, Y. & Keider, I. (1986). The two sides of the tactics of influence: Agent vs. target. *Journal of Occupational Psychology, 59,* 25–39.

Erikson, E. (1950). *Childhood and Society.* New York: W. W. Norton.

Erikson, E. (1978). (Ed.). *Adulthood.* New York: W. W. Norton.

Eskilson, A. & Wiley, M. G. (1976). Sex composition and leadership in small groups. *Sociometry, 39,* 183–194.

Evans, C. R. & Dion, K. L. (1991). Group cohesion and performance: A meta-analysis. *Small Group Research, 22* (2), 175–186.

Evans, N. & Jarvis, D. (1986). The group attitude scale: A measure of attraction to group. *Small Group Behavior, 17* (2), 203–216.

Exline, R. V. (1957). Group climate as a factor in the relevance and accuracy of social perception. *Journal of Abnormal and Social Psychology, 55,* 382–388.

Falbo, T. (1977). The multidimensional scaling of power strategies. *Journal of Personality and Social Psychology, 35,* 537–548.

Farr, R. (1990). Waxing and waning of interest in societal psychology: A historical perspective. In H. Himmelweit & G. Gaskell (Eds.), *Societal Psychology* (pp. 46–65). Newbury Park, CA: Sage.

Farrell, M. P. (1976). Patterns in the development of self-analytic groups. *Journal of Applied Behavioral Science, 12,* 523–542.

Farrell, M. P. (1979). Collective projection and group structure: The relationship between deviance and projection in groups. *Small Group Behavior, 10,* 81–100.

Farrell, M. P. (1982). Artists' circles and the development of artists. *Small Group Behavior, 13* (4), 451–474.

Fensterheim, H. & Glazer, H. I. (1983). *Behavioral Psychotherapy.* New York: Brunner/Mazel.

Festinger, L. (1950). Informal social communication. *Psychological Review, 57,* 271–282.

Festinger, L. (1954). A theory of social comparison processes. *Human Relations, 7,* 117–140.

Festinger, L. (1957). *A Theory of Cognitive Dissonance.* New York: Harper & Row.

Fiedler, F. E. (1964). A contingency model of leadership effectiveness. In L. Berkowitz (Ed.), *Advances in Experimental Social Psychology* (Vol. 1, pp. 149–190). New York: Academic Press.

Fiedler, F. E. (1967). *A Theory of Leadership Effectiveness.* New York: McGraw-Hill.

Fisher, B. A. (1970a). Decision emergence: Phases in group decision making. *Speech Monographs, 37,* 53–66.

Fisher, B. A. (1970b). The process of decision modification in small discussion groups. *Journal of Communication, 20,* 51–64.

Fisher, B. A. (1980). *Small Group Decision Making* (2d ed.). New York: McGraw-Hill.

Fisher, C. D. & Gitelson, R. (1983). A meta-analysis of the correlates of role conflict and ambi-

guity. *Journal of Applied Psychology, 68,* 320–333.

Fisher, R. (1964). Fractionating conflict. In R. Fisher (Ed.), *International Conflict and Behavioral Science: The Craigville Papers.* New York: Basic Books.

Fisher, R. & Ury, W. (1981). *Getting to Yes: Negotiating Agreements Without Giving In.* Boston: Houghton-Mifflin.

Flapan, D. & Fenchel, G. H. (1987). Terminations. *Group, 11,* 131–143.

Flowers, M. L. (1977). A laboratory test of some implications of Janis' groupthink hypothesis. *Journal of Personality and Social Psychology, 35,* 888–896.

Foa, U. G. (1957). Relation of worker's expectation to satisfaction with supervisor. *Personnel Psychology, 10,* 161–168.

Folberg, J. & Taylor, A. (1984). *Mediation: A Comprehensive Guide to Resolving Conflicts Without Litigation.* San Francisco, CA: Jossey-Bass.

Forsyth, D. R. (1990). *Group Dynamics* (2d ed.). Pacific Grove, CA: Brooks/Cole.

Forsyth, D. R. & Schlenker, B. R. (1977). Attributing the causes of group performance: Effects of performance quality, task importance, and future testing. *Journal of Personality, 45,* 220–236.

Frank, F. & Anderson, L. R. (1971). Effects of task and group size upon group productivity and member satisfaction. *Sociometry, 34,* 135–149.

Freeze, L. & Cohen, B. P. (1973). Eliminating status generalization. *Sociometry, 36,* 177–193.

French, J. P. R., Jr. (1941). The disruption and cohesion of groups. *Journal of Abnormal and Social Psychology, 36,* 361–377.

French, J. P. R., Jr. & Raven, B. (1959). The bases of social power. In D. Cartwright (Ed.), *Studies in Social Power* (pp. 150–167). Ann Arbor, MI: Institute for Social Research.

French, W. L., Bell, C. H. & Zawacki, R. A. (Eds.). (1989). *Organization Development* (3d ed.). Homewood, IL: BPI Irwin.

Freud, S. (1950). *Totem and Taboo.* New York: W. W. Norton.

Friedland, N. (1976). Social influence via threats.

Journal of Experimental Social Psychology, 12, 552–563.

Friedlander, F. (1987). The ecology of work groups. In J. Lorsch (Ed.), *Handbook of Organizational Behavior* (pp. 301–314). Englewood Cliffs, NJ: Prentice Hall.

Frost, P. J., Moore, L. F., Louis, M. R., Lundberg, C. C. & Martin, J. (Eds.) (1992). *Reframing Organizational Culture.* Newbury Park, CA: Sage.

Fuhriman, A. & Burlingame, G. M. (1990). Consistency of matter: A comparative analysis of individual and group process variables. *The Counseling Psychologist, 18* (1), 6–63.

Fuhrmann, B. S. & Washington, C. S. (1984a). Substance abuse and group work: Tentative conclusions. *Journal for Specialists in Group Work. 9* (1), 62–63.

Fuhrmann, B. S. & Washington, C. S. (1984b). Substance abuse: An overview. *Journal for Specialists in Group Work, 9* (1), 2–6.

Gabarro, J. J. (1987). The development of working relationships. In J. W. Lorsch (Ed.), *Handbook of Organizational Behavior* (pp. 172–189). Englewood Cliffs, NJ: Prentice Hall.

Galagan, P. (1986). Work teams that work. *Training and Development Journal, 11,* 33–35.

Gamson, W. A. (1961a). An experimental test of a theory of coalition formation. *American Sociological Review, 26,* 565–573.

Gamson, W. A. (1961b). A theory of coalition formation. *American Sociological Review, 26,* 373–382.

Gamson, W. A. (1964). Experimental studies of coalition formation. In L. Berkowitz (Ed.), *Advances in Experimental Social Psychology* (Vol. 1, pp. 82–110). New York: Academic Press.

Garland, J., Kolodny, R. & Jones, H. (1965). A model for stages of development in social work groups. In S. Bernstein (Ed.), *Explorations in Group Work.* Boston: Milford House.

Gaskell, G. (1990). Collective behavior in a societal context. In H. T. Himmelweit & G. Gaskell (Eds.), *Societal Psychology* (pp. 252–272). Newbury Park, CA: Sage.

Gazda, G. M. (1989). *Group Counseling: A Developmental Approach* (4th ed.). Boston: Allyn & Bacon.

Gazda, G. M., Childers, W. C. & Brooks, D. K. Jr. (1987). *Foundations of Counseling and Human Services.* New York: McGraw-Hill.

Geis, F. L., Brown, V., Jennings, J. & Corrado-Taylor, D. (1984). Sex vs. status in sex-associated stereotypes. *Sex Roles, 11,* 771–785.

Geller, G. M., Goodstein, L., Silver, M. & Sternberg, W. C. (1974) On being ignored: The effects of the violation of implicit rules of social interaction. *Sociometry, 37,* 541–556.

Gergen, K. J. & Gergen, M. M. (1988). Narrative and the self as a relationship. In L. Berkowitz (Ed.), *Advances in Experimental Social Psychology* (Vol. 21, pp. 17–56). New York: Academic Press.

Gergen, K. J. & Taylor, M. G. (1969). Social expectancy and self-presentation in a status hierarchy. *Journal of Experimental Social Psychology, 5,* 79–92.

Gersick, C. J. G. (1988). Time and transition in work teams: Toward a new model of group development. *Academy of Management Journal, 31,* 9–41.

Gewirtz, J. L. & Baer, D. M. (1958a). Deprivation and satiation of social reinforcers as drive conditions. *Journal of Abnormal and Social Psychology, 57,* 165–172.

Gewirtz, J. L. & Baer, D. M. (1958b). The effect of brief social deprivation on behaviors for a social reinforcer. *Journal of Abnormal and Social Psychology, 56,* 49–56.

Gibbard, G. & Hartman, J. (1973). The Oedipal paradigm in group development: A clinical and empirical study. *Small Group Behavior 4* (3), 305–354.

Gladstein, D. L. (1984). Groups in context: A model of task group effectiveness. *Administrative Science Quarterly, 29,* 499–517.

Gladstein, D. & Caldwell, D. (1985). Boundary management in new product teams. *Academy of Management Proceedings,* 161–165

Glaser, B. G. & Strauss, A. L. (1967). *The Discovery of Grounded Theory.* New York: Aldine Publishing Co.

Glass, D. C., Singer, J. E. & Friedman, L. N. (1969). Psychic cost of adaptation to an environmental stressor. *Journal of Personality and Social Psychology, 12,* 200–210.

Glickman, A. S., Zimmer, S., Montero, R. C., Guerette, P. J., Campbell, W. J., Morgan, B. & Salas, E. (1987). *The evolution of teamwork skills: An empirical assessment with implications for training* (Tech. Report 87–016). Orlando, FL: Office of Naval Research, Human Factors Division.

Goad, T. W. (1982). *Delivering Effective Training.* San Diego, CA: University Associates.

Goethals, G. R. & Zanna, M. P. (1979). The role of social comparison in choice shifts. *Journal of Personality and Social Psychology, 37,* 1469–1476.

Goetsch, G. G. & McFarland, D. D. (1980). Models of the distribution of acts in small discussion groups. *Social Psychology Quarterly, 43,* 173–183.

Goffman, E. (1967). *Interaction Ritual.* Chicago: Aldine.

Gold, M. (1990). Two "Field Theories." In S. Wheelan, E. Pepitone & V. Abt (Eds.), *Advances in Field Theory* (pp. 67–79). Newbury Park, CA: Sage.

Goldberg, S. C. (1955). Influence and leadership as a function of group structure. *Journal of Abnormal and Social Psychology, 51,* 119–122.

Good, L. R. & Good, K. C. (1974). Similarity of attitudes and attraction to a social organization. *Psychological Reports, 34,* 1071–1073.

Goodacre, D. M. (1951). The use of a sociometric test as a predictor of combat unit effectiveness. *Sociometry, 14,* 148–152.

Goodacre, D. M. (1953). Group characteristics of good and poor performing combat units. *Sociometry, 16,* 168–178.

Goodman, P. S., Devadas, R. & Hughson, T. L. G. (1988). Groups and productivity: Analyzing the effectiveness of self-managing teams. In J. P. Campbell & R. J. Campbell (Eds.), *Productivity in Organizations* (pp. 295–327). San Francisco: Jossey-Bass.

Gordon, T. (1970). *Parent Effectiveness Training.* New York: Wyden.

Graumann, C. F. (1986). The individualization of the social and the desocialization of the individual: Floyd H. Allport's contribution to social psychology. In C. F. Graumann & S. Moscovici (Eds.), *Changing Conceptions of Crowd Mind and Behavior* (pp. 97–116). New York: Springer-Verlag.

Graumann, C. F. & Kruse, L. (1990). The environment: Social construction and psychological problems. In H. T. Himmelweit & G. Gaskell (Eds.), *Societal Psychology* (pp. 212–229). Newbury Park, CA: Sage.

Greene, C. N. (1989). Cohesion and productivity in work groups. *Small Group Behavior, 20,* 70–86.

Griffitt, W. (1966). Interpersonal attraction as a function of self-concept and personality similarity-dissimilarity. *Journal of Personality and Social Psychology, 4,* 581–584.

Griffitt, W. & Veitch, R. (1974). Preacquaintance attitude similarity and attraction revisited: Ten days in a fall-out shelter. *Sociometry, 37,* 163–173.

Gross, E. (1954). Primary functions of small groups. *American Journal of Sociology, 60,* 24–30.

Gross, N., McEachern, A. W. & Mason, W. S. (1958). Role conflict and its resolution. In E. E. Maccoby, T. M. Newcomb & E. L. Hartley (Eds.), *Readings in Social Psychology* (3d ed.) (pp. 447–459). New York: Henry Holt.

Guetzkow, H. & Dill, W. R. (1957). Factors in the organizational development of task-oriented groups. *Sociometry, 20,* 175–204.

Guetzkow, H. & Simon, H. A. (1955). The impact of certain communication nets upon organization and performance in task-oriented groups. *Management Science, 1,* 233–250.

Gustafson, J. P. & Cooper, L. (1979). Unconscious planning in small groups. *Human Relations, 32* (12), 1039–1064.

Hackman, J. R. (1969). Toward understanding the role of tasks in behavioral research. *Acta Psychologica, 39,* 97–128.

Hackman, J. R. (1983). *A Normative Model of Work Team Effectiveness.* Technical Report No. 2, Research Program on Group Effectiveness. Yale School of Organization and Management, New Haven, CT.

Hackman, J. R. (1987). The design of work teams.

In J. W. Lorsch (Ed.), *Handbook of Organizational Behavior* (pp. 315–342). Englewood Cliffs, NJ: Prentice Hall.

Hackman, J. R. (1989). *Groups That Work (And Those That Don't)*. San Francisco, CA: Jossey-Bass.

Hackman, J. R., Brousseau, K. R. & Weiss, J. A. (1976). The interaction of task design and group performance strategies in determining group effectiveness. *Organizational Behavior and Human Performance, 16*, 350–365.

Hackman, J. R. & Morris, C. G. (1975). Group tasks, group interaction process, and group effectiveness: A review and proposed integration. In L. Berkowitz (Ed.), *Advances in Experimental Social Psychology* (Vol. 8, pp. 47–99). New York: Academic Press.

Hackman, J. R. & Oldham, G. R. (1980). *Work Redesign*. Reading, MA: Addison-Wesley.

Hardin, G. (1968). The tragedy of the commons. *Science, 162*, 1243–1248.

Hardy, C. & Latane, B. (1986). Social loafing on a cheering task. *Social Science, 71* (2–3), 165–172.

Hare, A. P. (1962). *Handbook of Small Group Research*. New York: Free Press.

Hare, A. P. (1967). Small group development in the relay assembly testroom. *Sociological Inquiry, 37*, 169–182.

Hare, A. P. (1976). *Handbook of Small Group Research* (2d ed.). New York: Free Press.

Hare, A. P. (1982). *Creativity in Small Groups*. Newbury Park, CA: Sage.

Hare, A. P. & Naveh, D. (1984). Group development at Camp David Summit, 1978. *Small Group Behavior, 15* (3), 299–318.

Hare, A. P. & Naveh, D. (1986). Conformity and creativity: Camp David. *Small Group Behavior, 17*, 243–268.

Harkins, S. G., Latane, B. & Williams, K. (1980). Social loafing: Allocating effort or taking it easy? *Journal of Experimental Social Psychology, 16*, 457–465.

Harkins, S. G. & Petty, R. E. (1982). Effects of task difficulty and task uniqueness on social loafing. *Journal of Personality and Social Psychology, 43*, 1214–1229.

Harkins, S. G. & Szymanski, K. (1987). Social loafing and social facilitation: New wine in old

bottles. In C. Hendrick (Ed.), *Review of Personality and Social Psychology: Group Processes and Intergroup Relations* (Vol. 9, pp. 167–188). Newbury Park, CA: Sage.

Harper, N. L. & Askling, L. R. (1980). Group communication and quality of task solution in a media production organization. *Communication Monographs, 47*, 77–100.

Harre, R. (1984). *Personal Being*. Cambridge, MA: Harvard University Press.

Hartman, J. J. (1979). Small group methods of personal change. *Annual Review of Psychology, 30*, 453–476.

Harvey, J. B. (1974). The Abilene paradox: The management of agreement. *Organizational Dynamics, 3*, 63–80.

Hatch, E. J. & Guerney, B. (1975). A pupil relationship enhancement program. *Personnel and Guidance Journal, 54*, 103–105.

Haythorn, W. (1953). The influence of individual members on the characteristics of small groups. *Journal of Abnormal and Social Psychology, 48*, 276–284.

Heider, F. (1958). *The Psychology of Interpersonal Relations*. New York: Wiley.

Heinen, J. S. & Jacobson, E. J. (1976). A model of task group development in complex organziations and a strategy of implementation. *Academy of Management Review, 1*, 98–111.

Heinicke, C. M. & Bales, R. F. (1953). Developmental trends in the structure of small groups. *Sociometry, 16*, 7–38.

Hembroff, L. A. (1982). Resolving status inconsistency: An expectation states theory and test. *Social Forces, 61*, 183–205.

Hembroff, L. A. & Myers, D. E. (1984). Status characteristics: Degrees of task relevance and decision process. *Social Psychology Quarterly, 47*, 337–346.

Hensley, T. R. & Griffin, G. W. (1986). Victims of groupthink: The Kent State University Board of Trustees and the 1977 gymnasium controversy. *Journal of Conflict Resolution, 30*, 497–531.

Herek, G., Janis, I. L. & Huth, P. (1987). Decision-making during international crises: Is quality of process related to outcome? *Journal of Conflict Resolution, 31*, 203–226.

Hershey, P. & Blanchard, K. H. (1976). Leader effectiveness and adaptability description (LEAD). In J. W. Pfeiffer & J. E. Jones (Eds.), *The 1976 Annual Handbook for Group Facilitators* (Vol. 5). LaJolla, CA: University Associates.

Hershey, P. & Blanchard, K. H. (1977). *Management of Organizational Behavior: Utilizing Human Resources* (3d ed.). Englewood Cliffs, NJ: Prentice Hall.

Hershey, P. & Blanchard, K. H. (1982). *Management of Organizational Behavior: Utilizing Human Resources* (4th ed.). Englewood Cliffs, NJ: Prentice Hall.

Hill, T. E. & Schmitt, N. (1977). Individual differences in leadership decision making. *Organizational Behavior and Human Performance, 19,* 353–367.

Hill, W. F. (1974). Systematic group development—SGD therapy. In A. Jacobs & W. Spradlin (Eds.), *The Group as Agent of Change.* New York: Behavioral Publications.

Hill, W. F. (1977). Hill Interaction Matrix (HIM): The conceptual framework, derived rating scales, and an updated bibliography. *Small Group Behavior, 8,* 251–268.

Hill, W. F. & Gruner, L. (1973). A study of development in open and closed groups. *Small Group Behavior, 4* (3), 355–382.

Hiltrop, J. M & Rubin, J. Z. (1982). Effect of intervention mode and conflict of interest on dispute resolution. *Journal of Personality and Social Psychology, 42,* 665–672.

Himmelweit, H. T. (1990). Societal psychology: Implications and scope. In H. T. Himmelweit & G. Gaskell (Eds.), *Societal Psychology* (pp. 17–45). Newbury Park, CA: Sage.

Himmelweit, H. T. & Gaskell, G. (Eds.). (1990). *Societal Psychology.* Newbury Park, CA: Sage.

Hirokawa, R. Y. (1980). A comparative analysis of communication patterns within effective and ineffective decision-making groups. *Communication Monographs, 47,* 312–321.

Hirokawa, R. Y. (1984). Does consensus really result in higher quality group decisions? In G. M. Phillips & J. T. Wood (Eds.), *Emergent Issues in Human Decision Making* (pp. 40–49). Carbondale, IL: Southern Illinois University Press.

Hirota, K. (1953). Group problem solving and communication. *Japanese Journal of Psychology, 24,* 176–177.

Hirschhorn, L. (1987). *The Workplace Within.* Cambridge, MA: MIT Press.

Hoffman, L. R. (1982). Improving the problem-solving process in managerial groups. In R. A. Guzzo (Ed.), *Improving Group Decision Making in Organizations* (pp. 95–126). New York: Academic Press.

Hofstede, G. & Boddewyn, J. J. (1977). Introduction: Power in organizations. *Inter-national Studies of Management and Organization, 7,* 3–7.

Hogan, R. (1975). Theoretical egocentrism and the problem of compliance. *American Psychologist, 30,* 533–539.

Hollander, E. P. (1960). Competence and conformity in the acceptance of influence. *Journal of Abnormal and Social Psychology, 61,* 365–369.

Hollander, E. P. (1978). *Leadership Dynamics: A Practical Guide to Effective Relationships.* New York: Free Press/Macmillan.

Hollander, E. P. (1985). Leadership and power. In G. Lindzey & E. Aronson (Eds.), *Handbook of Social Psychology* (Vol. 2, 3d ed., pp. 485–537). New York: Random House.

Hollander, E. P & Offermann, L. R. (1990). Power and leadership in organizations: Relationships in transition. *American Psychologist, 45* (2), 179–189.

Holmes, J. G. & Miller, D. T. (1976). Interpersonal conflict. In J. W. Thibaut, J. T. Spence & R. C. Carson (Eds.), *Contemporary Topics in Social Psychology.* Morristown, NJ: General Learning Press.

Holsti, O. R. (1969). *Content Analysis for the Social Sciences and Humanities.* London: Addison-Wesley.

Horai, J. (1977). Attributional conflict. *Journal of Social Issues, 33* (1), 88–100.

House, R. J. (1971). A path goal theory of leader effectiveness. *Administrative Science Quarterly, 16,* 321–338.

Hsu, F. L. K. (1971). Psychosocial homeostasis and Jen: Conceptual tools for advancing psychological anthropology. *American Anthropologist, 73,* 23–44.

Huey, W. C. & Rank, R. C. (1984). Effects of counselor and peer-led assertive training on black adolescent aggression. *Journal of Counseling Psychology, 31,* 95–98.

Husband, R. W. (1940). Cooperative versus solitary problem solution. *Journal of Social Psychology, 11,* 405–409.

Ingham, A. G., Levinger, G., Graves, J. & Peckman, V. (1974). The Ringelmann effect: Studies of group size and group performance. *Journal of Personality and Social Psychology, 10,* 371–384.

Ivancevich, J. M. & Matteson, M. T. (1980). *Stress at Work: A Managerial Perspective.* Glenview, IL: Scott, Foresman.

Ivancevich, J. M. & Matteson, M. T. (1987). *Organizational Behavior and Management.* Plano, TX: Business Publications, Inc.

Ivey, A. E. (1976). Counseling psychology, the psychoeducator model, and the future. *The Counseling Psychologist, 6,* 72–75.

Izard, C. E. (1960a). Personality similarity and friendship. *Journal of Abnormal Psychology, 61,* 47–51.

Izard, C. E. (1960b). Personality similarity, positive affect and interpersonal attraction. *Journal of Abnormal and Social Psychology, 61,* 484–485.

Jackson, J. M. & Harkins, S. G. (1985). Equity in effort: An explanation of the social loafing effect. *Journal of Personality and Social Psychology, 49,* 1199–1206.

Jacobs, R. C. & Campbell, D. T. (1961). The perpetuation of an arbitrary tradition through several generations of a laboratory microculture. *Journal of Abnormal and Social Psychology, 62,* 649–658.

Jacques, E. (1951). *The Changing Culture of the Factory.* London: Tavistock.

Jago, A. G. (1978). Configural cue utilization in implicit models of leadership behavior. *Organizational Behavior and Human Performance, 22,* 474–496.

Janis, I. L. (1972). *Victims of Groupthink.* Boston: Houghton Mifflin.

Janis, I. L. (1982). *Victims of Groupthink* (2d ed.). Boston: Houghton Mifflin.

Janis, I. L. (1983). Groupthink. In H. H. Blumberg, A. P. Hare, V. Kent & M. F. Davis (Eds.), *Small Groups and Social Interaction* (Vol. 2, pp. 39–46). New York: Wiley.

Janis, I. L. (1985). International crisis management in the nuclear age. *Applied Social Psychology Annual, 6,* 63–86.

Janis, I. L. (1989). *Crucial Decisions: Leadership in Policymaking and Crisis Management.* New York: Free Press.

Janis, I. L. & Mann, L. (1977). *Decision Making: A Psychological Analysis of Conflict, Choice, and Commitment.* New York: Free Press.

Janoff, S. (1992). The influence of legal education on moral reasoning. *Minnesota Law Review, 76* (2), 193–238.

Johnson, C. (1974). Planning for termination of the group. In P. Glasser, R. Sarri & R. Vinter (Eds.), *Individual Change Through Small Groups* (pp. 258–265). New York: Free Press.

Johnson, D. W. (1980). Group processes: Influences of student-student interaction on school outcomes. In J. H. McMillan (Ed.), *The Social Psychology of School Learning.* New York: Academic Press.

Johnson, D. W. & Johnson, R. T. (1989). *A Meta-Analysis of Cooperative, Competitive, and Individualistic Goal-Structures.* Hillsdale, NJ: Erlbaum.

Johnson, D. W., Johnson, R. T. & Smith, K. A. (1986). Academic conflict among students: Controversy and learning. In R. S. Feldman (Ed.), *The Social Psychology of Education* (pp. 199–231). New York: Cambridge University Press.

Johnson, D. W., Maruyama, G., Johnson, R., Nelson, D. & Skon, L. (1981). Effects of cooperative, competitive and individualistic goal structures on achievement: A meta-analysis. *Psychological Bulletin, 89,* 47–62.

Johnson, M. P. & Ewens, W. (1971). Power relations and affective style as determinants of confidence in impression formation in a game situation. *Journal of Experimental Social Psychology, 7,* 98–110.

Johnson, T. J., Feigenbaum, R., & Weiby, M. (1964). Some determinants and consequences of the teacher's perception of causation. *Journal of Educational Psychology, 55,* 237–246.

Jones, E. E. (1985). Major developments in social psychology during the past five decades. In G. Lindzey & E. Aronson (Eds.), *Handbook of Social Psychology* (Vol. 1, 3d ed., pp. 487–508). New York: Random House.

Jones, E. E. & Davis, K. E. (1965). From acts to dispositions: The attribution process in person perception. In L. Berkowitz (Ed.), *Advances in Experimental Social Psychology* (Vol. 2, pp. 219–266). New York: Academic Press.

Jones, J. (1982). *The Team Development Inventory.* La Jolla, CA: University Associates.

Jones, J. & Bearley, W. L. (1986). *Group Development Assessment (GDA Questionnaire and Trainer Guide).* King of Prussia, PA: Organization Design and Development, Inc.

Jones, M. O. (1990). A folklore approach to emotions in work. *American Behavioral Scientist, 3,* 278–286.

Jones, M. O., Moore, M. D. & Snyder, R. C. (1988). *Inside Organizations: Understanding the Human Dimension.* Newbury Park, CA: Sage.

Jones, R. A., Hendrick, C. & Epstein, Y. M. (1979). *Introduction to Social Psychology.* Sunderland, MA: Sinauer Associates.

Kandel, D. B. (1978). Similarity in real-life adolescent friendship pairs. *Journal of Personality and Social Psychology, 36,* 306–312.

Kano, S. (1971). Task characteristics and network. *Japanese Journal of Educational Social Psychology, 10,* 55–66.

Kanter, R. M. (1983). *The Change Masters.* New York: Simon & Schuster.

Katz, D. & Kahn, R. L. (1966). *The Social Psychology of Organizations.* New York: Wiley.

Katz, D. & Kahn, R. L. (1978). *The Social Psychology of Organizations* (2d ed.). New York: Wiley.

Katz, D., Kahn, R. L. & Adams, J. S. (1980). *The Study of Organizations.* San Francisco: Jossey-Bass.

Katz, G. M. (1982). Previous conformity, status, and the rejection of the deviant. *Small Group Behavior, 13,* 403–422.

Katz, I. (1970). Experimental studies in Negro-White relationships. In L. Berkowitz (Ed.), *Advances in Experimental Social Psychology* (Vol. 5, 71–117). New York: Academic Press.

Katz, R. (1978). The influence of job longevity on employee reactions to task characteristics. *Human Relations, 31,* 703–725.

Katz, R. & Tushman, M. (1979). Communication patterns, project performance, and task characteristics: An empirical evaluation and integration in an R & D setting. *Organization Behavior and Group Performance, 23,* 139–162.

Katz, R. & Tushman, M. (1981). An investigation into the managerial roles and career paths of gatekeepers and project supervisors in a major R & D facility. *R & D Management, 11,* 103–110.

Kaul, T. J. & Bednar, R. L. (1986). Experiential group research: Results, questions, and suggestions. In S. L. Garfield & A. E. Bergin (Eds.), *Handbook of Psychotherapy and Behavior Change* (3d ed., pp. 671–714). New York: Wiley.

Kelley, H. H. (1979). *Personal Relationships: Their Structures and Processes.* Hillsdale, NJ: Erlbaum.

Kelley, H. H. & Shapiro, M. M. (1954). An experiment on conformity to group norms where conformity is detrimental to group achievement. *American Sociological Review, 19,* 557–567.

Kemery, E. R., Bedeian, A. G., Mossholder, K. W. & Touliatos, J. (1985). Outcomes of role stress: A multisample constructive replication. *Academy of Management Review, 28,* 363–375.

Kernberg, O. F. (1978). Leadership and organizational functioning: Organizational regression. *International Journal of Group Psychotherapy, 28,* 3–25.

Kerr, N. L. (1982). Social transition schemes: Model, method, and applications. In H. Brandstatter, J. H. Davis & G. Stocker-Kreichgauer (Eds.), *Group Decision Making* (pp. 59–79). London: Academic Press.

Kerr, N. L. (1983). Motivation losses in small groups: A social dilemma analysis. *Journal of Personality and Social Psychology, 45,* 819–828.

Kerr, N. L. & Bruun, S. E. (1981). Ringelmann revisited: Alternative explanations for the social loafing effect. *Personality and Social Psychology Bulletin, 7,* 224–231.

Kerr, N. L. & Bruun, S. E. (1983). Dispensability of member effort and group motivation losses: Free-rider effects. *Journal of Personality and Social Psychology, 44,* 78–94.

Kerr, S., Schriesheim, C. A., Murphy, C. J. & Stogdill, R. M. (1974). Toward a contingency theory of leadership based upon the consideration and initiating structure literature. *Organizational Behavior and Human Performance, 12,* 62–82.

Ketchum, L. (1984). How redesigned plants really work. *National Productivity Review, 3,* 246–254.

Kidd, J. S. & Campbell, D. T. (1955). Conformity to groups as a function of group success. *Journal of Abnormal and Social Psychology, 51,* 390–393.

Kidder, L. H. (1981). *Research Methods in Social Relations* (4th ed.). New York: Holt, Rinehart & Winston.

Kihlstrom, J. F. (1987). Introduction to the special issue: Integrating Personality and Social Psychology. *Journal of Personality and Social Psychology, 53* (6), 989–992.

Killian, L. M. (1952). The significance of multiple-group membership in disaster. *American Journal of Sociology, 57,* 309–314.

Kilmann, R. H. & Thomas, K. W. (1978). Four perspectives on conflict management: An attributional framework for organizing descriptive and normative theory. *Academy of Management Journal, 32,* 687–704.

Kipnis, D. (1974). *The Powerholders.* Chicago: University of Chicago Press.

Kipnis, D. (1984). The use of power in organizations and in interpersonal settings. In S. Oskamp (Ed.), *Applied Social Psychology Annual* (Vol. 5, pp. 179–210). Newbury Park, CA: Sage.

Kipnis, D., Castell, P. J., Gergen, M. & Mauch, D. (1976). Metamorphic effects of power. *Journal of Applied Psychology, 61,* 127–135.

Kipnis, D., Schmidt, S. M., Swaffin-Smith, C. & Wilkinson, I. (1984). Patterns of managerial influence: Shotgun managers, tacticians, and bystanders. *Organizational Dynamics, 12* (3), 58–67.

Kirchler, E. & Davis, J. H. (1986). The influence of member status differences and task type on group consensus and member position change. *Journal of Personality and Social Psychology, 51,* 83–91.

Kleck, R. E. & Rubinstein, C. (1975). Physical attractiveness, perceived attitude similarity and interpersonal attraction in an opposite-sex encounter. *Journal of Personality and Social Psychology, 31,* 107–114.

Klein, M. & Christiansen, J. (1969). Group composition, group structure and group effectiveness of basketball teams. In J. W. Loy, Jr. & G. S. Kenyon (Eds.), *Sport, Culture and Society: A Reader on the Sociology of Sport* (pp. 397–408). London: Collier-MacMillan.

Kleiner, R. J. & Okeke, B. (1990). Level of aspiration theory and quality of life in cross cultural research. In S. Wheelan, E. Pepitone & V. Abt (Eds.), *Advances in Field Theory* (pp. 244–262). Newbury Park, CA: Sage.

Kogan, N. & Wallach, M. A. (1967). Group risk taking as a function of members' anxiety and defensiveness. *Journal of Personality, 35,* 50–63.

Kohn, M. L. & Schooler, C. (1969). Class, occupation, and orientation. *American Sociological Review, 34,* 659–678.

Kohn, M. L. & Schooler, C. (1978). The reciprocal effects of the substantive complexity of work and intellectual flexibility: A longitudinal assessment. *American Journal of Sociology, 84,* 24–52.

Kolodny, H. F. & Dresner, B. (1986). Linking arrangements and new work designs. *Organizational Dynamics, 14* (3), 33–51.

Kolodny, H. F. & Kiggundu, M. N. (1980). Towards the development of a sociotechnical systems model in woodlands mechanical harvesting. *Human Relations, 33,* 623–645.

Komorita, S. S. & Brinsberg, D. (1977). The effects of equity norms in coalition formation. *Sociometry, 40,* 351–361.

Komorita, S. S. & Lapworth, C. W. (1982). Cooperative choice among individuals versus groups in an n-person dilemma situation. *Journal of Personality and Social Psychology, 42,* 487–496.

Kramer, R. M. & Brewer, M. B. (1984). Effects of

group identity on resource use decisions in a simulated commons dilemma. *Journal of Personality and Social Psychology, 46,* 1044–1057.

Kramer, S. A. (1990). *Positive Endings in Psychotherapy: Bringing Meaningful Closure to Therapeutic Relationships.* San Francisco: Jossey-Bass.

Krebs, D. & Adinolfi, A. A. (1975). Physical attractiveness, social relations and personality style. *Journal of Personality and Social Psychology, 31,* 245–253.

Kriesberg, L. (1973). *The Sociology of Social Conflicts.* Englewood Cliffs, NJ: Prentice Hall.

Kushnir, T. (1984). Social psychological factors associated with the dissolution of dyadic business partnerships. *Journal of Social Psychology, 122,* 181–188.

Kuypers, B. C., Davies, D. & Glaser, K. (1986). Developmental arrestations in self-analytic groups. *Small Group Behavior, 17* (3), 269–302.

Kuypers, B. C., Davies, D. & Hazewinkel, A. (1986). Developmental patterns in self-analytic groups. *Human Relations, 39,* 793–815.

LaCoursiere, R. (1974). A group method to facilitate learning during the stages of a psychiatric affiliation. *International Journal of Group Psychotherapy, 24,* 342–351.

Lakin, M. (Ed.). (1979). What has happened to the small group? (Special Issue). *Journal of Applied Behavioral Science, 15* (3).

Lamm, H. & Myers, D. G. (1978). Group induced polarization of attitudes and behavior. In L. Berkowitz (Ed.), *Advances in Experimental Social Psychology* (Vol. 11, pp. 145–195). New York: Academic Press.

Landsberger, H. A. (1958). *Hawthorne Revisited.* Ithaca, NY: Cornell University.

Lange, A. J. & Jakubowski, P. (1976). *Responsible Assertive Behavior: Cognitive/Behavioral Procedures for Trainers.* Champaign, IL: Research Press.

Lanzetta, J. T. & Roby, T. B. (1956). Effects of work-group structure and certain task variables on group performance. *Journal of Abnormal and Social Psychology, 53,* 307–314.

Lanzetta, J. T. & Roby, T. B. (1957). Group learning and communication as a function of task

and structure "demands." *Journal of Abnormal and Social Psychology, 55,* 121–131.

Lanzetta, J. T. & Roby, T. B. (1960). The relationship between certain group process variables and group problem-solving efficiency. *Journal of Social Psychology, 52,* 135–148.

Larsen, O. N. & Hill, R. J. (1958). Social structure and interpersonal communication. *American Journal of Sociology, 63,* 497–505.

Larson, C. E. & LaFasto, F. M. J. (1989). *Team Work: What Must Go Right/What Can Go Wrong.* Newbury Park, CA: Sage.

Latane, B. (1981). The psychology of social impact. *American Psychologist, 36,* 343–356.

Latane, B. & Darley, J. M. (1968). Group inhibition of bystander intervention in emergencies. *Journal of Personality and Social Psychology, 10,* 215–221.

Latane, B., Eckman, J. & Joy, V. (1966). Shared stress and interpersonal attraction. *Journal of Experimental Social Psychology, 1,* 80–94.

Latane, B., Williams, K. & Harkins, S. (1979). Many hands make light the work: The causes and consequences of social loafing. *Journal of Personality and Social Psychology, 37,* 822–832.

Latham, G. P. (1988). Human resource training and development. *Annual Review of Psychology* (pp. 545–582). Palo Alto, CA: Annual Reviews.

Laughlin, P. R. (1988). Collective induction: Group performance, social combination processes, and mutual majority and minority influence. *Journal of Personality and Social Psychology, 54,* 254–267.

Lawler, E. J. (1975). An experimental study of factors affecting the mobilization of revolutionary coalitions. *Sociometry, 38,* 163–179.

Lawler, E. J. & Thompson, M. E. (1978). Impact of a leader's responsibility for inequity on subordinate revolts. *Social Psychology Quarterly, 41,* 264–268.

Lawler, E. J. & Thompson, M. E. (1979). Subordinate response to a leader's cooperation strategy as a function of type of coalition power. *Representative Research in Social Psychology, 9,* 69–80.

Lawler, E. J. & Youngs, G. A., Jr. (1975). Coalition formation: An integrative model. *Sociometry, 38,* 1–17.

Lawson, E. D. (1964a). Reinforced and non-reinforced four-man communication nets. *Psychological Reports, 14,* 287–296.

Lawson, E. D. (1964b). Reinforcement in group problem-solving with arithmetic problems. *Psychological Reports, 14,* 703–710.

Lawson, E. D. (1965). Change in communication nets, performance and morale. *Human Relations, 18,* 139–147.

Lax, D. A. & Sebenius, J. K. (1986). *The Manager as Negotiator.* New York: Free Press.

Lazarus, A. (1977). *In The Mind's Eye.* New York: Guilford Press.

Leach, E. (1982). *Social Anthropology.* Oxford: Oxford University Press.

Leana, C. R. (1985). A partial test of Janis' groupthink model: Effects of group cohesiveness and leader behavior on defective decision making. *Journal of Management, 11,* 5–17.

Leary, M. R. (1978). Self-presentational components of leadership. Dissertation. University of Florida, Gainesville.

Leavitt, H. J. (1951). Some effects of certain communication patterns on group performance. *Journal of Abnormal and Social Psychology, 46,* 38–50.

Le Bon, G. (1895). *The Crowd.* New York:Viking. Reprint 1960.

Ledford, G. E., Lawler, E. E. & Mohrman, S. A. (1988). The quality circle and its variations. In J. P Campbell & R. J. Campbell (Eds.), *Productivity in Organizations* (pp. 255–294). San Francisco: Jossey-Bass.

Leonard, R. L., Jr. (1975). Self-concept and attraction for similar and dissimilar others. *Journal of Personality and Social Psychology, 31,* 926–929.

Levinson, D. J., Darrow, C. N., Klein, E. B., Levinson, M. H. & McKee, B. (1978). *The Seasons of a Man's Life.* New York: Knopf.

Levitt, B. & March, J. G. (1988). Organizational Learning. *Annual Review of Sociology, 14,* 319–340.

Lewin, K. (1936). *Principles of Topological Psychology.* New York: McGraw-Hill.

Lewin, K. (1943). Forces behind food habits and methods of change. *Bulletin of the National Research Council, 108,* 35–65.

Lewin, K. (1947a). Frontiers in group dynamics, I. *Human Relations, 1,* 5–41.

Lewin, K. (1947b). Frontiers in group dynamics, II. *Human Relations, 1,* 143–158.

Lewin, K. (1951). *Field Theory in Social Science* (D. Cartwright, Ed.). New York: Harper.

Lewin, K., Dembo, T., Festinger, L. & Sears, P. S. (1944). Level of aspiration. In J. McV. Hunt (Ed.), *Personality and the Behavior Disorders* (pp. 333–378). New York: Ronald.

Lewin, K., Lippitt, R. & White, R. K. (1939). Patterns of aggressive behavior in experimentally created "social climates." *Journal of Social Psychology, 10,* 217–299.

Lewis, B. F. (1978). An examination of the final phase of a group development theory. *Small Group Behavior, 9* (4), 507–517.

Lieberman, M. A. (1980). Group methods. In F. H. Kanfer & A. P. Goldstein (Eds.), *Helping People Change.* New York: Pergamon.

Lieberman, M., Yalom, I. & Miles, M. (1973). *Encounter Groups: First Facts.* New York: Basic Books.

Likert, R. (1961). *New Patterns of Management.* New York: McGraw-Hill.

Likert, R. (1967). *The Human Organization.* New York: McGraw-Hill.

Lindskold, S. (1986). GRIT: Reducing distrust through carefully introduced conciliation. In S. Worchel & W. G. Austin (Eds.), *Psychology of Intergroup Relations* (2d ed., pp. 305–322). Chicago, IL: Nelson-Hall.

Lindskold, S., Han, G. & Betz, B. (1986). Essential elements of communication in GRIT strategy. *Personality and Social Psychology Bulletin, 12,* 179–186.

Littlepage, G. E., Cowart, L. & Kerr, B. (1989). Relationships between group environment scales and group performance and cohesion. *Small Group Behavior, 20,* 50–61.

Lockheed, E. & Hall, K. (1976). Conceptualizing sex as a status characteristic: Applications to leadership training strategies. *Journal of Social Issues, 32,* 111–124.

Lott, A. J. & Lott, B. E. (1961). Group cohesiveness, communication level and conformity. *Journal of Abnormal and Social Psychology, 62,* 408–412.

Lott, D. F. & Sommer, R. (1967). Seating arrangements and status. *Journal of Personality and Social Psychology, 7,* 90–95.

Louis, M. R. (1981). A cultural perspective on organizations. *Human Systems Management, 2,* 246–258.

Louis, M. R. (1983). Organizations as culture bearing milieux. In L. R. Pondy, P. J. Frost, G. Morgan & T. C. Dandridge (Eds.), *Organizational Symbolism* (pp. 39–54). Greenwich, CT: JAI Press.

Luft, J. (1984). *Group Processes: An Introduction to Group Dynamics.* Palo Alto, CA: Mayfield.

Lundgren, D. (1971). Trainer style and patterns of group development. *The Journal of Applied Behavioral Science, 7* (6), 689–709.

Lundgren, D. & Knight, D. (1978). Sequential stages of development in sensitivity training groups. *The Journal of Applied Behavioral Science, 14* (2), 204–222.

Lyden, F. J. (1975). Using Parson's functional analysis in the study of public organizations. *Administrative Science Quarterly, 20,* 59–69.

Lyle, J. (1961). Communication, group atmosphere, productivity and morale in small task groups. *Human Relations,* 369–379.

Maccoby, E. E. (1980). *Social Development.* New York: Harcourt, Brace, Jovanovich.

Maccoby, E. E. & Jacklin, C. N. (1974). *The Psychology of Sex Differences.* Stanford, CA: Stanford University Press.

MacIntyre, A. (1988). *Whose Justice? Which Rationality?* Notre Dame, IN: University of Notre Dame Press.

MacNeil, M. K. & Sherif, M. (1976). Norm change over subject generations as a function of arbitrariness of prescribed norms. *Journal of Personality and Social Psychology, 34,* 762–773.

Magnusson, D. (1981). *Toward a Psychology of Situations: An Interactional Perspective.* Hillsdale, NJ: Erlbaum.

Magnusson, D. & Endler, N. S. (Eds.). (1977). *Personality at the Crossroads: Current Issues in Interactional Psychology.* Hillsdale, NJ: Erlbaum.

Mahoney, T. A. (1967). Managerial perception of organizational effectiveness. *Management Science, 14* (2B), 76–91.

Maier, N. R. F. (1950). The quality of group decisions as influenced by the discussion leader. *Human Relations, 3,* 155–174.

Maier, N. (1970). Male vs. female discussion leaders. *Personnel Psychology, 23,* 455–461.

Maier, N. R. F. & Solem, A. R. (1952). The contribution of a discussion leader to the quality of group thinking: The effective use of minority opinions. *Human Relations, 5,* 277–288.

Manis, M., Cornell, S. D. & Moore, J. C. (1974). Transmission of attitude-relevant information through a communication chain. *Journal of Personality and Social Psychology, 30,* 81–94.

Mann, R. D. (1966). The development of the member-trainer relationship in self-analytic groups. *Human Relations, 19* (1), 85–115.

Mann, R. D. (1975). Winners, losers and the search for equality in groups. In C. L. Cooper (Ed.), *Theories of Group Processes.* New York: Wiley.

Mann, L. (1977). The effect of stimulus queues on queue-joining behavior. *Journal of Personality and Social Psychology, 35,* 437–442.

Mann, R. D., Gibbard, G. & Hartman, J. (1967). *Interpersonal Styles and Group Development.* New York: John Wiley and Sons.

Manz, C. C. & Sims, H. P. (1987). Leading workers to lead themselves: The external leadership of self-managing work teams. *Administrative Science Quarterly, 32,* 106–128.

Markova, I. (1990). Medical ethics: A branch of societal psychology. In H. T. Himmelweit & G. Gaskell (Eds.), *Societal Psychology* (pp. 112–137). Newbury Park, CA: Sage.

Markovsky, B., Smith, L. F. & Berger, J. (1984). Do status interventions persist? *American Sociological Review, 49,* 373–382.

Marquart, D. I. (1955). Group problem solving. *Journal of Social Psychology, 41,* 103–113.

Marquis, D. G., Guetzkow, H. & Heyns, R. W. (1951). A social psychological study of the decision-making conference. In H. Guetzkow (Ed.), *Groups, Leadership and Men* (pp. 55–67). Pittsburgh: Carnegie Press.

Marsh, L. L. (1931). Group therapy by the psychological equivalent of the revival. *Mental Hygiene, 15,* 328–349.

Martens, R. & Landers, D. M. (1972). Evaluation potential as a determinant of coaction effects. *Journal of Experimental Social Psychology, 8,* 347–359.

Martin, E. & Hill, W. F. (1957). Toward a theory of group development. *International Journal of Group Psychotherapy, 7* (1), 20–30.

Martin, M. W. & Sell, J. (1985). The effect of equating status characteristics on the generalization process. *Social Psychology Quarterly, 48,* 178–182.

Maslow, A. J. (1962). *Toward a Psychology of Being.* Princeton, NJ: Van Nostrand.

Mayadas, N. & Glasser, P. (1985). Termination: A neglected aspect of social group work. In M. Sundel, P. Glasser, R. Sarri & R. Vinter (Eds.), *Individual Change Through Small Groups* (2d ed., pp. 251–261). New York: Free Press.

Mayo, E. (1945). *The Social Problems of an Industrial Civilization.* Cambridge, MA: Harvard University Press.

Mayo, G. D. & DuBois, P. H. (1987). *The Complete Book of Training: Theory, Principles and Technique.* San Diego, CA: University Associates.

Mayr, E. (1963). *Populations, Species and Evolution.* Cambridge, MA: Belknap Press of Harvard University Press.

McClelland, D. C. (1975). *Power: The Inner Experience.* New York: Irvington.

McClelland, D. C. (1985). How motives, skills, and values determine what people do. *American Psychologist, 40,* 812–825.

McClelland, D. C., Atkinson, J. W., Clark, R. A. & Lowell, E. L. (1953). *The Achievement Motive.* New York: Appleton-Century-Crofts.

McCrae, R. R. & Costa, P. T. (1982). Self-concept and the stability of personality: Cross-sectional comparisons of self-reports and ratings. *Journal of Personality and Social Psychology, 43,* 1282–1292.

McCranie, E. W. & Kimberly, J. C. (1973). Rank inconsistency, conflicting expectations and injustice. *Sociometry, 36,* 152–176.

McGillicuddy, N. B., Pruitt, D. G. & Syna, H. (1984). Perceptions of firmness and strength in negotiation. *Personality and Social Psychology Bulletin, 10,* 402–409.

McGoldrick, M., Pearce, J. K. & Giordano, J. (Eds.). (1982). *Ethnicity and Family Therapy.* New York: Guilford Press.

McGoldrick, M. & Rohrbaugh, M. (1987). Researching ethnic family stereotypes. *Family Process, 26* (March), 89–99.

McGrath, J. E. (1984). *Groups: Interaction and Performance.* Englewood Cliffs, NJ: Prentice Hall.

McGregor, D. (1960). *The Human Side of Enterprise.* New York: McGraw-Hill.

Mead, G. H. (1934). *Mind, Self and Society.* Chicago: University of Chicago Press.

Medow, H. & Zander, A. (1965). Aspirations of group chosen by central and peripheral members. *Journal of Personality and Social Psychology, 1,* 224–228.

Melnick, M. J. & Chemer, M. M. (1974). Effects of group social structure on the success of basketball teams. *Research Quarterly, 45,* 1–8.

Merton, R. K. & Kitt, A S. (1950). Contributions to the theory of reference group behavior. In R. K. Merton & P. F. Lazarsfeld (Eds.), *Studies in the Scope and Method of "The American Soldier."* New York: Free Press.

Messe, L. A., Aronoff, J. & Wilson, J. P. (1972). Motivation as a mediator of the mechanisms underlying role assignments in small groups. *Journal of Personality and Social Psychology, 24,* 84–90.

Messe, L. A., Stollak, G. E., Larson, R. W. & Michaels, G. Y. (1979). Interpersonal consequences of person perception in two social contexts. *Journal of Personality and Social Psychology, 37,* 369–379.

Messick, D. M. & Thorngate, W. B. (1967). Relative gain maximization in experimental games. *Journal of Experimental Social Psychology, 3,* 85–101.

Meyerson, D. E. (1991). Acknowledging and uncovering ambiguities in cultures. In P. J. Frost, L. F. Moore, M. R. Louis, C. C. Lundberg & J. Martin, *Reframing Organizational Culture* (pp. 254–270). Newbury Park, CA: Sage.

Michener, H. A. & Burt, M. R. (1975a). Components of "authority" as determinants of compliance. *Journal of Personality and Social Psychology, 31,* 606–614.

Michener, H. A. & Burt, M. R. (1975b). Use of social influence under varying conditions of legitimacy. *Journal of Personality and Social Psychology, 32,* 398–407.

Michener, H. A. & Lawler, E. J. (1975). The endorsement of formal leaders: An integrative model. *Journal of Personality and Social Psychology, 31,* 216–223.

Miles, M. (1971). *Learning to Work in Groups.* New York: Teachers College Press.

Milgram, S. (1963). Behavioral study of obedience. *Journal of Abnormal and Social Psychology, 67,* 371–378.

Milgram, S. (1964). Group pressure and action against a person. *Journal of Abnormal and Social Psychology, 69,* 137–143.

Milgram, S. (1965). Liberating effects of group pressure. *Journal of Personality and Social Psychology, 1,* 127–134.

Milgram, S. (1974). *Obedience to Authority.* New York: Harper and Row.

Miller, C. E., Jackson, P., Mueller, J. & Schersching, C. (1987). Some social psychological effects of group decision rules. *Journal of Personality and Social Psychology, 52,* 325–332.

Miller, C. E. & Wong, J. (1986). Coalition behavior: Effects of earned versus unearned resources. *Organizational Behavior and Human Decision Processes, 38,* 257–277.

Miller, E. J. (1959). Technology, territory, and time: The internal differentiation of complex production systems. *Human Relations, 12,* 245–272.

Miller, N. E. & Dollard, J. (1941). *Social Learning and Imitation.* New Haven: Yale University Press.

Mills, C. W. (1959). *The Sociological Imagination.* London: Oxford University Press.

Mills, T. M. (1953). Power relations in three-person groups. *American Sociological Review, 18,* 351–357.

Mills, T. M. (1964). *Group Transformation: An Analysis of a Learning Group.* Englewood Cliffs, NJ: Prentice Hall.

Mills, T. M. (1967). *The Sociology of Small Groups.* Englewood Cliffs, NJ: Prentice Hall.

Mintzberg, H. (1973). *The Nature of Managerial Work.* New York: Harper & Row.

Mischel, W. & Peake, P. (1982). Beyond déjà vu in the search for cross-situational consistency. *Psychological Review, 89,* 730–755

Misumi, J. (1985). *The Behavioral Science of Leadership.* Ann Arbor, MI: University of Michigan Press.

Mitchell, R. R. (1975). Relationships between personal characteristics and change in sensitivity training groups. *Small Group Behavior, 6,* 414–420.

Moorhead, G. (1982). Groupthink: Hypothesis in need of testing. *Group and Organization Studies, 7,* 429–444.

Moorhead, G. & Montanari, J. R. (1986). An empirical investigation of the groupthink phenomenon. *Human Relations, 39,* 399–410.

Moreland, R. L. & Levine, J. M. (1988). Group dynamics over time: Development and socialization in small groups. In J. E. McGrath (Ed.), *The Social Psychology of Time* (pp. 151–181). Beverly Hills, CA: Sage.

Morgenthau, H. (1970). *Politics Among Nations.* New York: Academic Press.

Morran, D. K., Robison, F. F. & Stockton, R. (1985). Feedback exchange in counseling groups: An analysis of message content and receiver acceptance as a function of leader versus member delivery, session, and valance. *Journal of Counseling Psychology, 32,* 57–67.

Morris, W. N. & Miller, R. S. (1975). The effects of consensus-breaking and consensus pre-empting partners on reduction of conformity. *Journal of Experimental Social Psychology, 11,* 215–223.

Moscovici, S. (1976). *Social Influence and Social Change.* London: Academic Press.

Moscovici, S. (1985). Social influence and conformity. In G. Lindzey & E. Aronson (Eds.), *Handbook of Social Psychology* (Vol. 1, 3d ed., pp. 347–412). New York: Random House.

Moscovici, S. (1990). The generalized self and mass society. In H. T. Himmelweit & G. Gaskell (Eds.), *Societal Psychology* (pp. 66–91). Newbury Park, CA: Sage.

Mosher, R. L. & Sprinthall, N. A. (1970). Psychological education in secondary schools: A program to promote individual and human development. *American Psychologist, 25,* 911–924.

Mosher, R. L. & Sprinthall, N. A. (1971). Psychological education: A means to promote personal development during adolescence. *The Counseling Psychologist, 2* (4), 3–82.

Mulder, M. (1960). Communication structure, decision structure and group performance. *Sociometry, 23,* 1–14.

Mullen, J. H. (1965). Differential leadership modes and productivity in a large organization. *Academy of Management Journal, 8,* 107–126.

Murnighan, J. K. (1978). Models of coalition formation: Game theoretic, social psychological, and political perspectives. *Psychological Bulletin, 85,* 1130–1153.

Murnighan, J. K. (1986). Organizational coalitions: Structural contingencies and the formation process. In R. J. Lewicki, B. H. Sheppard & M. H. Bazerman (Eds.), *Research on Negotiations in Organizations.*(Vol. 1, pp. 155–174). Greenwich, CT: JAI Press.

Murphy, G. L., Murphy, L. B. & Newcomb, T. M. (1937). *Experimental Social Psychology.* New York: Harper.

Murphy, L. R. & Hurrell, J. J., Jr. (1987). Stress management in the process of occupational stress reduction. *Journal of Managerial Psychology, 2,* 18–23.

Nakamura, C. Y. (1958). Conformity and problem solving. *Journal of Abnormal and Social Psychology, 56,* 315–320.

Near, J. P. (1978). Comparison of developmental patterns in groups. *Small Group Behavior, 9,* 493–506.

Neimeyer, G. J. & Merluzzi, T. V. (1982). Group structure and group process. *Small Group Behavior, 13* (2), 150–164.

Nelson-Jones, R. (1988). The counselling psychologist as developmental educator. *The Australian Counselling Psychologist, 4,* 55–66.

Nelson-Jones, R. (1992). *Group Leadership: A Training Approach.* Pacific Grove, CA: Brooks/Cole.

Neugarten, B. L. (July, 1979). Time, age and the life cycle. *The American Journal of Psychiatry, 136* (7), 887–894.

Newcomb, T. M. (1956). The prediction of interpersonal attraction. *American Psychologist, 11,* 575–586.

Newcomb, T. M. (1961). *The Acquaintance Process.* New York: Holt.

Nicholls, J. R. (1985). A new approach to situational leadership. *Leadership and Organization Development Journal, 6* (4), 2–7.

Nisbet, R. A. (1969). *Social Change and History.* London: Oxford University Press.

Nixon, H. L. (1979). *The Small Group.* Englewood Cliffs, NJ: Prentice Hall.

Northen, H. (1969). *Social Work with Groups.* New York: Columbia University Press.

Offermann, L. R. & Gowing, M. K. (1990). Organizations of the future: Changes and challenges. *American Psychologist, 45* (2), 95–108.

Orkin, M. (1987). Balanced strategies for Prisoner's Dilemma. *Journal of Conflict Resolution, 31,* 186–191.

Orvis, B. B., Kelley, H. H., & Butler, D. (1976). Attributional conflict in young couples. In J. H. Harvey, W. J. Ickes, & R. E. Kidd (Eds.), *New Directions in Attribution Research* (Vol. 1). Hillsdale, NJ: Erlbaum.

Parsons, T. (1961). An outline of the social system. In T. Parsons, E. Shils, K. D. Naegele & J. R. Pitts (Eds.), *Theories of Society* (pp. 30–79). New York: Free Press.

Parsons, T., Bales, R. F. & Shils, E. A. (1953). *Working Papers in the Theory of Action.* Glencoe, IL: Free Press.

Pearce, J. L., Stevenson, W. B. & Porter, L. W. (1986). Coalitions in the organizational context. In R. J. Lewicki, B. H. Sheppard & M. H. Bazerman (Eds.), *Research on Negotiation in Organizations* (Vol. 1, pp. 97–115). Greenwich, CT: JAI Press.

Pennings, J. M. (1980). *Interlocking Directorates.* San Francisco, CA:Jossey-Bass.

Pepitone, A. (1981). Lessons from the history of social psychology. *American Psychologist, 36,* 972–985.

Pepitone, A. & Kleiner, R. J. (1957). The effects of threat and frustration on group cohesiveness. *Journal of Abnormal and Social Psychology, 54,* 192–199.

Pepitone, E. (1990). Social comparison, relative deprivation and pupil interaction: Homogeneous vs. heterogeneous classrooms. In S. Wheelan, E. Pepitone & V. Abt (Eds.), *Advances in Field Theory* (pp. 165–176). Newbury Park, CA: Sage.

Peters, T. J. & Waterman, R. H. (1982). *In Search of Excellence.* New York: Warner.

Pettigrew, A. M. (1979). On studying organizational cultures. *Administrative Science Quarterly, 24,* 570–581.

Pettigrew, T. (1988). Influencing policy with social psychology. *Journal of Social Issues, 44* (2), 205–219.

Pfeffer, J. & Salancik, G. R. (1978). *The External Control of Organizations: A Resource Dependence Perspective.* New York: Harper & Row.

Piper, W. E. & Perrault, E. L. (1989). Pretherapy preparation for group members. *International Journal of Group Psychotherapy, 39* (1), 17–34.

Poza, E. J. & Markus, M. L. (1980). Success story: The team approach to work-restructuring. *Organizational Dynamics, 8,* 3–25.

Pritchard, R. D., Jones, S., Roth, P., Stuebing, K. & Ekeberg, S. (1988). Effects of group feedback, goal setting, and incentives on organizational productivity. *Journal of Applied Psychology, 73* (2), 337–358.

Pruitt, D. G. (1981). *Negotiation Behavior.* New York: Academic Press.

Pruitt, D. G. (1983). Strategic choice in negotiation. *American Behavioral Science, 27,* 167–194.

Pruitt, D. G. (1987). Creative approaches to negotiation. In D. J. D. Sandole & I. Sandole-Staroste (Eds.), *Conflict Management and Problem Solving: Interpersonal to International Applications* (pp. 62–76). London: Frances Pinter.

Pruitt, D. G. & Carnevale, P. J. D. (1982). The development of integrative agreements. In V. J. Derlega & J. Grezlak (Eds.), *Cooperative and Helping Behavior* (pp. 151–181). New York: Academic Press.

Pruitt, D. G. & Rubin, J. Z. (1986). *Social Conflict: Escalation, Stalemate and Settlement.* New York: Random House.

Pugh, M. D. & Wahrman, R. (1983). Neutralizing sexism in mixed-sex groups: Do women have to be better than men? *American Journal of Sociology, 88,* 746–762.

Raven, B. H. & Rietsema, J. (1957). The effects of varied clarity of group goal and group path upon the individual and his relation to the group. *Human Relations, 10,* 29–44.

Raven, B. H. & Rubin, J. Z. (1976). *Social Psychology: People in Groups.* New York: John Wiley.

Rawlins, W. K. (1984). Consensus in decision-making groups: A conceptual history. In G. M. Phillips & J. T. Wood (Eds.), *Emergent Issues in Human Decision Making* (pp. 19–39). Carbondale, IL: Southern Illinois University Press.

Reckman, R. F. & Goethals, G. R. (1973). Deviancy and group orientation as determinants of group composition preferences. *Sociometry, 36,* 419–423.

Reddin, W. J. (1970). *Managerial Effectiveness.* New York: McGraw-Hill.

Reed, B. G. (1979). Differential reactions by male and female group members to a group experience in the presence of male and female authority figures. Doctoral dissertation, University of Cincinnati.

Regan, D. T. & Totten, J. (1975). Empathy and attribution: Turning observers into actors. *Journal of Personality and Social Psychology, 32,* 850–856.

Reilly, M. E. (1978). A case study of role conflict: Roman Catholic priests. *Human Relations, 31,* 77–90.

Reitan, H. T. & Shaw, M. E. (1964). Group membership, sex composition of the group and conformity behavior. *Journal of Social Psychology, 64,* 45–51.

Rendle, G. R. (1983). Conflict in a t-group as a source of polar energy and inclusive equilibrium in a group: A case study. Doctoral dissertation. Temple University.

Rewald, J. (1973). *History of Impressionism.* Greenwich, CT: New York Graphic Society.

Reynolds, P. D. (1979). *Ethical Dilemmas and Social Science Research.* San Francisco: Jossey-Bass.

Ridgeway, C. L. (1982). Status in small groups:

The importance of motivation. *American Sociological Review, 47*, 76–88.

Rinat, R. I. (1987). The effects of situational and personality variables on the responses to an economic crunch. Doctoral dissertation. Columbia University. Ringelmann, M. (1913). Research on animate sources of power: The work of man. *Annales de l'Institut National Agronomique*, 2e serie–tome XII, 1–40.

Rioch, M. J. (1975). "All we like sheep"–(Isaiah 53:6)–Followers and leaders. In A. D. Colman & W. H. Bexton (Eds.), *Group Relations Reader* (pp. 159–177). San Rafael, CA: Associates Printing and Publishing Co.

Riordan, C. (1983). Sex as a general status characteristic. *Social Psychology Quarterly, 46*, 261–267.

Riordan, C. & Riggiero, J. (1980). Producing equal-status interracial interaction: A replication. *Social Psychology Quarterly, 43*, 131–136.

Robbins, S. P. (1974). *Managing Organizational Conflict*. Englewood Cliffs, NJ: Prentice Hall.

Roethlisberger, F. J. & Dickson, W. J. (1939). *Management and the Worker*. Cambridge, MA: Harvard Press.

Rogers, E. (1962). *Diffusion of Innovations*. New York: The Free Press of Glencoe.

Romanelli, E. & Tushman, M. (1986). Inertia, environments, and strategic choice: A quasi-experimental design for comparative-longitudinal research. *Management Science, 32*, 608–621.

Rose, A. (1952). *Union Solidarity*. Minneapolis: The University of Minnesota Press.

Rosenberg, S. W. & Wolfsfeld, G. (1977). International conflict and the problem of attribution. *Journal of Conflict Resolution, 21*, 75–103.

Rosenhan, D. (1973). On being sane in insane places. *Science, 179*, 250–258.

Rosenthal, R. (1971). Teacher expectations and their effects upon children. In G. S. Lesser (Ed.), *Psychology and Educational Practice*. Glenview, IL: Scott, Foresman.

Rosenthal, R. (1976). *Experimenter Effects in Behavioral Research* (Rev. ed.). New York: Appleton-Century-Crofts.

Rosenthal, R. & Jacobson, L. (1968). *Pygmalion in the Classroom*. New York: Holt, Rinehart & Winston.

Rosenthal, R. & Rubin, D. B. (1978). Interpersonal expectancy effects: The first 345 studies. *Behavioral and Brain Sciences, 3*, 377–415.

Ross, I. & Zander, A. (1957). Need satisfaction and employee turnover. *Personnel Psychology, 10*, 327–338.

Ross, L. (1977). The intuitive psychologist and his shortcomings: Distortions in the attribution process. In L. Berkowitz (Ed.), *Advances in Experimental Social Psychology* (Vol. 10). New York: Academic Press.

Rothbart, M. & John, O. P. (1985). Social categorization and behavioral episodes: A cognitive analysis of the effects of intergroup contact. *Journal of Social Issues, 41* (3), 81–104.

Royle, M. H. (1983). Factors affecting the integration of women into Marine Corps units. Dissertation. Claremont Graduate School.

Rubin, J. Z. (1980). Experimental research on third-party intervention in conflict: Toward some generalizations. *Psychological Bulletin, 87*, 379–391.

Rubin, J. Z. (1983). Negotiation. *American Behavioral Science, 27*, 135–147.

Rubin, J. Z. & Brown, B. R. (1985). *The Social Psychology of Bargaining and Negotiation*. New York: Academic Press.

Rugel, R. P. & Meyer, D. J. (1984). The Tavistock group: Empirical findings and implications for group therapy. *Small Group Behavior, 15*, 361–374.

Runkel, P., Lawrence, M., Oldfield, S., Rider, M. & Clark, C. (1971). Stages of group development: An empirical test of Tuckman's hypothesis. *The Journal of Applied Behavioral Science, 7* (2), 180–193.

Rusbult, C. E. (1983). A longitudinal test of the investment model: The development (and deterioration) of satisfaction and commitment in heterosexual involvements. *Journal of Personality and Social Psychology, 45*, 101–117.

Rusbult, C. E., Zembrodt, I. M. & Gunn, L. K. (1982). Exit, voice, loyalty, and neglect: Responses to dissatisfaction in romantic involvements. *Journal of Personality and Social Psychology, 43*, 1230–1242.

Ryan, E. D. & Lakie, W. L. (1965). Competitive and noncompetitive performance in relation to achievement motive and manifest anxiety. *Journal of Personality and Social Psychology, 1*, 342–345.

Rychlak, J. F. (1965). The similarity, compatibility or incompatibility of needs in interpersonal selection. *Journal of Personality and Social Psychology, 2*, 334–340.

Ryff, C. D. (1987). The place of personality and social structure research in social psychology. *Journal of Personality and Social Psychology, 53* (6), 1192–1202.

Sampson, E. E. (1989). The debate on individualism: Indigenous psychologies of the individual and their role in personal and societal functioning. *American Psychologist, 43*, 15–22.

Sashkin, M. (1984). Participative management is an ethical imperative. *Organizational Dynamics, 12*, 4–22.

Schacter, S. (1951). Deviation, rejection and communication. *Journal of Abnormal and Social Psychology, 46*, 190–207.

Schacter, S. (1959). *The Psychology of Affiliation.* Stanford, CA: Stanford University Press.

Schacter, S., Ellertson, N., McBride, D., & Gregory, D. (1951). An experimental study of cohesiveness and productivity. *Human Relations, 4*, 229–238.

Schaible, T. D. & Jacobs, A. (1975). Feedback III: Sequence effects, enhancement of feedback acceptance and group attractiveness by manipulation of the sequence and valence of feedback. *Small Group Behavior, 6*, 151–173.

Schein, E. H. (1958). The development of organization in small problem-solving groups. Final Report, Sloan Project. No. 134. MIT.

Schein, E. H. (1980). *Organizational Psychology* (3d ed.). Englewood Cliffs, NJ: Prentice Hall.

Schein, E. H. (1983). The role of the founder in creating organizational culture. *Organizational Dynamics, 12*, 13–28.

Schein, E. H. (1985). *Organizational Culture and Leadership.* San Francisco: Jossey-Bass.

Schein, E. H. (1987). *The Clinical Perspective in Fieldwork.* Newbury Park, CA: Sage.

Schein, E. H. (1988). *Process Consultation* (rev. ed.). Reading, MA: Addison-Wesley.

Schein, E. H. (1990). Organizational culture. *American Psychologist, 45* (2), 109–119.

Schein, E. H. (1991). What is culture? In P. J. Frost, L. F. Moore, M. R. Louis, C. C. Lundberg & J. Martin (Eds.), *Reframing Organizational Culture* (pp. 243–253). Newbury Park, CA: Sage.

Schlenker, B. R., Nacci, P., Helm, B. & Tedeschi, J. T. (1976). Reactions to coercive and reward power: The effects of switching influence modes on target compliance. *Sociometry, 39*, 316–323.

Schmitt, D. R. (1981). Performance under cooperation or competition. *American Behavioral Scientist, 24*, 649–679.

Schmuck, P. & Schmuck, R. (1990). Democratic participation in small-town schools. *Educational Researcher, 19* (8), 14–19.

Schutz, W. C. (1958). *FIRO: A Three Dimensional Theory of Interpersonal Behavior.* New York: Rinehart.

Schutz, W. C. (1966). *The Interpersonal Underworld.* Palo Alto, CA: Science and Behavior Books.

Schwartz, A. M. (1988). *Hate Groups in America: A Record of Bigotry and Violence.* New York: The Anti-Defamation League of B'nai B'rith.

Schwartz, H. & Jacobs, J. (1979). *Qualitative Sociology: A Method to the Madness.* New York: Free Press.

Schwartz, H. & Schwartz, C. G. (1955). Problems in participant observation. *American Journal of Sociology, 60*, 343–354.

Seashore, S. E. (1954). *Group Cohesiveness in the Industrial Work Group.* Ann Arbor: The University of Michigan Press.

Sermat, V. (1964). Cooperative behavior in a mixed-motive game. *Journal of Social Psychology, 62*, 217–239.

Shaffer, D. R. & Sadowski, C. (1975). This table is mine: Respect for marked barroom tables as a function of gender, of spatial marker, and desirability of locale. *Sociometry, 38*, 408–419.

Shaffer, J. & Galinsky, M. D. (1989). *Models of Group Therapy* (2d ed.). Englewood Cliffs, NJ: Prentice Hall.

Shapiro, E. G. (1975). Effects of expectations of future interaction on reward allocations in dyads: Equity or equality? *Journal of Personality and Social Psychology, 31*, 873–880.

Shaw, J. I. & Condelli, L. (1986). Effects of compliance outcome and basis of power on the powerholder-target relationship. *Personality and Social Psychology Bulletin, 12,* 236–246.

Shaw, M. E. (1954a). Some effects of problem complexity upon problem solution efficiency in different communication nets. *Journal of Experimental Psychology, 48,* 211–217.

Shaw, M. E. (1954b). Some effects of unequal distribution of information upon group performance in various communication nets. *Journal of Abnormal and Social Psychology, 49,* 547–553.

Shaw, M. E. (1955). A comparison of two types of leadership in various communication nets. *Journal of Abnormal and Social Psychology, 50,* 127–134.

Shaw, M. E. (1958). Some effects of irrelevant information upon problem-solving by small groups. *Journal of Social Psychology, 47,* 33–37.

Shaw, M. E. (1959a). Acceptance of authority, group structure and the effectiveness of small groups. *Journal of Personality, 27,* 196–210.

Shaw, M. E. (1959b). Some effects of individually prominent behavior upon group effectiveness and member satisfaction. *Journal of Abnormal and Social Psychology, 59,* 382–386.

Shaw, M. E. (1976). *Group Dynamics: The Psychology of Small Group Behavior* (2d ed.). New York: McGraw-Hill.

Shaw, M. E. (1981). *Group Dynamics: The Psychology of Small Group Behavior* (3d ed.). New York: McGraw-Hill.

Shaw, M. E. & Blum, J. M. (1965). Group performance as a function of task difficulty and the group's awareness of member satisfaction. *Journal of Applied Psychology, 49,* 151–154.

Shaw, M. E. & Harkey, B. (1976). Some effects of congruency of member characteristics and group structure upon group behavior. *Journal of Personality and Social Psychology, 34,* 412–418.

Shaw, M. E. & Reitan, H. T. (1969). Attribution of responsibility as a basis for sanctioning behavior. *British Journal of Social and Clinical Psychology, 8,* 217–226.

Shaw, M. E. & Rothschild, G. H. (1956). Some effects of prolonged experience in communication nets. *Journal of Applied Psychology, 40,* 281–286.

Shaw, M. E., Rothschild, G. H. & Strickland, J. F. (1957). Decision processes in communication nets. *Journal of Abnormal and Social Psychology, 54,* 323–330.

Shaw, M. E. & Shaw, L. M. (1962). Some effects of sociometric grouping upon learning in a second grade classroom. *Journal of Social Psychology, 57,* 453–458.

Shea, G. P. & Guzzo, R. A. (1987a). Group effectiveness: What really matters? *Sloan Management Review, 3,* 25–31.

Shea, G. P. & Guzzo, R. A. (1987b). Groups as human resources. In K. M. Rowland & G. R. Ferris (Eds.), *Research in Personnel and Human Resources Management* (Vol. 5, pp. 323–256). Greenwich, CT: JAI Press.

Shelley, H. P. (1954). Levels of aspiration phenomena in small groups. *Journal of Social Psychology, 40,* 149–164.

Sherif, M. (1936). *The Psychology of Social Norms.* New York: Harper.

Sherif, M. & Sherif, C. (1953). *Groups in Harmony and Tension.* New York: Harper and Row.

Sherif, M. & Sherif, C. W. (1956). *An Outline of Social Psychology.* New York: Harper and Row.

Sieber, J. E. (Ed.). (1991). *Sharing Social Science Data: Advantages and Challenges.* Newbury Park, CA: Sage.

Siehl, C. & Martin, J. (1988). Organizational culture: A key to financial performance? In B. Schneider (Ed.), *Organizational Climate and Culture.* San Francisco, CA: Jossey-Bass.

Silberman, M. (1990). *Active Training.* San Diego, CA: University Associates.

Silberman, M. & Wheelan, S. A. (1980). *How to Discipline without Feeling Guilty: Assertive Relations with Children.* Champaign, IL: Research Press.

Simmel, G. (1978). *The Philosophy of Money.* London: Routledge & Kegan Paul.

Simon, H. A. (1976). *Administrative Behavior: A Study of Decision-Making Processes in Administrative Organizations* (3d ed.). New York: Free Press.

Simpson, J. A. & Wood, S. (1992). Where is the group in social psychology? In S. Worchel, W. Wood & J. A. Simpson (Eds.), *Group Process and Productivity* (pp. 1–12). Newbury Park, CA: Sage.

Simpson, R. L. (1959). Vertical and horizontal communication in formal organizations. *Administrative Science Quarterly, 4,* 188–196.

Singer, J. E. & Shockley, V. L. (1965). Ability and affiliation. *Journal of Personality and Social Psychology, 1,* 95–100.

Skypnek, B. J. & Snyder, M. (1982). On the self-perpetuating nature of stereotypes about women and men. *Journal of Experimental Social Psychology, 18,* 277–291.

Slater, P. (1966). *Microcosm.* New York: Wiley.

Slater, P. (1970). *The Pursuit of Loneliness: American Culture at the Breaking Point.* Boston: Beacon Press.

Slavin, R. E. (1985). Cooperative learning: Applying contact theory in desegregated schools. *Journal of Social Issues, 41*(3), 45–61.

Slavin, R. E. (1986). Cooperative learning: Engineering social psychology in the classroom. In R. S. Feldman (Ed.), *The Social Psychology of Education* (pp. 153–171). New York: Cambridge University Press.

Smith, C. R., Williams, L. & Willis, R. H. (1967). Race, sex and belief as determinants of friendship acceptance. *Journal of Personality and Social Psychology, 5,* 127–137.

Smith, P. B. (1975). Controlled studies of the outcome of sensitivity training. *Psychological Bulletin, 82,* 597–622.

Smith, P. B. (1980). The outcomes of sensitivity training and encounter. In P. B. Smith (Ed.), *Small Groups and Personal Change* (pp. 25–55). London: Methuen.

Smith, P. B., Wood, H. & Smale, G. G. (1980). The usefulness of groups in clinical settings. In P. B. Smith (Ed.), *Small Groups and Personal Change* (pp. 106–153). London: Methuen.

Smith, R. J. & Cook, P. E. (1973). Leadership in dyadic groups as a function of dominance and incentives. *Sociometry, 36,* 561–568.

Smoke, W. H. & Zajonc, R. B. (1962). On the reliability of group judgements and decisions. In J. H. Criswell, H. Solomon & P. Suppes (Eds.), *Mathematical Methods in Small Group Processes.* Stanford, CA: Stanford University Press.

Snadowsky, A. M. (1969). Group effectiveness as a function of communication network, task complexity, and leadership type. *Dissertation Abstracts International, 30* (5A), 2155.

Solomon, L. (1960). The influence of some types of power relationships and game strategies upon the development of interpersonal trust. *Journal of Abnormal and Social Psychology, 61,* 223–230.

Sommer, R. (1969). *Personal Space: The Behavioral Basis of Design.* Englewood Cliffs, NJ: Prentice Hall.

Sorrentino, R. M. & Sheppard, B. H. (1978). Effects of affiliation-related motives on swimmers in individual versus group competition: A field experiment. *Journal of Personality and Social Psychology, 36,* 704–714.

Spence, J. T. (1985). Achievement American style: The rewards and costs of individualism. *American Psychologist, 40,* 1285–1295.

Spitz, H. & Sadock, B. J. (1973). Small interactional groups in the psychiatric training of graduate nursing students. *Journal of Nursing Education, 12,* 6–13.

Spradley, J. P. (1979). *The Ethnographic Interview.* New York: Holt, Rinehart & Winston.

Spradley, J. P. (1980). *Participant Observation.* New York: Holt, Rinehart & Winston.

Sprinthall, N. A. (1980). Psychology for secondary schools: The saber-tooth curriculum revisited? *American Psychologist, 35,* 336–347.

Stanford, G. (1977). *Developing Effective Classroom Groups.* New York: Hart.

Stasser, G. & Titus, W. (1985). Pooling of unshared information in group decision making: Biased information sampling during discussion. *Journal of Personality and Social Psychology, 48,* 1467–1478.

Staub, E. (1990). Genocide and mass killing: Cultural-societal and psychological origins. In H. T. Himmelweit & G. Gaskel (Eds.), *Societal Psychology* (pp. 230–251). Newbury Park, CA: Sage.

Staw, B. M., Sandelands, L. E. & Dutton, J. E. (1981). Thread-rigidity effects in organizational behavior: Multi-level analysis. *Administrative Science Quarterly, 26,* 501–524.

Steiner, I. D. (1972). *Group Process and Productivity.* New York: Academic Press.

Steiner, I. D. (1974). Whatever happened to the group in social psychology? *Journal of Experimental Social Psychology, 10,* 94–108.

Steiner, I. D. (1986). Paradigms and groups. In L. Berkowitz (Ed.), *Advances in Experimental Social Psychology* (pp. 251–289). Orlando, FL: Academic Press.

Sternberg, R. J. & Soriano, L. J. (1984). Styles of conflict resolution. *Journal of Personality and Social Psychology, 47,* 115–126.

Stevenson, H. W. & Odom, R. D. (1962). The effectiveness of social reinforcement following two conditions of social deprivation. *Journal of Abnormal and Social Psychology, 65,* 429–431.

Stevenson, W. B., Pearce, J. L. & Porter, L. (1985). The concept of "coalition" in organization theory and research. *Academy of Management Research, 10,* 256–268.

Stiles, W. B., Tupler, L. A. & Carpenter, J. C. (1982). Participants' perceptions of self-analytic group sessions. *Small Group Behavior, 13,* 237–254.

Stock, D. & Thelen, H. (1958). *Emotional Dynamics and Group Culture.* New York: New York University Press.

Stockton, R. & Morran, D. K. (1980). The use of verbal feedback in counseling groups: Toward an effective system. *Journal for Specialists in Group Work, 5,* 10–14.

Stockton, R. & Morran, D. K. (1981). Feedback exchange in personal growth groups: Receiver acceptance as a function of valence, session, and order of delivery. *Journal of Counseling Psychology, 28,* 490–497.

Stogdill, R. M. (1948). Personal factors associated with leadership: A survey of the literature. *Journal of Psychology, 25,* 35–71.

Stogdill, R. M. (1950). Leadership, membership and organization. *Psychological Bulletin, 47,* 1–14.

Stogdill, R. M. (1972). Group productivity, drive and cohesiveness. *Organizational Behavior and Human Performance, 8,* 26–43.

Stogdill, R. M. (1974). *Handbook of Leadership.* New York: The Free Press.

Stone, G. (1962). Appearance and the self. In A. Rose (Ed.), *Human Behavior and Social Processes.* Boston, MA: Houghton Mifflin.

Stone, P., Dunphy, D., Smith, M. & Ogilvie, D. (Eds.). (1966). *The General Inquirer: A Computer Approach to Content Analysis.* Cambridge, MA: MIT Press.

Stoner, J. A. F. (1961). A comparision of individual and group decisions under risk. Master's Thesis. Massachusetts Institute of Technology.

Strauss, A. (1977). Sociological theories of personality. In R. J. Corsini (Ed.), *Current Personality Theories.* Itasca, IL: Peacock.

Strodtbeck, F. L. & Mann, R. D. (1956). Sex role differentiation in jury deliberations. *Sociometry, 19,* 3–11.

Strumpel, B. (1990). Macroeconomic processes and societal psychology. In H. T. Himmelweit & G. Gaskell (Eds.), *Societal Psychology* (pp. 193–211). Newbury Park, CA: Sage.

Strupp, H. H. & Hausman, H. J. (1953). Some correlates of group productivity. *American Psychologist, 8,* 443–444.

Sullivan, H. S. (1953). *The Interpersonal Theory of Psychiatry.* New York: Norton.

Sumner, W. G. (1906). *Folkways.* New York: Ginn.

Sundstrom, E. (1986). *Work Places.* New York: Cambridge University Press.

Sundstrom, E. & Altman, I. (1989). Physical environments and work group effectiveness. In L. L. Cummings & B. Staw (Eds.), *Research in Organizational Behavior* (Vol. 11, pp. 175–209). Greenwich, CT: JAI Press.

Sundstrom, E., De Meuse, K P. & Futrell, D. (1990). Work teams: Applications and effectiveness. *American Psychologist, 45* (2), 120–133.

Swann, W. B. (1987). Identity negotiation: Where two roads meet. *Journal of Personality and Social Psychology, 53* (6), 1038–1051.

Swingle, P. G. & Santi, A. (1972). Communication in non-zero sum games. *Journal of Personality and Social Psychology, 23,* 54–63.

Sykes, R. E., Larntz, K. & Fox, J. C. (1976). Proximity and similarity effects on frequency of interaction in a class of naval recruits. *Sociometry, 39,* 263–269.

Tajfel, H. (1974). Social identity and intergroup behavior. *Social Science Information, 13,* 65–93.

Tajfel, H. (1981). *Human Groups and Social Cate-*

gories. Cambridge: Cambridge University Press.

Tajfel, H. (1982). Social psychology of intergroup relations. *Annual Review of Psychology, 33,* 1–39.

Tajfel, H. (Ed.). (1984). *The Social Dimension: European Developments in Social Psychology* (Vols. 1 & 2). Cambridge: Cambridge University Press.

Teichman, Y. (1974). Predisposition for anxiety and affiliation. *Journal of Personality and Social Psychology, 29,* 405–410.

Thelen, H. A. (1954). *Dynamics of Groups at Work.* Chicago: University of Chicago Press.

Thelen, H. A. (1974). Reactions to Group Situations Test. *The 1974 Handbook for Group Facilitators.* LaJolla, CA: University Associates.

Thelen, H. A., Hawkes, T. H. & Strattner, N. S. (1969). *Role Perception and Task Performance of Experimentally Composed Small Groups.* Chicago: The University of Chicago Press.

Theodorson, G. A. (1962). The function of hostility in small groups. *The Journal of Social Psychology, 256,* 57–66.

Thibault, J. W. (1950). An experimental study of the cohesiveness of underprivileged groups. *Human Relations, 3,* 251–278.

Thompson, P. C. (1982). Quality circles at Martin Marietta Corporation, Denver/Aerospace/Michoud Division. In R. Zager & M. Roscow (Eds.), *The Innovative Organization* (pp. 3–20). New York: Pergamon.

Travis, L. E. (1925). The effect of a small audience upon eye-hand coordination. *Journal of Abnormal and Social Psychology, 20,* 142–146.

Travis, L. E. (1928). The influence of the group upon the stutterer's speed in free association. *Journal of Abnormal and Social Psychology, 23,* 45–51.

Triplett, N. (1898). The dynamogenic factors in pace-making and competition *American Journal of Psychology, 9,* 507–533.

Trotter, W. (1916). *Instincts of the Herd in Peace and War.* London: Hogarth Press.

Trujillo, N. (1986). Toward a taxonomy of small group interaction-coding systems. *Small Group Behavior, 17,* 371–394.

Tuckman, B. W. (1965). Developmental sequences in small groups. *Psychological Bulletin, 63,* 384–399.

Tuckman, B. W. & Jensen, M. A. C. (1977). Stages in small group development revisited. *Group and Organizational Studies, 2,* 419–427.

Turner, R. H. & Killian, L. M. (1957). *Collective Behavior.* Englewood Cliffs, NJ: Prentice Hall.

Turney, J. R. (1970). The cognitive complexity of group members, group structure and group effectiveness. *Cornell Journal of Social Relations, 5,* 152–165.

Tye, L. (July 29, 1990). Hate crimes on rise in U.S. *Boston Sunday Globe* (pp. 1, 14). Boston, MA.

Van de Ven, A. H. & Walker, G. (1984). The dynamics of interorganizational coordination. *Administrative Science Quarterly, 29,* 598–621.

Van Maanen, J. & Schein, E. H. (1979). Toward a theory of organizational socialization. In B. Staw & L. L. Cummings (Eds.), *Research in Organization Behavior* (Vol. 1, pp. 209–269). Greenwich, CT: JAI Press.

Van Zelst, R. H. (1952). Validation of a sociometric regrouping procedure. *Journal of Abnormal and Social Psychology, 47,* 299–301.

Vecchio, R. P. (1987). Situational leadership theory: An examination of a prescriptive theory. *Journal of Applied Psychology, 72,* 444–451.

Verdi, A. F. & Wheelan, S. (1992). Developmental patterns in same-sex and mixed-sex groups. *Small Group Research, 23* (3), 356–378.

Vinacke, W. E. & Arkoff, A. (1957). Experimental study of coalitions in the triad. *American Sociological Review, 22,* 406–415.

Vinokur, A. & Burnstein, E. (1974). Effects of partially shared persuasive arguments on group-induced shifts: A group problem-solving approach. *Journal of Personality and Social Psychology, 29,* 305–315.

Vinokur, A., Burnstein, E., Sechrest, L. & Wortman, P. M. (1985). Group decision making by experts: Field study of panels evaluating medical technologies. *Journal of Personality and Social Psychology, 49,* 70–84.

Von Bertalanffy, L. (1968). *Organismic Psychology*

and Systems Theory. Barre, MA: Clark University Press.

Von Bertalanffy, L. (1976). General systems theory: A critical review. In J. Beishon & G. Peters (Eds.), *Systems Behaviour* (pp. 30–40). London: Harper & Row, Ltd.

Von Bertalanffy, L. (1981). *A Systems View of Man.* Boulder, CO: Westview Press, Inc.

Vroom, V. H. (1973). A new look at managerial decision making. *Organizational Dynamics, 1,* 66–80.

Vroom, V. H. (1974). Decision making and the leadership process. *Journal of Contemporary Business, 3,* 47–64.

Vroom, V. H. (1976). Leadership. In M. D. Dunnette (Ed.), *Handbook of Industrial and Organizational Psychology.* Chicago: Rand McNally.

Vroom, V. H. & Jago, A. G. (1978). On the validity of the Vroom/Yetton model. *Journal of Applied Psychology, 63,* 151–162.

Vroom, V. H. & Yetton, P. W. (1973). *Leadership and Decision Making.* Pittsburgh, PA: University of Pittsburgh Press.

Wahrman, R. & Pugh, M. D. (1974). Sex, nonconformity and influence. *Sociometry, 37,* 137–147.

Walster, E., Aronson, V., Abrahams, D. & Rottman, I. (1966). Importance of physical attractiveness in dating behavior. *Journal of Personality and Social Psychology, 4,* 508–516.

Walton, R. E. (1985). From control to commitment in the workplace. *Harvard Business Review, 63* (2), 76–84.

Warriner, C. H. (1956). Groups are real: A reaffirmation. *American Sociological Review, 21,* 549–554.

Washburn, S. L. (1962). *Social Life of Early Man.* London: Methuen.

Watzlawick, P., Beavin, J. H. & Jackson, D. (1967). *Pragmatics of Human Communication: A Study of Interactional Patterns, Pathologies and Paradoxes.* New York: W. W. Norton.

Watzlawick, P., Weakland, J. H. & Fisch, R. (1974). *Change: Principles of Problem Formation and Problem Resolution.* New York: W. W. Norton.

Webster's Ninth *New Collegiate Dictionary* (1989). Springfield, MA: Merriam-Webster.

Weick, K. E. (1980). The management of eloquence. *Executive, 6,* 18–21.

Weick, K. E. (1985). Sources of order in underorganized systems: Themes in recent organizational theory. In Y. S. Lincoln (Ed.), *Organizational Theory and Inquiry: The Paradigm Revolution.* Beverly Hills, CA: Sage.

Weigel, R. H., Wiser, P. I. & Cook, S. W. (1975). The impact of cooperative learning experiences on cross-ethnic relations and attitudes. *Journal of Social Issues, 31* (1), 219–244.

Weisbord, M. R. (1987). *Productive Workplaces.* San Francisco: Jossey-Bass.

Wheaton, B. (1974). Interpersonal conflict and cohesiveness in dyadic relationships. *Sociometry, 37,* 328–248.

Wheelan, S. (1974). Sex differences in the functioning of small groups. Dissertation. University of Wisconsin.

Wheelan, S. (June, 1978). The effect of personal growth and assertive training on female sex role self-concept. *Group and Organizational Studies, 3* (2), 239–243.

Wheelan, S. (1990). *Facilitating Training Groups.* New York: Praeger.

Wheelan, S. & Abraham, M. (1993). The concept of intergroup mirroring: Reality or illusion? *Human Relations.* (In press)

Wheelan, S. & Abt, V. (1990). Field theory and the construction of social problems: A relational perspective. In S. Wheelan, E. Pepitone & V. Abt (Eds.), *Advances in Field Theory* (pp. 80–89). Newbury Park, CA: Sage.

Wheelan, S. & Bastas, E. (1979). Should doctors be more assertive? *Behavioral Medicine,* August, 39–41.

Wheelan, S. & Conway, C. (1991). Group development as a framework to understand and promote school readiness to engage in an OD project. *The Journal of Educational and Psychological Consultation, 2* (1), 59–71.

Wheelan, S. & Krasick, C. (1993). The emergence, transmission, and acceptance of themes in a temporary organization. *Group and Organization Studies* (In press)

Wheelan, S. & McKeage, R. (1993). Developmental patterns in small and large groups. *Small Group Research, 24* (1), 60–83.

Wheelan, S. & Stivers, E. (1990). Group dynamics,

action research and intergroup relations. In S. Wheelan, E. Pepitone & V. Abt (Eds.), *Advances in Field Theory* (pp. 197–209). Newbury Park, CA: Sage.

Wheelan, S. & Verdi, A. F. (1992). Differences in male and female patterns of communication in groups: A methodological artifact? *Sex Roles: A Journal of Research, 27* (1/2), 1–15.

Wheelan, S., Verdi, A. F. & McKeage, R. (In process). *The Group Development Observation System: Origins and Applications.*

Whitaker, D. S. (1974). *Reactions to Group Situations Test.* LaJolla, CA: University Associates.

Whitaker, D. S. & Lieberman, M. A. (1964). *Psychotherapy Through the Group Process.* New York: Atherton Press.

White, R. K. & Lippitt, R. (1960). *Autocracy and Democracy.* New York: Harper & Row.

Whyte, W. F. (1943a). A challenge to political scientists. *American Political Science Review, 37,* 692–697.

Whyte, W. F. (1943b). A slum sex code. *American Journal of Sociology, 49* (1), 24–31.

Whyte, W. F. (1943c). Social organization in the slums. *American Sociological Review, 8* (1), 34–39.

Whyte, W. F. (1955). *Street Corner Society* (2d ed.). Chicago: University of Chicago Press.

Whyte, W. F. (1957). *The Organization Man.* New York: Doubleday.

Whyte, W. F. (1961). *Men at Work.* Homewood, IL: Dorsey Press and Richard D. Irwin.

Whyte, W. F. (1969). *Organizational Behavior: Theory and Application.* Homewood, IL: Richard D. Irwin and Dorsey Press.

Whyte, W. F. (1992). Comments for the SCS critics. In P. J. Frost, L. F. Moore, M. R. Louis, C. C. Lundberg & J. Martin (Eds.), *Reframing Organizational Culture* (pp. 234–240). Newbury Park, CA: Sage.

Whyte, W. F. & Whyte, K. K. (1984). *Learning from the Field: A Guide from Experience.* Beverly Hills, CA: Sage.

Wiesz, J. R., Rothbaum, F. M., & Blackburn, T. C. (1984). Standing out and standing in: The psychology of control in America and Japan. *American Psychologist, 39,* 955–969.

Wilkins, A. L. & Ouchi, W. G. (1983). Efficient cultures: Exploring the relationship between culture and organizational performance. *Administrative Science Quarterly, 28,* 468–481.

Willerman, B. & Swanson, L. (1953). Group prestige in voluntary organizations. *Human Relations, 6,* 57–77.

Williams, K. B., Harkins, S. & Latane, B. (1981). Identifiability as a deterrent to social loafing: Two cheering experiments. *Journal of Personality and Social Psychology, 40,* 303–311.

Winter, S. (1976). Developmental stages in the roles and concerns of group co-leaders. *Small Group Behavior, 7* (3), 349–362.

Wolfers, A. (1959). The actors in international politics. In W. Fox (Ed.), *Theoretical Aspects of International Relations* (pp. 83–106). Notre Dame, IN: Notre Dame University Press.

Worchel, S. (1986). The role of cooperation in reducing intergroup conflict. In S. Worchel & W. G. Austin (Eds.), *Psychology of Intergroup Relations* (2d ed., pp. 288–304) Chicago: Nelson-Hall.

Worchel, S., Axsom, D., Ferris, F., Samaha, C. & Schwietzer, S. (1978). Factors determining the effect of intergroup cooperation on intergroup attraction. *Journal of Conflict Resolution, 22,* 429–439.

Worchel, S., Coutant-Sassic, D. & Grossman, M. (1992). A developmental approach to group dynamics: A model and illustrative research. In S. Worchel, W. Wood & J. A. Simpson (Eds.), *Group Process and Productivity* (pp. 181–202). Newbury Park, CA: Sage.

Worchel, S., Lind, E. A. & Kaufman, K. H. (1975). Evaluations of group products as a function of expectations of group longevity, outcome of competition, and publicity of evaluations. *Journal of Personality and Social Psychology, 31,* 1089–1097.

Worchel, S., Wood, W. & Simpson, J. A. (Eds.). (1992). *Group Process and Productivity.* Newbury Park, CA: Sage.

Worchel, S. & Yohai, S. M. L. (1979). The role of attribution in the experience of crowding. *Journal of Experimental Social Psychology, 15,* 91–104.

Wrong, D. H. (1961). The oversocialized conception of man in modern sociology. *American Sociological Review, 26,* 183–193.

Wrong, D. H. (1979). *Power.* New York: Harper.

Wyer, R. S. (1966). Effects of incentive to perform well, group attraction and group acceptance on conformity in a judgmental task. *Journal of Personality and Social Psychology, 4,* 21–26.

Yalom, I. D. (1970). *The Theory and Practice of Group Psychotherapy.* New York: Basic Books.

Yalom, I. D. (1975). *The Theory and Practice of Group Psychotherapy.* (2d ed.) New York: Basic Books.

Yalom, I. D. (1983). *Inpatient Group Psychotherapy.* New York: Basic Books.

Yalom, I. D. (1985). *The Theory and Practice of Group Psychotherapy* (3d ed.). New York: Basic Books.

Yankelovich, D., Zetterberg, H., Shanks, M. & Strumpel, B. (1985). *The World at Work.* New York: Octagon.

Youngs, G. A., Jr. (1986). Patterns of threat and punishment reciprocity in a conflict setting. *Journal of Personality and Social Psychology, 51,* 541–546.

Yukl, G. A. (1981). *Leadership in Organizations.* Englewood Cliffs, NJ: Prentice Hall.

Zacarro, S. J. (1984). Social loafing: The role of task attractiveness. *Personality and Social Psychology Bulletin, 10,* 99–106.

Zajonc, R. B. (1965). Social facilitation. *Science, 149,* 269–274.

Zander, A. (1971). *Motives and Goals in Groups.* New York: Academic Press.

Zander, A. (1979). The psychology of group processes. *Annual Review of Psychology, 30,* 417–452.

Zander, A. (1982). *Making Groups Effective.* San Francisco, CA: Jossey-Bass.

Zander, A. & Medow, H. (1963). Individual and group levels of aspiration. *Human Relations, 16,* 89–105.

Zander, A. & Newcomb, T. (1967). Group levels of aspiration in United Fund campaigns. *Journal of Personality and Social Psychology, 6,* 157–162.

Zimbardo, P. G. (1975). Transforming experimental research into advocacy for social change. In M. Deutsch & H. A. Hornstein (Eds.), *Applying Social Psychology* (pp. 33–66). Hillsdale, NJ: Erlbaum.

Zimbardo, P. G., Haney, C., Banks, W. & Jaffe, D. (April 8, 1973). A Pirandeloian prison: The mind is a formidable jailer. *New York Times Magazine,* 38–60.

Zola, E. (1886). *The Masterpiece.* (Trans. K. Woods, 1946). New York: Howell & Soskin.

Zurcher, L. A. (1969). Stages of development in poverty program neighborhood committees. *Journal of Applied Behavioral Science, 5,* 223–251.

NAME INDEX

Abraham, M., 137, 270
Abrahams, D., 63, 270
Abt, V., 124, 271
Adams, J. S., 139, 144, 241, 255
Adams, S, 111, 241
Adelson, J. P., 152, 241
Adinolfi, A. A., 63, 257
Agazarian, Y., ix, 2, 61, 135, 188, 241
Alberti, R., 210, 241
Alderfer, C. P., 142, 241
Allison, S. T., 106, 107, 108, 241
Allport, F. H., 102, 123, 150, 241
Allport, G., 2, 241
Altman, I., 114, 268
Altman, L. S., 154, 241
Ames, R., 129, 241
Amir, Y., 13, 152, 177, 179, 180, 241, 242
Ancona, D. G., 27, 135, 138, 139, 147, 155, 241
Anderson, A. B., 87, 96, 242
Anderson, L. R., 110, 152, 249
Anderson, R. C., 72, 111, 151, 242
Anstorp, T., 131, 188, 247
Argyle, M., 111, 151, 242
Argyris, C., 50, 131, 242
Aries, E., 152, 242
Arkoff, A., 79, 151, 270
Aronoff, J., 44, 260
Aronson, E., 36, 242
Aronson, V., 63, 270

Asch, S., 6, 40, 41, 61, 95, 124, 150, 151, 242
Askling, L. R., 106, 252
Astley, W. G., 147, 242
Atkin, R. S., 110, 244
Atkinson, J. W., 62, 260
Axelrod, R., 82, 242
Axsom, D., 82, 271

Babad, E., 13, 54, 126, 152, 177, 179, 180, 242
Back, K., 12, 26, 32, 35, 96, 97, 149, 151, 242
Baer, D. M., 62, 250
Bales, R. F., 2, 9, 12, 17, 22, 32, 55, 98, 101, 109, 151, 156, 177, 178, 179, 242, 244, 252, 263
Banas, P. A., 77, 242
Bandura, A., 204, 242, 243
Banks, W., 6, 272
Barnard, C. I., 175, 243
Baron, R. M., 125, 243
Barrera, M., 188, 243
Bartol, K. M., 152, 243
Bass, B. M., 2, 4, 128, 151, 243
Bassin, M., 115, 153, 243
Bastas, E., 209, 210, 271
Bavelas, A., 29, 151, 243
Bearley, W. L., 170, 255
Beavin, J. H., 49, 270
Beck, A. T., 204, 243
Becker, L. J., 81, 244
Beckman, L. J., 129, 243

273

SUBJECT INDEX